SCHOLASTIC

LITERACY PLACE

IT WORKS...AND KIDS LIKE IT!

SCHOLASTIC

SCHOLASTIC

LITERACY PLACE

IT WORKS...AND KIDS LIKE IT!

Manageable Instructional Plans

Literacy Place follows a clear, consistent pattern of instruction and provides support for all learners. The Teacher's Edition includes explicit skills instruction and integrates the language arts.

The Strongest System for Beginning Readers

Literacy Place provides direct instruction in phonics and phonological awareness and fully reflects current and confirmed research.

Assessment Tools to Monitor and Modify Instruction

Literacy Place features focused assessment that informs instruction and measures progress. The program offers strategies targeting students who need skills intervention, language-development support, and enrichment.

Power and Confidence for the Information Age

Literacy Place uses technology as an integral part of learning while connecting the classroom to the real world.

The Matrix

Grade	PERSONAL LITERACY **Personal Voice** We communicate in our unique voices as we grow and learn.	INTELLECTUAL LITERACY **Problem Solving** People have the power to solve problems.	SOCIAL LITERACY **Teamwork** Successful teams depend on the collaboration of individuals.
K	**Stories About Us** **Big Idea** We listen to, tell, and create stories. **Mentor** Grandmother: *Honey Wada* **Place** Storytelling Corner **Project** "All About Me" Class Book	**See It, Solve It** **Big Idea** We see problems and find solutions. **Mentor** Clay Animator: *Becky Wible* **Place** Claymator's Studio **Project** Dramatization	**All Together Now!** **Big Idea** We share and help each other. **Mentor** Pizza Maker: *Kwaku Twumasi* **Place** Restaurant **Project** Big Book of Menus
1	**Hello!** **Big Idea** We share what we like. **Mentor** Author: *Donald Crews* **Place** Writer's Home **Project** Scrapbook	**Problem Patrol** **Big Idea** There are many kinds of problems. **Mentor** Veterinarian: *Fay Vittetoe* **Place** Veterinarian's Office **Project** Pet Care Guide	**Team Spirit** **Big Idea** It's fun to do things together. **Mentor** Soccer Coach: *Danny Prenat* **Place** Soccer Stadium **Project** Game Rule Book
2	**Snapshots** **Big Idea** Our actions tell about us. **Mentor** Photographer: *Bruce Thorson* **Place** Sports Arena **Project** Exhibit	**Super Solvers** **Big Idea** There may be more than one way to solve a problem. **Mentor** Toy Designer: *Mary Rodas* **Place** Toy Company **Project** Safety Poster Campaign	**Lights! Camera! Action!** **Big Idea** Creative teams produce great performances. **Mentor** Theater Director: *Judith Martin* **Place** Children's Theater **Project** Play Production
3	**What's New?** **Big Idea** We learn about our world through new experiences. **Mentor** Wilderness Guide: *Keith Jardine* **Place** Wilderness School **Project** Anecdote	**Big Plans** **Big Idea** Making and using plans can help us solve problems. **Mentor** Architect: *Jack Catlin* **Place** Construction Site **Project** Floor Plan	**On the Job** **Big Idea** Teams work best when they use each member's strengths to get the job done. **Mentor** Art Director: *Max Jerome* **Place** Ad Agency **Project** Ad Campaign
4	**Chapter by Chapter** **Big Idea** We are always adding to our life story. **Mentor** Author: *Jerry Spinelli* **Place** Bookstore **Project** Personal Narrative	**What an Idea!** **Big Idea** People solve problems by inventing new things. **Mentor** Inventor: *Julie Lewis* **Place** Inventor's Office **Project** Invention Marketing Plan	**Discovery Teams** **Big Idea** When we work as a team, we learn new things about our world. **Mentor** Astronaut: *Dr. Mae Jemison* **Place** Space Center **Project** Multimedia Presentation
5	**Making a Difference** **Big Idea** Each of us is inspired by the lives of others. **Mentor** Musician: *Joseph Shabalala* **Place** Concert Hall **Project** Tribute	**It's a Mystery** **Big Idea** We can solve mysteries using reason, logic, and intuition. **Mentor** Forensic Chemist: *Lilly Gallman* **Place** Detective Headquarters **Project** Investigative Report	**Voyagers** **Big Idea** We depend on a network of people when we explore. **Mentor** Travel Agent: *Marie French* **Place** Travel Agency **Project** Travel Magazine

scholastic.com
Look for the Unit-by-Unit Extensions in the Literacy Place area.

PERSONAL LITERACY

Creative Expression

People express themselves in many creative ways.

Express Yourself

Big Idea We express ourselves through songs, sounds, stories, dance, and art.
Mentor Author: *Pat Mora*
Place Author's Studio
Project Storybook

Imagine That!

Big Idea Imagination lets us look at things in new ways.
Mentor Muralist: *William Walsh*
Place Artist's Studio
Project Story Mural

Story Studio

Big Idea People express themselves through stories and pictures.
Mentor Author & Artist: *Tomie dePaola*
Place Author's Studio
Project Picture Book

Hit Series

Big Idea A creative idea can grow into a series.
Mentor Author & Illustrator: *Joanna Cole & Bruce Degen*
Place Publishing Company
Project New Episode

The Funny Side

Big Idea Sometimes humor is the best way to communicate.
Mentor Cartoonist: *Robb Armstrong*
Place Cartoonist's Studio
Project Comic Strip

In the Spotlight

Big Idea We use our creativity to reach an audience.
Mentor Drama Coach: *José García*
Place Actor's Workshop
Project Stage Presentation

INTELLECTUAL LITERACY

Managing Information

Finding and using information helps us live in our world.

I Spy!

Big Idea Information is all around us.
Mentor Farmer: *Steven Powell*
Place Gardening Center
Project Garden Journal

Information Finders

Big Idea Information comes from many sources.
Mentor Marine Biologist: *Laela Sayigh*
Place Aquarium
Project Big Book of Information

Animal World

Big Idea We use information to understand the interdependence of people and animals.
Mentor Zoo Curator: *Lisa Stevens*
Place Zoo
Project Zoo Brochure

Time Detectives

Big Idea Finding information in stories and artifacts brings the past to life.
Mentor Archaeologist: *Dr. Ruben Mendoza*
Place Archaeological Site
Project Time Capsule

Nature Guides

Big Idea Gathering and using information help us understand and describe the natural world.
Mentor Park Ranger: *Veronica Gonzales-Vest*
Place National Park Headquarters
Project Field Guide

America's Journal

Big Idea Considering different points of view gives us a fuller understanding of history.
Mentor Historian/Author: *Russell Freedman*
Place Historical Museum
Project Historical Account

SOCIAL LITERACY

Community Involvement

Communities are built on the contributions of the people who live there.

Join In!

Big Idea We help our community.
Mentor Singer/Songwriter: *Tom Chapin*
Place Performance Stage
Project Community Sing

Home Towns

Big Idea We are all members of a community.
Mentor Mayor: *Steve Yamashiro*
Place Mayor's Office
Project Visitor's Map

Lend a Hand

Big Idea People can make a difference in their communities.
Mentor Police Officer: *Nadine Jojola*
Place Police Station
Project Community Expo

Community Quilt

Big Idea In a community, some things continue and some things change.
Mentor Community Garden Director: *Lorka Muñoz*
Place Community Garden
Project Community Quilt

It Takes a Leader

Big Idea In every community there are people who inspire others to take action.
Mentor Editor: *Suki Cheong*
Place Newspaper Office
Project Op-Ed Page

Cityscapes

Big Idea Cities depend on the strengths and skills of the people who live and work there.
Mentor Urban Planner: *Karen Heit*
Place Urban Planner's Office
Project Action Plan

Components

Pupil's Editions & Teacher's Editions

K

Literacy Place Kindergarten provides a rich learning environment including Big Books, Read Alouds, Sentence Strips, Audiocassettes, Phonics Manipulatives, Workbooks, Teacher Editions, and much more.

1

Grades 1-5

- Literacy Place brings you what you would expect from Scholastic—authentic, award-winning children's literature.
- Our Teacher's Editions are easy to use, and provide explicit skills instruction.
- You'll also find a management CD-ROM to help you customize instruction to state and district standards.

2

3

scholastic.com
Check it out! You'll find a wealth of professional support resources, plus a lot of great stuff for kids and parents.

4

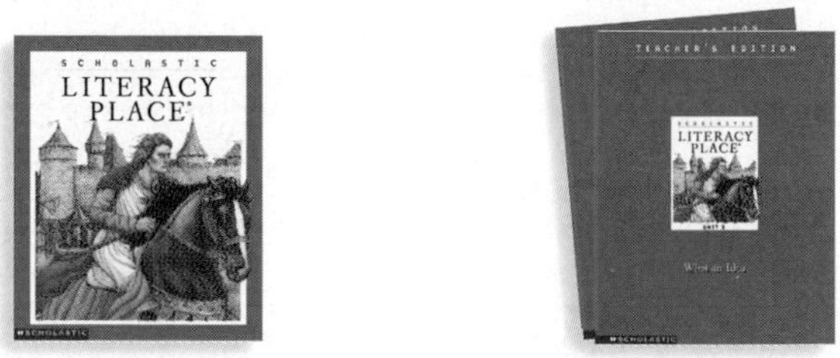

5

Pupil's Editions **Teacher's Editions**

Support Materials

Practice

Literacy Place includes comprehensive practice resources.

- ✔ My Reading Workbook (1)
- ✔ Workshop and Project Cards (K-2)
- ✔ Practice Books (1-5)
- ✔ Spelling Resource Book (1-5)
- ✔ Grammar Resource Book (1-5)
- ✔ Handwriting Practice Book (K-3)
- ✔ ESL/ELD Resource Book (K-5)
- ✔ Skills Overhead Transparencies (2-5)
- ✔ Vocabulary Overhead Transparencies (2-5)
- ✔ Place Cards (3-5)

Assessment

Literacy Place provides a wide range of assessment and evaluation options. (K-5)

- ✔ Placement Tests
- ✔ Assessment Handbook
- ✔ Classroom Management Forms
- ✔ Selection Tests (for every story!)
- ✔ Unit Tests (Forms A and B)
- ✔ Oral Reading Assessment
- ✔ Scholastic Reading Inventory
- ✔ TAAS Preparation and Practice Book
- ✔ Assessment System CD-ROM

Technology

We set the industry standard.

- ✔ Phonics Practice CD-ROM (K-2)
- ✔ WiggleWorks Plus CD-ROM (K-2)
- ✔ Smart Place CD-ROM (3-5)
- ✔ Scholastic Management Suite (K-5)
- ✔ Staff Development Videos (K-5)
- ✔ Meet the Mentor Videos (K-5)
- ✔ Scholastic Network (K-5)
- ✔ Selection Audiocassettes (1-5)
- ✔ Classroom Resources CD-ROM (K-5)

Scholastic Solutions

Only Scholastic can offer you the diverse range of materials you need for your classroom. Please call 1-800-Scholastic for a catalog. Ask about these exciting products:

- ✔ High-Frequency Readers (K-1)
- ✔ Sound and Letter Books (K-1)
- ✔ Big Books/Little Books (K-2)
- ✔ Phonemic Awareness Kit (K-2)
- ✔ Phonics Readers (K-3)
- ✔ Phonics Chapter Books (1-3)
- ✔ Phonics Workbooks (K-2)
- ✔ Guided Reading Program (K-5)
- ✔ Bilingual Support (K-5)
- ✔ Solares (K-5)
- ✔ Transition Program (3-6)
- ✔ Sprint Plus Intervention (3-6)
- ✔ READ 180 (4-8)
- ✔ Reading Counts! (K-8)

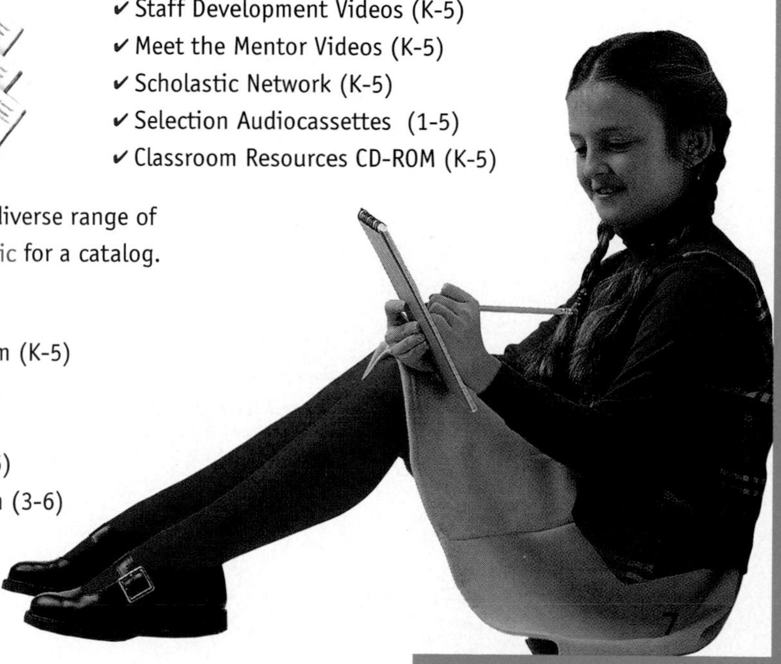

Advisors

Program Consultants

SKILLS, STRATEGIES, INSTRUCTION
James Bauman
Professor, University of Georgia,
Athens, Georgia

PHONICS AND EARLY READING
Wiley Blevins
Consultant and Educational Writer
New York, New York

ESL/ELD
Jacqueline Kiraithe-Cordova
Professor, California State, California

STAFF DEVELOPMENT
Nancy Cummings
Western Director of Implementation
Success For All School Restructuring
Phoenix, Arizona

BILINGUAL EDUCATION
James Cummins
Professor, Ontario Institute for
Studies in Education
Ontario, Canada

EARLY LITERACY DEVELOPMENT
Nell K. Duke
Michigan State University

ASSESSMENT/WRITING
Adele Fiderer
Consultant and Educational Writer
Scarsdale, New York

HANDWRITING
Steve Graham
Professor, University of Maryland
College Park, Maryland

WRITING
Shelley Harwayne
Director of Manhattan New School
New York, New York

SPELLING
Richard E. Hodges
Professor, University of Puget Sound
Tacoma, Washington

SPELLING
Louisa Moats
County Office of Education
Sacramento, California

VOCABULARY
William E. Nagy
Assistant Professor, University of Illinois
Champaign-Urbana, Illinois

FLEXIBLE GROUPING
Michael Opitz
Professor, University of Colorado
Boulder, Colorado

ESL/ELD
Robert Parker
Consultant, Brown University
Providence, Rhode Island

ESL/ELD
Cao Anh Quan
ESOL Program Specialist
Tallahassee, Florida

ESL/ELD
Kim Quan Nguyen-Lam
California State University
Long Beach, California

WRITING
Michael Strickland
Author, Consultant
Orange, New Jersey

Teacher Reviewers

Kim Andrews
Fourth Grade Reviewer
Baltimore, Maryland

Shirley Beard
Fourth Grade Reviewer
El Paso, Texas

Barbara Bloom
Fifth Grade Reviewer
Wall Lake, Iowa

Sherry Brown
Third Grade Reviewer
Georgetown, Texas

Lisa Buchholz
First Grade Reviewer
Wheaton, Illinois

Kathy Burdick
Fifth Grade Reviewer
Austin, Texas

Marianne Chorba
Fourth Grade Reviewer
Baltimore, Maryland

Peggy Colley
Third Grade Reviewer
Rocky Face, Georgia

Carol Curry
Third Grade Reviewer
Tallahassee, Florida

Claire Dale
First Grade Reviewer
National City, California

Mildred DeStefano
First Grade Reviewer
Brooklyn, New York

Doris Dillan
Grade Two Reviewer
San Jose, California

Oneaster Drummer
First Grade Reviewer
Cincinnati, Ohio

Ethel Durham
Third Grade Reviewer
Grand Rapids, Michigan

Patty Ernst
Second Grade Reviewer
Naples, New York

Alzada Fowler
First Grade Reviewer
Lake Helen, Florida

Jane Ginn
First Grade Reviewer
Rohnert Park, California

Amy Gordon
Third Grade Reviewer
New City, New York

Janet Gray
Fourth Grade Reviewer
Lake Helen, Florida

Velma Gunn
Fourth Grade Reviewer
New Rochelle, New York

Annie Ruth Harris
Third Grade Reviewer
Decatur, Alabama

Barbara Ann Hawkins
Second Grade Reviewer
Hamer, South Carolina

Amy Hom
Second Grade Reviewer
New York, New York

Min Hong
First Grade Reviewer
Brooklyn, New York

Susan Howe
Third Grade Reviewer
Ellicott City, Maryland

Barbara Jansz
First Grade Reviewer
Naperville, Illinois

Michele Jessen
First Grade Reviewer
El Paso, Texas

Ellen W. Johnson
Second Grade Reviewer
Chalfont, Pennsylvania

Vera Johnson
First Grade Reviewer
Uniondale, New York

Carol Kaiser
Third Grade Reviewer
Los Angeles, California

Karen Kolsky
Third Grade Reviewer
Philadelphia, Pennsylvania

Judy Keyak
Second Grade Reviewer
St. Petersburg, Florida

Jacqueline Krass
Second Grade Reviewer
Gulfport, Mississippi

Warren Livesley
Fourth Grade Reviewer
New York, New York

Libby Lesley
First Grade Reviewer
San Angelo, Texas

Dora I. Magana
Fourth Grade Reviewer
El Paso, Texas

Tim Mason
Second Grade Reviewer
Willington Florida

Carol Mercer
Fourth Grade Reviewer
National City, California

Betty Milburn
Third Grade Reviewer
Grand Prairie, Texas

Jane Moore
Third Grade Reviewer
Dallas, Texas

Sandy Nolan
Third Grade Reviewer
Salem, Wisconsin

Carol Ochs
Fifth Grade Reviewer
Noble, Oklahoma

Lynn Olson
Fifth Grade Reviewer
Omaha, Nebraska

Cynthia Orange
Second Grade Reviewer
Bronx, New York

Sue Panek
Fourth Grade Reviewer
Hawthorne, New Jersey

Deborah Peale
Fourth Grade Reviewer
Miami, Florida

Arturo Perez
Second Grade Reviewer
Ventura, California

Jeanette Reber
First Grade Reviewer
Rock Hill, South Carolina

Charlene Richardson
Fourth Grade Reviewer
Everett, Washington

Daria Rigney
Fifth Grade Reviewer
Brooklyn, New York

Andrea Ruff
First Grade Reviewer
Brooklyn, New York

Carol Shirmang
First Grade Reviewer
Palatine, Illinois

Wendy Smiley
Fourth Grade Reviewer
Syracuse, New York

Barbara Solomon
Second Grade Reviewer
Hempstead, New York

Alicia Sparkman
First Grade Reviewer
Plant City, Florida

Elaine Steinberg
Third Grade Reviewer
Fresh Meadows, New York

Bobby Stern
Third Grade Reviewer
Winston-Salem, North Carolina

Laura Stewart
First Grade Reviewer

Kate Taylor
Fifth Grade Reviewer
Baltimore, Maryland

Vasilika Terss
Second Grade Reviewer
St. Louis, Missouri

Linda Thorn
Fifth Grade Reviewer
Cranford, New Jersey

Gayle Thurn
Second Grade Reviewer
Piedmont, South Carolina

Jerry Trotter
Fifth Grade Reviewer
Chicago, Illinois

Julia Tucker
First Grade Reviewer
Hampton, Virginia

Patricia Viales
First Grade Reviewer
Salinas, California

Janielle Wagstaff
Second Grade Reviewer
Salt Lake City, Utah

Gail Weber
Fourth Grade Reviewer
Sherman Oaks, California

Elizabeth White
First Grade Reviewer
Bronx, New York

Karla Hawkins-Windeline
Second Grade Reviewer
Hickman, Nebraska

National Advisory Council

Barbara R. Foorman, Ph. D.
Professor of Pediatrics
Director of the Center for
Academic and Reading Skills
Houston, TX

Dr. Wilmer Cody
Commissioner of Education
Kentucky State Department
of Education
Frankfort, KY

Ms. Judy Mountjoy
Vice President
The National PTA
Chicago, IL

Ms. Anne Bryant
Executive Director
National School Boards
Association
Alexandria, VA

Dr. Anthony Alvarado
Chancellor for Instruction
San Diego City Schools
San Diego, CA

TEACHER'S EDITION

SCHOLASTIC

LITERACY PLACE®

UNIT 5

Information Finders

Literacy Place Authors

Cathy Collins Block
Professor, Curriculum and Instruction, Texas Christian University

Linda B. Gambrell
Professor, Education, University of Maryland at College Park

Virginia Hamilton
Children's Author; Winner of the Newbery Medal, the Coretta Scott King Award and the Laura Ingalls Wilder Lifetime Achievement Award

Douglas K. Hartman
Associate Professor of Language and Literacy, University of Pittsburgh

Ted S. Hasselbring
Co-Director of the Learning Technology Center and Professor in the Department of Special Education at Peabody College, Vanderbilt University

Adria Klein
Professor, Reading and Teacher Education, California State University at San Bernardino

Hilda Medrano
Dean, College of Education, University of Texas-Pan American

Gay Su Pinnell
Professor, School of Teaching and Learning, College of Education, Ohio State University

D. Ray Reutzel
Provost/Academic Vice President, Southern Utah University

David Rose
Founder and Executive Director of the Center for Applied Special Technology (CAST); Lecturer, Harvard University Graduate School of Education

Alfredo Schifini
Professor, School of Education, Division of Curriculum Instruction, California State University, Los Angeles

Delores Stubblefield Seamster
Principal, N.W. Harllee Elementary, Dallas, Texas; Consultant on Effective Programs for Urban Inner City Schools

Quality Quinn Sharp
Author and Teacher-Educator, Austin, Texas

John Shefelbine
Professor, Language and Literacy Education, California State University at Sacramento

Gwendolyn Y. Turner
Associate Professor of Literacy Education, University of Missouri at St. Louis

Acknowledgments and credits appear on pages R115–R116, which constitute an extension of this copyright page.

Published by Scholastic Inc. Printed in the U.S.A.

ISBN 0-439-07887-3 (National)

3 4 5 6 7 8 9 10 14 07 06 05 04 03 02 01 00

TABLE OF CONTENTS

Information Finders

THEME
Information comes from many sources

Trade Book Library

UNIT AT A GLANCE

READ

LITERATURE	PHONICS	COMPREHENSION	VOCABULARY	LISTENING/ SPEAKING/ VIEWING
WEEK 1  *Fish Faces* pp. T24–T49	☑ **DIGRAPHS** *sh, th*, p. T22 ☑ **HOMOPHONES**, p. T56	☑ **MAIN IDEA/DETAILS**, p. T54	☑ **HIGH-FREQUENCY:** *more, belongs*, p. T20 • **STORY WORDS:** *fish, waves, mouth, nose, eyes, fins*, p. T21	• **MAKE FISH-FACE PUPPETS**, p. T69 • **WRITE A BOOK REPORT**, p. T69 • **READ ABOUT HOW FISH MOVE**, p. T70 • **MAKE A CLASS BOOK**, p. T70
WEEK 2 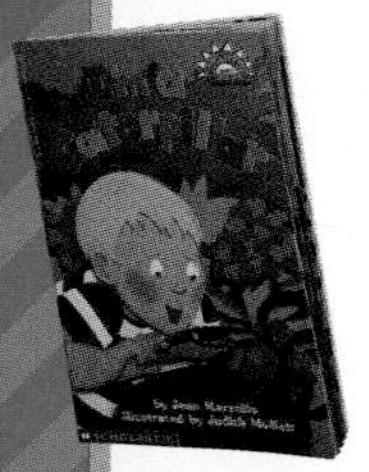 *I'm a Caterpillar* pp. T82–T110	☑ Words With /ô/*all, aw*, p. T80 ☑ **VOWEL** /ā/*ay, ai*, p. T116	☑ **SEQUENCE**, p. T114	☑ **HIGH-FREQUENCY:** *next, all*, p. T78 • **STORY WORDS:** *munch, wait, grow, wet, dry, straw*, p. T79	• **CREATE A WORD BUTTERFLY**, p. T129 • **MAKE A BUTTERFLY BOOK**, p. T129 • **EXPLORE SOUNDS**, p. T130 • **INTERVIEW THE CATERPILLAR**, p. T130
WEEK 3 * "The Garden" from Frog and Toad Together* pp. T146–T157	☑ **VOWEL** /ō/*oa*, p. T144 ☑ **INFLECTIONAL ENDING** *-ed* /d/, /t/, p. T164	☑ **SETTING**, p. T162	☑ **HIGH-FREQUENCY:** *was, grow*, p. T142 • **STORY WORDS:** *frog, garden, work, plant, flower, seeds*, p. T143	• **WRITE ABOUT YOUR SENSES**, p. T177 • **PUT SOUNDS IN A SETTING**, p. T177 • **TOAD SAYS . . .**, p. T178 • **MAKE A FROG AND TOAD BOOK**, p. T178
WEEK 4  *Daniel's Dinosaurs* pp. T190–T213	☑ **VOWEL** /ē/*y, ey*, p. T188 ☑ **COMPOUND WORDS**, p. T220	**FANTASY/REALITY**, p. T218	☑ **HIGH-FREQUENCY:** *school, their*, p. T186 • **STORY WORDS:** *library, supermarket, city, office, teacher, shark*, p. T187	• **COMPARE SHARKS AND DINOSAURS**, p. T233 • **WRITE ABOUT DANIEL'S SHARKS**, p. T233 • **INTERVIEW DANIEL'S DINOSAUR**, p. T234 • **CREATE A SHARK EXHIBIT**, p. T234
WEEK 5  *The Plant Castle* pp. T250–T265	☑ **VOWEL** /ō/*o, ow*, p. T248 ☑ *r*-**CONTROLLED VOWEL** /är/*ar*, p. T270	☑ **COMPARE/CONTRAST**, p. T268	☑ **HIGH-FREQUENCY:** *mother, girl*, p. T246 • **STORY WORDS:** *desert, butterfly, forest, fruits, leaves, trees*, p. T247	• **GROW A PLANT**, p. T283 • **GIVE A TOUR**, p. T283 • **CREATE CATEGORIES**, p. T284 • **MAKE A MAP**, p. T284

WEEK 6

Unit Wrap-Up
pp. T285–T301

TRADE BOOK LIBRARY

- *Lost!* by David McPhail
  EASY
- *Animal Tracks* by Arthur Dorros
  CHALLENGE
- *Owl at Home* by Arnold Lobel
  AVERAGE

✓ = TESTED SKILL ✔ = TESTED WORD

WRITE		EXTEND SKILLS		
SPELLING/ GRAMMAR, USAGE, MECHANICS	**WRITING**	**INTEGRATED CURRICULUM**	**REAL WORLD SKILLS/ STUDY SKILLS**	**LEVELED RESOURCES**
✓**SPELLING:** Words With *sh* and *th,* pp. R4–R5 ✓**GRAMMAR, USAGE, MECHANICS:** Word Order, pp. R6–R7	✓**SHARED WRITING:** Book of Facts, p. T60 • **JOURNAL,** p. T24	• **MATH:** How Many Are Left?, p. R8 • **SCIENCE:** From Mouth to Fin, p. R8 • **SOCIAL STUDIES:** Where Fish Live, p. R9 • **THE ARTS:** Fish Shapes, p. R9	• **MEET THE MENTOR VIDEO,** p. T9 • **READ ALOUD:** *Three Days on a River Bed in a Red Canoe,* p. T64 • **TECHNOLOGY:** pp. T20, T22, T29, T47, T53, T56, T58, T61, T64, T69	• **PHONICS READERS:** *Shhh! See the Sea* • **PHONICS CHAPTER BOOK:** *Let's Go on a Museum Hunt* • **MY BOOKS:** *Six Shaggy Things Going to Sea* • **GUIDED READING PROGRAM**
✓**SPELLING:** Words With *all* and *aw,* pp. R12–R13 ✓**GRAMMAR, USAGE, MECHANICS:** Capitalizing the Word *I,* pp. R14–R15	✓**SHARED WRITING:** Description, p. T120 • **JOURNAL,** p. T82	• **MATH:** Larger Than Life?, p. R16 • **SCIENCE:** From an Egg, p. R16 • **SOCIAL STUDIES:** Butterfly Territory, p. R17 • **THE ARTS:** Paint a Butterfly, p. R17	• **WORKSHOP 1:** How to Keep an Observation Log, p. T131 ✓**STUDY SKILLS:** Graphic Aids: Diagrams, p. T124 • **TECHNOLOGY:** pp. T78, T80, T93, T99, T113, T116, T121, T125, T130	• **PHONICS READERS:** *Dinosaur Hall, Paws and Claws, The Frog Trail, A Rain Forest Day* • **PHONICS CHAPTER BOOK:** *Let's Go on a Museum Hunt* • **MY BOOKS:** *The Awful Bug; Small Daniel; Anna Jane, the Pain; Waiting for Suzy* • **GUIDED READING PROGRAM**
✓**SPELLING:** Words With *oa,* pp. R20–R21 ✓**GRAMMAR, USAGE, MECHANICS:** Homophones, pp. R22–R23	✓**SHARED WRITING:** Poem, p. T168 • **JOURNAL,** p. T146	• **MATH:** Days of Toad's Life, p. R24 • **SCIENCE:** Frogs and Toads, p. R24 • **SOCIAL STUDIES:** Gardens in Our Town, p. R25 • **THE ARTS:** Music for Seeds, p. R25	✓**STUDY SKILLS:** Follow Directions, p. T172 • **TECHNOLOGY:** pp. T142, T144, T149, T153, T161, T164, T166, T171, T173, T177	• **PHONICS READERS:** *The Hungry Toad, Goat's Book, Small Animals with Big Names, See the Sea* • **PHONICS CHAPTER BOOK:** *Let's Go on a Museum Hunt* • **MY BOOKS:** *Rabbit's New Coat, Don't Be Bored* • **GUIDED READING PROGRAM**
✓**SPELLING:** Compound Words, pp. R28–R29 ✓**GRAMMAR, USAGE, MECHANICS:** Verbs: Past Tense, pp. R30–R31	✓**SHARED WRITING:** Fantasy, p. T224 • **JOURNAL,** p. T190	• **MATH:** Dinosaur Footprints, p. R32 • **SCIENCE:** Dinosaur Facts, p. R32 • **SOCIAL STUDIES:** A Dinosaur in My Neighborhood, p. R33 • **THE ARTS:** Make a Fossil, p. R33	• **WORKSHOP 2:** How to Make a Nature Poster, p. T235 • **READ ALOUD:** *An Alphabet of Dinosaurs,* p. T228 • **TECHNOLOGY:** pp. T186, T188, T201, T211, T217, T220, T228, T234	• **PHONICS READERS:** *Baby Pig at School, Donkey and Monkey* • **PHONICS CHAPTER BOOK:** *Let's Go on a Museum Hunt* • **MY BOOKS:** *Monkey See, Monkey Do; Father's Backpack; Sunflowers* • **GUIDED READING PROGRAM**
✓**SPELLING:** Words With *o* and *ow,* pp. R36–R37 ✓**GRAMMAR, USAGE, MECHANICS:** Words That Compare, pp. R38–R39	✓**SHARED WRITING:** Personal Narrative, p. T274 • **JOURNAL,** p. T250	• **MATH:** Read a Garden Map, p. R40 • **SCIENCE:** How Trees Change, p. R40 • **SOCIAL STUDIES:** Map the Neighborhood, p. R41 • **THE ARTS:** Fill a Greenhouse, p. R41	✓**STUDY SKILLS:** Test-Taking Strategies, p. T278 • **TECHNOLOGY:** pp. T246, T248, T255, T263, T267, T270, T272, T275, T279, T284	• **PHONICS READERS:** *Follow It!, Bow's Bows* • **PHONICS CHAPTER BOOK:** *Let's Go on a Museum Hunt* • **MY BOOKS:** *Don't Go So Slow!, Sunflowers* • **GUIDED READING PROGRAM**

✓ **WRITING PROCESS:** Description of a Place Visited

PROJECT: Make a Big Book of Information

✓ **PRESENTATION SKILL:** Listen to Get Information

TECHNOLOGY: WiggleWorks Plus

UNIT TRADE BOOK LIBRARY

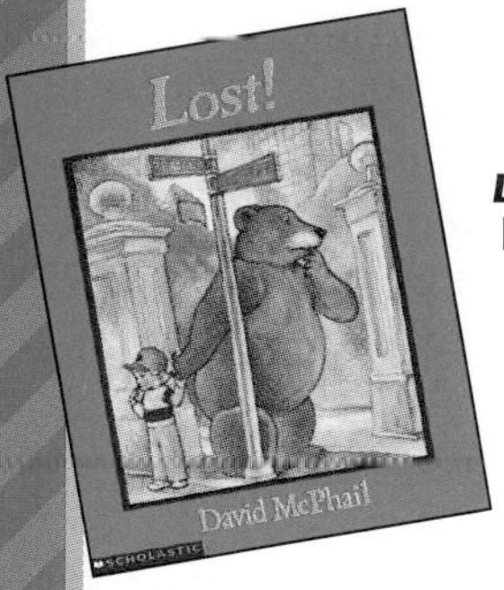

***Lost!* by David McPhail**

Challenge
Average
▶ Easy

***Animal Tracks* by Arthur Dorros**

▶ Challenge
Average
Easy

***Owl at Home* by Arnold Lobel**

Challenge
▶ Average
Easy

BOOKS FOR INDEPENDENT READING

EASY

Bugs!
by Fred and Patricia McKissack
Children's Press, 1988
✸ ◆ ▲
This very accessible book introduces insects to the early reader.

Danny and the Dinosaur
by Syd Hoff
Scholastic, 1990
▲ ✸ ◆
This easy-to-read story tells about Danny and his friend, the museum dinosaur.

Everything Grows
by Raffi
Illustrated by Bruce McMillan
Crown, 1989 ✸ ▲ ◆
Lively photographs of an African-American brother and sister and of growing things accompany the text of Raffi's song.

Ladybugs and Other Insects
by Pascale de Bourgoing
Scholastic, 1993 ✸ ▲ ◆
Transparent overlays help to reveal basic information about insects.

AVERAGE

Amazing Fish
by Mary Ling
Knopf/Eyewitness Junior, 1991 ▲ ✸
This photo-illustrated book introduces the reader to many kinds of fish.

The Dinosaur Who Lived in My Backyard
by B. G. Hennessey
Illustrated by Susan Davis
Scholastic, 1992 ✸ ◆
A child imagines what it would be like to bring back the dinosaurs.

Going Fishing
by Rachel Warner
Scholastic, 1992 ★ ■
In Bangladesh, Suroth and his father catch everything except fish.

Pinky and Rex
by James Howe
Atheneum, 1990 ▲ ★
Rex visits the museum to see dinosaurs with her friend Pinky.

CHALLENGE

My Visit to the Aquarium
by Aliki
HarperCollins, 1993
✸ ★ ■
This big, beautiful book introduces readers to the wonders of the aquarium.

Nessa's Fish
by Nancy Luenn
Illustrated by Neil Waldman
Scholastic, 1992 ■ ✸ ✚
Nessa, an Inuit girl, goes ice-fishing with her grandmother and uses her wits to keep animals away from their catch.

The Race of Toad and Deer
by Pat Mora
Illustrated by Maya Itzna Brooks
Orchard Books, 1995 ■ ✚
In this Guatemalan folk tale, Toad races proud Deer—and gets some help from his friends.

When the Woods Hum
by Joanne Ryder
Morrow, 1991 ✸ ◆
A father and daughter observe the coming of the cicadas, as the father did 17 years earlier.

BOOKS WITH PHONIC ELEMENTS

Arthur's Funny Money
by Lillian Hoban
Harper, 1981
(long *e*)

Boats
by Anne Rockwell
Dutton, 1985
(long *o*)

Clifford's Puppy Days
by Norman Bridwell
Scholastic, 1989
(long *e*, long *a*)

How My Parents Learned to Eat
by Ina Friedman
Illustrated by Allen Say
Houghton Mifflin, 1984
(*ed*, /t/, /d/)

Mr. Tall and Mr. Small
by Barbara Brenner
Holt, 1994
(*all*)

KEY

■ Cultural Connections
★ Social Studies
▲ Kid Picks
◆ Math
✸ Science
✚ The Arts

Books in Other Languages

SPANISH

Daniel y los dinosaurios
by Mary Carmine
Illustrated by Martin Baynton
Scholastic, 1993 ▲ ✷ ◆
A trip to the aquarium reveals that Daniel does love something other than dinosaurs.

El desierto es mi madre/The Desert Is My Mother
by Pat Mora
Illustrated by Francisco Mora
Arte Publico Press, 1994
■ ★
Pat Mora writes a poetic, bilingual tribute to the desert of the Southwest.

El encanto del caracol
by Joanne Ryder
Illustrated by Lynne Cherry
Scholastic, 1994 ✷ ◆
A child experiences a garden from the size and perspective of a snail.

Las huellas de los animales
by Arthur Dorros
Scholastic, 1994 ✷ ◆
A guessing-game format enables young readers to identify animal tracks.

¡Insectos!
by Fred and Patricia McKissack
Children's Press, 1988
✷ ◆
This very simple book introduces insects to the early reader.

La pesca de Nessa
by Nancy Luenn
Illustrated by Neil Waldman
Libros Colibri, 1995
■ ✷ ✚
Nessa, an Inuit girl, goes ice-fishing with her grandmother and uses her wits to keep animals away from their catch.

Mis cinco sentidos
by Aliki
Harper Arco Iris, 1995
▲ ✷
This simple book focuses on common experiences associated with each sense.

CHINESE

Bugs and Other Garden Creatures
by Toskiki Kobayashi
Multicultural Distributing Center ■ ✷
Chinese-language text introduces the small creatures of the garden. (also available in Japanese)

KOREAN

Amazing Fish
by Mary Ling
Shen's, 1990 ■ ✷
Photos and simple Korean text introduce the reader to many kinds of fish.

Technology

You'll find this Scholastic technology referenced in the Literacy Place Teacher's Editions.

AUDIO

Literacy Place Listening Library
Selections from the student anthology as well as every Big Book in grades K–2 are available on audiocassette.

VIDEO

Literacy Place Meet the Mentor
One Meet-the-Mentor video per unit gives children an opportunity to meet a real-life professional who models ways in which literacy is used in his or her career.

SOFTWARE

WiggleWorks Plus
Scholastic (Win/Mac)
This CD-ROM component for Kindergarten through Grade 2 of Literacy Place supports children's language development. These activities integrate reading, writing, listening, and speaking.

Scholastic Reading Counts!
Formerly known as The Electronic Bookshelf, this interactive reading motivation and management program is for students at all reading levels.

I Spy
Scholastic (Win/Mac)
These scavenger-hunt games build reading, math, problem-solving, and logic skills.

Usborne's Animated First Thousand Words
Usborne/Scholastic (Win/Mac)
This fun-to-use vocabulary tool introduces pre- and beginning readers to 1,000 common English and Spanish words.

INTERNET

www.scholasticnetwork.com
This comprehensive online curriculum service for grades K–8 features unit-by-unit extensions for Literacy Place.

www.scholastic.com
Scholastic's corporate web site includes Literacy Place resources and unit-related Internet links.

Other Sites
The Internet is growing and changing every day, so be sure to preview all sites before your students visit them.

For more information about Scholastic's technology, please call 1-800-SCHOLASTIC.

LAUNCH THE UNIT

BASELINE ASSESSMENT

The Baseline Assessment activity helps you determine the conceptual level at which each child starts the unit. Repeat the task at the end of the unit. Have children draw pictures of various sources of information, such as television, newspapers, books, computers, and the library. Save these pictures to use for comparison at the end of the unit.

K-W-L

Start a K-W-L chart for Information Finders that you will return to at the end of the unit. Ask children the following questions:

- Where do you get most of your information?
- Where would you go to get more information about something you were interested in learning about?

What do we know?	What do we want to know?	What did we learn?

Set Up the Place: Aquarium

Young children are often enthralled by the underwater world, and are eager to learn more about it. A classroom aquarium is an ideal place for children to investigate marine life while gaining hands-on experience with gathering and managing information. Transform a corner of your classroom into a workplace model of an aquarium. The learning center is an appropriate setting for cooperative and self-directed activities.

Idea File: Aquarium

- Invite children to help organize and maintain their aquarium with a list of tasks that need doing, such as: "Make a sign-out sheet for books in the aquarium library."
- Create a collection of facts about the ocean or its inhabitants on separate index cards. Encourage children to add cards to the file. You might have them develop categories for the facts and sort the cards into sections.
- Encourage cooperative groups to take charge of a "tank" in the aquarium and fill it with murals or collages of aquatic plants and animals. Children can gain experience synthesizing information as they write labels for their displays.
- Choose a name for your classroom aquarium and use banners, calendars, and posters.
- Use a calendar to keep track of the children's activities in the aquarium and to schedule special events.
- Ask children to suggest new and interesting words for the "Underwater Words" list.

"I keep a logbook. I write down anything I learn from the tapes and pictures."

—LAELA SAYIGH

Meet the Mentor: Laela Sayigh

View the Video

Before viewing the mentor video, explain that Laela Sayigh is a marine biologist—someone who studies the animals and plants that live in the sea. Her particular interest is dolphins.

- Ask children to watch and listen for tools that Laela Sayigh uses to listen to dolphins.

Think About the Video

After viewing, give children time to discuss their thoughts and opinions about the video with questions such as:

> **What did you learn from watching and listening to this video?**

> **Do you think dolphins say their names? What do you think dolphin whistles mean?**

> **What did you enjoy about the video?**

Invite volunteers to imitate the sounds of different animals. Have the class identify the animals.

Viewing as a Learning Tool

Teach/Model Help children understand that setting a purpose for listening can help them to focus on what they want to learn.

Think Aloud *My purpose for listening to the video was to find out why Laela Sayigh was spending so much time listening to dolphins. As I watched and listened to the video, I found out that she wanted to understand what the dolphins were saying with their whistles.*

Practice/Apply Ask children to share their purposes for listening to the video and how their purposes helped them learn about the dolphins.

Real-World Skills

- Identify a main idea and support it with details.
- Distinguish between fantasy and reality.
- Research, synthesize, and report facts.
- Appreciate the perspective and experience of other generations.
- Use observation to draw conclusions.
- Use listening as a learning tool.

Preview of Workshops and Project

The Workshops and Project will give children an opportunity to apply to hands-on activities what they have learned about the mentor and place.

Workshop 1
How to Keep an Observation Log
(T131–T134)
Children will record the sights and sounds of nature in a log.

Workshop 2
How to Make a Nature Poster
(T235–T238)
Children choose a natural environment and design a Nature Poster to present information.

Project
How to Make a Big Book of Information
(T292–T295)
Children will select information, write text, and draw illustrations for their own Big Book about a sea plant or animal.

Big Book

Share the Big Book

THEME CONNECTION In this book, children learn that there are many different ways to find information about things you are interested in. Sometimes asking the right question does the trick.

Preview and Predict

USE PICTURE CLUES Read the Big Book title and the name of the author/illustrator. Show children the cover. Ask them to describe all the things they see that have to do with writing and sending a letter.

MAKE PREDICTIONS Flip through several pages with children and show them that the story is told through letters. Encourage children to predict what the story will be about.

> **Who do you think Mr. Blueberry is? Who do you think is writing to him?**

> **What do you think the whale has to do with the story?**

Write children's responses on the chalkboard or on chart paper.

Read the Big Book

CHECK COMPREHENSION As you read the Big Book with children, track the print. After reading the first two letters, pause to discuss the following questions:

> **Why does Emily write to Mr. Blueberry?**

> **What does Mr. Blueberry think of Emily's whale? Why does he think that?**

> **What do you think will happen next?**

Each time Emily asks a questions, let children respond with their own ideas and make predictions about how Mr. Blueberry might respond.

DISCUSS VOCABULARY As you continue reading, discuss the meanings of unfamiliar words as they come up.

Respond to the Big Book

Personal Response

SHARE OPINIONS

Give children an opportunity to share their thoughts and opinions about the story. You may wish to prompt discussion with questions such as:

> **Why doesn't Mr. Blueberry believe that Emily has a whale in her pond?**

> **What does Emily do to take care of her whale?**

> **What was your favorite letter? Why did you like it?**

> **Do you think Mr. Blueberry is a good teacher? Would you like to have him as your teacher? Why or why not?**

THEME CONNECTIONS

Looking at different sources helps us learn new things about our world. Discuss Emily's love of whales and her curiosity about them. Ask children to name their favorite animal and to share any information they might have about it. Ask:

> **Where would you go to find out more information?**

Telling a Whale of a Tale

USING YOUR IMAGINATION

To help children understand that we learn about the world in many different ways—including using our imaginations—invite them to join you in a story circle.

- Start a story and then go around the circle, letting each child take a turn adding a sentence to the story.
- Encourage children to make the story as funny, fanciful, and fantastic as they can. Here are some story starters you might use:
  - **Yesterday I was home and there was a giant goldfish in my bathtub.**
  - **One day a monkey followed me home from the zoo.**
  - **I think I saw a dinosaur in my back yard.**

FAMILY LITERACY NIGHT

Involve families every step of the way and close the unit with a Family Literacy Night. See page T298 for details.

Home Involvement

TAKE HOME

A two-way partnership between the school and the home will help to improve children's learning. Distribute the following items for children to take home and read with their families:

- *Family Letter* in the **Literacy-at-Home Kit**
- *Family Literacy Newsletter* on **pages T3–T4** of the **Practice Book**
- *Family Newsletter* on **page T171** of the **Literacy Place Spelling Teacher's Resource Book**
- **My Books** and **Phonics Readers**

Family Literacy Tips

TEACHER'S EDITION

In the Teacher's Edition you'll find these valuable tips at point of use.

- **FAMILY TALK** Children's school performance benefits from talking about school events at home. See the activities on pages T49, T91, and the 10-minute activity on page T257.
- **HOME-SCHOOL CONNECTION** Children take selected books home to read to a family member in the activities on pages T58, T63, T118, T123, T166, T171, T222, T227, T272, and T277.
- **FAMILY LITERACY** Reading together is most effective if family members use a specific reading strategy. See the activity on page T111 and the tip on page T215 for reading aloud.
- **FAMILY LITERACY RESOURCES** The tip on page T193 encourages families to share written material from home or the library to promote children's special interests. The ALA web site in the tip on page T265 provides resource lists of books for children.

Internet

Suggest that parents visit the Scholastic web site at **www.scholastic.com** for links to valuable resources. Parents can learn all about their children's favorite books, authors, and characters.

Fish Faces

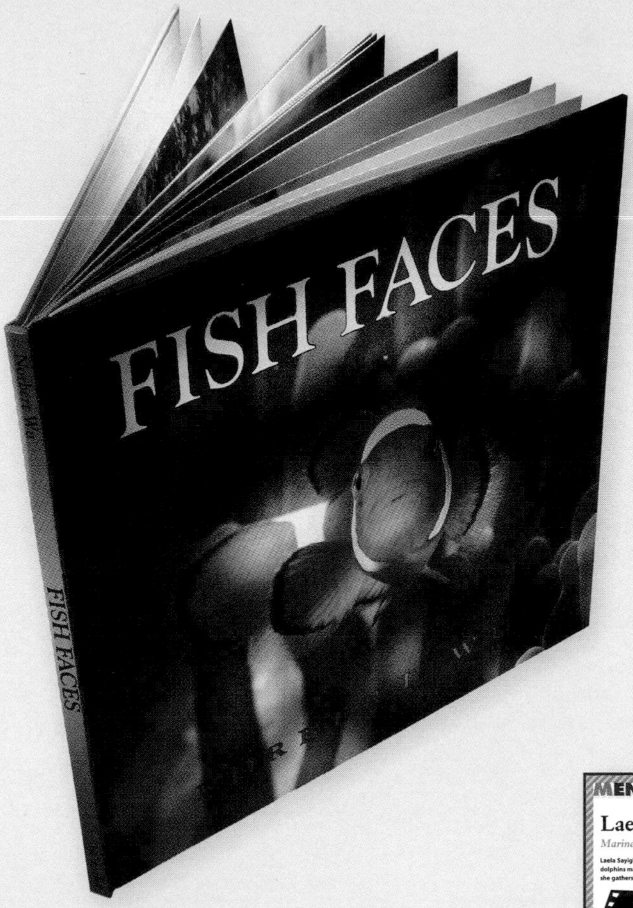

Main Selection
Genre: Photo Essay

Paired Selection
Genre: Profile

WEEK 1 TESTED SKILLS

- **Vocabulary**
- **Daily Phonics: Digraphs *sh, th***
- **Key Comprehension Skill: Main Idea/Details**
- **Homophones**
- **Spelling: Words With Digraphs *sh, th***
- **Grammar, Usage, Mechanics: Word Order**

Technology Connection

BUILD BACKGROUND Send children surfing to the National Aquarium in Baltimore at **www.aqua.org** to find more fantastic fish faces and facts. There's also something fishy going on at the Monterey Bay "E-Quarium," at **www.mbayaq.org.**

Selection Summary

This photo essay gives children an up-close look at various kinds of fish. Readers are face to face with flat fish, round fish, spotted fish, dotted fish, fish with spikes, and many more. The selection pays particular attention to specific parts of the fish, including the nose and eyes.

PAIRED SELECTION Dolphins are the focus of marine biologist Laela Sayigh's work. She works closely with them, studying how they make their sounds.

Author

NORBERT WU is both a marine biologist and underwater photographer. He loves to observe and photograph fish in their natural habitat. He believes that fish have their own personalities. Another book by Mr. Wu is *Life in the Oceans.*

Weekly Organizer

Visit Our Web Site
www.scholastic.com

Fish Faces

	DAY 1	DAY 2
READ and Introduce Skills • VOCABULARY • PHONICS • COMPREHENSION • LISTENING • SPEAKING • VIEWING 	**BUILD BACKGROUND,** p. T19 ▲ **VOCABULARY,** p. T20 ▲ ✱ Practice Book, p. 5 **DAILY PHONICS:** ▲ ■ Digraphs *sh, th,* pp. T22–T23 Practice Book, pp. 6, 7 **PREVIEW AND PREDICT,** p. T24 **READ:** ▲ ✱ ■ *Fish Faces,* pp. T24–T33 **COMPREHENSION:** Main Idea/Details, p. T27	**READ:** ▲ ■ ✱ *Fish Faces,* pp. T34–T49 **DAILY PHONICS:** Homophones, p. T39 **GENRE:** Photo Essay, p. T43 **COMPREHENSION:** Draw Conclusions, p. T45 Summarize, p. T47
WRITE and Respond • GRAMMAR • USAGE • MECHANICS • SPELLING • WRITING	**SHARED WRITING,** p. T19 **JOURNAL:** p. T21 **QUICKWRITE:** Predict, p. T33 **SPELLING:** Pretest: Words With Digraphs *sh, th,* p. R4 Spelling Resource Book, p. 109 **GRAMMAR, USAGE, MECHANICS:** Teach/Model: Word Order, p. R6 **ORAL LANGUAGE,** p. T33	**SHARED WRITING:** Prewrite, p. T49 Practice Book, p. 14 **SPELLING:** Vocabulary Practice, p. R4 Spelling Resource Book, pp. 110–112 **GRAMMAR, USAGE, MECHANICS:** Practice, p. R6 **ORAL LANGUAGE,** p. T49
EXTEND SKILLS and Apply to Literature • SKILLS • INTEGRATED LANGUAGE ARTS • INTEGRATED CURRICULUM • GUIDED READING • INDEPENDENT READING	**READ ALOUD,** p. T33 **GUIDED READING,** pp. R2–R3 **INTEGRATED CURRICULUM:** Math, p. R8 The Arts, p. R9 **TRADE BOOKS** • *Lost!* • *Owl at Home* • *Animal Tracks* 	**READ ALOUD,** p. T49 **GUIDED READING,** p. R2–R3 **INTEGRATED CURRICULUM:** Science, p. R8 Social Studies, p. R9

TECHNOLOGY and **REAL-WORLD SKILLS**	**WIGGLEWORKS PLUS CD-ROM** Magnet Board, pp. T20, T22 **SCHOLASTIC NETWORK** Finding the Facts, p. T29	**WIGGLEWORKS PLUS CD-ROM** Language Development, p. T47

MODIFY INSTRUCTION

● INTERVENTION ▲ ESL/ELD ■ EXTRA HELP
✳ GIFTED & TALENTED ✓ = TESTED SKILL

DAY 3	DAY 4	DAY 5
READ: ▲ ■ "Mentor Profile: Laela Sayigh," pp. T50–T51 ✓ **COMPREHENSION:** ▲ ■ Main Idea/Details, pp. T54–T55 Practice Book, pp. 9, 10 ✓ **DAILY PHONICS:** ▲ ■ Homophones, p. T56 Practice Book, pp. 12, 13 **BUILDING FLUENCY,** p. T58 **FOCUS ON HIGH-FREQUENCY WORDS,** p. T59 **FOCUS ON PHONICS,** p. T59	**VOCABULARY REVIEW,** p. T62 ✓ **DAILY PHONICS:** Homophones, p. T63	**READING ASSESSMENT,** p. T66 Selection Test, p. T67 Conference Decoding Test, p. T67
RESPOND: ▲ ✳ Think About Reading, p. T52 Practice Book, p. 18 **WRITE LABELS,** p. T53 ✓ **SPELLING:** Write/Proofread, p. R5 Spelling Resource Book, p. 113 ✓ **GRAMMAR, USAGE, MECHANICS:** Practice, p. R7 **ORAL LANGUAGE,** p. T53	**SHARED WRITING:** ▲ ■ Book of Facts, p. T60 Practice Book, p. 14 ✓ **SPELLING:** Study/Review, p. R5 Spelling Resource Book, p. 161 ✓ **GRAMMAR, USAGE, MECHANICS:** Apply, p. R7 **ORAL LANGUAGE,** p. T61	**WRITING ASSESSMENT,** p. T68 Child Model Children's Writing Rubric ✓ **SPELLING:** Posttest, p. R5 Spelling Resource Book, p. 163 ✓ **GRAMMAR, USAGE, MECHANICS:** Assess, p. R7 **ORAL LANGUAGE,** p. T68
READ ALOUD, p. T59 **GUIDED READING,** pp. R2–R3 **OPTIONAL MATERIALS,** p. T58 Phonics Reader #36: *Shhh!*	**READ ALOUD,** p. T65 **GUIDED READING,** pp. R2–R3 **EXTEND VOCABULARY:** Review Vocabulary, p. T62 **OPTIONAL MATERIALS,** p. T63 Phonics Reader #54: *See the Sea* **READ ALOUD:** *Three Days on a River in a Red Canoe,* p. T64	**READ ALOUD,** p. T70 **GUIDED READING,** pp. R2–R3 **INTEGRATED LANGUAGE ARTS:** Make Fish-Face Puppets, p. T69 Write a Book Report, p. T69 Make a Class Book, p. T70 Read About How Fish Move, p. T70
WIGGLEWORKS PLUS CD-ROM Presentation Tools, p. T53 Magnet Board, p. T56 **WORKSHOP 1,** pp. T132–T134	**WIGGLEWORKS PLUS CD-ROM** Writing Skills, pp. T61, T64 **WORKSHOP 1,** pp. T132–T134	**WIGGLEWORKS PLUS CD-ROM** Viewing Skills, p. T69 **WORKSHOP 1,** pp. T132–T134

Weekly Assessment

ASSESSMENT PLANNING

USE THIS CHART TO PLAN YOUR ASSESSMENT OF THE WEEKLY READING OBJECTIVES.

- **Informal Assessment is ongoing and should be used before, during and after reading.**
- **Formal Assessment occurs at the end of the week on the selection test.**
- **Note that intervention activities occur throughout the lesson to support children who need extra help with skills.**

YOU MAY CHOOSE AMONG THE FOLLOWING PAGES IN THE ASSESSMENT HANDBOOK.

- **Informal Assessment**
- **Anecdotal Record**
- **Portfolio Checklist and Evaluation Forms**
- **Self-Assessment**
- **English Language Learners**
- **Using Technology to Assess,**
- **Test Preparations**

SKILLS AND STRATEGIES	Informal Assessment
COMPREHENSION Main Idea/Details	**OBSERVATION p. T27** • Did children use the text and pictures to identify the main idea? **QUICKCHECK p. T54** • Can children recognize the main idea of the selection? **CHECK PRACTICE BOOK p. 9** **CONFERENCE p. T66**
DAILY PHONICS Digraphs *sh, th* Homophones	**OBSERVATION pp. T29, T39** • Can children recognize words with *sh* and *th*? • Can children identify words that sound alike but are spelled differently? **CHECK PRACTICE BOOK pp. 6, 12** **DICTATION pp. T23, T57**
VOCABULARY Story Words **fish mouth eyes** **nose fins waves** High-Frequency **more belongs**	**OBSERVATION p. T62** • Did children identify story words? • Did children identify high-frequency words? **CHECK PRACTICE BOOK p. 5**

Formal Assessment	**INTERVENTION** and Instructional Alternatives	
SELECTION TEST • Questions 1–3 check children's mastery of the key strategy, main idea/details. **UNIT TEST**	**If children need help with main idea/details, then go to:** • **Instructional Alternatives, p. T55** • **Review, p. R43** • **Reteach, p. R55**	
DECODING TEST • See p. T67 **SELECTION TEST** • Questions 4–7 check children's ability to recognize words with *sh* and *th* and homophones. **UNIT TEST**	**If children need help identifying words with *sh* and *th*, then go to:** • **Intervention Activity, p. T59** • **Review, p. R49** • **Reteach, p. R57** **If children need help identifying homophones, then go to:** • **Review, p. R46** • **Reteach, p. R57**	
SELECTION TEST • Questions 8–10 check children's recall of high-frequency words and story words. **UNIT TEST**	**If children need additional practice with the vocabulary words, then go to:** • **Intervention Activity, p. T59** • **Extend Vocabulary, p. T62** • **Integrated Language Arts Activity, p. T69**	

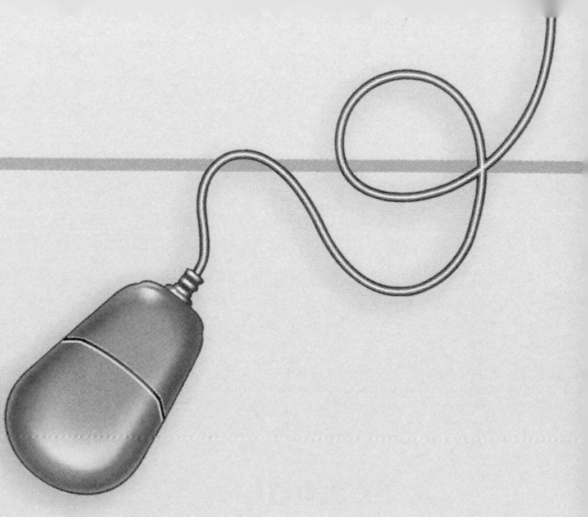

Technology

The technology in this lesson helps teachers and children develop the skills they need for the 21st century. Look for integrated technology activities on every day of instruction.

DAY 1
Finding the Facts

- Children search **www.scholasticnetwork.com** to answer a question about dolphins.

www.scholasticnetwork.com

DAY 2
Language Development

- Children read **WiggleWorks Plus** My Book and then rewrite and redraw the last page.

WiggleWorks Plus CD-ROM

DAY 3
Presentation Tools

- Children use **WiggleWorks Plus** PlaceMaker to draw and label parts of a fish.

DAY 4
Writing Skills

- Children use **WiggleWorks Plus** Unit Writer to write a journal entry about an imaginary canoe trip.

WiggleWorks Plus CD-ROM

DAY 5
Viewing Skills

- Children create fish puppets and then videotape a puppet show version of the book.

Build Background

Some selections use photographs with the text. Fish Faces *has photographs that show fish in an amazing variety of shapes, colors, and patterns.*

Activate Prior Knowledge

DISCUSS PHOTO ESSAYS Explain that a photo essay gives information about a topic through both photographs and words. Ask children to describe books they have seen that have photographs.

SHARE EXPERIENCES Ask children if they have ever seen fish in an aquarium, pet store, or fish tank.

> **Where have you seen fish?**

> **What did those fish look like?**

SHARED WRITING *Book of Facts*

INTRODUCE Have children brainstorm what they know about fish. Have children write or dictate their facts on fish-shaped paper. Display the fish on a bulletin board under the head *Fishy Facts We Know.*

DAY 1 OBJECTIVES

CHILDREN WILL:

READ 30 MINUTES

- Build Background
- Vocabulary
- Daily Phonics: Digraphs *sh, th*
- *Fish Faces*, pp. 8–17
- Key Comprehension Skill: Main Idea/Details

WRITE 30 MINUTES

- Shared Writing: Introduce Writing a Book of Facts
- Quickwrite: Set a Purpose
- Spelling: Words With Digraphs *sh, th*
- Grammar, Usage, Mechanics: Word Order
- Oral Language

EXTEND SKILLS 30 MINUTES

- Integrated Curriculum
- Read Aloud
- Guided Reading

RESOURCES

- Practice Book, pp. 5–7
- Spelling Resource Book, p. 109

MODIFY Instruction

ESL/ELD

▲ Preview the photos in the story, comparing color, size, and shape. Review *-er* comparison ending. Then brainstorm a list of words that describe fish. Verify understanding as you list the describing words in categories such as: Colors (blue, grey), Shapes (round, flat), and Patterns (stripes, dots). **(CATEGORIZE)**

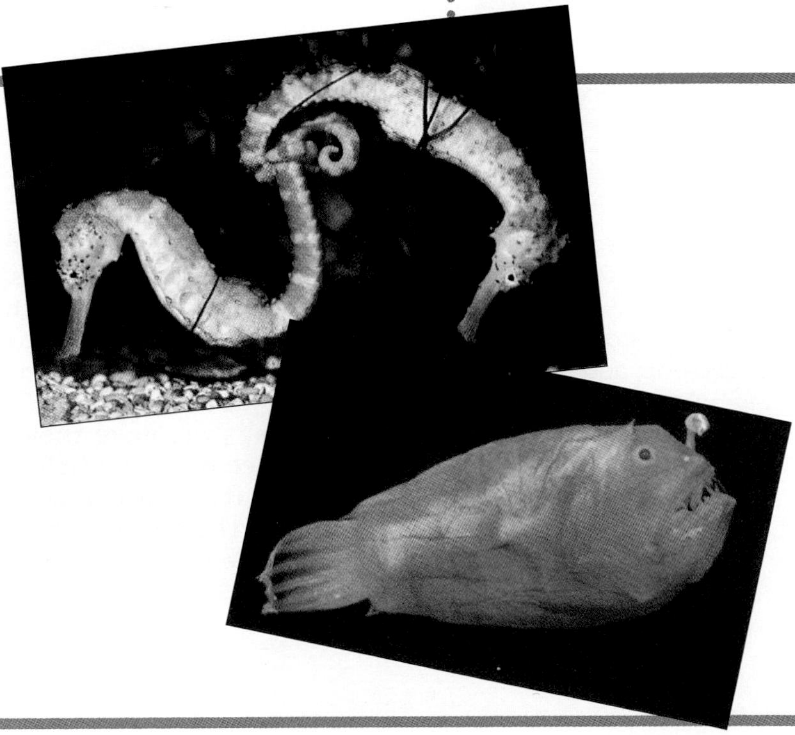

VOCABULARY

High-Frequency Words

VOCABULARY

HIGH-FREQUENCY

more belongs

STORY WORDS

fish waves

mouth nose

eyes fins

A TEACH/MODEL

INTRODUCE HIGH-FREQUENCY WORDS Write the high-frequency words ***more*** and ***belongs*** in sentences on the chalkboard. Read the sentences aloud, underline the high-frequency words, and ask children if they recognize them. You may wish to use these sentences:

Can you tell us more about fish?

This book about fish belongs to me.

Ask volunteers to dictate sentences using the high-frequency words. Add these to the chalkboard.

B PRACTICE/APPLY

FOCUS ON SPELLING Write each high-frequency word on a note card. Read each aloud. Then do the following:

ROUTINE

1. **Display one card at a time, and ask children to state each word aloud.**
2. **Have children spell each word aloud.**
3. **Ask children to write each word in the air as they state aloud each letter. Then have them write each word on a sheet of paper or in their Journals.**

MAINTAIN VOCABULARY Add the note cards to the **Word Wall.** Then review the following high-frequency words on the wall: ***which, make, were,*** and ***way.***

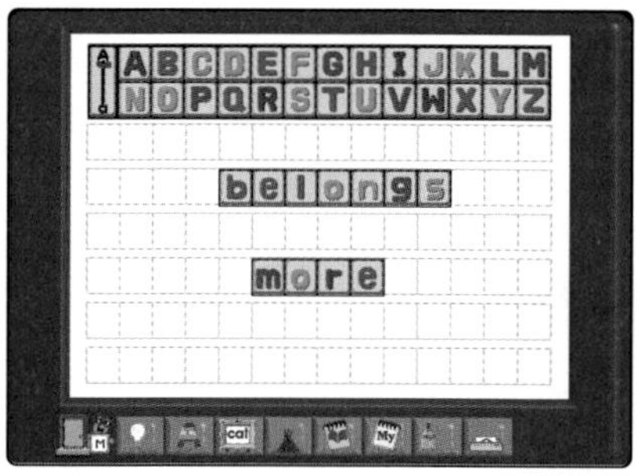

TECHNOLOGY

For children needing additional practice with high-frequency words prior to reading the story, have them build, explode, and rebuild each high-frequency word on the **WiggleWorks Plus** Magnet Board.

MODIFY Instruction

ESL/ELD

▲ To reinforce the meaning of the selection words, model and have English language learners draw their own picture of a fish and label the *mouth, eyes, nose, fins.* Have them draw a *wave* near the fish and label it. Finally, have them write the title of their picture on top: *FISH.* **(MULTISENSORY TECHNIQUES)**

GIFTED & TALENTED

✳ Have children write one sentence each using high-frequency words. Then have children cover the high-frequency words with sticky notes. Ask partners to exchange sentences. Have children fill in missing words and check their answers by lifting up the sticky notes. **(WORK IN PAIRS)**

Story Words

Ⓐ TEACH/MODEL

INTRODUCE STORY WORDS

The selection also contains the following story words: ***fish, waves, mouth, nose, eyes, fins.***

- Write these words on the chalkboard, read them aloud, and discuss their meanings if necessary.
- Point out previously taught sound-spelling correspondences, **/ā/*a-e*, /ō/*o-e*,** and **/sh/*sh*.**
- Using colored chalk, create a visual clue for each word—a simple outline of a ***fish,*** a wavy line for ***wave,*** and so on.

PRACTICE BOOK p. 5

Ⓑ PRACTICE/APPLY

BUILD STORY BACKGROUND

Discuss fish with children.

- Have volunteers tell about fish they have seen, either live or in books, films, or on TV.
- Invite children to imagine what it would be like to go underwater and see the fish up close.
- Then have children draw an underwater scene with fish.

WRITE TO READ

When completed, have children write a sentence about their pictures using one or more of the story words.

PLAY CHARADES

Write the story words on index cards, one word per card. Have partners take turns drawing word cards, one card per child. Children should read their word cards without letting their partners see the words. Then children should take turns acting out the meanings of their words while their partners try to guess the words.

JOURNAL

Ask children to write a sentence using each **high-frequency word** in their Journals. You might suggest the following sentence starters:

I need more ____.

That belongs ____.

SELECTION WORDS With Digraphs *sh, th*

fish	mouths
shine	that
there	thin
thousands	

SKILLS TRACE

DIGRAPHS *sh, th* TESTED

Introduce	pp. T22–T23
Practice	pp. T29, T58–T59
Review	p. R49
Reteach	p. R57

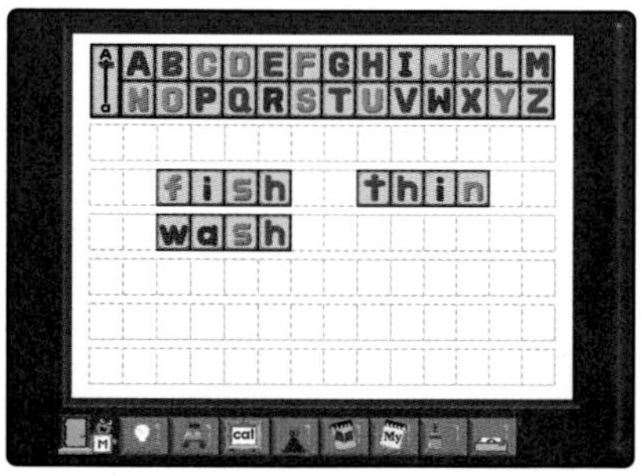

TECHNOLOGY

Have children build words with *sh* and *th* on the **WiggleWorks Plus** Magnet Board.

- Begin with the words ***fish*** and ***thin.***
- Have children search for other words in classroom books.

DAILY PHONICS

Digraphs sh, th

A PHONOLOGICAL AWARENESS

RHYME Read aloud the rhyme "Little Bo Peep" from the *Big Book of Rhymes and Rhythms* 1A, page 33. As you read, stress the words that contain ***sh*** and ***th: sheep*** and ***them.***

- When children are comfortable with the rhyme, have them read along with you.
- Frame the words ***sheep*** and ***them.*** Point out the consonant digraph.

Little Bo Peep
Little Bo Peep has lost her sheep,
And doesn't know where to find them,
Leave them alone,
And they'll come home,
Wagging their tails behind them.
them

Big Book of Rhymes and Rhythms 1A, p. 33

ORAL BLENDING Say the following word parts and ask children to blend them. Provide modeling and corrective feedback as needed.

/sh/ . . . eep	/sh/ . . . ine	fi . . . /sh/
/th/ . . . in	/th/ . . . ick	wi . . . /th/

B CONNECT SOUND-SPELLING

INTRODUCE CONSONANT DIGRAPHS *sh, th* Explain that there are pairs of consonant letters that are called digraphs. A digraph is two different letters that together stand for one sound. Write the words ***shark*** and ***thumb*** on the chalkboard. Model how to blend the words.

THINK ALOUD *I can put the letters* ***sh, a, r,*** *and* ***k*** *together to make the word* ***shark.*** *Let's say the sounds slowly as I move my finger under the letters. Listen to the sound that* ***sh*** *stands for in the word* ***shark.*** *The sound of* ***sh*** *is* ***/sh/.*** Now let's repeat for ***th*** *and the word* ***thumb.***

MODIFY Instruction

ESL/ELD

▲ To help English language learners remember the *th* and *sh* sounds, have them draw or cut out a picture of a *ship* and a *fish*, a *thumb* and a *mouth*. Have them say each word, write it, and circle the digraph. Model correct pronunciation for any children inclined to drop the *-h* in *th*. **(PICTURE CLUES)**

EXTRA HELP

■ Children can hold *sh* and *th* and these word-part cards: *in, ine, ink, op, ut, ank*. A child with a digraph stands next to a child with a word part. Then they blend the parts together to say a word and decide if it's a real word. **(HANDS-ON LEARNING)**

- On the chalkboard, write ***sip, sock, sort, tick, torn, tree.*** In the first three words, have children replace ***s*** with ***sh*** and say the new word. In the next three, have them replace ***t*** with ***th.***

sh		th
wi __	ba __	fi __
pa __	pu __	di __

- Create a chart like the one shown. Have volunteers add final ***sh*** or ***th*** to form words.

PHONICS MAINTENANCE Review the following sound-spellings: **/sh/*sh*, /th/*th*, /st/*st*, /sn/*sn*, /ch/*ch*, /hw/*wh*,** and **/ē/*ea, ee*.** Say one of the sounds. Have a volunteer write on the chalkboard the spelling that stands for the sound. Continue with all the sounds.

C PRACTICE/APPLY

BLEND WORDS To practice using the sound-spellings and to review previous sound-spellings, list the following words and sentences on the chalkboard. Have children read each chorally. Model blending as needed.

shop shine sheep those
cheap wheel steep snap
That dish is thin.
Some fish have sharp teeth.

DICTATON Dictate the following words for children to spell: ***shape, thin, chat, wheel, step.***

BUILD WORDS Write the digraphs ***sh*** and ***th*** and these word parts on the chalkboard: ***ine, ake, op, ade, ud, row, ank, ing.*** Allow children time to build as many words as possible by adding the digraphs to the word parts. Children can write their words on separate sheets of paper. **(INDEPENDENT WORK)**

DIGRAPH TIC-TAC-TOE

Give each child a sheet of paper and nine paper markers. Have children draw tic-tac-toe grids and write ***sh*** or ***th*** in each of the squares. Say words that begin or end with ***sh*** or ***th.*** If children hear **/sh/,** they can cover a ***sh*** on their grid. If they hear **/th/,** they can cover a ***th.*** The object is to cover three digraphs in a row, across, down, or on a diagonal.

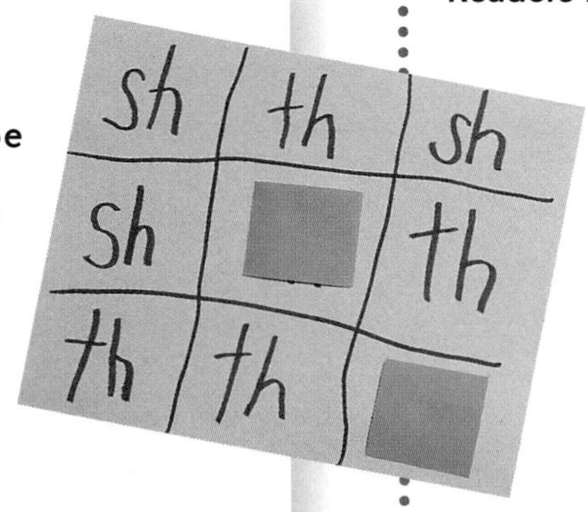

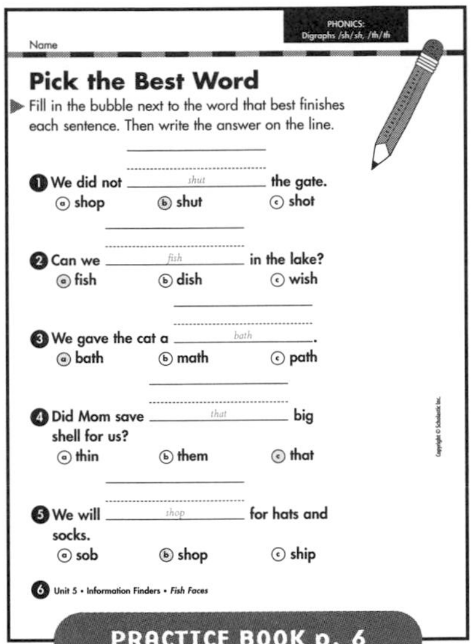
PHONICS: Digraphs /sh/sh, /th/th
Name
Pick the Best Word
Fill in the bubble next to the word that best finishes each sentence. Then write the answer on the line.
1 We did not ______ the gate. (a) shop (b) shut (c) shot
2 Can we ______ in the lake? (a) fish (b) dish (c) wish
3 We gave the cat a ______. (a) bath (b) math (c) path
4 Did Mom save ______ big shell for us? (a) thin (b) them (c) that
5 We will ______ for hats and socks. (a) sob (b) shop (c) ship
6 Unit 5 • Information Finders • *Fish Faces*

PRACTICE BOOK p. 6

PHONICS: Digraphs /sh/sh, /th/th
Name
Thin Fish
Say each picture name. If you hear /th/ in the word, write th. If you hear /sh/, write sh.
Unit 5 • Information Finders • *Fish Faces* 7

PRACTICE BOOK p. 7

DECODABLE TEXT

For practice reading decodable text, see ***Scholastic Decodable Readers #55–57.***

For additional phonics instruction and review, see ***Scholastic Phonics A, pp. 131–132, 157–158.***

COMPREHENSION

Preview and Predict

Show children the cover and read aloud the title and the author's name. Tell children that the author, Norbert Wu, is a marine biologist like the mentor Laela Sayigh. Have children preview the selection.

> **What do you think this selection is about? Will it tell facts about fish or will it tell a story about fish? How do you know?**

> **In what ways are fish faces the same as people's faces? How are they different?**

Help children make predictions before they read by asking a question:

> **What do you think you will learn about fish?**

JOURNAL

Make Predictions

Ask children to write their predictions in their Journal. Encourage them to record what they discover about fish as they read.

Set a Purpose

Help children set their own purposes for reading the selection. For example, they might want to look for the largest or the smallest fish. Then have them read page 9.

8

PHOTO ESSAY

CLASSROOM Management

WHOLE CLASS

On-Level Use the questions, Think Alouds, and Skills and Strategies lessons to guide children through a reading of the selection.

Below-Level Have children listen to the selection on audiocassette prior to the whole class reading to familiarize themselves with the selection format and vocabulary.

INDEPENDENT

Above-Level You might choose to have above-level children read the selection independently while you do a guided reading of the selection with the rest of the class. When they have finished, have these children rejoin the group to participate in the selection discussion.

9

One fish, two fish, three fish, more
Fish that dart and dip and slide
9

SKILLS AND STRATEGIES

Revisit the selection for skills instruction.

✓ = Tested Skill

COMPREHENSION

✓ **Main Idea/Details** T27

PHONICS

✓ **Digraphs *sh, th*** T29

Homophones T39

GENRE

Photo Essay T43

SMALL GROUP TO WHOLE CLASS

ESL/ELD Have children who need extra help listen to the story on the audiocassette prior to the whole class reading. This will help them to become familiar with the story sequence and vocabulary. Make sure that the children pay attention to the pre- and post-listening activities. **(AUDIO CLUES)**

COMPREHENSION

1 MAIN IDEA/DETAILS

> **How are the fish on these pages alike? Why are they grouped together?** *(The fish on these pages are alike because they all look like they are flying through the water. They are grouped together because their fins look alike.)*

2 PICTURE DETAILS

> **The fish on these pages almost look like they are flying through the water! Where are the fins on these fish? Point to them. How do you think the fins help the fish?** *(Possible answer: The fish move their fins to propel themselves through the water.)*

SELF-MONITORING STRATEGY

Use Illustrations

THINK ALOUD *As I read through this selection, I pay careful attention to the pictures. The photographs provide important details and information about the selection. Picture details help support the main idea of the selection.*

10

MODIFY Instruction

ESL/ELD

▲ Use visuals and gestures to clarify the meaning of *wings*. Verify children's understanding of the main idea of asking: *What do you see on these pages? Do all the fish seem to have wings?* Then ask: *What else has wings?* Encourage children to role-play a creature with wings. **(GUIDED QUESTIONS)**

EXTRA HELP

■ Brainstorm with the children a list of words that describe how fish move. Examine the word *glide*, demonstrate its meaning, and have children pantomime the action. **(ACT IT OUT)**

11

Fish that glide on fins like wings

1

2

11

MATH

Ask children to complete the **How Many Are Left**? activity on **page R8**, where they'll make up subtraction problems using the number of animals in pictures. This will give children practice with subtraction.

CONNECTING TO FICTION

Children may have enjoyed reading or listening to *Swimmy* by Leo Lionni, *One Fish Two Fish Red Fish Blue Fish* by Dr. Seuss, and other stories about fish. Ask children to bring in these and other stories to share with the class. Help them compare the stories and illustrations in the books.

SKILLS AND STRATEGIES

COMPREHENSION

Main Idea/Details

TEACH/MODEL

Explain to children that the main idea of a selection tells what it is mostly about. The details give more information about the main idea.

> **Pictures and words in a selection often give details that support the main idea.**

THINK ALOUD *The title* Fish Faces *gives me a clue that the main idea of this selection has to do with fish. Next, I can look for details that will tell me more.*

PRACTICE/APPLY

Have children complete a Main Idea chart to identify some details about fish.

> **What have you learned so far about fish?**

> **What part of their bodies do fish use to move?**

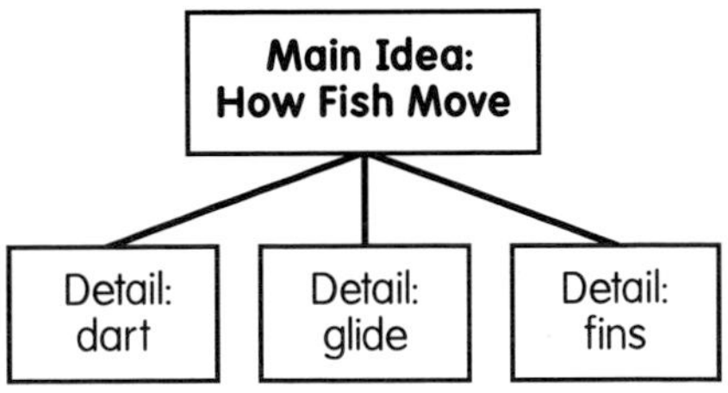

INFORMAL ASSESSMENT

OBSERVATION

Did children:

✔use the text and pictures to identify the main idea?

✔recognize details that support the main idea?

See pages T54–T55 for a full lesson on Main Idea/Details.

COMPREHENSION

3 MAIN IDEA/DETAILS

> The first pages told us about the different ways fish move. What details about fish do these pages tell us? *(We learn about the different shapes of fish.)*

12

Flat fish, round fish
A very long and thin fish

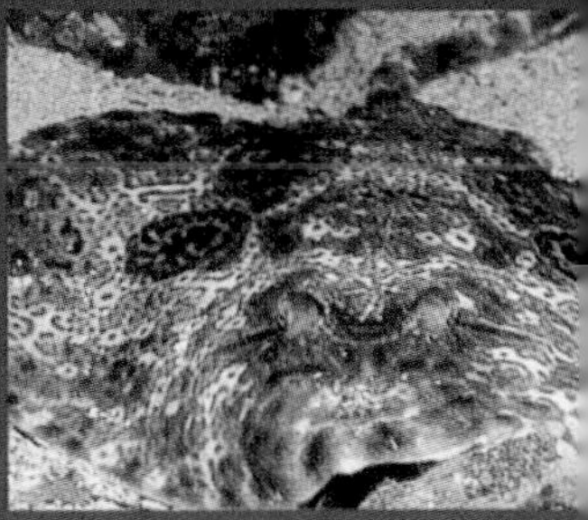

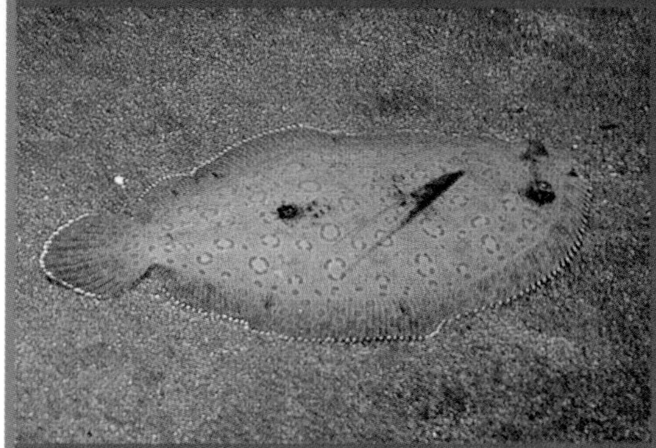

3

12

MODIFY Instruction

ESL/ELD

▲ Help children understand that these two pages are all about the different shapes of fish. As you read the text have children point to the shape word and then to the fish being described. Then ask them to practice using these words to describe different objects in the classroom. **(MAKE CONNECTIONS)**

EXTRA HELP

■ You may need to help children identify the main idea. Ask them to describe the fish on these pages. Write the words on the chalkboard. Help children see that *flat, round, long,* and *thin* describe the shape of fish; these details support the main idea. **(GUIDED READING)**

13

THE ARTS

Have children complete the **Fish Shapes** activity on **page R9**, where they'll combine various geometric forms to create original fish shapes.

TECHNOLOGY

Finding the Facts After they've read the paired selection on dolphins, have children visit **www.scholasticnetwork.com** and click on Dolphins. Ask them to find the answer to the question: "Do dolphins have families?"

DAILY PHONICS

Digraphs *sh, th*

CONNECT SOUND-SPELLING

TEACH/MODEL Review with children that digraphs are two letters that together stand for one sound.

- Write the word ***shine*** on the chalkboard and read it aloud, stressing the beginning sound **/sh/**. Have a volunteer underline the letters ***sh***.
- Write the word ***with*** on the chalkboard and read it aloud, stressing the final sound **/th/**. Have a volunteer underline the letters ***th***.

PHONICS MAINTENANCE Review the following sound-spellings: digraphs ***sh, th; r***-controlled vowels ***ar, ur, er, ir, or.***

PRACTICE/APPLY

BLEND WORDS Ask children to find the words ***fish*** and ***thin*** on page 12.

- Write ***fish*** and ***thin*** on the chalkboard and underline ***sh*** and ***th***. Help children chorally read the words.
- For additional practice, encourage children to look for other words in the selection with the digraphs ***sh*** and ***th***. List and chorally read the words they find.

INFORMAL ASSESSMENT
OBSERVATION

As children read, can they:

✔ recognize words with ***sh*** and ***th***?

✔ blend words with ***sh*** and ***th***?

COMPREHENSION

4 MAIN IDEA/DETAILS

> **How would you state the main idea of what you learn about the fish on these two pages?** *(Fish have different colors and markings on their bodies.)*

5 COMPARE/CONTRAST

> **These fish are all very colorful. That's one way the fish are alike. What are some ways they are different?** *(Possible answer: The size, shape, and color of the fish are often different.)*

INTERVENTION TIP

Sentence Structure

Children may be confused by the fact that there are very few complete sentences in this selection. Make sure children realize that some of the words that make up complete sentences are left out, but that the text is always referring to the fish in the pictures.

14

Spotted fish, dotted fish
4
14

MODIFY Instruction

ESL/ELD

▲ Ask children to tell about other details that will support the main idea. Ask: *What are some colors fish can be? Are all the dots and spots the same colors and size?* Help children use describing words to make full sentences about the fish. **(GUIDED QUESTIONS)**

EXTRA HELP

■ Help children match the words *spotted, dotted, lines, stripes,* and *waves* to the patterns on the fish. Write the describing words on the chalkboard and ask children to draw a picture for each word. Then have them label their pictures. **(MAKE CONNECTIONS)**

15

Fish with lines and stripes and waves
5
15

TEACHER TIP

"Children are fascinated by undersea life—it's one of those commonly shared fascinations, on a par with dinosaurs. Although the text of this selection focuses attention on fish, the photographs provide wonderful information about the underwater environment. *Fish Faces* is a great beginning point for an exploration of coral reefs and undersea plant life."

COMPREHENSION

6 PICTURE CLUES

> **Look at the picture of the fish on these pages. Which fish has spikes? Which fish has spines? Which fish has branches?** *(Possible answer: The brown-and-white fish (big picture) has spikes, the porcupine fish (inset on p. 17 lower right) and the one above it have spines, and the other two have branches.)*

7 DRAW CONCLUSIONS

> **How might it be helpful for these fish to have spikes and spines and branches? How could these features help the fish if another fish wanted to eat them?** *(Possible answer: Spikes, spines, and branches might keep other fish away.)*

SELF-MONITORING STRATEGY

Word Attack

THINK ALOUD *When I first read* ***Fish with spikes and spins and branches****, I knew that* ***spins*** *did not belong in this sentence. I know the right word begins with* ***s*** *and is part of the fish in the picture.*

> What do you think the word is?

> How does the word *spin* change if I add an *e* to the end of the word?

> Look at the word *spine.* Let's slowly sound it out together. Read the word. *Spine.*

16

Fish with spikes and spines and branches
6
16

MODIFY Instruction

ESL/ELD

▲ Use photos of other objects with spines, spikes, or branches to reinforce understanding. Have children trace along the spines of the fish to show you the parts that look like spikes and branches. Be sure children realize that the spikes and branches are sharp fins. **(USE VISUALS)**

GIFTED & TALENTED

✷ Fish have different ways of protecting themselves; some have spikes, others use camouflage or speed. Challenge children to select a fish from the story and draw a picture showing how this fish might protect itself. Ask children to share their drawings with their classmates. **(HANDS-ON-LEARNING)**

17

CONNECTING TO THEME

Discuss with children how the author organizes the information in *Fish Faces*. Children should mention that there is information about how fish move and how fish look. Encourage them to notice how the selection is organized as they read on.

Quickwrite

PREDICT
Ask children to describe what they think is interesting about the selection so far. Give children an opportunity to refine the predictions they made before reading. Have children predict what will happen next.

DAILY LANGUAGE PRACTICE

SPELLING
DAY 1: Administer the Pretest for Words with Digraphs *sh, th*. **See page R4.**

GRAMMAR, USAGE, MECHANICS
DAY 1: Teach and Model Word Order. **See page R6.**

ORAL LANGUAGE
Write the following sentence on the chalkboard. Work with children to correct the errors.

You did learn what about fith?
(What did you learn about fish?)

DAY 1 WRAP-UP

READ ALOUD *To develop children's oral vocabularies, spend five to ten minutes reading from a selection of your choice.*

GUIDED READING *Meet with the **red** and **blue** reading groups and assign Independent Center activities.* ***See pages R2–R3.***

COMPREHENSION

DAY 2 OBJECTIVES

CHILDREN WILL:

READ 35 MINUTES

- **Fish Faces, pp. 18–33**
- **Mentor Profile: Laela Sayigh, Marine Biologist, pp. 34–35**
- **Daily Phonics: Homophones**

WRITE 25 MINUTES

- **Shared Writing: Prewrite Book of Facts**
- **Spelling: Words With Digraphs *sh, th***
- **Grammar, Usage, Mechanics: Word Order**
- **Oral Language**

EXTEND SKILLS 30 MINUTES

- **Integrated Curriculum**
- **Read Aloud**
- **Guided Reading**

RESOURCES

- **Practice Book, page 14**
- **Spelling Resource Book, pp. 110–112**

Reread

You may wish to have children independently reread the first part of the selection before beginning Day 2 reading.

8 SUMMARIZE

> **What have you learned about fish so far?** *(Answers should include something about the way fish move and how they look.)*

9 MAIN IDEA/DETAILS

> **What is the main idea of this page?** *(Fish have different kinds of mouths.)*

18

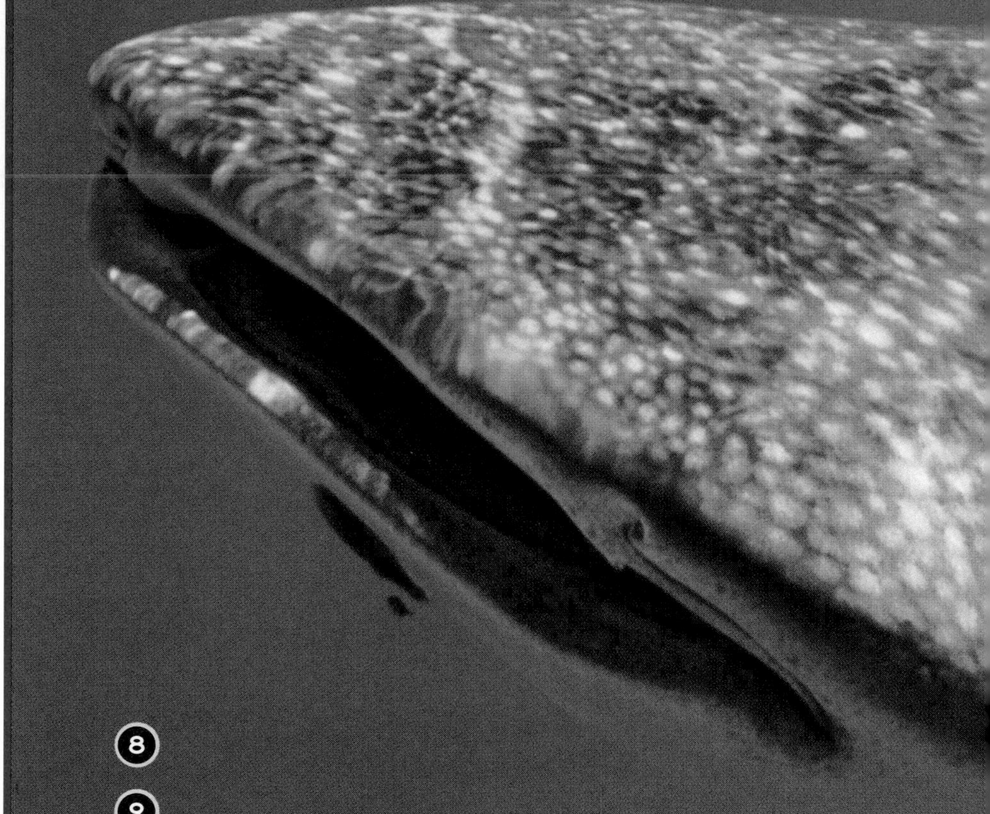

8

9

Fish with mouths that open wide
Mouth like a tube, mouth like a beak
Mouth that belongs to a monster of the deep

18

MODIFY Instruction

ESL/ELD

▲ Help children summarize what they have learned about fish by going back to the beginning and paging through the story. Ask: *What did you learn about colors? What did you learn about shapes?* Encourage children to restate what they have learned. **(RETELL)**

EXTRA HELP

■ Children may need help summarizing what they have learned so far. Encourage children to use the pictures to help them recall details about fish. **(USE VISUALS)**

19

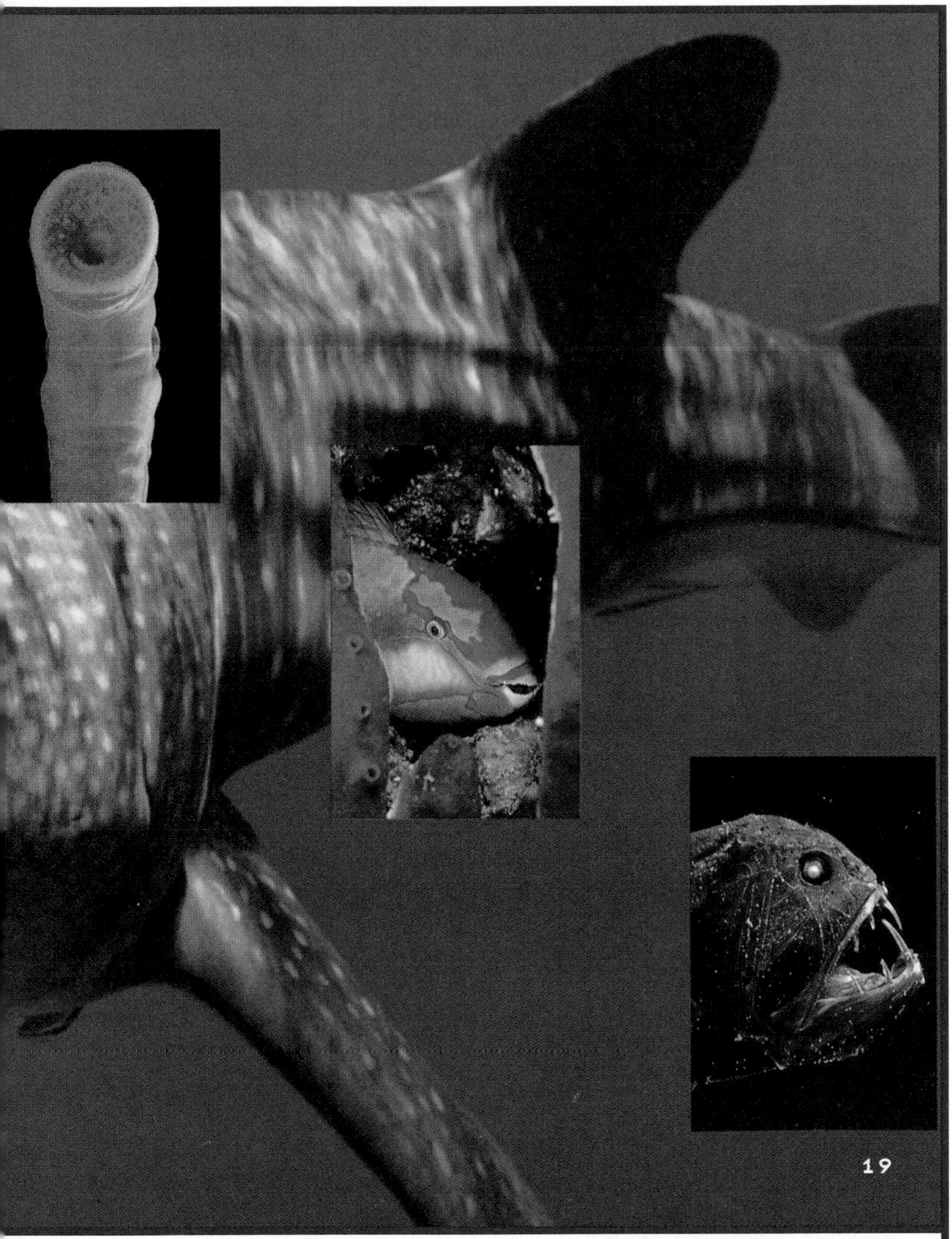

VISUAL LITERACY

Ask children to close their eyes while you read aloud a page from *Fish Faces*. Encourage children to try to picture the fish that you are describing. Then have children draw the fish as you described it.

DAILY PHONICS

Final *e*

CONNECT SOUND-SPELLING

TEACH/MODEL Review with children the effect that final ***e*** has on the vowel sound.

- Write the word ***spin*** on the chalkboard and have children read it aloud.
- Add final ***e*** to ***spin*** and have children read the new word ***spine*** aloud.

PRACTICE/APPLY

BLEND WORDS Write the following pairs of words in two columns on the chalkboard or on chart paper: ***fin, fin; slid, slid; strip, strip; shin, shin; mad, mad.***

- Ask children to add an ***e*** to the end of the second word in each pair.
- Have children blend the new word.
- Read the word pairs aloud together.

fin	fine
slid	slide
strip	stripe
shin	shine
mad	made

COMPREHENSION

10 MAKE INFERENCES

> **What do you think the author means when he says that some fish have noses that are "hard to ignore"?** *(Possible answer: The nose is so big or so strange-looking that you almost don't notice the rest of the fish.)*

11 MAKE PREDICTIONS

> **We've read about fishes' fins, bodies, mouths, and noses. What part of a fish do you think we will read about next?** *(Answers should reflect an awareness of the parts of a fish's body, eyes, and tails that have not yet been mentioned.)*

INTERVENTION TIP

Homophones

Write the words ***knows*** and ***would*** on the chalkboard and read them aloud with children. Explain that homophones are words that sound the same but have different spellings and different meanings. Have children find homophones for ***knows*** and ***would*** on this page. Then invite them to use the words ***knows*** and ***nose*** and ***would*** and ***wood*** in sentences of their own.

20

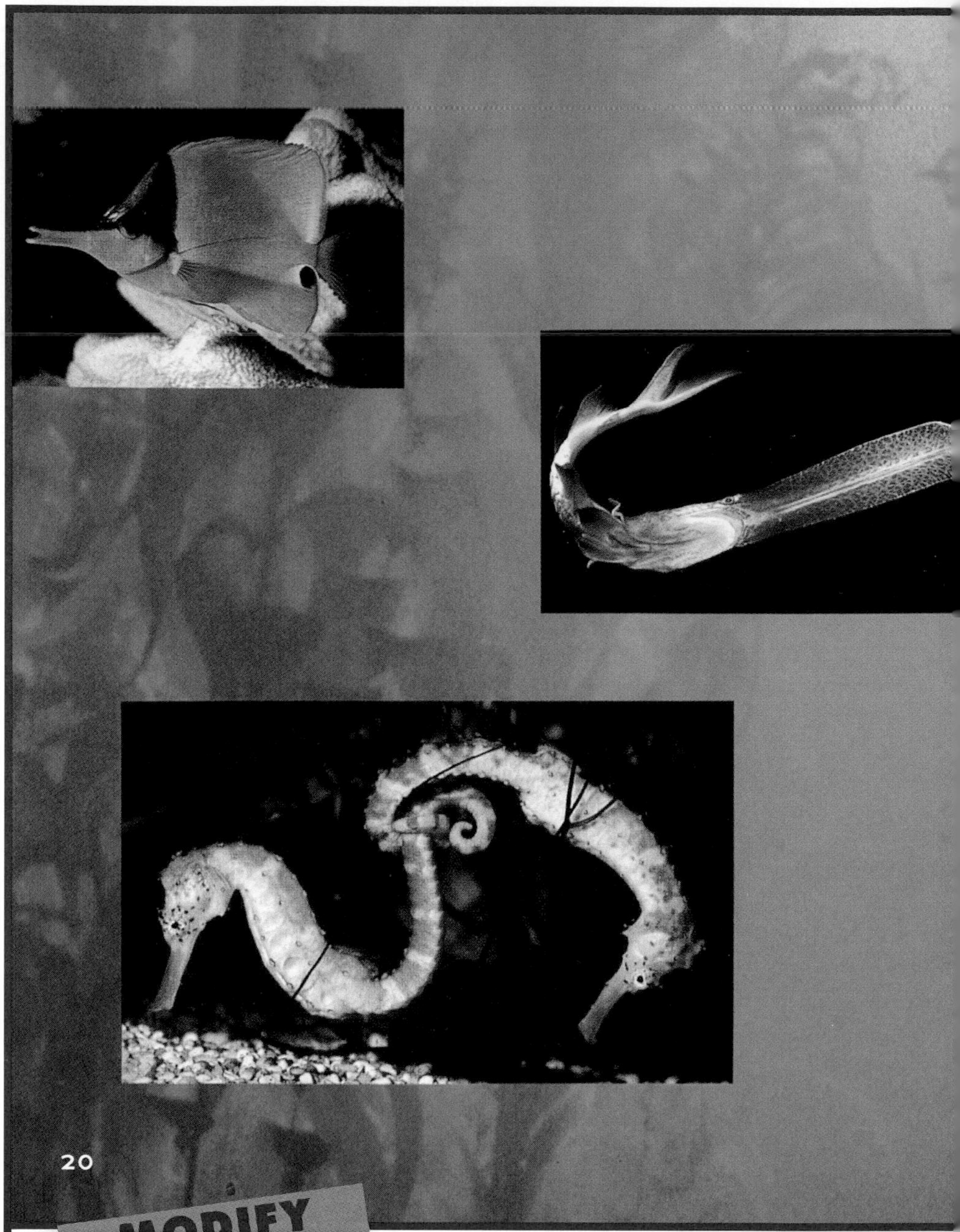

MODIFY Instruction

ESL/ELD

▲ Help English language learners infer that the phrase "hard-to-ignore" means something that is strange or very remarkable. Encourage children to go back through the pictures they have seen so far and point to other details that they find hard to ignore. **(MAKE CONNECTIONS)**

GIFTED & TALENTED

✳ Have children work in pairs and find out more about a specific fish they are interested in. Provide books with information about sea life for them to refer to. Invite children to share what they learn with their classmates. **(RESEARCH)**

21

(10)

A long nose, a flat nose, a hard-to-ignore nose
A nose that looks like it could cut wood
A nose that shines in the dark!

(11)

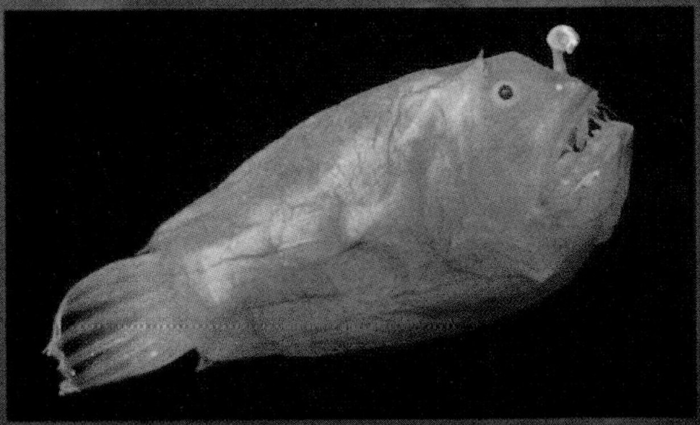

21

DAILY PHONICS

l-Blends

CONNECT SOUND-SPELLING

TEACH/MODEL Review *l*-blends with children.

- Write the word ***slide*** on the chalkboard and underline the beginning consonant letters ***sl***.
- Say ***slide*** aloud, extending each sound. Explain that ***sl*** is a consonant blend. You hear the sounds of both letters that make up a consonant blend.

PRACTICE/APPLY

BLEND WORDS Ask children to find the word ***flat*** on page 21.

- Write ***flat*** on the chalkboard and underline the consonant blend ***fl***. Encourage children to blend the word.
- Ask children to suggest other words that begin with ***fl***. List them on the chalkboard.
- Encourage children to look for other words in the selection with *l*-blends. Add these to the list on the chalkboard. Have children blend these words. *(**slide**, page 9; **glide**, page 11; **flat**, page 12)*

VISUAL LITERACY

Ask children to create a Main Idea/Details chart as they reread *Fish Faces*.

Main Idea: Fish Faces
Detail: fierce
Detail: long
Detail: green eyes

ORAL LANGUAGE

Using the photographs in the selection, have children describe one of the fish in their own words. Partners can take turns describing and listening.

COMPREHENSION

12 **COMPARE/CONTRAST**

> **What do you notice about the eyes of the fish on these pages? In what ways are they the same? How are they different?** *(Possible answers: The fish on these pages all have different color eyes; two of the fish have red eyes.)*

22

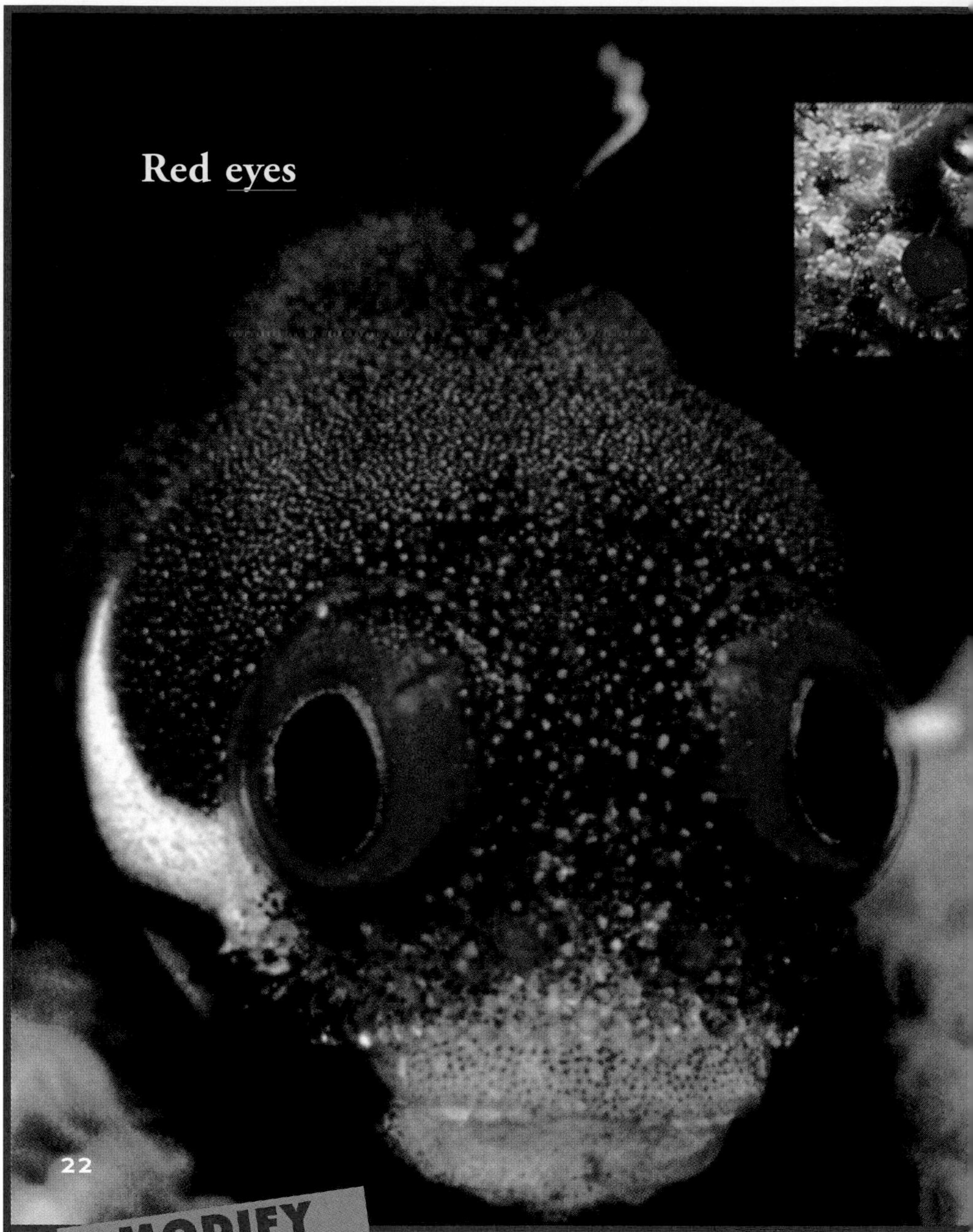

MODIFY Instruction

ESL/ELD

▲ Ask English language learners to compare and contrast as many details as they can about the fish on these pages. Ask: *What colors do you see? What shapes do you see? What kinds of noses do these fish have? Mouths?* **(USE VISUALS)**

GIFTED & TALENTED

✳ Are red eyes and green eyes uncommon for fish? Suggest that children review the photographs of the fish in *Fish Faces* to find out how many of the fish shown in the photographs have red eyes, green eyes, or eyes of other colors. **(USE VISUALS)**

23

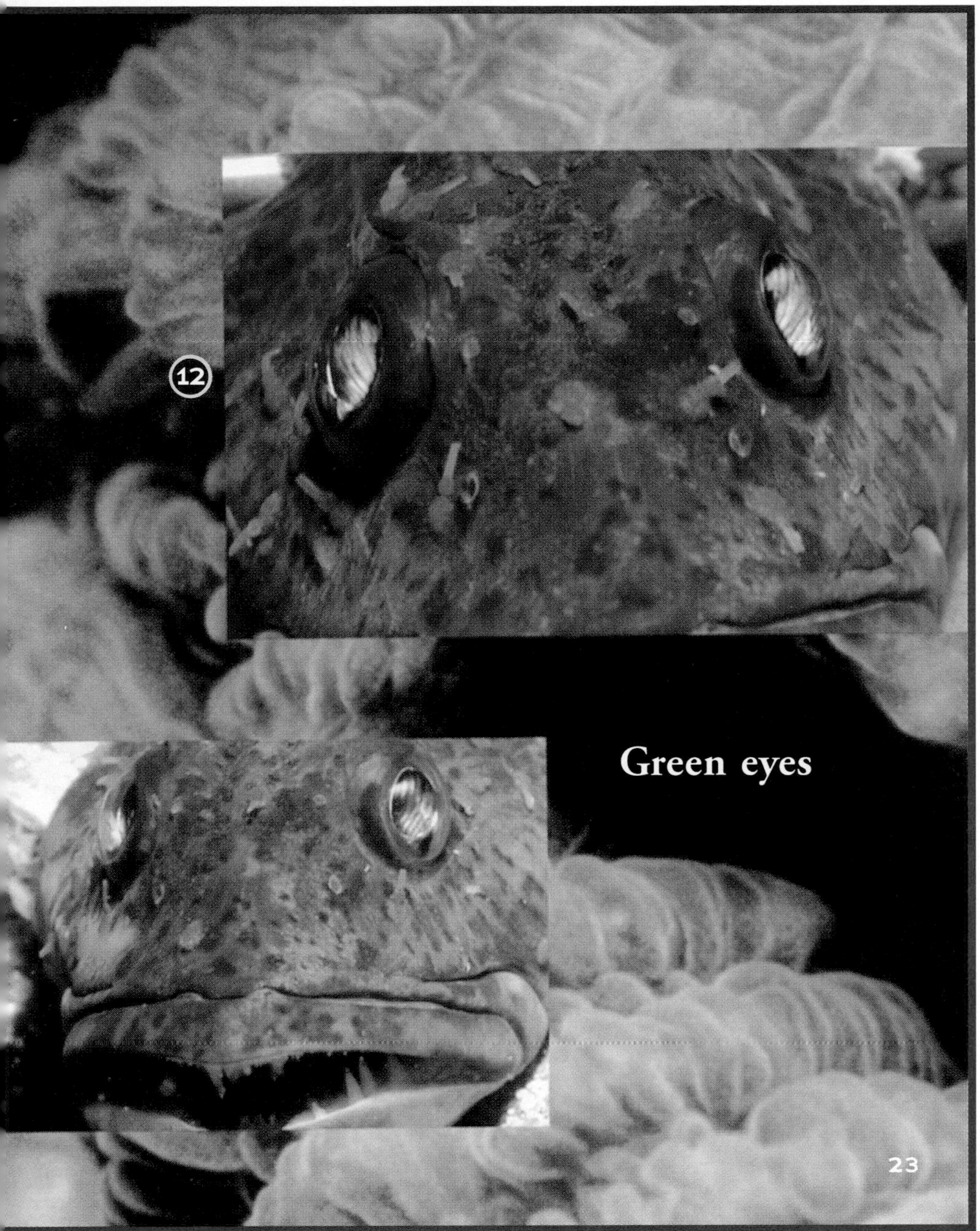

12

SCIENCE

Ask children to complete the **From Mouth to Fin** activity on **page R8** where they'll draw a fish and label its basic body parts.

TEACHER TIP

"The photographs in *Fish Faces* can be used to inspire descriptive writing. Try brainstorming descriptive words about one fish with the class and then work as a group to write a description on chart paper. Ask children to choose a fish and write their own descriptions."

DAILY PHONICS

Homophones

TEACH/MODEL

Remind children that homophones are words that sound alike but are spelled differently and mean different things.

- Write ***I*** and ***eye*** on the chalkboard.
- Read these sentences aloud and ask children which of the two words they hear in each sentence:
  I see a spotted fish.
  It has a shiny green eye.

PRACTICE/APPLY

Have children find the word ***red*** on page 22.

- Ask children what the word ***red*** means.
- Have children think of a word that sounds like ***red*** but has a different meaning.
- Ask children to make up sentences using the homophones ***red*** and ***read.***

INFORMAL ASSESSMENT
OBSERVATION

As children read, note if they can:

✔ identify words that sound alike but are spelled differently.

✔ use homophones correctly in sentences.

See pages T56–T57 for a full skills lesson on Homophones.

COMPREHENSION

13 COMPARE/CONTRAST

> **How are the pretend eyes on the fish different from the real eyes?** *(The real eyes are in the fish's head; the pretend eye is on its side.)*

14 MAKE INFERENCES

> **Why do you think the fish have pretend eyes?** *(Possible answer: The eyes could scare off enemies.)*

24

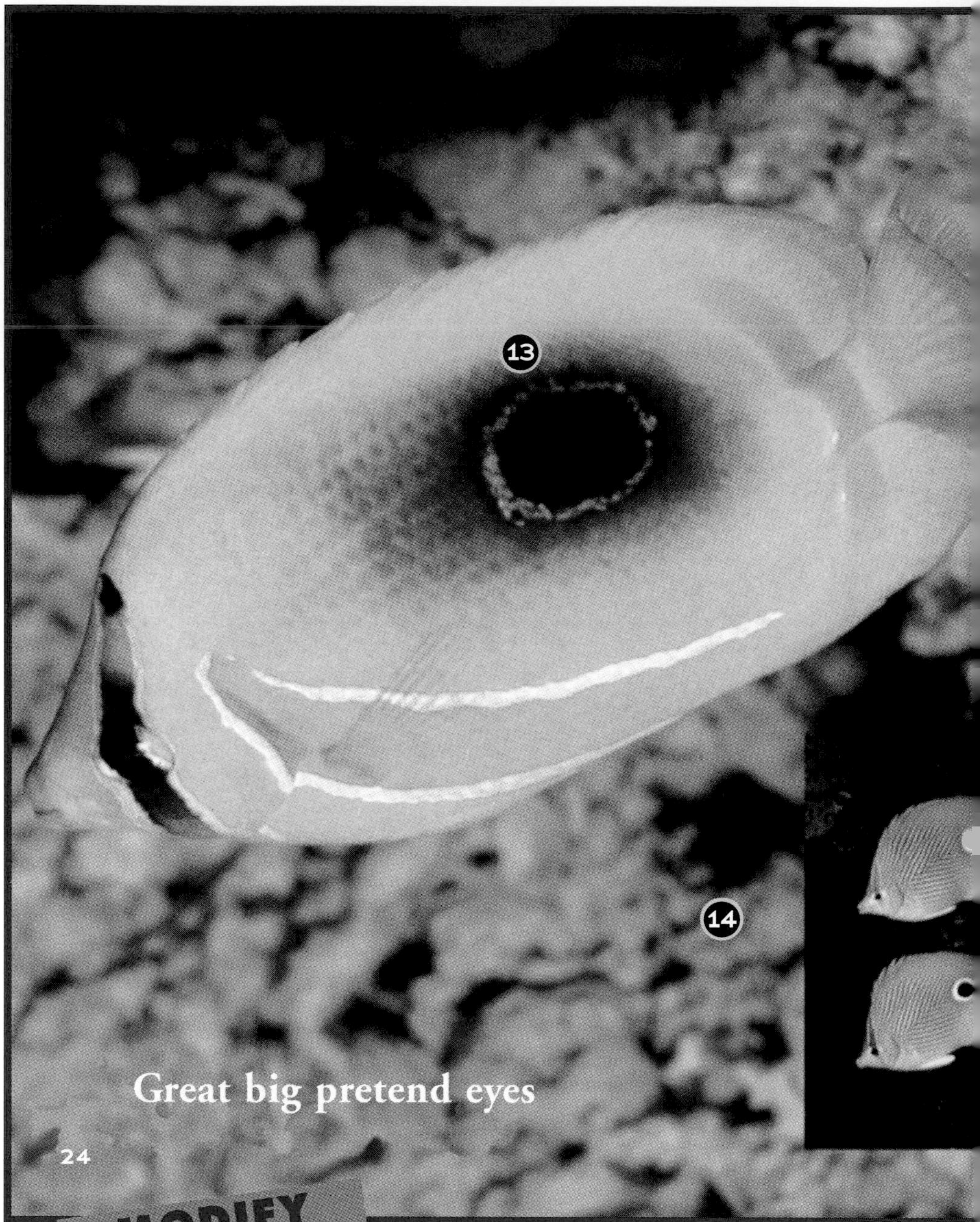

Great big pretend eyes

24

MODIFY Instruction

ESL/ELD

▲ Help children compare the pretend eyes to the real eyes. Ask: *Which eye on the fish is a "great big" one? Is it really an eye? Where are the real eyes? Are they bigger or smaller than the pretend eyes?* **(PICTURE CLUES)**

EXTRA HELP

■ Ask children to point to the fish's head. Then have them locate the fish's tail. Ask which eye is on the fish's head and which eye is close to the fish's tail. Guide children to see that the real eyes are on the fish's head; the pretend eyes are close to the fish's tail. **(GUIDED QUESTIONS)**

25

Eyes that are hooded
25

VISUAL LITERACY

Discuss with children how the pictures and the words work together. Point out how the pictures help the reader figure out what "pretend eyes" and "hooded eyes" are. Ask children to make a list of words that describe fish.

WORD STUDY

Ask children to find the word *hooded* on page 25. Have children read aloud and spell the word. Display a coat or sweatshirt with a hood to the class. Remind children that a hood is something that goes over your head. Then ask them to discuss *eyes that are hooded* based on what they know about a hood.

DAILY PHONICS

r-Blends

CONNECT SOUND-SPELLING

TEACH/MODEL Review *r*-blends with children.

- Write the word ***green*** on the chalkboard and underline the beginning consonant letters ***gr.***
- Say ***green*** aloud, extending the sounds. Explain that ***gr*** is a consonant blend. You hear the sounds of both letters that make up a consonant blend.

PRACTICE/APPLY

BLEND WORDS Ask children to find the word ***great*** on page 24.

- Write the word ***great*** on the chalkboard and underline the consonant blend ***gr.*** Have children blend ***great.***
- Ask children to suggest other words that begin with ***gr.*** List them on the chalkboard.
- Encourage children to look through the selection to find other words with ***r*** as the second letter. Add these to the list on the chalkboard. Have children blend these words. (***branches,*** page 16; ***pretend,*** page 24; ***friendly,*** page 28)

COMPREHENSION

15 **Main Idea/Details**

> **What details have we learned about fish so far?** *(They move in different ways, have different shapes, markings, and features, and have different kinds of mouths, noses, and eyes.)*

26

Eyes that shine
26

MODIFY Instruction

ESL/ELD

▲ Help children make a web organizer to summarize the details they have learned about fish. Place the word *fish* in the central ring, and ask children for subcategories to place around it (colors, shapes). Have children add details to each of the subcategories. **(GRAPHIC DEVICE)**

EXTRA HELP

■ Summarizing what has gone on before will reinforce children's understanding of the text. Have children use their own words to talk about the most important ideas in the selection so far. **(SUMMARIZE)**

27

Eyes that stick up like periscopes
15
27

WORD STUDY

Share with children that *periscope* is an instrument used for looking at things. Point out that the word part *peri* means *all around or about. Scope* means *to watch or look at.*

CULTURAL CONNECTION

In many cultures, certain fish have become symbols. In China, the fish *(yu)* symbolizes happiness and plenty. In Japan, the carp is a symbol of strength and endurance because it can swim up rapids. On Children's Day, May 5, wind socks shaped like carp are hung in front of each house.

SKILLS AND STRATEGIES

GENRE

Photo Essay

TEACH/MODEL

Tell children that a photo essay gives information using words and photographs. Guide children to see what makes a photo essay different from other kinds of selections.

THINK ALOUD *As I read this selection, I notice that the words tell me important details, but the photographs tell me even more about the fish.*

PRACTICE/APPLY

Invite children to look through the selection and talk about details in the pictures that are not discussed in the text.

COMPREHENSION

16 MAIN IDEA/DETAILS

> **What is the main idea of these pages? What are the details that support the main idea?** *(The main idea of this page is that fish have different faces. There are pictures of friendly faces and fierce faces that support this idea.)*

17 DRAW CONCLUSIONS

> **What makes the fish on page 28 look friendly? What makes the fish on page 29 look fierce?** *(The mouth and eyes are what make the fish on page 28 seem friendly. The teeth make the fish on page 29 look fierce.)*

28

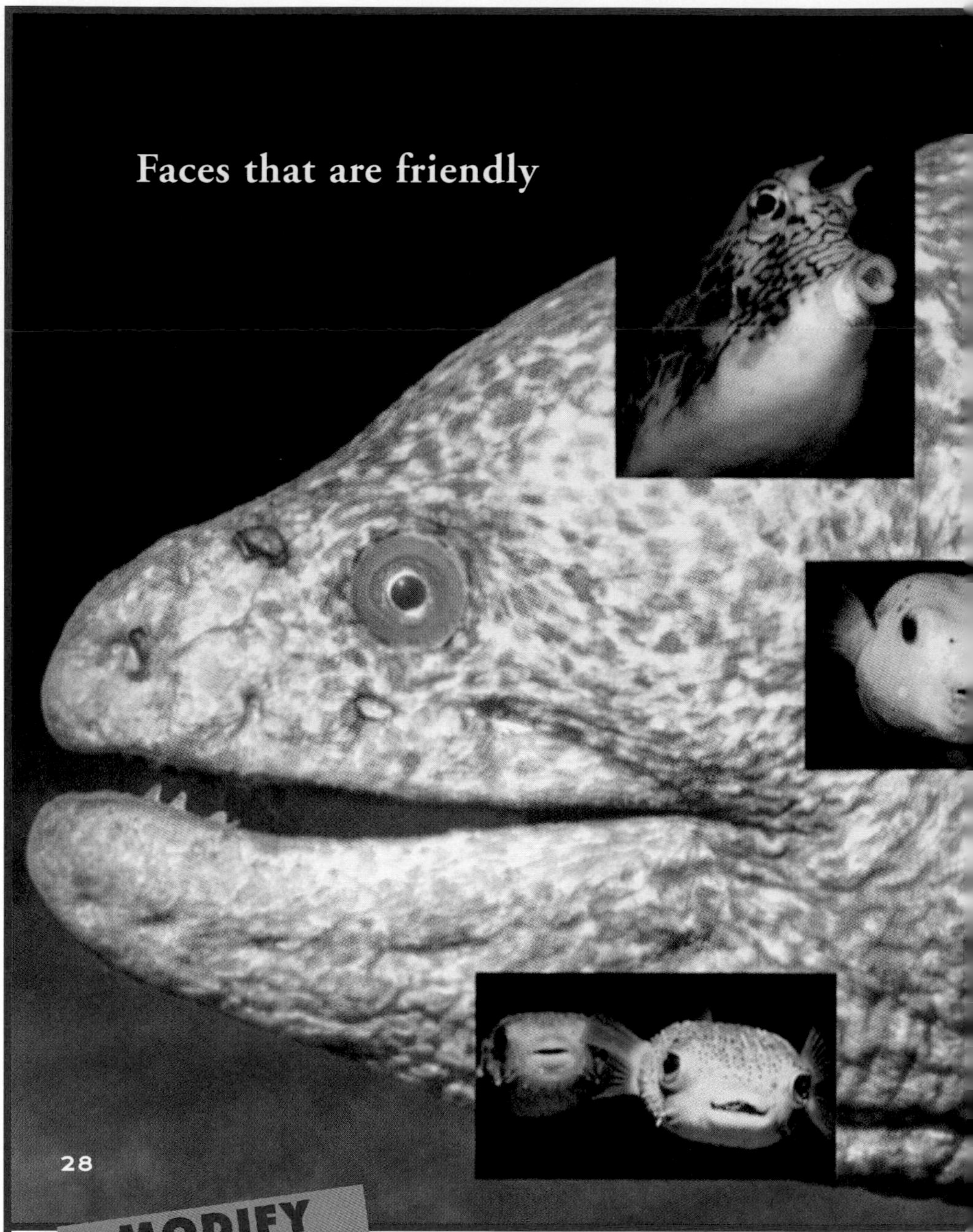
Faces that are friendly
28

MODIFY Instruction

ESL/ELD

▲ Ask children for other words that mean *funny* (silly) and *fierce* (scary). Help children draw conclusions about the fish faces on these pages by asking either/or questions: *Does this fish have a funny face or a fierce face? Is this a happy or a sad face?* **(GUIDED QUESTIONS)**

EXTRA HELP

■ Children may need help understanding the descriptive words in the story. Ask children to look through the pictures and think of words that describe the expressions on the faces of the fish. Guide children to use words such as *happy, kind, angry, silly, and fierce.* **(CONTEXT CLUES)**

29

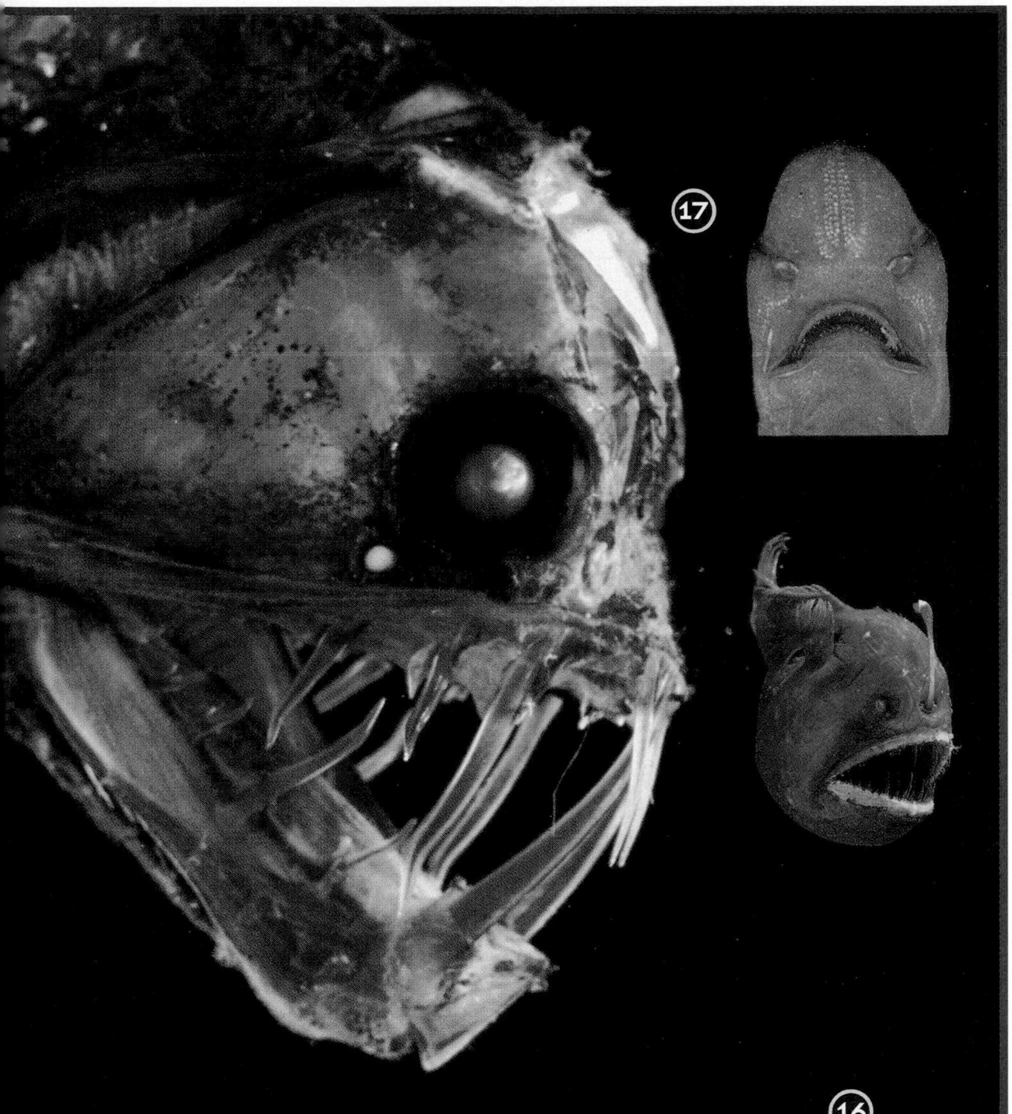

(17)

(16)

Faces that are fierce

29

WORD STUDY

Point out to children that fish often swim together in a group. Ask children if they know what you call a group of fish. Help them recognize that a group of fish is called a ***school.*** Then ask them to give another meaning for the word ***school*** and use it in a sentence of their own.

MENTOR

Marine biologist Laela Sayigh uses a special microphone to listen to dolphins. What special equipment do you think Norbert Wu uses to take fish photos?

SKILLS AND STRATEGIES

COMPREHENSION

Draw Conclusions

TEACH/MODEL

Help children understand that when they draw conclusions, they use what they already know as well as facts from the story to understand the information presented.

THINK ALOUD *When I read this book, I notice that some fish have long teeth and some fish have spines. I know how sharp teeth and spines can be, so I can figure out that some fish have teeth and spines to protect themselves.*

PRACTICE/APPLY

As they reread the selection, invite children to use what they know as well as story information to draw conclusions about fish. Suggest to children that they can use the graphic organizer below to help them draw conclusions.

Clues from the story	+	What I already know	=	My conclusion

COMPREHENSION

18 Draw Conclusions

> **I know that sometimes animals have special features that help them survive. Why do you think these fish have spines?** *(They probably have spines to protect themselves from being attacked by other fish.)*

19 Picture Details

> **Which fish on these pages look sad? Which look mad?** *(Possible answers: The fish on page 30 look sad and the fish on page 31 look mad.)*

30

Faces that could be sad or mad 18
30

MODIFY Instruction

ESL/ELD

▲ Focus on picture details with some pantomime fun. Have one child select a word from the story and use gestures, facial expressions, or board drawings to convey its meaning to classmates. The first child to guess the correct word selects a new word. **(PANTOMIME)**

EXTRA HELP

■ To help children connect the text to the pictures, invite them to slide their hands from left to right over the specific picture elements as you describe them. You may wish to use this picture tracing technique with other pages. **(MULTISENSORY TECHNIQUES)**

31

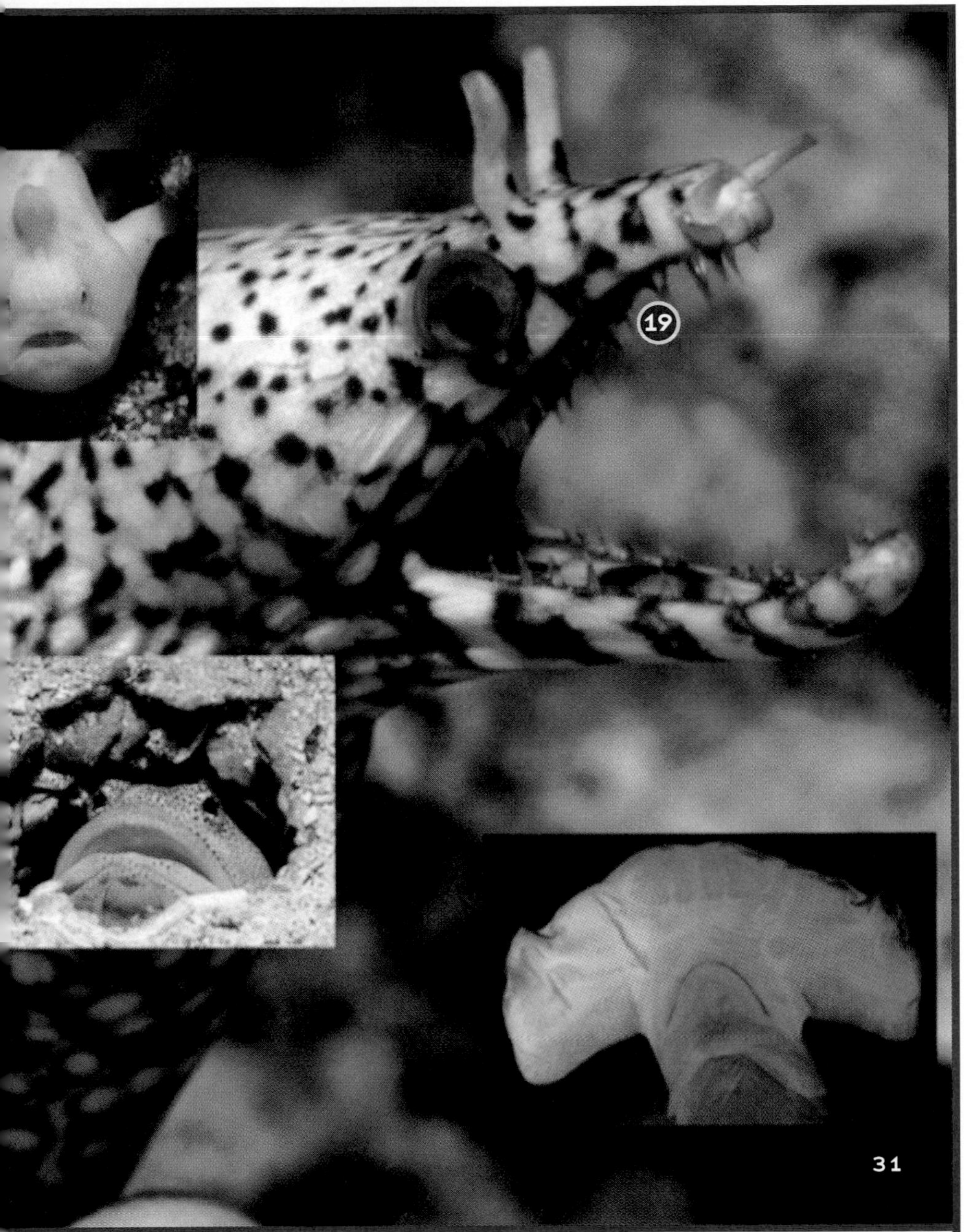

SOCIAL STUDIES

Ask children to complete the **Where Fish Live** activity on **page R9,** where they'll look at a map to locate the different bodies of water in which fish live.

TECHNOLOGY

Language Development Have children read the **WiggleWorks Plus** My Book *The Pet Show.* Ask them to rewrite and redraw the last page so the prize is for a fish with the funniest face. Encourage them to use story words.

SKILLS AND STRATEGIES

COMPREHENSION

Summarize

TEACH/MODEL

Review with children that a summary gives the most important information about a story.

- Think about what the most important information is in *Fish Faces.*
- Ask yourself what are some of the important things you have learned about fish.

THINK ALOUD *When I want to summarize what I've read so far, I think about how I can give the most important information. I would want my summary to say that not all fish look alike. I'd want to include the important things I've learned so far about fish in my summary, using my own words.*

PRACTICE/APPLY

Invite partners to take turns summarizing parts of the selection for each other. Encourage them to use the pictures to help them complete their summaries.

COMPREHENSION

20 MAIN IDEA/DETAILS

> **How would you describe the main idea of this selection to someone who hasn't read it? What would you say the selection is about? What details would you share?**

(Possible answer: The selection is mainly about different fish and how some fish look alike and some fish look different. Some details include information about fish eyes, mouths, and noses.)

JOURNAL

Revisit Predictions

Ask children to look back at their predictions and record how they were or were not confirmed by the end of the selection.

32

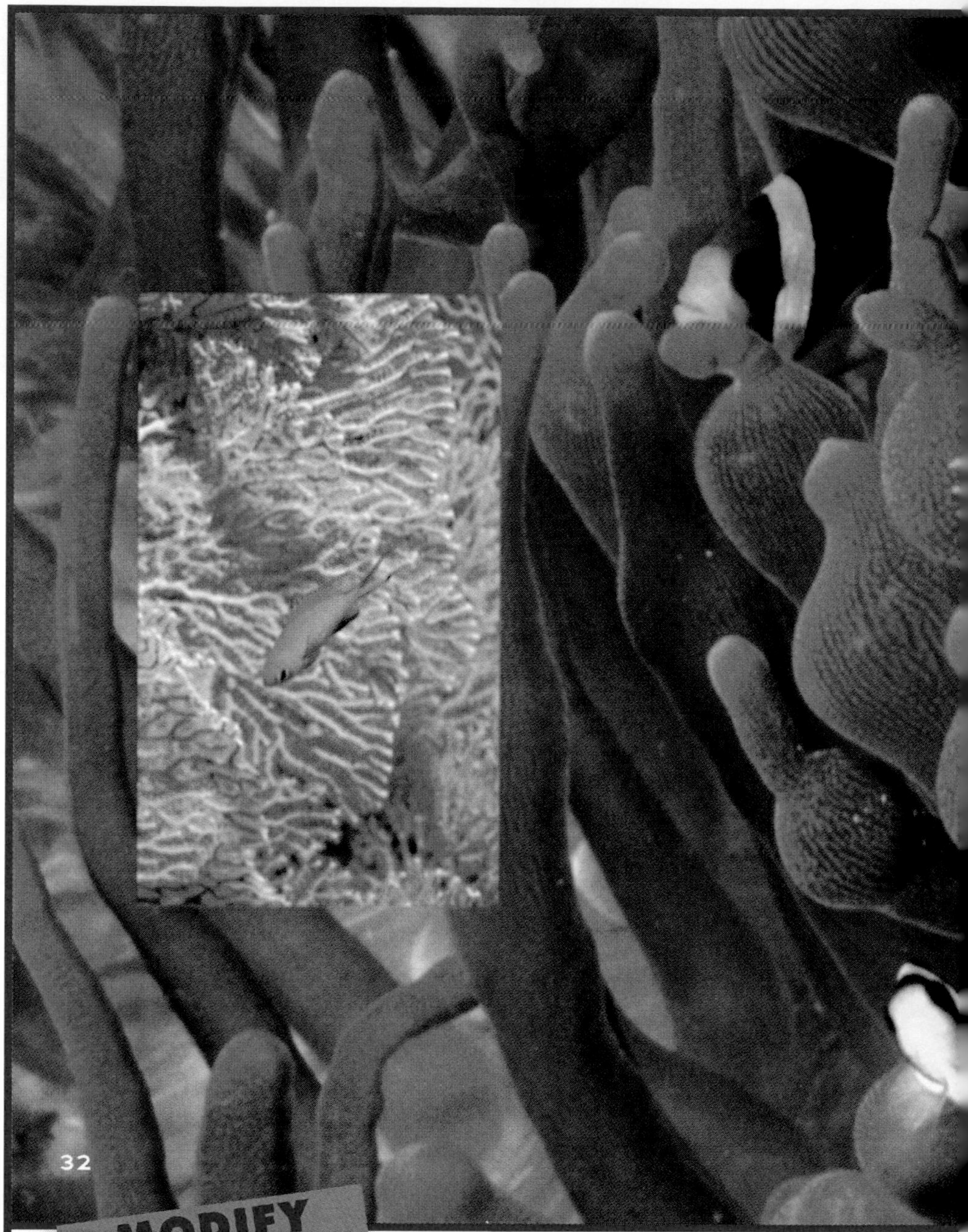

MODIFY Instruction

ESL/ELD

▲ Help children express the main idea of this story in a single sentence: *There are many different kinds of fish.* Reinforce the meaning of "thousands more" in the text by asking children to name other things they know of that come in "thousands." (stars, people, or dollars) **(MAKE CONNECTIONS)**

GIFTED & TALENTED

✷ Encourage children to learn more fish facts. Have children locate picture books and photo essays in the library that will help them learn more about fish. Suggest that children share their research results with their classmates. **(RESEARCH)**

33

One fish, two fish, three fish, four
Deep in the ocean, there are thousands more! 20
33

WORKSHOP

You may wish to introduce the Workshop on this day. Set aside specific times over the next two weeks for children to work on this ongoing activity.

Book of Facts

SHARED WRITING

PREWRITE Explain that *Fish Faces* is a fact book that gives information about fish. Tell children they will be writing a book of facts about themselves. Have them begin to develop their ideas by completing the fact chart on **Practice Book page 14.**

DAILY LANGUAGE PRACTICE

SPELLING PRACTICE

DAY 2: Practice Words with Digraphs *sh, th.* **See page R4.**

GRAMMAR, USAGE, MECHANICS

DAY 2: Practice Word Order. **See page R6.**

ORAL LANGUAGE

DAY 2: fish some have spiky, charp fins. *(Some fish have spiky, sharp fins.)*

DAY 2 WRAP-UP

READ ALOUD *Spend five to ten minutes reading from a selection of your choice.*

GUIDED READING *To extend reading, meet with the **green** and **yellow** reading groups and assign Independent Center activities.* ***See pages R2–R3.***

COMPREHENSION

DAY 3 OBJECTIVES

CHILDREN WILL:

READ 25 MINUTES

- "Mentor Profile: Laela Sayigh," pp. 34–35
- Assess Comprehension
- Key Comprehension Skill: Main Idea/Details
- Daily Phonics: Homophones

WRITE 35 MINUTES

- Respond: Write Labels
- Spelling: Words With Digraphs *sh, th*
- Grammar, Usage, Mechanics: Word Order
- Oral Language

EXTEND SKILLS 30 MINUTES

- Integrated Curriculum
- Read Aloud
- Guided Reading

RESOURCES

- Practice Book, pp. 8–13
- Spelling Resource Book, p. 113

▶ Preview

Remind children that the subject of this profile is Laela Sayigh, the marine biologist they met in the mentor video. Encourage children to look at the pictures in the profile.

1 MAIN IDEA/DETAILS

> **Why does Laela Sayigh study dolphins?** *(Possible answer: She wants to know how dolphins make sounds.)*

2 SUMMARIZE

> **What would you tell a friend about Laela Sayigh? How does she gather and organize information?** *(She is a marine biologist who studies dolphin sounds. She records the sounds and takes notes.)*

34

MENTOR

Read Together!

Laela Sayigh

Marine Biologist

1

Laela Sayigh studies dolphins. She wants to know how dolphins make sounds from their throats. Here's how she gathers and uses information at work.

Laela Sayigh records the sounds dolphins make.

She records new facts on her computer.

34

MODIFY Instruction

ESL/ELD

▲ Help children summarize the way Laela Sayigh gets information about dolphins. Then lead a discussion about how children could learn more about an animal they are interested in. Ask: *What animal are you curious about? What do you want to know?* **(RELATE TO REAL LIFE)**

EXTRA HELP

■ For children who need help understanding *Fish Faces,* reread the selection with them. Have children point to the photographs as you read the accompanying text. **(READ ALOUD)**

35

VISUAL LITERACY

Help children identify which picture goes with the text. Discuss how the text *tells* about what Laela Sayigh does, while the photos *show* what she does. Ask children if the pictures help them better understand what a marine biologist does.

Name MENTOR: Laela Sayigh

Animal Information

What animal would you like to learn more about? Write your ideas in the Research Notebook to finish each sentence.

The animal I want to know more about:

What I want to find out:

How I will learn more about my animal:

Where I will write what I learn:

To the Teacher: The mentor for *Information Finders* is Marine Biologist Laela Sayigh. She will share with children how she gathers and uses information about dolphins.

Unit 5 • Information Finders • *Fish Faces* 11

PRACTICE BOOK p. 11

COMPREHENSION

Think About Reading

Below are the **answers** to the *Think About Reading* questions.

1. *The story names flat, round, and very long and thin fish.*
2. *Some fish noses are hard to ignore because they have special shapes, they are sharp, or they glow in the dark.*
3. *Possible responses: Spikes and spines might protect fish from bigger fish or other sea animals.*
4. *Possible responses: This story is about real fish, and photographs show them clearly.*
5. *Possible responses: Both have learned a lot about sea animals. (Paired Selection)*

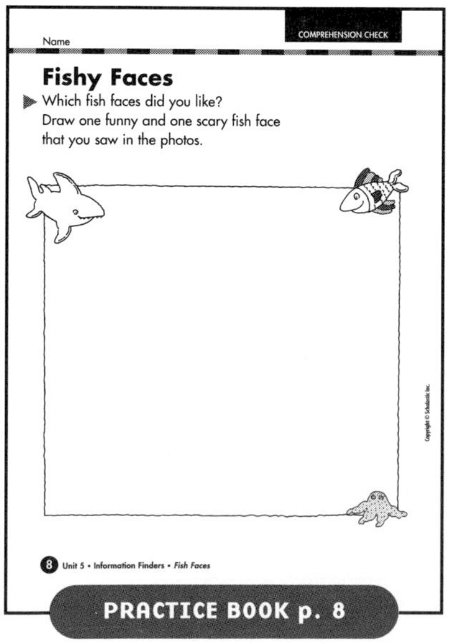
Name

COMPREHENSION CHECK

Fishy Faces

Which fish faces did you like? Draw one funny and one scary fish face that you saw in the photos.

8 Unit 5 • Information Finders • *Fish Faces*

PRACTICE BOOK p. 8

36

RESPOND

Think About Reading

1. What three different fish shapes does the story name?
2. Why are some fish noses hard to ignore?
3. Why do some fish have spikes and spines?
4. Why do you think <u>Fish Faces</u> shows photographs instead of drawings?
5. How is the author of <u>Fish Faces</u> like Laela Sayigh?

36

MODIFY Instruction

ESL/ELD

▲ Read each question to children, and have pairs look back in the story together to find the answer. Have children read aloud the portion of the page that answers the question. Beginning English language learners may point to picture clues to show understanding. **(WORK IN PAIRS)**

GIFTED & TALENTED

✳ Encourage children to include plants and other creatures in the background of their fish pictures. Write labels for these background details, as well as for the parts of their fish. **(INNOVATE)**

37

Write Labels

Fish Faces showed many different fish. Draw your own picture of a fish. Write labels on your picture to show the different parts of the fish. You may want to label the mouth, eye, fin, and tail.

Literature Circle

Talk about some ways the fish in Fish Faces are different from each other. Which fish do you think is the most unusual? Why?

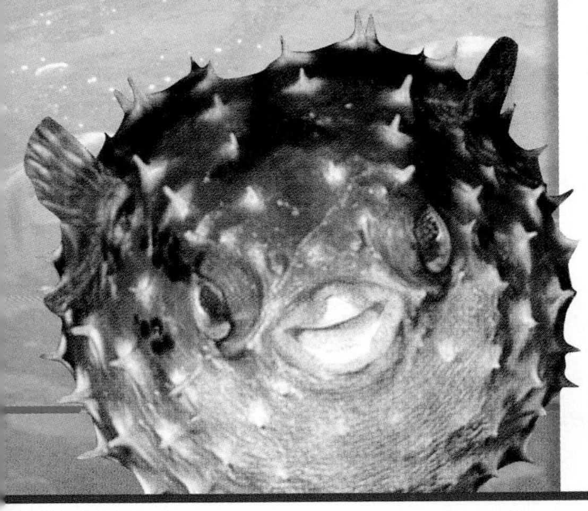

Author
Norbert Wu

Wouldn't it be fun to take pictures under water? Norbert Wu thinks so. His job isn't all fun, though. Sometimes he is chased by sharks. He has even been run over by an iceberg! Still, Wu likes taking underwater photos and sharing them with other people.

More Books by Norbert Wu

- Life in the Ocean
- A City Under the Sea: Life in a Coral Reef
- Beneath the Waves: Exploring the Hidden World of the Kelp Forest

37

RESPOND

Write Labels

Before children begin to write, have them think about these questions:

- **What shape and colors will the fish be?**
- **What parts of the fish will need labels?**

Children may wish to add an appropriate underwater background to their labeled fish drawings and display them on a class bulletin board.

Literature Circle

Encourage the groups to participate in a conversation in which they compare their choices for most unusual fish and their reasons for choosing these fish.

DAILY LANGUAGE PRACTICE

SPELLING

DAY 3:
Write Spelling Words With Digraphs *sh, th*. **See page R5.**

GRAMMAR, USAGE, MECHANICS

DAY 3:
Practice Word Order. **See page R7.**

ORAL LANGUAGE

I made a fish wit a nose big.
(I made a fish with a big nose.)

TECHNOLOGY

Presentation Tools Have children use **WiggleWorks Plus** PlaceMaker to draw and label parts of a fish. Ask them to print the drawings and cut them out. Then the class can put the pieces together to create a big mix-and-match fish.

AUTHOR/ILLUSTRATOR STUDY

You can find information about author and photographer Norbert Wu at **www.ag-editions.com.** You will also find underwater photos using the Image Catalog.

COMPREHENSION
Main Idea/Details

QUICKCHECK

Can children:

- ✔ recognize the main idea of the selection?
- ✔ recognize the details in the selection that support the main idea?
- ✔ understand that some details support the main idea and some details do not?

If YES, go on to Practice/Apply.

If NO, start at Teach/Model.

Ⓐ TEACH/MODEL

USE ORAL LANGUAGE Write the following sentences on strips of paper, one sentence per strip. Have children read them aloud. Have a volunteer point out the sentence that states the main idea. Ask three or more volunteers to point out the supporting detail sentences.

Some rabbits turn white in winter.

Many creatures have protective coloring.

Some moths look like dead leaves.

My dog likes to run and play.

Tigers' stripes help them hide in tall grass.

The main idea is **the sentence with the most important information.** The details **tell about the main idea.**

MODIFY Instruction

ESL/ELD

▲ Children can make a bulletin board to demonstrate main idea and details. They can start with a large index card that says, "Fish have different kinds of eyes." Then they can place small illustrated words all around to show details such as *green*, *hooded*, or *shiny*. **(MULTISENSORY TECHNIQUES)**

EXTRA HELP

■ Provide a main idea statement such as *Playgrounds are good places to play.* Ask children to suggest reasons or details as to why this statement is true. Help children understand that their ideas are all supporting the main idea. **(ASSIST IN PROCESS)**

SKILLS TRACE

MAIN IDEA/DETAILS TESTED

Introduce	pp. T54–T55
Practice	p. T27
Reteach	p. R55

CONNECT TO THE TRADE BOOKS

Select one of the unit trade books. Read aloud the title and discuss the cover illustration.

- Have children make predictions about what they might learn while reading this book. Record their predictions on chart paper or the chalkboard.
- Read a few pages at a time and stop to help children identify the topic or main idea. Ask children what details support this main idea.
- Record children's responses on an outline or idea map and review main idea and details.

To determine the main idea, have children:

1. Read the text and look at the pictures for the most important information.
2. Look for details that support the main idea.

LITERATURE CONNECTION

THINK ALOUD *When I started reading* Fish Faces *the text and pictures gave me facts about long fish, mad fish, and more! These details helped me to be sure that the main idea was different kinds of fish.*

B PRACTICE/APPLY

USE PRACTICE BOOK

Have children revisit page 8 of *Fish Faces.* Read aloud the text. Ask children to discuss the main idea of *Fish Faces.* Help them to see that the main idea is different kinds of fish. Now have pairs of children practice the skill by completing **Practice Book page 9.**

C ASSESS

APPLY INSTRUCTIONAL ALTERNATIVES

Based on children's completion of **Practice Book page 9,** determine if children were able to identify the main idea and details in *Fish Faces.* The instructional alternatives below will aid you in pinpointing children's level of proficiency. Consider the appropriate instructional alternative to promote further skill development.

To reinforce the skills, distribute **page 10** of the **Practice Book.**

INSTRUCTIONAL ALTERNATIVES

	If the child . . .	Then
Proficient	Correctly identifies the main idea and supporting details	• Have the child apply this skill independently to a more challenging nonfiction selection. • Present a main idea sentence along with supporting detail sentences. Have the child identify the main idea and the supporting details.
Apprentice	Can identify main idea and supporting details in a simple exercise but has difficulty applying the concept to a longer selection	• Have the child work with others to brainstorm the main idea and supporting details in a simple, familiar selection.
Novice	Cannot distinguish the main idea from supporting details and often identifies a supporting detail as the main idea	• Provide the child with main idea and supporting detail sentences and work with the child to distinguish the difference between them. • Complete the Reteach lesson on p. R55.

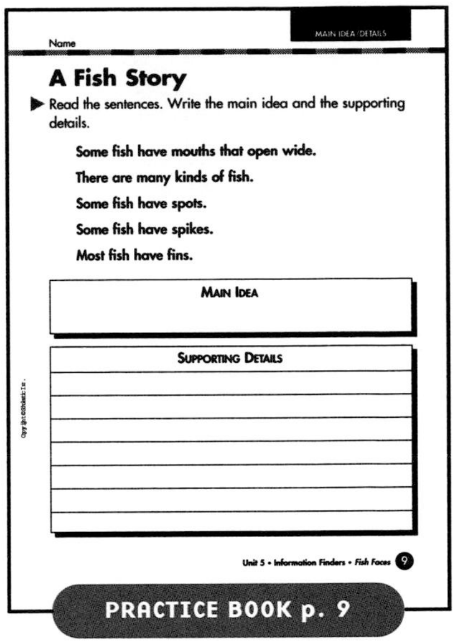
Name MAIN IDEA/DETAILS

A Fish Story

▶ Read the sentences. Write the main idea and the supporting details.

Some fish have mouths that open wide.
There are many kinds of fish.
Some fish have spots.
Some fish have spikes.
Most fish have fins.

MAIN IDEA

SUPPORTING DETAILS

Unit 5 • Information Finders • Fish Faces 9

PRACTICE BOOK p. 9

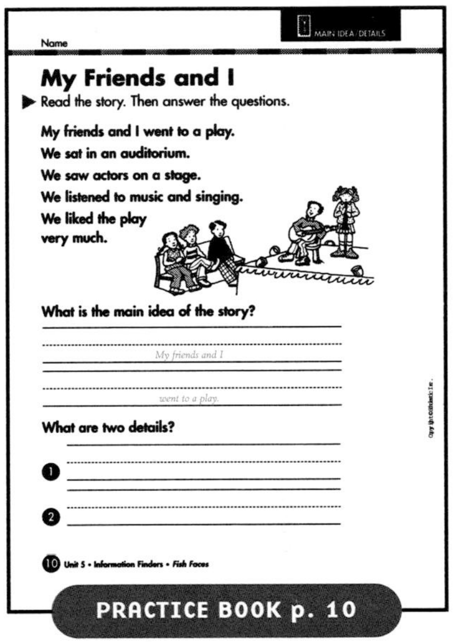
Name MAIN IDEA/DETAILS

My Friends and I

▶ Read the story. Then answer the questions.

My friends and I went to a play.
We sat in an auditorium.
We saw actors on a stage.
We listened to music and singing.
We liked the play very much.

What is the main idea of the story?

My friends and I went to a play.

What are two details?

1
2

10 Unit 5 • Information Finders • Fish Faces

PRACTICE BOOK p. 10

SELECTION WORDS: HOMOPHONES

eye	red
four	there
great	two
nose	wood
one	

SKILLS TRACE

HOMOPHONES TESTED

Introduce	pp. T56–T57
Practice	pp. T39, T63
Review	p. R46
Reteach	p. R64

TECHNOLOGY

Have children write sentences on the **WiggleWorks Plus** Magnet Board using the following words: ***one, won, two, to, wood, would, red, read, four, for.***

DAILY PHONICS

Homophones

A TEACH/MODEL

INTRODUCE HOMOPHONES Ask children to listen as you read this nonsense rhyme:

> How much wood would a woodchuck chuck if a woodchuck could chuck wood?

- Have children identify the two words that sound alike but have different meanings: ***wood*** and ***would.***
- Write ***wood*** and ***would*** on the chalkboard and point out that the two words are spelled differently.
- Have volunteers use ***wood*** and ***would*** in sentences.

Explain that ***wood*** and ***would*** are homophones. They sound alike, but they have different meanings and different spellings.

PHONICS MAINTENANCE Review the following sound-spellings: ***/ā/a-e; /ē/ee, ea.*** Write each of the following words on the chalkboard. Read each word aloud, and define it if necessary: ***sail, main, tail, pail, see, real, steal, knead.*** Have volunteers write a homophone for each word that has a different spelling for the vowel sound.

sail	sale	see	sea
main	mane	real	real
tail	tale	steal	steel
pail	pale	knead	need

MODIFY Instruction

ESL/ELD

▲ To help children assimilate information, pause before introducing a new pair of homophones. Offer visual clues whenever possible. Ask fluent peers to help their classmates make word cards to help them practice recognizing homophones. **(ASSIST IN PROCESS)**

EXTRA HELP

■ Write homophone pairs on word cards. Give one card to each child and help them read their words aloud. Children with homophone pairs should get together and make up two sentences that use their words. **(WORK IN PAIRS)**

B PRACTICE/APPLY

IDENTIFY HOMOPHONES To give children practice in recognizing homophones, write the following sentences on the chalkboard:

> The vet knows a healthy dog's nose is cool and wet.
>
> The boat store is having a sail sale.
>
> *Wags* is a tale about a dog with a bushy tail.
>
> The main thing about a lion is the mane.

Read the sentences aloud and have volunteers identify and underline the two words in each sentence that are homophones.

NAME HOMOPHONES Write these selection words from the selections on a chart:

one	two	wood	red
four	there	nose	great

Read the words aloud and ask volunteers to suggest a homophone for each word. Then work as a group to compose sentences using each homophone pair.

DICTATION Dictate the following words for children to spell: ***date, green, eat.***

Name HOMOPHONES

I See the Sea

▶ Read the words in the box. Then write the name of the picture on the line. Cut out the cards. With a friend, pick a card and say a sentence for the word on each side.

two	sea
sun	plane
one	no
ant	write

12 Unit 5 • Information Finders • Fish Faces

PRACTICE BOOK p. 12

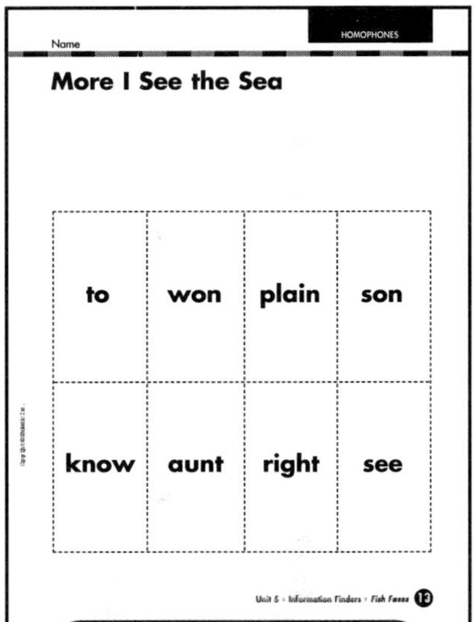

Name HOMOPHONES

More I See the Sea

to	won	plain	son
know	aunt	right	see

Unit 5 • Information Finders • Fish Faces 13

PRACTICE BOOK p. 13

DECODABLE TEXT

For practice reading decodable text, see ***Scholastic Decodable Reader #58.***

For additional phonics instruction and review, see ***Scholastic Phonics A, p. 238.***

HOMOPHONE RIDDLES

Share this riddle with children:

Why won't a grizzly wear shoes?
Because it likes going bearfoot!

Help children recognize the homophones ***bear*** and ***bare*** that are basic to the riddle. Then challenge children to use homophones and come up with their own silly riddles to ask the class.

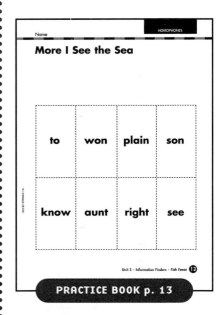

Building Fluency

Phonics Reader

Guide children through a reading of **Phonics Reader #36** *Shhh!* For a detailed lesson plan, see **Phonics Reader Teacher's Guide Part A, pages 82–83.** While children read, note how well they:

- **blend words,**
- **recognize high-frequency words,**
- **read with speed, accuracy, and expression.**

You may wish to have children reread the story with a partner.

* See Phonics Readers Take-Home Books 37–72 for reproducible format.

More Support Materials . . .

Trade Book Library

For additional leveled reading practice, have children read one of the following:

Animal Tracks
Challenge

Owl at Home
Average

Lost!
Easy

Phonics and Word Building Kit

Have children build words with digraphs ***sh*** and ***th*** using the digraph and phonogram cards.

Home-School Connection

Send home *Shhh!* and *Six Shaggy Things*. Have children read the books to a family member.

My Book

For additional practice with digraphs, have children read *Six Shaggy Things*. It is also available on **WiggleWorks Plus.**

Intervention

For children who need extra help . . .

FOCUS ON HIGH-FREQUENCY WORDS

Write the words ***more*** and ***belongs*** on note cards. Then follow this procedure:

- State each word as children repeat it.
- Have children spell the word aloud as you point to each letter.
- Have children write each word in their Journal.
- Provide children with simple sentences containing each word. Help them to read the sentences. Allow ample time for them to practice reading the words and sentences before rereading *Fish Faces.*

Some children may need a large number of repetitions before these words become sight words. Brief, daily reviews and frequent rereadings of previous stories containing these words will be helpful.

FOCUS ON PHONICS

Provide time for children to play with the decodable words they encountered in the selection, such as ***fish*** and ***thin.***

- Make each word using magnetic letters or letter cards as children observe.
- Have children trace the letters in each word with their fingers, as you say the sounds with them.
- Mix the letters and have children respell the words.
- Model blending as needed.

PROFESSIONAL DEVELOPMENT

GAY SU PINNELL

What Are Homophones?

Homophones are words that sound the same but have different meanings and spellings. The spellings of homophones are critical because they provide clues to the word's meaning. It is helpful to have children read and write these words in multiple contexts.

DAY 3 WRAP-UP

READ ALOUD *To conclude each reading session and develop children's oral vocabularies, read aloud a book of your choice. If the book contains chapters, you might choose to read only one chapter a day.*

GUIDED READING *Meet with the* ***red*** *and* ***blue*** *reading groups and assign Independent Center activities.*
See pages R2–R3.

DAY 4 OBJECTIVES

CHILDREN WILL:

READ 30 MINUTES

- **Reread *Fish Faces***

WRITE 30 MINUTES

- **Shared Writing: Book of Facts**
- **Spelling: Words With Digraphs**
- **Grammar, Usage, Mechanics: Word Order**
- **Oral Language**

EXTEND SKILLS 30 MINUTES

- **Vocabulary**
- **Daily Phonics: Homophones**
- **Read Aloud: *Three Days on the River in a Red Canoe***
- **Guided Reading**

RESOURCES

- **Practice Book, pp. 14, 15**
- **Spelling Resource Book, p. 161**

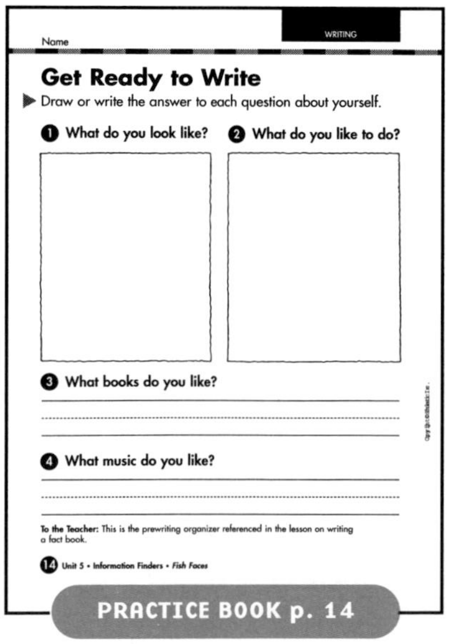

Name WRITING

Get Ready to Write

▶ Draw or write the answer to each question about yourself.

1. What do you look like?
2. What do you like to do?
3. What books do you like?
4. What music do you like?

To the Teacher: This is the prewriting organizer referenced in the lesson on writing a fact book.

14 Unit 5 • Information Finders • Fish Faces

PRACTICE BOOK p. 14

SHARED WRITING

Book of Facts

SELECTION CONNECTION Using *Fish Faces* as a model, children will write a book of facts about themselves.

THINK ABOUT WRITING Ask children to discuss some fact books that they have read or seen. Talk with children about how writing a fact book like *Fish Faces* involves:

- gathering information and discovering facts.
- getting photographs.

INTRODUCE THE WRITING EVENT Let children know that they will develop a fact book about themselves. Have them think about what information they would like to include in their fact book.

TEACH/MODEL

PUT IT IN CONTEXT Have children look back at page 14 of *Fish Faces*. Ask: What information does the writer share?

Ask children to answer these questions about themselves to help them begin their book of facts.

- What do you look like?
- What do you like to do?

Help children organize facts about themselves on a chart:

FACTS ABOUT ME		
What I Look Like	What I Like to Do	Other Facts About Me

GRAMMAR CONNECTION Have children compare the different word order in your questions and their answers.

MODIFY Instruction

ESL/ELD

▲ To help children write their facts, model how you would write a factual story about yourself. Write, gesture, and say, *I am tall. I have brown hair. I like to teach. I like to read. My favorite color is red. My favorite animal is a dog.* Display your story and a list of other words for reference. **(MODEL)**

EXTRA HELP

■ Support children who need extra help discovering facts about themselves by having them work with a partner to answer the questions about themselves and the things they like. **(BRAINSTORM)**

WRITE

BOOK OF FACTS

- Have children choose photographs or draw pictures of themselves.
- Then have children select the facts from their Facts Chart that they want to use with their pictures to tell about themselves.
- Have children write the facts they choose in sentences, then attach their photographs or drawings to their papers.
- Gather the pages into a class book of facts. Give children an opportunity to read their pages aloud to the class.

ASSESS

PERFORMANCE-BASED ASSESSMENT

The following questions will help children assess their work:

✔ **Do my facts create a word picture of me?**

✔ **Would someone who does not know me well learn something about me from these facts?**

Children may wish to develop this piece through the writing process described on pages T292–T295.

DAILY LANGUAGE PRACTICE

SPELLING

DAY 4:

Review Words With Digraphs *sh, th.*

See page R5.

GRAMMAR, USAGE, MECHANICS

DAY 4:

Apply Word Order. **See page R7.**

ORAL LANGUAGE

I wis could I read a book thick.

(I wish I could read a thick book.)

TECHNOLOGY

Writing Skills
Encourage children to use the Unit Writer to create their Book of Facts. Suggest that they use the Record Tool, the Paint Tools, and stamp art.

Extend Vocabulary

more

belongs

Review High-Frequency Words

Write the high-frequency words ***more*** and ***belongs*** on note cards. Then write the following incomplete sentences on the chalkboard:

All this stuff _____ to Ben.

He has _____ stuff than anyone!

Read aloud each incomplete sentence and have children place the appropriate high-frequency word note card in each blank space. Then help children to chorally read the sentences.

TEACHER TIP

"Make and distribute copies of the vocabulary cards on pages R22–R67. Have children use these cards for additional practice."

Review Story Words

Write the selection words ***fish, waves, mouth, nose, eyes,*** and ***fins*** on note cards. Then write the following incomplete sentences on sentence strips:

This _____ is flat.

It has big, black _____ to see with.

Its _____ looks round when the fish opens it.

Its _____ looks like a beak.

It has yellow _____ on its tail.

It has _____ that help it swim.

Read aloud the incomplete sentences and have children place the appropriate story word note card in the blank space. Then help children to chorally read the sentences.

my fish has a fat nose.

FISHY SHOW AND TELL

Ask children to draw pictures of fish. Then, on the back of their pictures, have children use describing words and the vocabulary words to write about their fish. Encourage children to take turns showing and telling about their fish. You may also wish to create a fish tank bulletin board on which to display the fish.

Building Fluency

Phonics Reader

Guide children through a reading of **Phonics Reader #54** *See the Sea.* For a detailed lesson plan, see **Phonics Reader Teacher's Guide Part B, pages 50–51.** While children read, note how well they:

- **blend words,**
- **recognize high-frequency words,**
- **read with speed, accuracy, and expression.**

You may wish to have children reread the story with a partner.

* See Phonics Readers Take-Home Books 37–72 for reproducible format.

More Support Materials . . .

Trade Book Library

For additional leveled reading practice, have children read one of the following:

Animal Tracks
CHALLENGE

Owl at Home
AVERAGE

Lost!
EASY

Phonics Chapter Book

For additional practice with homophones, have children read Chapter 1, "Charlie and Kate on the Trail," in Phonics Chapter Book 5, ***Let's Go on a Museum Hunt.***

Home-School Connection

Send home *See the Sea* and *Going to Sea.* Have children read the book to a family member.

My Book

For additional practice with homophones, have children read *Going to Sea.* This book is also available on **WiggleWorks Plus.**

Listen to the Read Aloud

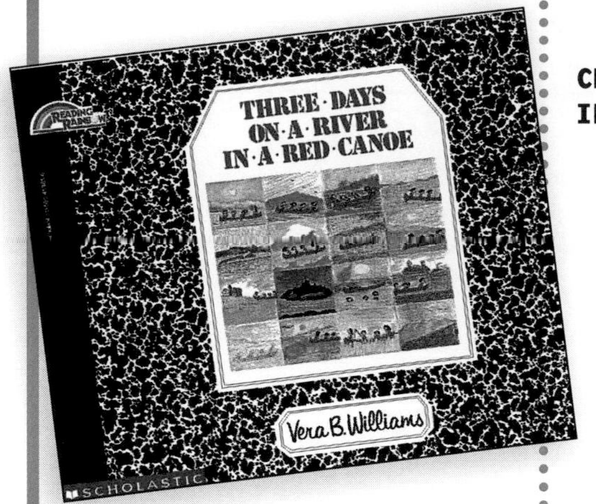

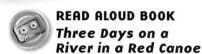

READ ALOUD BOOK
Three Days on a River in a Red Canoe

Introduce the Read Aloud

CREATE INTEREST

Spark children's interest in the Read Aloud by asking these questions: ***Have you ever been on a boat? What do you think a canoe trip would be like?***

Have cooperative groups decide on three things they'd most enjoy about a canoe trip. Encourage children to draw pictures to show their ideas.

Have groups share their pictures and ideas. You may also ask the groups to think about what parts of a canoe trip they might *not* enjoy.

Share the Read Aloud

MAKE PREDICTIONS

Show children the cover of the book and read the name of the author/illustrator. Ask children what clues the title and cover give about the book. Show the inside of the book and help them see that it's written as if it were a child's journal of the trip.

Begin reading aloud. Stop when you reach the page that shows all the things taken on the trip. Have children examine the picture. Then ask:

> **How do you think the people will use all these things on their trip?**

Continue reading. From time to time, pause and ask:

> **Is this canoe trip the way you thought it would be or is it different? How?**

Think About the Read Aloud

DISCUSSION

Have children share their thoughts and ideas about the story. You may want to prompt discussion by asking:

> **What did you enjoy most about this story?**

> **What did you learn about canoeing? What did you learn about camping?**

> **Did you like the way this book was written—as a child's journal? How did the maps, pictures, and diagrams help you understand what was happening?**

TECHNOLOGY

Writing Skills Have children write a journal entry about an imaginary canoe/camping trip, using the **WiggleWorks Plus** Unit Writer. Ask them to use plenty of descriptive words and encourage them to illustrate with clip art and simple drawings.

Focus on Language

FIGURATIVE LANGUAGE

Talk with children about how the book is written. It is written the way a child might tell about the adventures of a canoe trip—but it also includes good examples of figurative language.

ACTIVITY: REVISIT THE STORY

- Point out the simile in this sentence from page 12: "Here are Mom and Aunt Rosie paddling into a part of the river like a hot green tunnel." Ask children to tell what the words *like a hot green tunnel* tell them about the river.
- Explore the onomatopoeic words in this sentence from page 24: "The branches creaked and whooshed all night long." Ask children to imitate the sounds the trees made.

Make Connections

ORAL LANGUAGE

To *Fish Faces* Remind children that when they read *Fish Faces* they had a chance to meet many different faces "face to face." Ask children if they think any of the fish they met in *Fish Faces* were the same kind of fish the characters in this story encountered. Encourage children to explain the reasons for their answers.

To Children's Lives Point out how *Three Days on a River in a Red Canoe* shows the importance of managing information during a trip along a river. Encourage children to talk about times when they have had to manage information in this way. You may wish to start the discussion by asking if children have ever used a map to find their way, paddled in a canoe, or tied special knots in rope.

RESPOND TO WHAT IS VIEWED

TEACH/MODEL Talk about how the pictures, maps, and diagrams in this book tell part of the story.

THINK ALOUD *This book is written like a trip journal. The author uses words, pictures, maps, and diagrams to tell about her trip. When you look at the pages called "Our First Morning on the River," you see everything the group did that morning. There are just a few words on this page. Most of what we learn we learn from the pictures.*

PRACTICE/APPLY Have children examine the picture details in "Our First Morning on the River" and talk about them.

DAY 4 WRAP-UP

READ ALOUD *Spend five to ten minutes reading from a selection of your choice.*

GUIDED READING *Meet with the* ***green*** *and* ***yellow*** *reading groups and assign Independent Center activities.* ***See pages R2–R3.***

DAY 5 OBJECTIVES

CHILDREN WILL:

READ 30 MINUTES

- **Reading Assessment**
- **Daily Phonics: Digraphs *sh*, *th*; Homophones**

WRITE 30 MINUTES

- **Writing Assessment**
- **Spelling: Words With Digraphs *sh*, *th***
- **Grammar, Usage, Mechanics: Word Order**

EXTEND SKILLS 30 MINUTES

- **Integrated Language Arts**
- **Read Aloud**
- **Guided Reading**

RESOURCES

- **Selection Test**
- **Spelling Resource Book, p. 163**

REGROUPING TIP

- Assess and regroup children for leveled reading every six weeks.
- Use the results of your informal and formal assessments to regroup children as necessary.
- Be sure all children are involved in whole class and small group instruction throughout each day.

Reading Assessment

INFORMAL ASSESSMENT: OBSERVATION

PHONICS

Write the digraphs ***sh*** and ***th*** on note cards. Display one card and then the other and have the class state the sound and the letters in the digraph. Repeat this a few times, repeating or reversing the order. Note children who respond incorrectly or wait for classmates to respond before saying the sound.

HIGH-FREQUENCY WORDS

Write the following words on note cards: ***more, belongs.*** Display one card at a time and have the class read the word. Repeat this a few times, showing the two cards in different order. Note children who have difficulty recognizing either of the words.

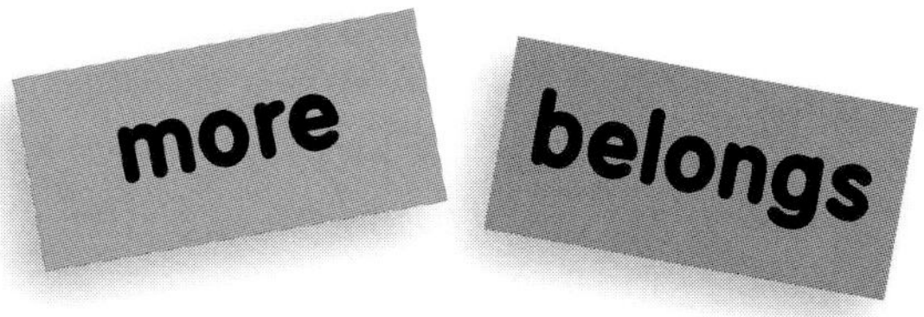

KEY SKILL: MAIN IDEA/DETAILS

Choose a nonfiction ***Phonics Reader*** or one of the ***My Books.*** Read the story with children. Then ask children to write a sentence or draw a picture to show the main idea.

CONFERENCE

Have children reread *Fish Faces*. As they reread, select several children to conference with. Ask them to do the following:

- read aloud a few pages of the selection.
- retell what they learned in their own words.
- explain what they do to figure out an unfamiliar word.

Fish Faces

Keep anecdotal records of the conferences. Place your findings in each child's assessment folder. Use the information to determine which children need additional support.

FORMAL ASSESSMENT

DECODING TEST

Make two copies of the assessment below. The assessment piece is designed to be used individually.

- Give one to the child and keep the other to record each child's errors.
- As the child reads aloud the words and sentences in the assessment boxes, record his or her attempts, corrections, errors, and passes.
- Once completed, keep each assessment piece in the child's portfolio as a running record of his or her emerging reading skills.

NAME: ______________________________ **DATE:** __________

A Have children read the following word list:

thin	**path**	**fish**	**were**	**more**
wish	**sheep**	**shade**	**way**	**which**
think	**bath**	**shine**	**belongs**	**make**
leash	**clash**	**trash**	**about**	**some**
grade	**thick**	**teeth**	**look**	**many**

B Have children read the following sentences:

- **Many fish have shiny fins.**
- **Some fish have sharp teeth in their mouths.**

C On a separate sheet of paper, have children write the following words and sentences:

- **wish fish thin teeth**
- **You can see fish in the sea.**
- **Those two fish are too thin.**

SELECTION TEST

Use the selection test to obtain a formal measure of children's mastery of the week's reading objectives.

TIME MANAGEMENT

Part C of the assessment can be administered to the whole class. Assess children throughout the entire day on Parts A and B. Each assessment should take no more than 2–3 minutes.

You may choose to assess children during independent reading time or Independent Center time. If you have a teacher's aide, allow him or her to give the assessment.

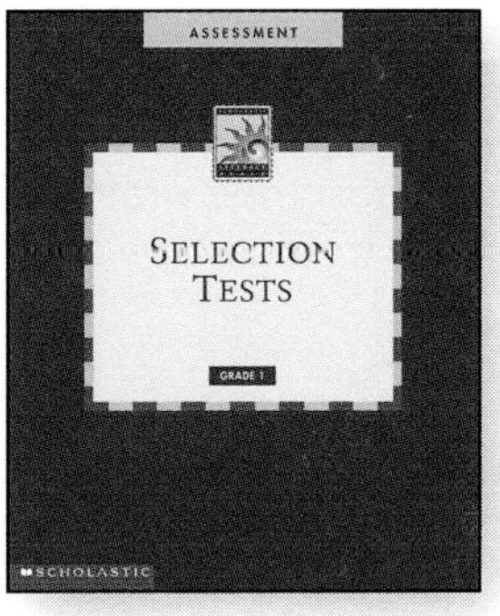

SELECTION TEST

Writing Assessment

Your facts go along well with your drawing of yourself.
You do a good job including detailed facts that tell about yourself.
You have also done a good job proofreading your work and correcting your errors.
I am happy and I like people.
I have yellow hair. I have 2 brothers.
I am 6 years old.
Proficient

Use the rubric below to assess children's writing.

CHILDREN'S WRITING RUBRIC

Proficient	• Child's writing includes facts that reflect his or her self-portrait or photograph. • The facts give a clear, detailed description of the child.	• The writing has been proofread and corrected for errors.
Apprentice	• Child's writing includes some facts that reflect a self-portrait or photograph. • The facts may not give clear, detailed descriptions.	• The writing may have been proofread, but may not have been corrected for errors.
Novice	• Child's writing includes few facts that reflect a self-portrait or photograph.	• The writing has not been proofread or corrected for errors.

DAILY LANGUAGE PRACTICE

SPELLING

DAY 5:
Administer the Posttest for Words With Digraphs *sh*, *th*. See page R5.

GRAMMAR, USAGE, MECHANICS

DAY 5:
Assess Word Order. See page R7.

ORAL LANGUAGE

A fis is always taking a baht?
(Is a fish always taking a bath?)

PORTFOLIO

Suggest that children add their drafts and revisions to their Literacy Portfolios.

Integrated Language Arts

VIEWING/LISTENING

Make Fish-Face Puppets

MATERIALS:
Construction paper
Crayons
Scissors Tape
Straws or Sticks

SUGGESTED GROUPING:
Cooperative groups, partners, or individuals

CHILDREN can look through the selection and choose a fish with an interesting feature—such as a long nose or spots. Using collage materials, crayons, and markers, have children draw and cut out their fish.

AFTER drawing, coloring, and cutting out the fish, children can tape them to straws or sticks.

HAVE children reread *Fish Faces* aloud, holding up their fish puppets when the text that describes their fish is read. For example, when "fish with lines" is read, children who made fish with lines could hold up their fish.

TECHNOLOGY

Viewing Skills Have children create their fish puppets in **WiggleWorks Plus** PlaceMaker or a familiar art program. Then have them work in teams to narrate and videotape their puppet show version of the book.

ORAL LANGUAGE

Write a Book Report

MATERIALS:
Anthology, pp. 8–33
Book Report form in *Community Involvement,* Unit 6, p. R92
Construction paper
Markers
Crayons
Tape or stapler

SUGGESTED GROUPING:
Individuals

ASK children to talk about the fish they liked best in the selection *Fish Faces.* Encourage children to discuss the main idea and details of the selection.

DISTRIBUTE Book Report forms to children. Have them fill in the title and write sentences describing what they enjoyed about the selection. Let them use the photographs from the Anthology to help them draw a picture of a favorite fish. You may wish to have children make Book Report covers for their work.

ENCOURAGE children to share their book reports. Children can write notes to each other about their book reports.

Children might want to include their Book Reports in their Literacy Portfolios.

Integrated Language Arts

WRITING

Make a Class Book

MATERIALS:
Anthology, pp. 8–33
Drawing paper

SUGGESTED GROUPING:
Whole class, individuals

HAVE children make a class book entitled *Our Favorite Fish.* Each child can select one kind of fish and use it as the basis of a page in the class book. Children can use *Fish Faces* or other books or magazines to come up with ideas.

CHILDREN can draw a picture of the fish, name it (if they know its name), and write a caption or label that tells two or three things about it.

HAVE children gather the pages together to create a class book. Call on volunteers to design a cover. Lend the book to your school library for display and check-out.

READING

Read About How Fish Move

Good For Grading

MATERIALS:
Anthology, pp. 8–33
Index cards

SUGGESTED GROUPING:
Partners

DISCUSS how fish move in many different ways like darting and gliding. Children may wish to pantomime fish movements.

ASK children to flip through *Fish Faces* and choose words that describe how fish move. Then write these movement words on index cards.

ENCOURAGE partners to take turns reading words from each other's cards. Have them act out these words.

GRADE by looking for a connection between the action words and the children's movements.

Action Verbs

TEACH/MODEL Make a list of action verbs such as ***dance, jump, sing.*** Ask children to pantomime each verb.

PRACTICE/APPLY Prompt children to brainstorm other action verbs and act them out. Have children guess the verb being pantomimed.

DAY 5 WRAP-UP

READ ALOUD *Spend five to ten minutes reading from a selection of your choice.*

GUIDED READING *Meet with the* ***blue*** *and* ***red*** *reading groups and assign Independent Center activities.* ***See pages R2–R3.***

I'm a Caterpillar

Main Selection
Genre: Nonfiction

Paired Selection
Genre: Poem
National Council of Teachers of English
Award for Excellence in Poetry for Children
Award-winning poet

WEEK 2 TESTED SKILLS

- Vocabulary
- Daily Phonics: Vowel /ô/ *all, aw*
  Vowel /ā/ *ay, ai*
- Key Comprehension Skill: Sequence
- Study Skills: Graphic Aids: Diagrams
- Spelling: Words With /ô/*all, aw*
- Grammar, Usage, Mechanics: Capitalizing the Word *I*

Technology Connection

Build Background Butterfly fun is waiting online in The Children's Butterfly Site at **www.mesc.usgs.gov.** Children can print out pages to color or visit the photo gallery and try to find the butterfly from the story.

Selection Summary

I'*m a Caterpillar* follows the life of a caterpillar. The reader first meets the caterpillar eating. Once it has eaten enough, the caterpillar hangs upside down on a tree, sheds its skin, and grows a shell. By the time it has left the shell, the caterpillar has become a butterfly. It visits flowers, eats, and lays eggs out of which hatch caterpillars. With the words "I'm a caterpillar," the process begins again.

PAIRED SELECTION In this poem, the poet discovers what caterpillars do.

Author

JEAN MARZOLLO has produced rhythmic picture books for children, easy-to-read and chapter books for early readers, novels for young adults, and nonfiction selections for parents. Another of her books is *Close Your Eyes.*

Weekly Organizer

Visit Our Web Site
www.scholastic.com

I'm a Caterpillar

	DAY 1	DAY 2
READ and Introduce Skills • VOCABULARY • PHONICS • COMPREHENSION • LISTENING • SPEAKING • VIEWING 	**BUILD BACKGROUND,** p. T77 ▲ ✓ **VOCABULARY,** p. T78 ▲ ✸ Practice Book, p. 16 ✓ **DAILY PHONICS:** ▲ ■ Vowel /ô/*all, aw*, pp. T80–T81 Practice Book, pp. 17, 18 **PREVIEW AND PREDICT,** p. T82 **READ:** ▲ ✸ ■ *I'm a Caterpillar*, pp. T82–T93 ✓ **COMPREHENSION:** Sequence, p. T85	**READ:** ▲ ■ ✸ *I'm a Caterpillar*, pp. T94–T110 "Caterpillars," p. T111 ✓ **DAILY PHONICS:** Words With /ô/*all, aw*, p. T95 Vowel /ā/*ay, ai*, p. T107 **COMPREHENSION:** Main Idea/Details, p. T101 **GENRE:** Nonfiction, p. T103
WRITE and Respond • GRAMMAR • USAGE • MECHANICS • SPELLING • WRITING	**SHARED WRITING,** p. T77 **JOURNAL,** p. T79 ✓ **SPELLING:** Pretest: Words With /ô/*all, aw*, p. R12 Spelling Resource Book, p. 114 ✓ **GRAMMAR, USAGE, MECHANICS:** Teach/Model: Capitalizing *I*, p. R14 **ORAL LANGUAGE,** p. T93	**SHARED WRITING:** Prewrite, p. T111 Practice Book, p. 24 ✓ **SPELLING:** Vocabulary Practice, p. R12 Spelling Resource Book, pp. 115–117 ✓ **GRAMMAR, USAGE, MECHANICS:** Practice, p. R14 **ORAL LANGUAGE,** p. T111
EXTEND SKILLS and Apply to Literature • SKILLS • INTEGRATED LANGUAGE ARTS • INTEGRATED CURRICULUM • GUIDED READING • INDEPENDENT READING	**READ ALOUD,** p. T93 **GUIDED READING,** pp. R10–R11 **TRADE BOOKS** • *Lost!* • *Owl at Home* • *Animal Tracks* 	**READ ALOUD,** p. T111 **GUIDED READING,** pp. R10–R11 **INTEGRATED CURRICULUM:** Math, p. R16 Social Studies, p. R17 The Arts, p. R17 Science, p. R16
TECHNOLOGY and **REAL-WORLD SKILLS**	**WIGGLEWORKS PLUS CD-ROM** Magnet Board, pp. T78, T80 **SCHOLASTIC NETWORK** Finding the Facts, p. T93 **WORKSHOP 2,** pp. T235–T238	**WIGGLEWORKS PLUS CD-ROM** Organizing Information, p. T99 **WORKSHOP 2,** pp. T235–T238

MODIFY INSTRUCTION

● INTERVENTION ▲ ESL/ELD ■ EXTRA HELP
✷ GIFTED & TALENTED ✓ = TESTED SKILL

DAY 3	DAY 4	DAY 5
✓ **COMPREHENSION:** ▲ ■ Sequence, pp. T114–T115 Practice Book, pp. 20, 21 ✓ **DAILY PHONICS:** ▲ ✷ Vowel /ā/*ay, ai,* p. T116 Practice Book, pp. 22, 23 **FLUENCY,** p. T118 ✓ **FOCUS ON HIGH-FREQUENCY WORDS,** p. T119 **FOCUS ON PHONICS,** p. T119	✓ **VOCABULARY REVIEW,** p. T122 **FLUENCY,** p. T123 ✓ **DAILY PHONICS:** Vowel /ā/*ay, ai,* p. T123	**READING ASSESSMENT,** p. T126 Selection Test Conference Decoding Test
RESPOND: ▲ Think About Reading, p. T112 Practice Book, p. 19 **WRITE CARTOON DIALOGUE,** p. T113 ✓ **SPELLING:** Write/Proofread, p. R13 Spelling Resource Book, p. 118 ✓ **GRAMMAR, USAGE, MECHANICS:** Practice, p. R15 **ORAL LANGUAGE,** p. T113	**SHARED WRITING** ▲ ■ Description, p. T120 Practice Book, p. 24 ✓ **SPELLING:** Study/Review, p. R13 Spelling Resource Book, p. 161 ✓ **GRAMMAR, USAGE, MECHANICS:** Apply, p. R15 **ORAL LANGUAGE,** p. T121	**WRITING ASSESSMENT,** p. T128 Child Model Children's Writing Rubric ✓ **SPELLING:** Posttest, p. R13 Spelling Resource Book, p. 163 ✓ **GRAMMAR, USAGE, MECHANICS:** Assess, p. R15 **ORAL LANGUAGE,** p. T128
READ ALOUD, p. T119 **GUIDED READING,** pp. R10–R11 **OPTIONAL MATERIALS,** p. T118 Phonics Reader #51: *Dinosaur Hall* Phonics Reader #52: *Paws and Claws*	**READ ALOUD,** p. T125 **GUIDED READING,** pp. R10–R11 **EXTEND VOCABULARY:** Review High-Frequency Words, p. T122 Review Story Words, p. T122 **OPTIONAL MATERIALS,** p. T123 Phonics Reader #49: *The Frog Trail* Phonics Reader #50: *A Rain Forest Day* ✓ **STUDY SKILLS:** Graphic Aids: Diagrams, p. T124	**READ ALOUD,** p. T130 **GUIDED READING,** pp. R10–R11 **INTEGRATED LANGUAGE ARTS:** Create a Word Butterfly, p. T129 Make a Butterfly Book, p. T129 Explore Noises and Sounds, p. T130 Interview the Caterpillar, p. T130
WIGGLEWORKS PLUS CD-ROM Language Development, p. T113 **WIGGLEWORKS PLUS CD-ROM** Magnet Board, p. T116 **WORKSHOP 2,** pp. T235–T238	**WIGGLEWORKS PLUS CD-ROM** Presentation Tools, p. T125 **WORKSHOP 2,** pp. T235–T238	**AUDIO** Speaking Skills, p. T130 **WORKSHOP 2,** pp. T235–T238

Weekly Assessment

ASSESSMENT PLANNING

USE THIS CHART TO PLAN YOUR ASSESSMENT OF THE WEEKLY READING OBJECTIVES.

- **Informal Assessment is ongoing and should be used before, during and after reading.**
- **Formal Assessment occurs at the end of the week on the selection test.**
- **Note that Intervention activities occur throughout the lesson to support students who need extra help with skills.**

YOU MAY CHOOSE AMONG THE FOLLOWING PAGES IN THE ASSESSMENT HANDBOOK.

- **Informal Assessment**
- **Anecdotal Record**
- **Portfolio Checklist and Evaluation Forms**
- **Self-Assessment**
- **English Language Learners**
- **Using Technology to Assess**
- **Test Preparations**

SKILLS AND STRATEGIES	Informal Assessment
COMPREHENSION Sequence	**OBSERVATION p. T85** • Did children recognize the sequence of events in the story so far? **QUICKCHECK p. T114** • Can children follow the sequence of events? **CHECK PRACTICE BOOK p. 20** **CONFERENCE p. T126**
DAILY PHONICS Vowel /ô/*all, aw* Vowel /ā/*ay, ai*	**OBSERVATION pp. T95, T107** • Did children recognize and blend words with /ô/*all, aw*? • Did children recognize and blend words with /ā/*ay, ai*? **CHECK PRACTICE BOOK pp. 17, 22** **DICTATION pp. T81, T117**
VOCABULARY Story Words **munch** **straw** **grow** **wait** **dry** **wet** High-Frequency **next** **all**	**OBSERVATION p. T122** • Did children identify story words? • Did children identify high-frequency words? **CHECK PRACTICE BOOK p. 16**

Formal Assessment	INTERVENTION and Instructional Alternatives	Planning Notes
SELECTION TEST • Questions 1–3 check children's mastery of the key strategy, sequence. **UNIT TEST**	If children need help with sequence, then go to: • **Instructional Alternatives, p. T115** • **Review, p. R44** • **Reteach, p. R55**	
DECODING TEST • See p. T127 **SELECTION TEST** • Questions 4–7 check children's ability to recognize words with /ô/*all, aw* and /ā/*ay, ai.* **UNIT TEST**	If students need help identifying words with /ô/*all, aw,* then go to: • **Intervention Activity, p. T119** • **Review, p. R47** • **Reteach, p. R58** If children need help identifying words with /ā/*ay, ai,* then go to: • **Review, p. R48** • **Reteach, p. R58**	
SELECTION TEST • Questions 8–10 check children's recall of high-frequency words and story words. **UNIT TEST**	If children need additional practice with the vocabulary words, then go to: • **Intervention Activity, p. T119** • **Extend Vocabulary, p. T122** • **Integrated Language Arts, p. T130**	

Technology

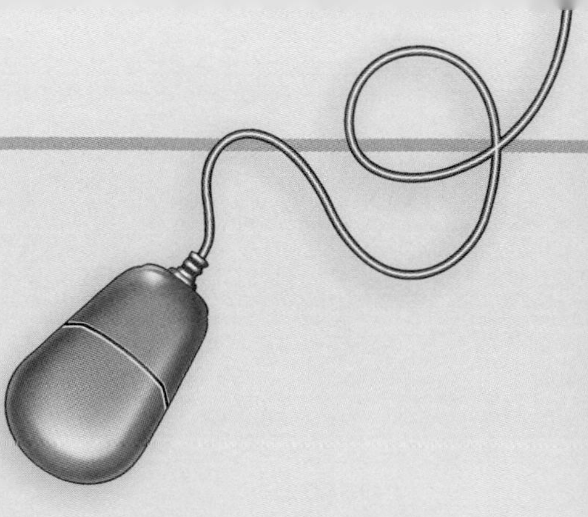

The technology in this lesson helps teachers and children develop the skills they need for the 21st century. Look for integrated technology activities on every day of instruction.

DAY 1 Finding the Facts	• Children use the Internet to research interesting butterfly facts.
DAY 2 Organizing Information	• Children learn how to format and organize a list of caterpillar characteristics.
DAY 3 Language Development	• Children rewrite a My Book and make speech bubbles to show dialogue.
DAY 4 Presentation Tools	• Children create a butterfly life cycle poster.
DAY 5 Speaking Skills	• Children conduct and tape record interviews with a caterpillar.

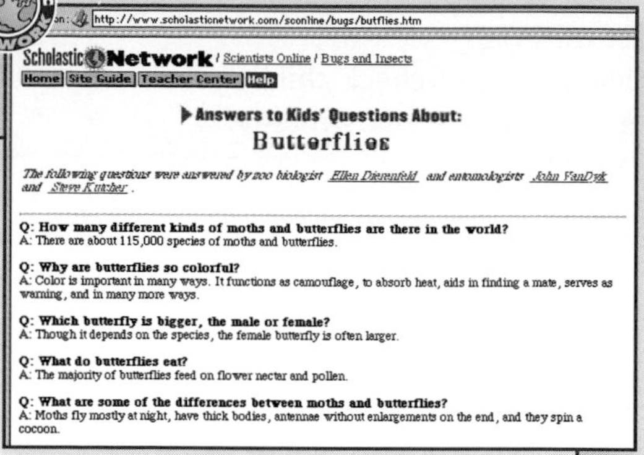

http://www.scholasticnetwork.com/sconline/bugs/butflies.htm

Scholastic Network / Scientists Online / Bugs and Insects

Home | Site Guide | Teacher Center | Help

Answers to Kids' Questions About:

Butterflies

The following questions were answered by zoo biologist Ellen Dierenfeld and entomologists John VanDyk and Steve Kutcher.

Q: How many different kinds of moths and butterflies are there in the world?
A: There are about 115,000 species of moths and butterflies.

Q: Why are butterflies so colorful?
A: Color is important in many ways. It functions as camouflage, to absorb heat, aids in finding a mate, serves as warning, and in many more ways.

Q: Which butterfly is bigger, the male or female?
A: Though it depends on the species, the female butterfly is often larger.

Q: What do butterflies eat?
A: The majority of butterflies feed on flower nectar and pollen.

Q: What are some of the differences between moths and butterflies?
A: Moths fly mostly at night, have thick bodies, antennae without enlargements on the end, and they spin a cocoon.

www.scholasticnetwork.com

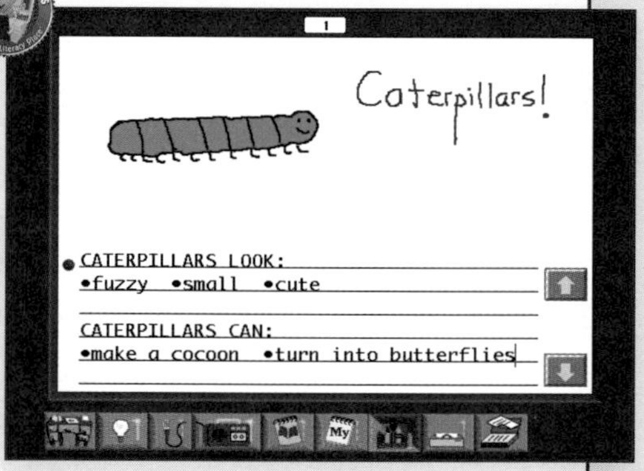

WiggleWorks Plus CD-ROM

WiggleWorks Plus CD-ROM

Build Background

Some nonfiction selections give information in an entertaining way. I'm a Caterpillar *is just such a selection. A caterpillar gives facts and information about its own life cycle.*

Activate Prior Knowledge

DISCUSS NONFICTION Explain to children that nonfiction selections give true facts and information. These selections often have pictures, drawings, charts, and diagrams to help the reader understand the information given.

SHARE INFORMATION Ask children to share what they know about caterpillars and butterflies.

> **What do caterpillars look like?**

> **Is there anything unusual about caterpillars?**

SHARED WRITING *Description*

INTRODUCE Explain that a description tells about something—what it looks like or what it does. Have children think about a caterpillar or other crawly thing. Ask each child to write a sentence or two describing how the crawly thing looks or what it does.

DAY 1 OBJECTIVES

CHILDREN WILL:

READ 40 MINUTES

- **Build Background**
- **Vocabulary**
- **High-Frequency Words**
- **Daily Phonics: Words With /ô/ *all, aw***
- ***I'm a Caterpillar*, pp. 38–49**
- **Key Comprehension Skill: Sequence**

WRITE 30 MINUTES

- **Shared Writing: Introduce Description**
- **Quickwrite: Return to Purposes**
- **Spelling: Words With /ô/ *all, aw***
- **Grammar, Usage, Mechanics: Capitalizing *I***
- **Oral Language**

EXTEND SKILLS 20 MINUTES

- **Read Aloud**
- **Guided Reading**

RESOURCES

- **Practice Book, pp. 16–18**
- **Spelling Resource Book, p. 114**

MODIFY Instruction

ESL/ELD

▲ Create a word web on the chalkboard, with *caterpillar* in the center and descriptive words, such as *furry, small, wiggly* around it. Encourage English language learners to use the words when they write their sentences. Make sure the children understand the meaning of the words. **(GRAPHIC DEVICE)**

VOCABULARY

High-Frequency Words

VOCABULARY

HIGH-FREQUENCY

next all

STORY WORDS

munch wait
grow wet
dry straw

Ⓐ TEACH/MODEL

INTRODUCE HIGH-FREQUENCY WORDS

Write the high-frequency words ***next*** and ***all*** in sentences on the chalkboard. Read the sentences aloud, underline the high-frequency words, and ask children if they recognize them.

The caterpillar ate all of the leaf.

What will happen to the caterpillar next?

Ask volunteers to dictate sentences using the high-frequency words. Add these to the chalkboard.

Ⓑ PRACTICE/APPLY

FOCUS ON SPELLING

Write each high-frequency word on a note card. Read each aloud. Then do the following:

next

all

ROUTINE

1. **Display one card at a time, and ask children to state each word aloud.**
2. **Have children spell each word aloud.**
3. **Ask children to write each word in the air as they state aloud each letter. Then have them write each word on a sheet of paper or in their journals.**

MAINTAIN VOCABULARY

Add the note cards to the **Word Wall.** Then review the following high-frequency words on the wall: ***which, make, were, way, more, belongs.***

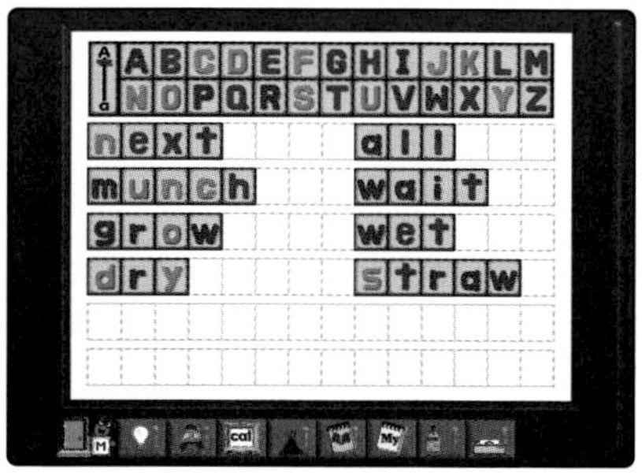

TECHNOLOGY

Have children practice with high-frequency and story words on the **WiggleWorks Plus** Magnet Board.

- Ask them to build several words on the Magnet Board.
- Have children explode all the words and then rebuild them.

MODIFY Instruction

ESL/ELD

▲ Use visuals and gestures to help children understand the vocabulary. Then ask a few questions to encourage use of the words: *What do you like to munch? When do you have to wait? Pretend you are wet. Do you know anything made of straw?* **(MAKE CONNECTIONS)**

GIFTED & TALENTED

✷ Working in pairs, children can take turns choosing a high-frequency word from the Word Wall. Have children who chose the word spell it aloud. The partner must locate the word, read it aloud, and use it in a sentence. **(WORK IN PAIRS)**

Story Words

Ⓐ TEACH/MODEL

INTRODUCE STORY WORDS

The story also contains the following story words—***munch, wait, grow, wet, dry, straw.***

- Write these words on the chalkboard, read them aloud, and discuss their meanings if necessary.
- Point out previously taught sound-spelling correspondences, such as **/e/**, **/u/**, and **/ch/**.
- If possible, provide a visual clue for each of the words. For example, show a drinking straw, a wet and dry paper towel, and pantomime the verbs ***munch, wait,*** and ***grow.***

Ⓑ PRACTICE/APPLY

BUILD STORY BACKGROUND

Discuss things that grow with children.

- Ask children to name things that grow. You may wish to suggest plants and baby animals.
- Have children close their eyes and picture things that grow. Ask: *How did these things look before they grew? How do they look after they've grown?*
- Have children draw before and after pictures of things that grow. They may wish to fold their papers in half and draw the before pictures on one side of the page and the after pictures on the opposite side.

WRITE TO READ

When children have completed their pictures, have each child write a sentence about his or her pictures using one or more of the story words.

WORD CATERPILLAR

Use construction paper to create a large-sized caterpillar. In bands on the caterpillar's side, write the high-frequency words *next* and *all* and the story words. Challenge children to "read the caterpillar"—that is, to start at the head and read each word, without a mistake, to the end of the caterpillar.

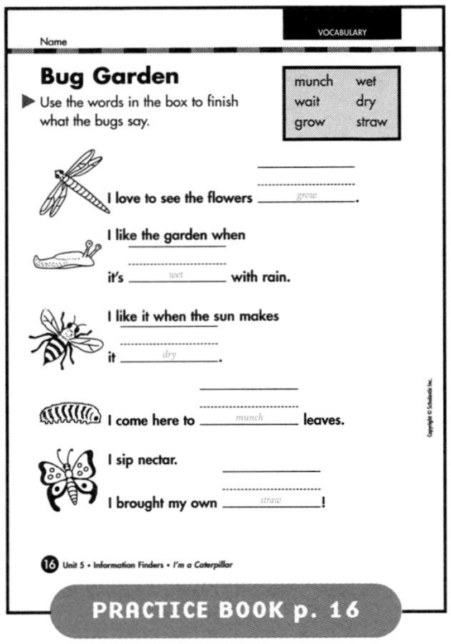

Name

VOCABULARY

Bug Garden

▶ Use the words in the box to finish what the bugs say.

munch	wet
wait	dry
grow	straw

I love to see the flowers ______.

I like the garden when it's ______ with rain.

I like it when the sun makes it ______.

I come here to ______ leaves.

I sip nectar. I brought my own ______!

16 Unit 5 • Information Finders • I'm a Caterpillar

PRACTICE BOOK p. 16

The puppy will grow a lot.

JOURNAL

Ask children to write a sentence in their Journals using each **high-frequency word**. You might suggest the following sentence starters:

Next, I will ______.

We all are ______.

SELECTION WORDS With /ô/ all, aw

all	awful
crawl	falls
straws	

SKILLS TRACE

Words With /ô/ all, aw TESTED

Introduce . . . . pp. T80–T81
Practice . . . . pp. T95, T119
Review . . . . p. R47
Reteach . . . . p. R58

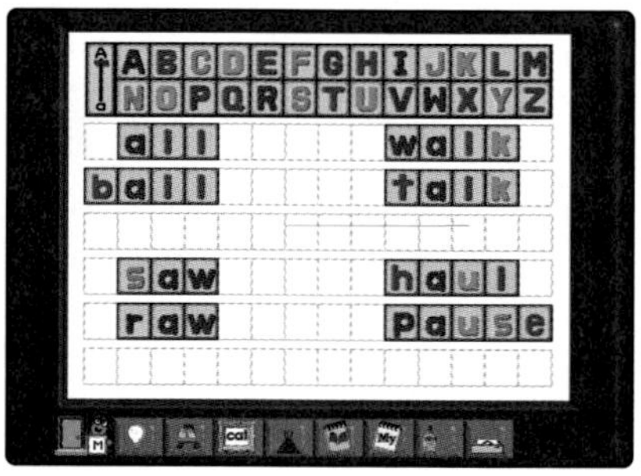

ABCDEFGHIJKLM
NOPQRSTUVWXYZ
all
walk
ball
talk
saw
haul
raw
pause

TECHNOLOGY

Have children build words with *-all, -alk, aw,* and *au* on the **WiggleWorks Plus** Magnet Board.

- Begin with the words *all, walk, saw,* and *haul.* Have children add or replace beginning consonants, digraphs, or blends to form new words.
- Suggest that children search classroom books for other words to add to the list.

DAILY PHONICS

Words With /ô/ all, aw

A PHONOLOGICAL AWARENESS

RHYME Read aloud "Humpty Dumpty" from the *Big Book of Rhymes and Rhythms 1B,* pages 16–17. As you read, stress the words with /ô/: ***wall, fall, all.***

- Have children read the rhyme along with you. Track the print as you read.
- Isolate the words ***wall, fall,*** and ***all*** and have children repeat them. Say the vowel sound /ô/. Ask children to name other words that contain this sound.

Humpty Dumpty
Humpty Dumpty sat on a wall,
Humpty Dumpty had a great fall.
All the king's horses
And all the king's men
Couldn't put Humpty together again.
wall

***Big Book of Rhymes and Rhythms 1B*, pp. 16–17**

ORAL BLENDING Say the following word parts, and have children blend them. Provide corrective feedback and modeling as needed.

- /s/ /ô/ (saw)
- /kl/ /ô/ (claw)
- /th/ /ô/ (thaw)

B CONNECT SOUND-SPELLING

INTRODUCE /ô/ *all, aw* Explain that the letters ***aw*** stand for /ô/ as in ***saw.*** Write ***saw*** on the chalkboard and underline the letters ***aw.*** Then write ***wall*** and underline the letters ***all.*** Explain that the vowel ***a*** stands for the /ô/ sound in words with ***all*** as in ***wall.***

THINK ALOUD *I can put the letters* **s, a,** *and* **w** *together to make* **saw.** *Let's say the sounds slowly. Listen to the sound that* **aw** *stands for in* **saw.** *The sound of* **aw** *is* /ô/.

MODIFY Instruction

ESL/ELD

▲ As you read "Humpty Dumpty," tell children to act out each /ô/ sound word when they hear it. For example, when you read *wall,* children stand straight; when you read *fall,* they fall down, and so on. **(ACT IT OUT)**

EXTRA HELP

■ Kinesthetic learners can build words by holding index cards with *all, aw,* and these letters: *b, c, f, h, j, p, s, t, w.* Children with the letters stand next to the child with the *all* card, say their sounds, blend them, and decide if they made a real word. Repeat for *aw.* **(HANDS-ON LEARNING)**

- Have children suggest other words with /ô/. List these words on a chart in separate columns according to the spelling pattern.
- Have children underline the letter or letters in each word that stand for /ô/. For words with *-all,* underline the whole spelling pattern.

Words With /ô/	
ball	claw
call	draw
fall	jaw
tall	paw
wall	saw

PHONICS MAINTENANCE Review the following sound-spellings: ***/ô/aw, all; /ch/ch, /sh/sh, /th/th, /hw/wh.*** Say one of these sounds. Have a volunteer write on the chalkboard the spelling that stands for the sound. Continue with all the sounds.

C PRACTICE/APPLY

BLEND WORDS To practice using the sound-spellings and review previous sound-spellings, list the following words and sentences on the chalkboard. Have children read each chorally. Model blending as needed.

all wall draw straw
child thin when ship
I sat next to him in the hall.
The cat has small paws.

DICTATION Dictate the following words for children to spell: ***straw, fall, thin, shell, which.***

BUILD WORDS Distribute the following letter and spelling pattern cards: ***aw, all, b, w, f, s, t, r, d.*** Allow children time to build as many words as possible using the cards. Children can write their words on a separate sheet of paper. **(INDEPENDENT WORK)**

BUILD A TALL WALL

Have children work with partners and use blocks or dominoes to build a wall. They can add a brick to the wall for every word with /ô/ they can state. Suggest that they record their words on a separate sheet of paper. Partners can see who can build a taller wall.

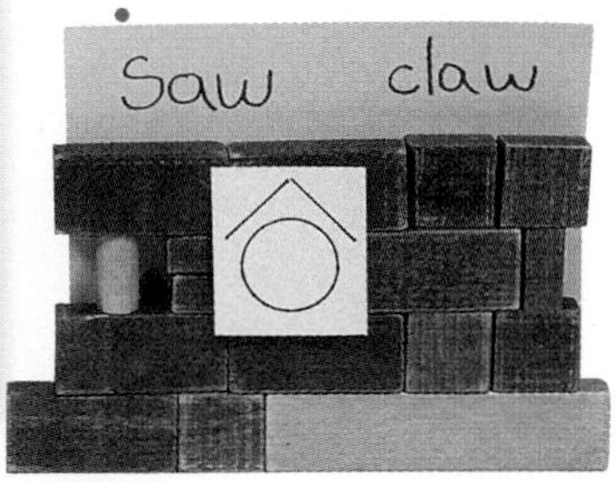

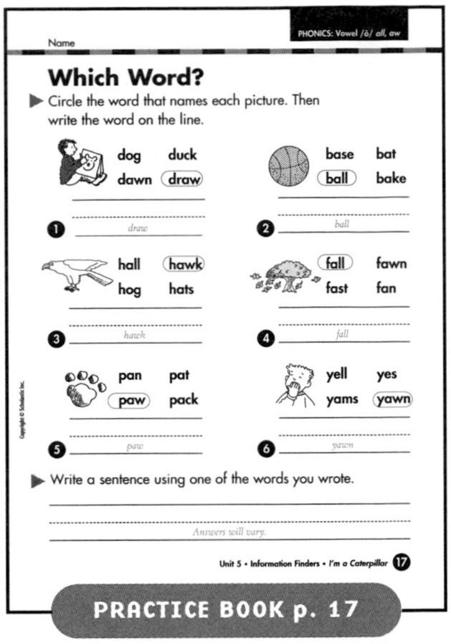
Name
PHONICS: Vowel /ô/ all, aw
Which Word?
Circle the word that names each picture. Then write the word on the line.
1. dog duck dawn draw — draw
2. base bat ball bake — ball
3. hall hawk hog hats — hawk
4. fall fawn fast fan — fall
5. pan pat paw pack — paw
6. yell yes yams yawn — yawn
Write a sentence using one of the words you wrote.
Answers will vary.
Unit 5 • Information Finders • I'm a Caterpillar 17

PRACTICE BOOK p. 17

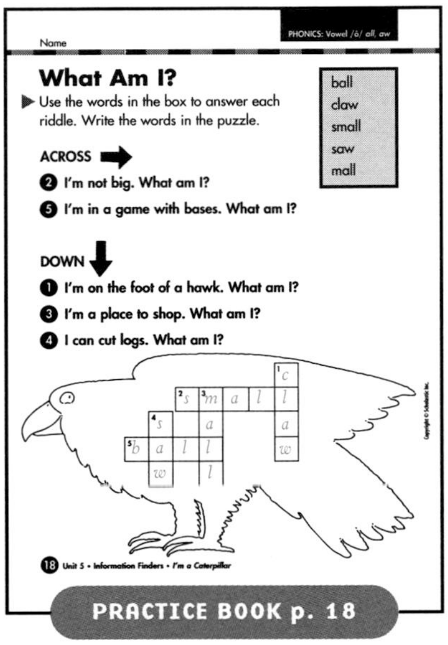
Name
PHONICS: Vowel /ô/ all, aw
What Am I?
Use the words in the box to answer each riddle. Write the words in the puzzle.
ball claw small saw mall
ACROSS
2 I'm not big. What am I?
5 I'm in a game with bases. What am I?
DOWN
1 I'm on the foot of a hawk. What am I?
3 I'm a place to shop. What am I?
4 I can cut logs. What am I?
18 Unit 5 • Information Finders • I'm a Caterpillar

PRACTICE BOOK p. 18

DECODABLE TEXT

For practice reading decodable text, see ***Scholastic Decodable Reader #59.***

For additional phonics instruction and review, see ***Scholastic Phonics A, pp. 219–220.***

COMPREHENSION

Preview and Predict

Read aloud the book title and the names of the author and illustrator. Have children look at the first few pictures in the story.

> **What is the story about?**

> **Do you think this is a story that is factual or make-believe? Why do you think so?**

Help children make predictions before they read by asking a question:

> **What do you think you will learn about caterpillars?**

JOURNAL

Make Predictions

Ask children to write their predictions in their Journals. Encourage them to refine their predictions, recording what they discover about caterpillars as they read.

Set a Purpose

Help children set their own purposes for reading the story. For example, they might want to learn more about caterpillars. Then have them read page 39.

38

NONFICTION

I'm a Caterpillar
Hello Reader! Level 1 SCIENCE Preschool–Grade 1
by Jean Marzollo
Illustrated by Judith Moffatt
SCHOLASTIC

38

CLASSROOM Management

WHOLE CLASS

On-Level Use the questions, Think Alouds, and the Skills and Strategies lessons to guide children through a reading of the story.

Below-Level Have children listen to the story on audiocassette before reading so they can familiarize themselves with story structure and vocabulary.

PARTNERS

Above-Level You may wish to have some children read the story independently or with a partner while you read with the rest of the class. If they are reading with a partner, encourage children to take turns reading aloud. Have these children rejoin the group to participate in the story discussion.

39

I'm a caterpillar.
Munch.
Crunch.
39

SKILLS AND STRATEGIES

Revisit the selection for skills instruction.

✓ = Tested Skill

COMPREHENSION

✓ **Sequence** T85

DAILY PHONICS

✓ **Words With /ô/ *all, aw*** T95

Vowel /ā/ *ay, ai* T107

GENRE

Nonfiction T103

SMALL GROUP TO WHOLE CLASS

ESL/ELD Have children who need extra help or who are acquiring English listen to the story on the audiocassette prior to the class reading. This will help them to become familiar with the story sequence and vocabulary. Have children do the pre- and post-listening activities. **(AUDIO CLUES)**

COMPREHENSION

40

① Cause and Effect

> **Why is the caterpillar getting bigger?** *(It's getting bigger because it is eating a lot.)*

② Picture Details

> **What is the caterpillar eating? How can you tell?** *(The caterpillar is eating leaves. I see that the caterpillar has taken bites out of the leaves.)*

③ Make Predictions

> **Why do you think the caterpillar stopped eating? What do you think will happen next?** *(Possible answer: The caterpillar is full and it is time for it to make its chrysalis.)*

SELF-MONITORING STRATEGY

Use Illustrations

Think Aloud *As I read this story, I'm going to pay careful attention to the pictures. The pictures are made from cut paper. The pictures and the text give me a lot of information about caterpillars.*

> What have you learned about caterpillars so far?

MODIFY Instruction

ESL/ELD

▲ In addition to using picture clues to see that the caterpillar is eating, point out to children that the caterpillar has gotten bigger. Have them compare the caterpillar on page 40 with the one on page 41. Ask, *How are the two pictures different?* **(PICTURE CLUES)**

EXTRA HELP

■ Help children understand that although *I'm a Caterpillar* is told by the caterpillar, it is not a fantasy story. It is a nonfiction selection because the narrator (the caterpillar) is sharing facts and information about caterpillars. **(MAKE CONNECTIONS)**

41

Munch. Crunch.
Munch. Crunch.

That's it. 3
No more food.
I'm done.

41

TEACHER TIP

"Tell children that the caterpillar in this story will become a monarch butterfly. These caterpillars eat milkweed leaves, which have toxic chemicals. The chemical won't harm them, but it stays in their bodies. The chemical is what gives the adult monarch butterfly such a bad taste."

SKILLS AND STRATEGIES

COMPREHENSION

Sequence

TEACH/MODEL

Remind children that when they think about sequence of events, they pay attention to what happened first, next, and last.

> **When you want to figure out the order in which things happen in a story, look for clues in the text and in the illustrations.**

THINK ALOUD *There is a certain order to the way things happen in* I'm a Caterpillar. *First, the caterpillar munches and crunches. Next, it grows bigger. Then the caterpillar stops eating. When I talk about what happens in order, I use words such as* first, next, *and* last *to help me.*

PRACTICE/APPLY

Help children fold a piece of paper into three equal parts. Label the parts, *First, Next,* and *Last.* Have children draw pictures to show what has happened to the caterpillars so far.

INFORMAL ASSESSMENT

OBSERVATION

Did children:

✔ recognize the sequence of events in the story so far?

✔ describe what happened to the caterpillar and relate the events in order?

✔ identify what happened first, next, and last?

See **pages T114–T115** for a full skills lesson on Sequence.

COMPREHENSION

4 SEQUENCE

> **What does the caterpillar do after it is done eating?** *(It hangs from a stem and waits.)*

5 MAKE PREDICTIONS

> **What do you think the caterpillar is waiting for?** *(Possible answer: The caterpillar is waiting to become a butterfly.)*

42

It's time to hang from a stem. 4
42

MODIFY Instruction

ESL/ELD

▲ Help English language learners keep track of sequence by listing the story events in order on the chalkboard:

What the Caterpillar Does:
1. Eats
2. Gets bigger
3. Stops eating
4. Hangs from a stem
5. Waits

(STEP BY STEP)

GIFTED & TALENTED

✳ As they read, have children keep track of the sequence described in the story with the stages of metamorphosis. Children can fold a piece of paper into four parts and draw pictures to represent each stage. **(MAKE CONNECTIONS)**

43

I wait,
and wait,
and wait. 5
43

CONNECTING TO FICTION

Children may have enjoyed reading or listening to *The Very Hungry Caterpillar* by Eric Carle, *If at First You Do Not See* by Ruth Brown, and other stories about caterpillars. Share some of these books with the class and invite children to compare the stories and illustrations in the books.

MENTOR

Have children think about the techniques Laela Sayigh uses to gather information about dolphins. Talk about which techniques she could apply to the study of caterpillars.

COMPREHENSION

6 Make Inferences

> **The caterpillar shivers, twists, and splits its skin. What's happening to the caterpillar?** *(Possible answer: The caterpillar is changing in some way.)*

44

44

MODIFY Instruction

ESL/ELD

▲ Children will understand the meaning of *shivers*, *twists*, and *splits* better if they use their bodies to demonstrate each action. Suggest that children pretend they are the caterpillar. Ask: *What does the caterpillar look like when it shivers? Twists? Splits it skin?* **(TOTAL PHYSICAL RESPONSE)**

EXTRA HELP

■ Have children compare the pictures on pages 42 and 44. Draw attention to the yellow and black caterpillar on page 42 and the yellow and black skin that is coming off on page 44. Help children see that the caterpillar's skin is being replaced with something new. **(MAKE CONNECTIONS)**

45

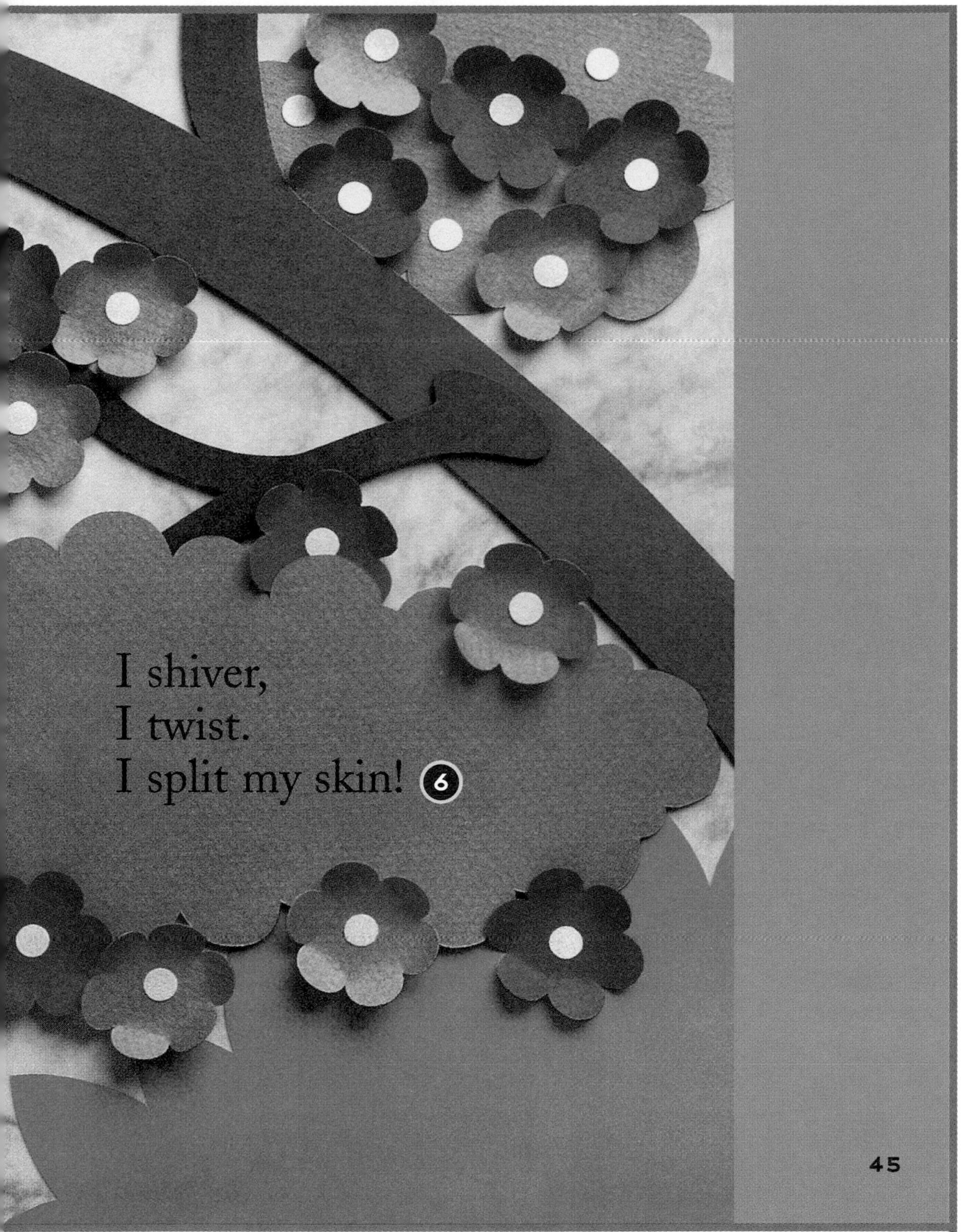

I shiver,
I twist.
I split my skin! 6

45

IDEA FILE

Monarch butterflies have been in North America for about two million years. Their habit of migrating began about 10,000 years ago, after the earth warmed and the milkweed plants—the host plant for monarch caterpillars—spread northward.

SKILLS AND STRATEGIES

COMPREHENSION

Make Inferences

TEACH/MODEL

Remind children that writers do not always tell readers everything about the events in their stories. Sometimes readers have to supply missing information.

> **Use pictures and other clues from the story along with what you already know to make decisions about things the author does not say.**

THINK ALOUD *When I read this part of the story and look at the pictures on the page, I know that the caterpillar is changing because it used to be black and yellow and now it is green and yellow.*

PRACTICE/APPLY

Ask children to make inferences about what is happening to the caterpillar. Write the following graphic organizer on the chalkboard and ask children to help you complete it.

STORY CLUES	WHAT I KNOW	INFERENCE

> **What story clues help you know that something is happening to the caterpillar?**

> **What do you think is going to happen next to the caterpillar?**

COMPREHENSION

7 SEQUENCE

> **What has happened to the caterpillar since it stopped eating?** *(The caterpillar attached itself to a stem. Its skin split and fell off. Then it grew a shell to protect the pupa.)*

8 PICTURE DETAILS

> **Compare the pictures on pages 46 and 47. How is a chrysalis different from a pupa?** *(Possible answers: The shape is different, the yellow markings have changed, and some black markings have appeared that weren't there before. The chrysalis looks different because it has grown a protective shell.)*

INTERVENTION TIP

Understanding a Science Concept

Some children who are familiar with caterpillars and cocoons may wonder why the cocoon step has been left out. Explain that a caterpillar that becomes a moth makes a cocoon. A butterfly caterpillar usually does not make a cocoon. The butterfly develops a protective shell called a chrysalis. The chrysalis is often brightly colored; a monarch butterfly's shell is soft green with gold spots.

46

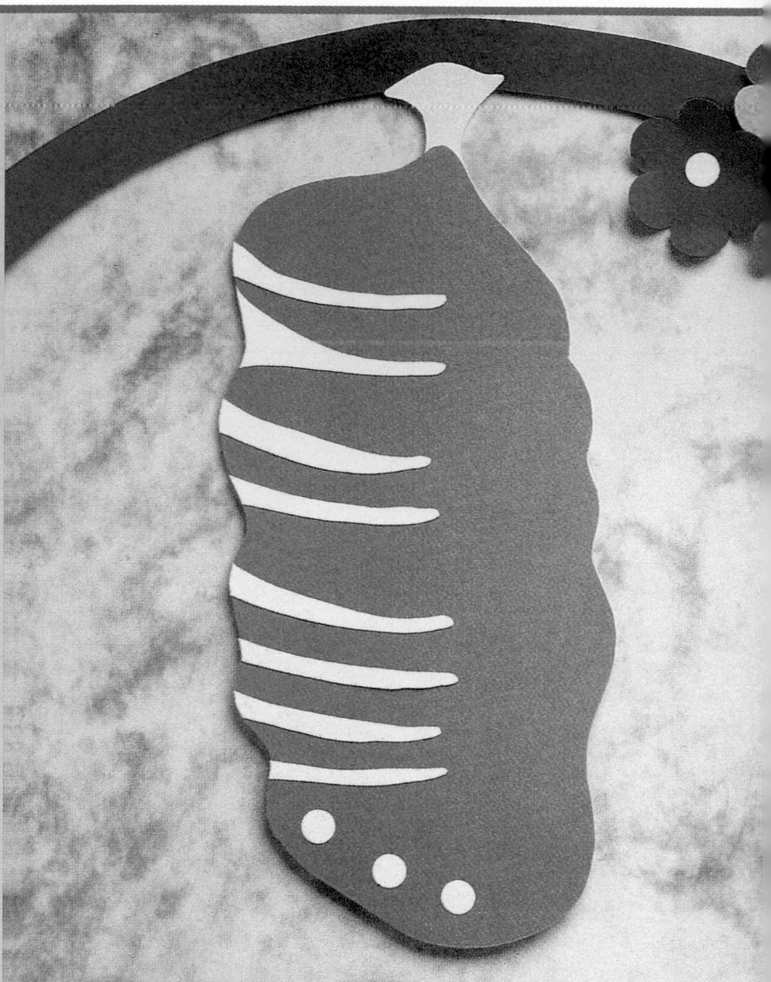

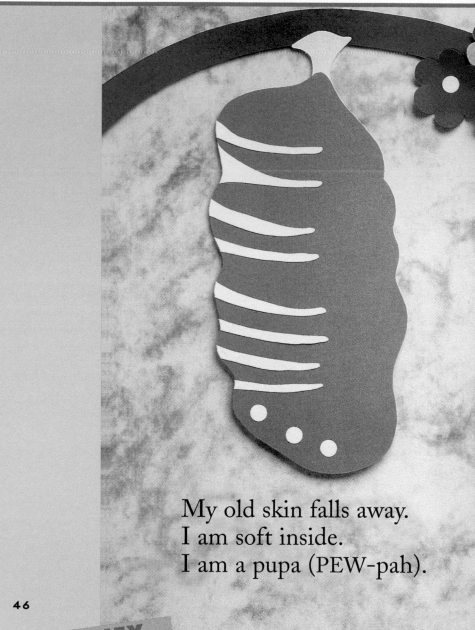

My old skin falls away.
I am soft inside.
I am a pupa (PEW-pah).

46

MODIFY Instruction

ESL/ELD

▲ As children compare the pictures on these pages, help English language learners list details:

Page 46	Page 47
bumpy sides	smooth sides
yellow dots	some black dots
no shell	shell

(COMPARE AND CONTRAST)

EXTRA HELP

■ You may need to help children pronounce the words in parentheses on pages 46 and 47. Model how to pronounce each word and help children see how the pronunciations are represented by the letter combinations in parentheses. **(MODEL)**

47

I grow a shell
to protect the pupa. 7
I am now a chrysalis
(KRIS-ah-lis).

8

47

CULTURAL CONNECTION

Each year during the Fourth of July Butterfly Count, more than 2000 people count every butterfly, caterpillar, and egg they find. They report their findings to the North American Butterfly Association, which publishes a report of the butterflies seen that year.

FAMILY TALK

Weather permitting, suggest that families do a butterfly count in their own garden or in a public garden. Invite children to make up names for any unfamiliar species or draw pictures of them. Encourage them to share their drawings and what they have learned about butterflies with the class.

COMPREHENSION

9 PICTURE DETAILS

> **Look at the chrysalis now. How has it changed?** *(Possible answer: The chrysalis is see-through. The caterpillar looks different; it is orange and black.)*

10 MAKE PREDICTIONS

> **The caterpillar asks "What will I be?" What do you think it will be?** *(Children may predict that the caterpillar is now a monarch butterfly.)*

11 SEQUENCE

> **The caterpillar's waiting time is almost over. Review what has happened to the caterpillar since it stopped eating.** *(Possible answer: The caterpillar shed its skin and became a pupa. Next it grew a shell and became a chrysalis. It kept changing and now it's almost ready to come out.)*

SELF-MONITORING STRATEGY

Use a Graphic Organizer

Help children keep track of the stages in the caterpillar's transformation. Encourage them to draw and label a picture of the caterpillar in each stage.

OPTION You may end the first day's reading here or have children continue reading the entire selection.

48

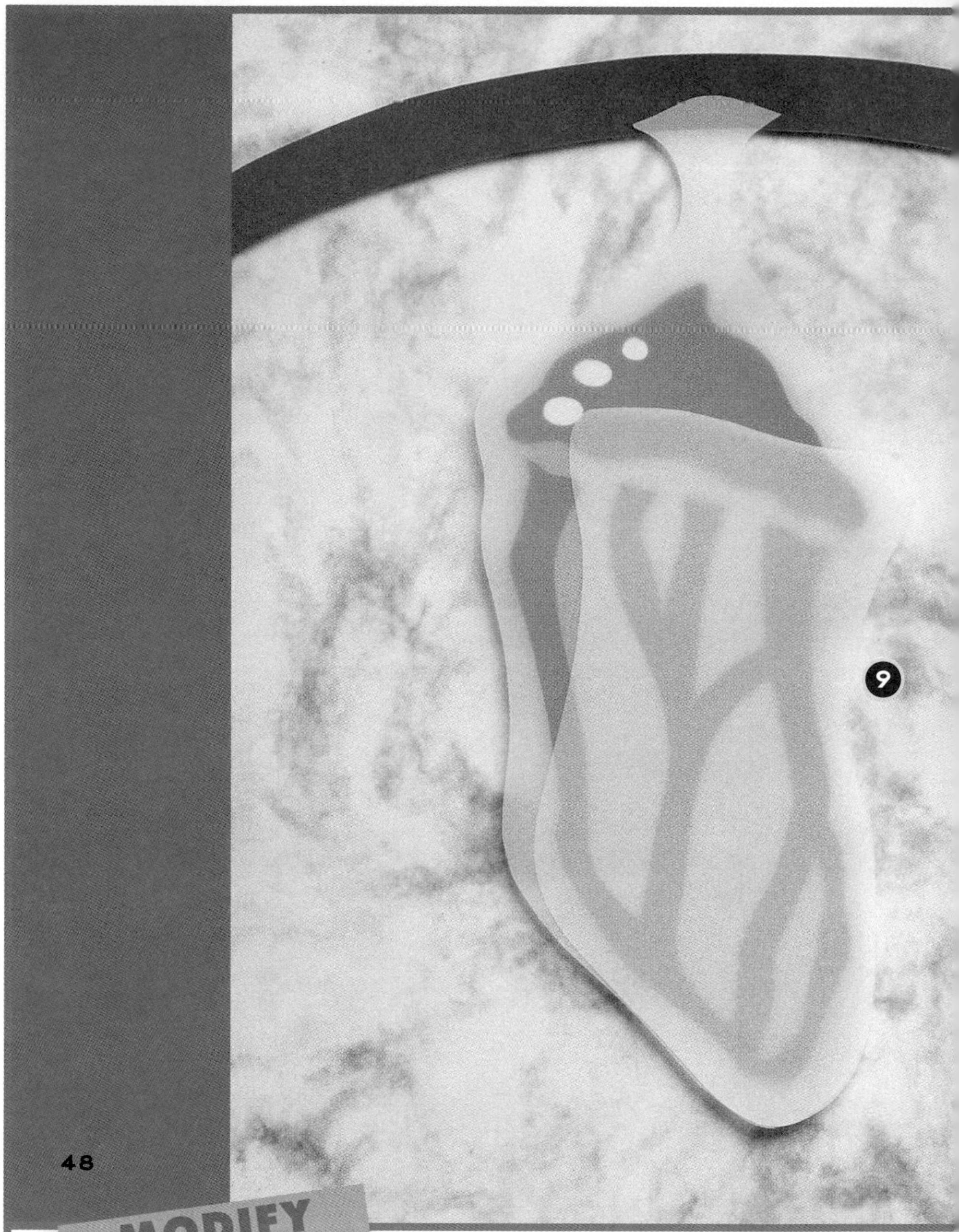

MODIFY Instruction

ESL/ELD

▲ Create a timeline of the caterpillar's changes to help children understand the sequence. Use these labels in order on the timeline: 1. Eats; 2. Gets bigger; 3. Stops eating; 4. Hangs from a stem; 5. Waits; 6. Skin splits; 7. Grows shell. Have children illustrate the timeline. **(SPIRALING)**

EXTRA HELP

■ Help children recall the stages in the caterpillar's transformation. Have children use the pictures in the story to help them remember how a caterpillar changes into a butterfly. Then ask children to predict what the caterpillar will be when it comes out of the chrysalis. **(PICTURE CLUES)**

49

I keep changing.
Soon I'll come out.
What will I be? 10 11
49

Quickwrite

RETURN TO PURPOSES

Ask children to describe what has happened to the caterpillar so far. Give them the opportunity to refine the predictions they made before reading and predict what will happen to the caterpillar next.

DAILY LANGUAGE PRACTICE

SPELLING

DAY 1:
Administer the Pretest for Words With /ô/ *all, aw.* **See page R12.**

GRAMMAR, USAGE, MECHANICS

DAY 1:
Teach and Model Capitalizing *I.* **See page R14.**

ORAL LANGUAGE

This is where i saw awl the bees.

(This is where I saw all the bees.)

CONNECTING TO THEME

Discuss with children how the author presents the information in *I'm a Caterpillar.* Help children see that the information is presented in the order in which it happens. Encourage children to continue to think about how the selection is organized as they read on.

TECHNOLOGY

Finding the Facts
Why do butterflies taste with their feet? Why are they so colorful? Ask students to research these questions in the Scientists Online area of **www.scholasticnetwork.com** where they should click on Bugs and Insects, then Butterflies.

DAY 1 WRAP-UP

READ ALOUD *To develop children's oral vocabularies, spend five to ten minutes reading from a selection of your choice.*

GUIDED READING *To extend reading, meet with the **green** and **yellow** reading groups and assign Independent Center activities. **See pages R10–R11.***

COMPREHENSION

DAY 2 OBJECTIVES

CHILDREN WILL:

READ 30 MINUTES

- *I'm a Caterpillar*, pp. 50–66
- Poem: "Caterpillars," p. 67
- Daily Phonics: Words With /ô/ *all, aw*

WRITE 30 MINUTES

- Shared Writing: Prewrite
- Spelling: Words With /ô/ *all, aw*
- Grammar, Usage, Mechanics: Capitalizing *I*
- Oral Language

EXTEND SKILLS 30 MINUTES

- Integrated Curriculum
- Read Aloud
- Guided Reading

RESOURCES

- Practice Book, p. 24
- Spelling Resource Book, pp. 115–117

▶ Reread

You may wish to have children independently reread the first part of the story before beginning Day 2 reading.

12 SUMMARIZE

> **What has happened to the caterpillar so far?** *(Possible answer: It ate, attached to a stem, shed its skin, grew a shell, and became a butterfly.)*

13 DRAW CONCLUSIONS

> **How does the butterfly get itself out of the shell?** *(It pushes and cracks the shell.)*

50

12
A butterfly!
Push.
Crack.
Wow!
I'm free! 13
50

MODIFY Instruction

ESL/ELD

▲ Help English language learners understand the events on these pages by having them role-play being a butterfly. In addition to acting out the transformation process, encourage children to say what the butterfly might say if it could speak. **(ROLE-PLAY)**

EXTRA HELP

■ Some children may need help understanding how the butterfly breaks out of its shell. Ask children if they have seen a baby bird break out of an egg. *How did it get out of the shell? Were its feathers wet when it first broke out?* Explain that the butterfly goes through a similar process. **(MAKE CONNECTIONS)**

51

14
My wings are all wet.
51

ORAL LANGUAGE

Point out the exclamation marks in the text on page 50. Remind children that an exclamation mark shows that something should be said with excitement. Ask volunteers to read the lines on page 50 the way they think the caterpillar (now a butterfly) might have said them.

MATH

Ask children to complete the **Larger Than Life?** activity on **page R16** in the illustrations in which they will use measurement skills to compare the size of all actual monarch butterfly with those shown.

DAILY PHONICS

Words With /ô/ *all, aw*

CONNECT SOUND-SPELLING

Teach/Model Write the words ***all*** and ***saw*** on the chalkboard.

> **The /ô/ sound in these words is made by the spelling pattern *all* and *aw*.**

> **Find and circle the *all* or *aw* spelling pattern in each word.**

THINK ALOUD *When I see the spelling pattern **aw**, I know the word will have the /ô/ sound as in **saw**. I also know that words with the spelling pattern **all** have the /ô/ sound, as in **ball**.*

Phonics Maintenance Review the following sound spellings: ***/ô/aw, all; /sh/sh; /th/th; /ch/ch; /hw/wh.***

PRACTICE/APPLY

Blend Words List the following words and sentences on the chalkboard. Have children read each chorally. Model blending as needed.

tall	mall	paw	yawn
ship	chin	thick	when

I saw a bug on the wall.

This ball is small.

INFORMAL ASSESSMENT
OBSERVATION

Did children:

✔ recognize words with ***/ô/all, aw***?

✔ blend words with ***/ô/all, aw***?

COMPREHENSION

14 MAKE PREDICTIONS

> **The butterfly's wings dry off and unfold. What do you think is going to happen next?** *(Possible answer: The butterfly will fly.)*

15 COMPARE/CONTRAST

> **Compare the picture of the butterfly on page 52 to the picture on page 50. How are they different?** *(Possible answer: The butterfly's wings on page 50 are all folded up. The butterfly's wings on page 52 are beginning to unfold and get bigger.)*

52

MODIFY Instruction

ESL/ELD

▲ Use a demonstration with paper to help English language learners understand what is happening to the butterfly. Draw a butterfly on the paper. Demonstrate folding and unfolding the sheet of paper. Then have children fold and unfold their own sheet of paper. **(DEMONSTRATE)**

GIFTED & TALENTED

✳ Encourage children to take turns retelling what they have learned so far while reading *I'm a Caterpillar*. You may wish to have children record their retellings for others to listen to. **(RETELL)**

53

My wings dry off.
They unfold.
14
53

WORD STUDY

Ask children to find the word *unfold* on page 53. Have children read it aloud. Then use a piece of paper to demonstrate the meaning of *fold* and *unfold.* Tell children that the prefix *un-* at the beginning of a word makes the word mean exactly the opposite. Help children think of other words to which *un-* can be added to make it mean the opposite. *(happy, unhappy; tie, untie)* List the words on the chalkboard and have volunteers underline the prefix *un-* in each word.

COMPREHENSION

16 **SEQUENCE**

> **Let's think about what has happened to the butterfly after it broke out of its shell. What happened first? Then what happened? What happened next?** *(Possible answer: First the butterfly broke out of its shell. Then the butterfly's wings unfolded. Next the butterfly flapped its wings and began to fly.)*

54

54

MODIFY Instruction

ESL/ELD

▲ To understand the sequence, encourage English language learners to look at the picture of the butterfly as you ask what happens after the wings dry off. Then ask, *Is the butterfly moving or not? How can you tell? How do you think the butterfly feels?* **(GUIDED QUESTIONS)**

EXTRA HELP

■ Invite children to imitate how the butterfly pushes its way out of the protective shell, unfolds its wings, and begins to fly. You may read pages 50–54 aloud as children act it out. **(ACT IT OUT)**

55

Flap. Flap.
Hey!
I can fly!
Ta-da! 16
55

SOCIAL STUDIES

Ask children to complete the **Butterfly Territory** activity on **page R17** where they'll record where they have seen butterflies around the school. Children will develop an awareness of the local geography.

TECHNOLOGY

Organizing Information Have children use the **WiggleWorks Plus** Unit Writer or a familiar word processor to create descriptive lists under these categories:
Caterpillars can . . .
Caterpillars look . . .
Caterpillars are . . .

COMPREHENSION

17 SEQUENCE

> **Now that the caterpillar is a butterfly, what does it do?** *(It visits flowers.)*

18 AUTHOR'S CRAFT

> **What words does the author use to tell you that the butterfly likes the nectar?** *(Yum!; Sip, Sip)*

19 DRAW CONCLUSIONS

> **How is a butterfly's mouth like a straw?** *(Possible answer: A butterfly's mouth is like a straw because it is long and thin; the butterfly drinks nectar through it.)*

56

MODIFY Instruction

ESL/ELD

▲ Help English language learners compare and contrast the way the butterfly and the caterpillar eat. Go back to pages 40 and 41. Ask: *What is the caterpillar doing?* Then have children look at the picture of the butterfly. Ask: *How is the butterfly eating?* **(PICTURE CLUES)**

EXTRA HELP

■ Help children understand that *Yum!* and *Sip, Sip* are words that help describe the butterfly drinking nectar. Ask children to find other words in *I'm a Caterpillar* that describe eating. (*munch, crunch*) **(MAKE CONNECTIONS)**

57

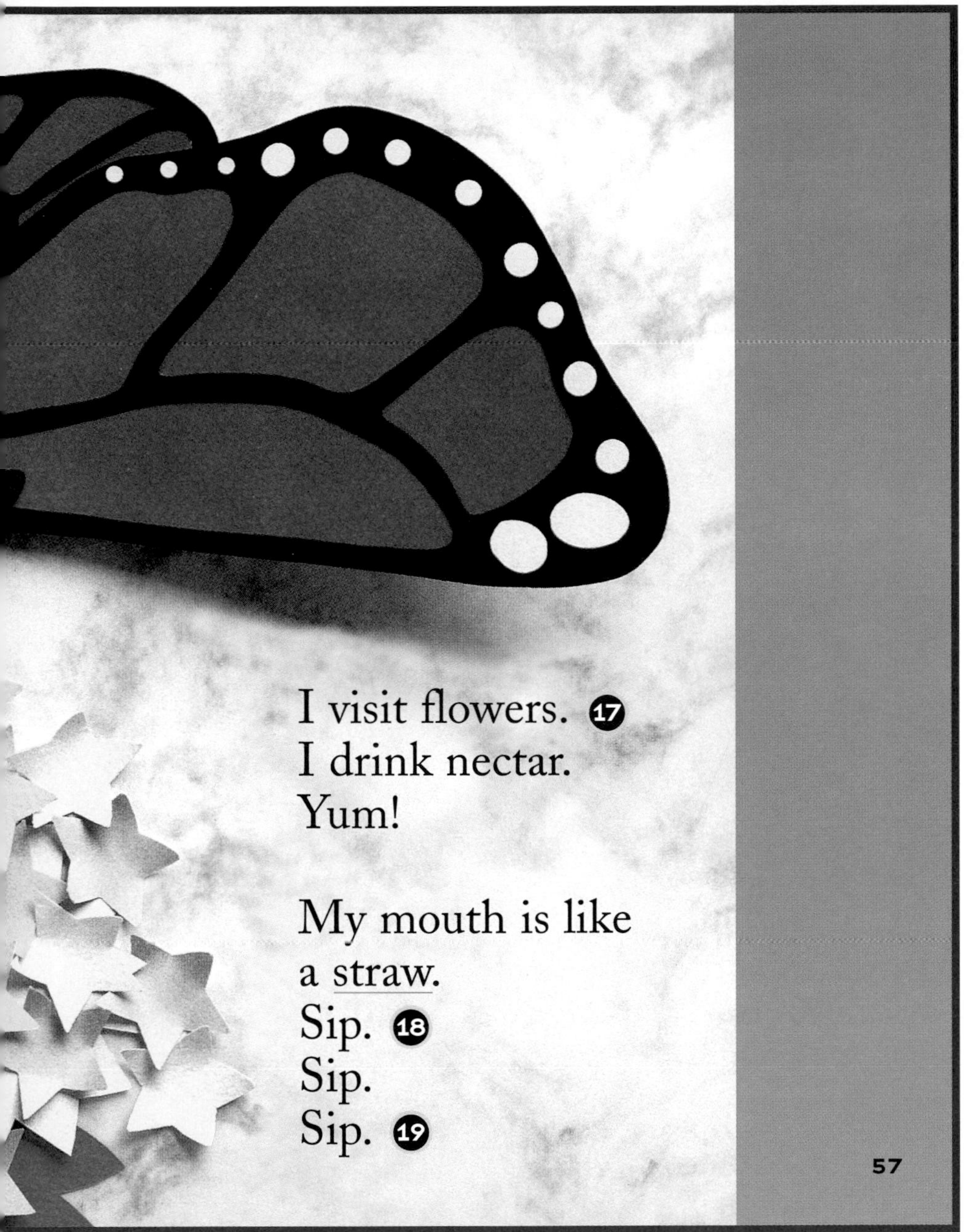

I visit flowers. 17
I drink nectar.
Yum!

My mouth is like
a straw.
Sip. 18
Sip.
Sip. 19

57

ORAL LANGUAGE

Read aloud the words on page 57 that describe the butterfly drinking the nectar from the flower: *Yum!, Sip, Sip.* Ask children to name other words that help describe eating; for example, *mmmmm* and *slurp.* Look back at the beginning of the story and remind children that *crunch* and *munch* helped to describe the caterpillar eating a leaf.

SKILLS AND STRATEGIES

COMPREHENSION

Main Idea/Details

TEACH/MODEL

Remind children that the main idea of a story tells what the story is mostly about. The details give more information about the main idea.

THINK ALOUD *When I look at this page, I know that it is mainly about the life of a butterfly. That's the main idea of the page. All the other information about the butterfly are the details.*

PRACTICE/APPLY

Have children complete a main idea chart to identify some of the details about the butterfly they observed.

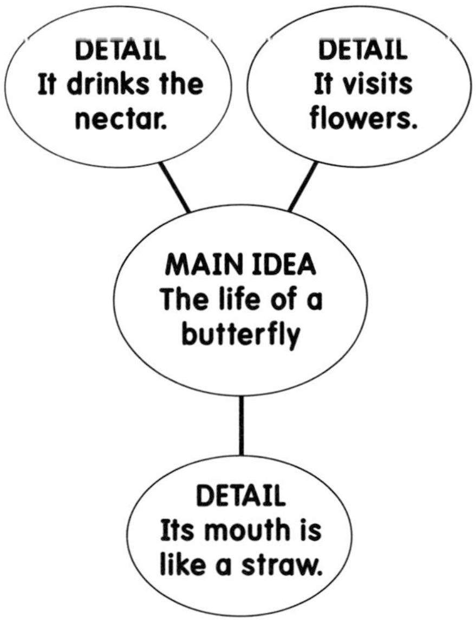

IF children need more support with Main Idea/Details,

THEN see the review lesson on page R43.

COMPREHENSION

20 PICTURE DETAILS

> **How do you know that the butterflies visited many flowers?** *(There are many flowers in this picture.)*

58

MODIFY Instruction

ESL/ELD

▲ Focus children's understanding on the significance of a mate for the butterfly. Paraphrase the information on this page: *The butterfly has a partner in life. The two of them will do many things together. They will visit flowers. They will also create more butterflies.* **(PARAPHRASE)**

THE ARTS

Ask children to complete the **Paint a Butterfly** activity on **page R17,** where they'll create a colorful pattern for a butterfly's wings. Children learn about real butterfly markings.

59

I have a mate. 20
We visit many flowers.
59

CULTURAL CONNECTION

The monarch butterfly makes one of nature's most amazing migrations. It can fly from Mexico to places as far away as Maine. On a map or a globe, trace the monarch butterfly's path. Have children make small notes to post on the map identifying the monarch's summer and winter homes.

SKILLS AND STRATEGIES

GENRE

Nonfiction

TEACH/MODEL

Explain to children that a nonfiction selection gives facts and information.

THINK ALOUD *When I read nonfiction such as* I'm a Caterpillar, *I learn new information. The text and the pictures give me facts and details about caterpillars. When I read nonfiction, I often want to learn even more about a subject.*

PRACTICE/APPLY

Invite children to share facts or information they learned about caterpillars and butterflies from this selection.

What I Learned

- Caterpillars eat a lot.
- Caterpillars shed their skin.
- Caterpillars make a hard shell.
- Caterpillars become butterflies.
- Butterflies visit flowers.

COMPREHENSION

21 Draw Conclusions

> **Why don't the birds like butterflies?** *(The birds don't like butterflies because they know the butterflies taste awful.)*

22 Picture Details

> **The butterflies aren't afraid of birds. What else in this picture do you think the butterflies might be afraid of? Why?** *(Possible answer: The butterflies might be afraid of the spider because they could get caught in the spider's web.)*

INTERVENTION TIP

Understand a Science Concept

Children may be interested to know how birds know that butterflies taste bad. Explain that the bright colors of the butterflies are what warn the birds to stay away. Remind children that the monarch butterfly gets its bad taste from the milkweed leaves it eats when it's a caterpillar. The milkweed taste stays with the monarch through its whole life as a butterfly.

60

We're not afraid of birds.
They know that 21
we taste awful.
60

MODIFY Instruction

ESL/ELD

▲ As you discuss picture details, check to make sure your English language learners can name all of the pictures they see on this page. List the words on the chalkboard as they point to the pictures, for example, *leaves, bird, butterfly, spider, web.* Make sure all of the children understand the words. **(KEY WORDS)**

EXTRA HELP

■ Help children recognize that the word *awful* has the same beginning sound as *all.* Write the word *awful* on the chalkboard and underline the letters *aw.* Tell children that /ô/ in *awful* is spelled the same as it is at the end of *saw.* **(PHONICS)**

61

IDEA FILE

You may wish to point out to children that the flowering bush in the illustration is a *buddleia* (BUD lee ah), or butterfly bush. It gets its name from the fact that its flowers are the favorites of butterflies.

WORD STUDY

To help children understand the meaning of *awful,* have them brainstorm synonyms for *awful*—that is, words that could take the place of *awful* in the sentence without changing the meaning of the sentence.

SKILLS AND STRATEGIES

DAILY PHONICS

Homophones

TEACH/MODEL

Remind children that homophones are words that sound alike, but have different meanings and spellings.

THINK ALOUD *I know that homophones can sometimes be confusing when you hear people say them. This is because the words sound alike. But when you see them written, it's easier to tell them apart because their spellings give you a clue.*

PRACTICE/APPLY

Help children explore homophones.

- Write the word ***no*** on the chalkboard and have children read it chorally. Then have them identify the homophone for ***no*** on page 60. *(know)*
- Write these words from the story on the chalkboard, and have children suggest a homophone for each one: ***to*** *(too, two);* ***I*** *(eye);* ***wait*** *(weight);* ***be*** *(bee).*

IF children need more support with Homophones,

THEN see page R46.

COMPREHENSION

23 SEQUENCE

> **What happens after the butterfly visits the flowers?** *(The butterfly will lay its eggs.)*

24 MAKE PREDICTIONS

> **Where do you think this female butterfly will lay her eggs?** *(She will lay her eggs on the leaf.)*

62

62

MODIFY Instruction

ESL/ELD

▲ Be sure English language learners understand what the result of "laying its eggs" is for the butterfly. Ask: *Why does a butterfly lay eggs?* If necessary, explain that baby caterpillars come from these eggs. **(ASSIST IN PROCESS)**

GIFTED & TALENTED

✷ Have children make a list of all the different creatures they know of that lay eggs. They may want to include extinct creatures like dinosaurs. Encourage children to share the list with the whole class. **(BRAINSTORM)**

63

Soon I will lay my eggs.
23 24
63

CULTURAL CONNECTION

Every year, monarch butterflies migrate to Mexico for the winter. Farmers in Mexico prepare their land by burning off old vegetation. In 1998, drought and bad weather conditions led to fires that threatened the monarchs' home. Fortunately, the rains arrived and saved their home.

CONNECTING TO THEME

Have children imagine that they are observing things that live in a garden like the one in *I'm a Caterpillar.* Ask them to name additional creatures they might find there. Then make a class picture of the garden and invite children to add pictures of garden creatures.

DAILY PHONICS

Vowel /ā/*ay, ai*

CONNECT SOUND-SPELLING

Teach/Model Write the word *lay* on the chalkboard.

- **The /ā/ sound in these words is made by the spellings *ai* and *ay*.**
- **Find and circle the spelling pattern that makes the /ā/ sound like the word.**

THINK ALOUD *When I see the spelling **ai** in the middle of a word such as **wait,** I know the letters stand for the /ā/ sound as in **train.** When I see the spelling pattern **ay** at the end of a word, I know that it, too, stands for the /ā/ sound of **train.***

Phonics Maintenance Review the following sound-spellings: ***/ô/ aw, all;* final *e; -ing.***

PRACTICE/APPLY

Blend Words List the following words and sentences. Have children read each chorally. Model blending.

rain	afraid	day
away	shine	cone
falling	going	

All of us wait for the train.
She saw her mail today.

INFORMAL ASSESSMENT
OBSERVATION

Did children:

✔recognize and blend words with /ā/ *ay, ai?*

COMPREHENSION

25 SEQUENCE

> **What happens after the butterfly lays her eggs?** *(The butterfly lays eggs that have thin shells. The shells break open and baby caterpillars crawl out. The caterpillars start eating leaves.)*

26 MAKE PREDICTIONS

> **What do you think will happen to the caterpillar? Why?** *(Possible answer: The new caterpillar will eat until it's time to hang from a stem and wait to change into a butterfly.)*

64

The eggs have thin shells.

Baby caterpillars crawl out.

64

MODIFY Instruction

ESL/ELD

▲ Help English language learners discuss sequence. Have them look carefully at the pictures as you ask: *Where does the butterfly lay its eggs? What happens to the eggs? What does the caterpillar do after it comes out of the egg?* **(GUIDED QUESTIONS)**

EXTRA HELP

■ Help children recognize that the vowel sound in *crawl* is /ô/, the same sound that is heard at the beginning of *awful* and at the end of *straw*. **(PHONICS)**

65

Hi! I'm a caterpillar.

Munch. Crunch. 25 26

65

VISUAL LITERACY

Discuss the four pictures on pages 64–65 with children. Help them see that the development from butterfly egg to a baby caterpillar is pictured here. Ask children to predict what will be on the next page. Guide them to understand that the pattern of development always begins and ends in the same way.

SCIENCE

Ask children to do the **From an Egg** activity on **page R16** where they'll explore creatures hatched from eggs. This activity will give children practice in categorizing.

DAILY PHONICS

Digraphs *ch, wh*

CONNECT SOUND-SPELLING

Teach/Model Review with children that digraphs are two letters that together stand for one sound.

- Write the word ***which*** on the chalkboard and have children count the letters.
- Say the word ***which.*** Then say it again, segmenting the sounds: **/hw/ /i/ /ch/.** Have children tell how many sounds they hear.
- Explain that five letters become three sounds because ***wh*** and ***ch*** are digraphs. Each stands for one sound.

PRACTICE/APPLY

Blend Words Give children practice with digraphs.

- Write ***hair, deer, part,*** and ***sick*** on the chalkboard. Have volunteers substitute ***ch*** for the beginning consonant letter in each word and read the new word.
- Write ***ten, my, mile,*** and ***bite*** on the chalkboard. Have volunteers substitute ***wh*** for the beginning consonant letter in each word and read the new word.

Have children go back through the selection and look for words with ***ch*** and ***wh.*** *(**munch, crunch** on pp. 39, 40, 41, and 65; **changing, what** on p. 49; **what** on p. 66)*

COMPREHENSION

27 SEQUENCE

> **In your own words, tell what happens to the egg.** *(Possible answer: The eggs become a caterpillar, then the caterpillar forms a chrysalis, next it becomes a butterfly. Then the butterfly lays an egg and the whole process starts again.)*

28 MAIN IDEA/DETAILS

> **What is the main idea of this story?** *(The main idea of the story is the life of a monarch butterfly.)*

Preview

Invite children to preview the poem by reading the title and studying the pictures that go with it.

1 SUMMARIZE

> **What is the poem about?** *(Possible answer: The poem is about caterpillars who do nothing but eat and grow so that they can become butterflies.)*

JOURNAL

Revisit Purposes for Reading

Ask children to look back at the purposes they set for reading and record whether their purposes were met.

66

caterpillar
What will happen
to me next?
Do you know?
27
eggs
chrysalis
butterfly
28
66

MODIFY Instruction

ESL/ELD

▲ List the following words on the chalkboard: *eggs, caterpillar, pupa, chrysalis, butterfly*. To help English language learners summarize a butterfly's life cycle, draw pictures for them and label each stage on an index card. Have pairs of children arrange the cards in order. **(MULTISENSORY TECHNIQUES)**

EXTRA HELP

■ Ask children to retell the life cycle of a butterfly in their own words. Encourage them to use the illustrations in the story to help them recall the order. **(RETELL)**

67 ▼

POEM

Caterpillar

What do caterpillars do?
Nothing much but chew and chew.

What do caterpillars know?
Nothing much but how to grow. ❶

They just eat what by and by
will make them be a butterfly,

But that is more than I can do
however much I chew and chew.

Aileen Fisher

67

FAMILY TALK

Caterpillars eat leaves. Have children talk with their families about other insects that eat leaves. Encourage them to make a list, or draw pictures of insects that eat leaves and plants.

Description
SHARED WRITING

PREWRITE Using *I'm a Caterpillar* as a model, talk about describing what something looks like or what it does. Tell children that later they will be writing a description of something from the story. Have children think about what they would like to describe and begin to complete the prewriting organizer on **Practice Book page 24.**

DAILY LANGUAGE PRACTICE

SPELLING
DAY 2:
Practice Words With /ô/ all, aw. **See page R12.**

GRAMMAR, USAGE, MECHANICS
DAY 2:
Practice Capitalizing the Word *I*. **See page R14.**

ORAL LANGUAGE
I hope i do not fal.
(I hope I do not fall.)

DAY 2 WRAP-UP

READ ALOUD *Spend five to ten minutes reading from a selection of your choice.*

GUIDED READING *Meet with the* ***red*** *and* ***blue*** *reading groups and assign Independent Center activities.* ***See pages R10–R11.***

COMPREHENSION

DAY 3 OBJECTIVES

CHILDREN WILL:

READ 30 MINUTES

- **Assess Comprehension**
- **Key Comprehension Skill: Sequence**
- **Daily Phonics: Vowel /ā/ *ay*, *ai***

WRITE 30 MINUTES

- **Respond: Cartoon Dialogue**
- **Spelling: Words With /ô/ *all*, *aw***
- **Grammar, Usage, Mechanics: Capitalizing *I***
- **Oral Language**

EXTEND SKILLS 30 MINUTES

- **Read Aloud**
- **Guided Reading**

RESOURCES

- **Practice Book, pp. 19–23**
- **Spelling Resource Book, p. 118**

Think About Reading

Below are the **answers** to the *Think About Reading* questions.

1. *A caterpillar turns into a pupa.*
2. *It becomes a chrysalis.*
3. *It becomes a butterfly.*
4. *The eggs become caterpillars.*

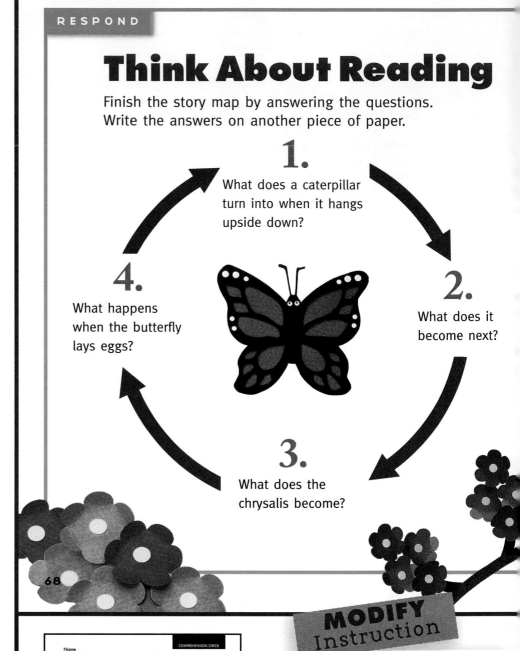

68

RESPOND

Think About Reading

Finish the story map by answering the questions. Write the answers on another piece of paper.

1. What does a caterpillar turn into when it hangs upside down?

2. What does it become next?

3. What does the chrysalis become?

4. What happens when the butterfly lays eggs?

68

MODIFY Instruction

ESL/ELD

▲ Make sure English language learners are familiar with cartoon dialogue. Before you begin the writing activity, bring in sample cartoons for them to use as models. Point out that the words in the balloons are the words the characters say. **(DEMONSTRATE)**

Name COMPREHENSION CHECK

Caterpillar Grows Up

▶ What does the caterpillar become? Draw a picture to show it. Then tell what a caterpillar does to turn into this!

Responses will vary.

Unit 5 • Information Finders • I'm a Caterpillar 19

PRACTICE BOOK, p. 19

69

Vrite Cartoon Dialogue

.t do you think a caterpillar a butterfly would say to each :r? Draw a caterpillar and a erfly on another piece of paper. e words for both animals to say ach other.

terature Circle

.t if the caterpillar in I'm a :rpillar could meet the poet wrote "Caterpillars"? What ht the caterpillar tell the t? What might the poet tell caterpillar?

Author
Jean Marzollo

Don't forget! That's good advice from Jean Marzollo. Marzollo knows that everyone has good ideas for writing. Still, it's easy to forget those good ideas. Then, when it's time to write, it can be hard to think up a good idea. That's why Marzollo writes down all her ideas right away.

More Books by
Jean Marzollo

- I Am Fire
- Happy Birthday, Martin Luther King
- Football Friends

69

TECHNOLOGY

Language Development Have children read the **WiggleWorks Plus** My Book *The Awful Bug.* Ask them to rewrite the text to describe a butterfly and redraw to show a butterfly. Have them add a speech bubble and words for the butterfly to say or think.

RESPOND

Write Cartoon Dialogue

Before children begin to draw or write, have them think about these questions:

- **What does a caterpillar spend its time doing?**
- **What does a butterfly do most of the time?**
- **What might a caterpillar and a butterfly say to each other?**

Children may want to sketch out their cartoons with pencils before using paint, markers, or other materials to do the actual drawing and writing.

Literature Circle

Encourage children to have a conversation speculating what the caterpillar and the poet might say to each other.

DAILY LANGUAGE PRACTICE

SPELLING

DAY 3: Write Words With /ô/ *all, aw.* **See page R13.**

GRAMMAR, USAGE, MECHANICS

DAY 3: Practice Capitalizing *I.* **See page R15.**

ORAL LANGUAGE

i know that butterflies taste alful.

(I know that butterflies taste awful.)

SKILLS TRACE

SEQUENCE TESTED

Introduce . . . . .pp. T114–T115
Practice . . . . .p. T85
Review . . . . .p. R44
Reteach . . . . .p. R55

CONNECT TO THE TRADE BOOKS

Select one of the unit trade books. Read aloud the title, and discuss the cover illustration.

- Have children make predictions about what might happen in the selection. Record their predictions on chart paper or the chalkboard.
- Read the selection a few pages at a time. Stop periodically to have children recall the sequential order of what happens in the selection. Record the events in order on chart paper.
- When you have finished, review the list of events and have children summarize what happened first, next, and last in the selection.

COMPREHENSION

Sequence

QUICKCHECK

Can children:

✔ follow the sequence of events?

✔ identify what happened first, next, then, and last?

If YES, go on to Practice/Apply.

If NO, start at Teach/Model.

A TEACH/MODEL

USE ORAL LANGUAGE

Ask children to describe a sequence in nature that repeats itself. For example, children could describe how some trees change colors, or how the sun moves across the sky. Ask children to describe what happens first, next, and last.

Then ask children to describe the sequence of events in *I'm a Caterpillar*. Explain to children that the **sequence of events is the order in which the important story events happen.** Point out that signal words such as ***first, next, then,*** and ***last*** can help show sequence. To determine the sequence of events, have children:

1. Read the selection and identify important events.
2. Look for signal words such as ***first, next, then,*** and ***last*** that tell the order in which events happened.

MODIFY Instruction

ESL/ELD

▲ To reinforce the concept of sequence, act out a sequence of events and have children describe each step. Then invite children to do the same. For example: (making a glass of chocolate milk) 1. Take a glass. 2. Pour the milk. 3. Pour in the syrup. 4. Stir. 5. Drink. **(SEQUENCE)**

EXTRA HELP

■ To help children understand a cyclical sequence, like the one presented in *I'm a Caterpillar*, have them create a circle chart, similar to the one on page 66 of the selection. Guide them by showing a familiar four-step sequence, such as the sun's movement in the sky. **(GRAPHIC DEVICE)**

LITERATURE CONNECTION

You may wish to revisit *I'm a Caterpillar* with children to review the major events in the life of a caterpillar.

THINK ALOUD *Thinking about sequence in the life of the butterfly is pretty easy. In its whole life, a butterfly goes through four stages: egg, caterpillar, chrysalis, butterfly. Those are the four stages shown on the circle chart at the end of the selection.*

B PRACTICE/APPLY

USE PRACTICE BOOK

Have pairs of children work together to complete **Practice Book, page 20.** Have children recall the four stages in the life of a caterpillar. **(PARTNERS)**

C ASSESS

APPLY INSTRUCTIONAL ALTERNATIVES

Based on children's completion of **Practice Book, page 20,** determine if they were able to recognize sequence in *I'm a Caterpillar*. The instructional alternatives below will aid you in pinpointing children's level of proficiency. Consider the appropriate instructional alternative to promote further skill development.

To reinforce the skills, distribute **page 21** of the **Practice Book.**

INSTRUCTIONAL ALTERNATIVES

	If the child . . .	Then . . .
Proficient	Recognizes sequence	• Have the child apply this skill independently to a more challenging story. • Summarize a process by telling the important steps in the correct order.
Apprentice	Recalls major story events, but cannot organize them into sequential order	• Describe a familiar process and have the child identify the important steps or stages, in order.
Novice	Does not recognize all major story events and does not organize any events in correct order	• Review the chart on page 66 of the selection. Guide the child to use the chart to retell the events in *I'm a Caterpillar*. • Use the Reteach lesson on page R55.

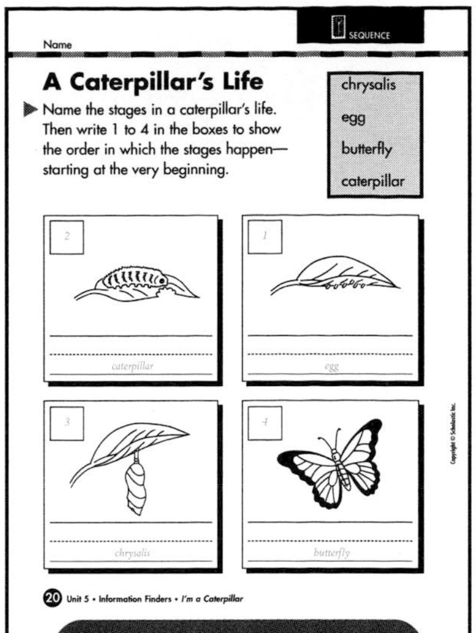
Name
SEQUENCE
A Caterpillar's Life
▶ Name the stages in a caterpillar's life. Then write 1 to 4 in the boxes to show the order in which the stages happen—starting at the very beginning.
chrysalis
egg
butterfly
caterpillar
20 Unit 5 • Information Finders • I'm a Caterpillar

PRACTICE BOOK p. 20

Name
SEQUENCE
In Order
▶ Put the pictures in order by writing the numbers 1, 2, 3, or 4 next to each picture. Then use the pictures to write a story.
Unit 5 • Information Finders • I'm a Caterpillar 21

PRACTICE BOOK p. 21

SELECTION WORDS With /ā/ ay, ai

wait

away

afraid

lay

SKILLS TRACE

VOWEL /ā/ (ay, ai) TESTED

Introduce . . . . p. T116
Practice . . . . p. T107
Review . . . . p. R48
Reteach . . . . p. R58

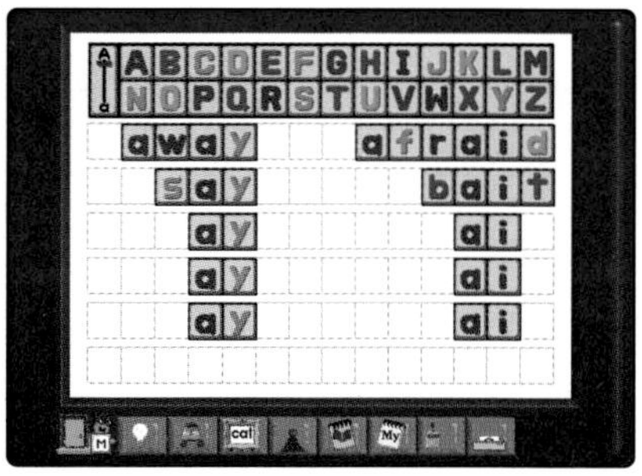

TECHNOLOGY

Have children practice *-ay* and *-ai* words using the **WiggleWorks Plus** Magnet Board.

- Start with the words ***away*** and ***afraid*** in two columns. Below them, add several pairs of ***ay*** and ***ai.***
- Have children add letters to the ***ay*** and ***ai*** pairs to make words.

DAILY PHONICS

Vowel /ā/ ay, ai

A PHONOLOGICAL AWARENESS

RHYME Chant the rhyme "Rain, Rain, Go Away" from the *Big Book of Rhymes and Rhythms 1B,* pages 14–15. As you chant, clap on the words with long ***a.***

- Frame the words ***rain, away, day,*** and ***play.*** Have children repeat them as you read each, stressing the **/ā/** sound.

Rain, Rain, Go Away
Rain, rain, go away,
Come again another day,
Little Johnny wants to play.
rain away

***Big Book of Rhymes and Rhythms 1B,* pp. 14–15**

ORAL BLENDING Say the following word parts. Ask children to blend them. Provide corrective feedback and modeling as needed.

/d/ /ā/ (day)	/l/ /ā/ (lay)	/s/ /ā/ (say)
/r/ /ā/ /n/ (rain)	/w/ /ā/ /t/ (wait)	/t/ /ā/ /l/ (tail)

B CONNECT SOUND-SPELLING

INTRODUCE *ā/ay, ai* Explain to children that the letters ***ay*** and the letters ***ai*** stand for **/ā/** as in the words ***say*** and ***train.*** Write the word ***train*** on the chalkboard and underline the letters ***ai.***

THINK ALOUD *I can put the letters **t, r, ai,** and **n** together to make the word **train.** Let's say the sounds slowly as I move my fingers under the letters. Listen to the sound that **ai** stands for in **train.** The sound of **ai** is* **/ā/.**

Repeat the process for the ***ay*** spelling of **/ā/** in the word ***way.***

MODIFY Instruction

ESL/ELD

▲ Keep a list of **ai** and **ay** words in appropriate categories. Start a chart similar to the following:

ai	ay
train	play
rain	day
wait	say

Have children say the words. Make sure they understand the words. **(CATEGORIZE)**

GIFTED & TALENTED

✳ Challenge children to work with a partner to create a chain of long a words spelled with *ai*. The first child says an *ai* word—*rain*. The next child changes that beginning or ending sound to form a different word. They should continue in this way to see how many different words they can form. **(WORD PLAY)**

- Ask children to suggest other words with */ā/ay* or */ā/ai*.
- List the words on chart paper and have volunteers underline the spelling for */ā/* in each word.

PHONICS MAINTENANCE Review the following sound-spellings: */ā/ai, ay; /ô/all, aw; l*-blends; *r*-blends; long *e (ea, ee)*. Say one of these sounds. Have a volunteer write on the chalkboard the spelling or spellings that stand for the sound. Continue with all the sounds.

C PRACTICE/APPLY

BLEND WORDS To practice using the sound-spellings and review previous sound-spellings, list the following words and sentences on the chalkboard. Have children read each chorally. Model blending as needed.

play	stay	train	grain
black	green	pea	bee

We will ride the train today.

Do you like to play in the rain?

DICTATION Dictate the following words for children to spell: ***may, nail, draw, clean.***

BUILD WORDS Distribute the following letter cards, or have children use their own sets: ***ay, ai, s, t, n, p, l, r, g, w.*** Give children time to build as many words as possible using the letter cards. Children can write their words on a separate sheet of paper. **(INDEPENDENT WORK)**

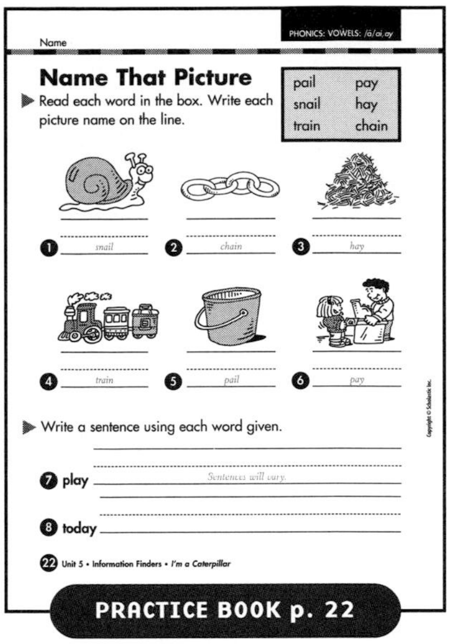
Name

PHONICS: VOWELS: /ā/ai, ay

Name That Picture

▶ Read each word in the box. Write each picture name on the line.

pail	pay
snail	hay
train	chain

1 snail 2 chain 3 hay

4 train 5 pail 6 pay

▶ Write a sentence using each word given.

7 play Sentences will vary.

8 today

22 Unit 5 • Information Finders • I'm a Caterpillar

PRACTICE BOOK p. 22

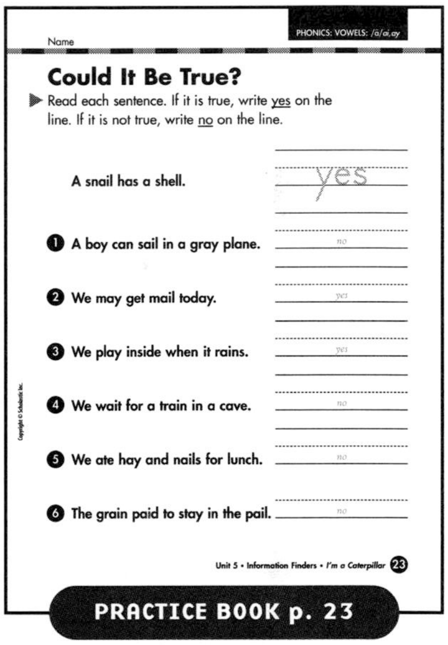
Name

PHONICS: VOWELS: /ā/ai, ay

Could It Be True?

▶ Read each sentence. If it is true, write yes on the line. If it is not true, write no on the line.

A snail has a shell. yes

1 A boy can sail in a gray plane. no

2 We may get mail today. yes

3 We play inside when it rains. yes

4 We wait for a train in a cave. no

5 We ate hay and nails for lunch. no

6 The grain paid to stay in the pail. no

Unit 5 • Information Finders • I'm a Caterpillar 23

PRACTICE BOOK p. 23

DECODABLE TEXT

For practice reading decodable text, see ***Scholastic Decodable Reader #60.***

For additional phonics instruction and review, see ***Scholastic Phonics A, pp. 215–216.***

1-2-3 RHYME

Three or more children can play this game. The first says a long *a* word spelled with *ay* or *ai*. The next child must say a rhyming word. The third child must use both words to create a rhyming sentence. Here's an example.

CHILD 1: *stay*

CHILD 2: *play*

CHILD 3: We can *play* if you *stay*.

Building Fluency

PHONICS READER

Guide children through a reading of **Phonics Reader #51,** *Dinosaur Hall* or **#52,** *Paws and Claws*. For a detailed lesson plan, see **Phonics Reader Teacher's Guide Part B, pages 44–47.** While children read, note how well they:

- **blend words,**
- **recognize high-frequency words,**
- **read with speed, accuracy, and expression.**

You may wish to have children reread the story with a partner.

* See Phonics Readers Take-Home Books 37–72 for reproducible format.

More Support Materials . . .

Trade Book Library

For additional leveled reading practice, have children read one of the following:

Animal Tracks
Challenge

Owl at Home
Average

Lost!
Easy

Phonics Chapter Book

For additional practice with **/ô/**, have children read Chapter 2, "This Hall Is for the Birds" in **Phonics Chapter Book 5,** *Let's Go on a Museum Hunt*.

Home-School Connection

Send home *Dinosaur Hall* and *Paws and Claws*. Have children read the books to a family member.

My Book

For additional practice with high-frequency words and the vowel sound **/ô/ *(all, aw)***, have children read *The Awful Bug* and *Small Daniel*. The My Books are also available on **WiggleWorks Plus.**

Intervention

For children who need extra support . . .

FOCUS ON HIGH-FREQUENCY WORDS

Write the words ***next*** and ***all*** on note cards. Then follow this procedure:

- State each word aloud and have children repeat it.
- Have children spell the word aloud as you point to each letter.
- Provide children with simple sentences containing each word. Help them to read the sentences. Allow ample time for them to practice reading the words and sentences before rereading *I'm a Caterpillar.*
- Some children may need a large number of repetitions before these words become sight words. Brief, daily reviews and frequent rereadings of previous stories containing these words will be helpful.

next   all

FOCUS ON PHONICS

Write the following words on index cards: ***fall, straw, awful, crawl, tall, small, wall, draw.***

- Help children read the word on each card.
- Then mix the cards. Have children sort the cards according to the spelling for **/ô/—*a*** before ***ll*** or ***aw.***
- Ask children to read the words in each group.

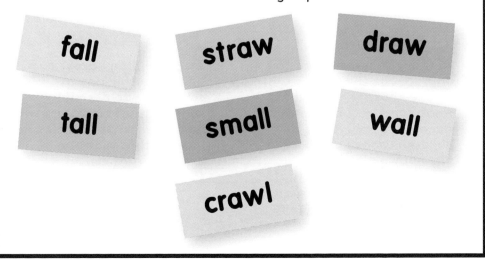

fall   straw   draw
tall   small   wall
crawl

PROFESSIONAL DEVELOPMENT

JOHN SHEFELBINE

How Fluency Develops

Fluent reading is a major goal of beginning reading instruction. Skilled readers are fluent because of their ability to instantaneously identify and process virtually all the letters in a word. The development of this ability depends on two critical components: (1) students' use of word identification strategies that focus attention on spelling patterns, and (2) a large amount of individualized reading practice in decodable materials that are not too difficult.

DAY 3 WRAP-UP

READ ALOUD *To conclude each reading session and develop children's oral vocabularies, read aloud a book of your choice. If the book contains chapters, you might choose to read only one chapter a day.*

GUIDED READING *Meet with the **green** and **yellow** reading groups and assign Independent Center activities.* ***See pages R10–R11.***

DAY 4 OBJECTIVES

CHILDREN WILL:

READ 20 MINUTES

- **Reread *I'm a Caterpillar***

WRITE 40 MINUTES

- **Shared Writing: Description**
- **Spelling: Words With /ô/ *all*, *aw***
- **Grammar, Usage, Mechanics: Capitalizing *I***
- **Oral Language**

EXTEND SKILLS 30 MINUTES

- **Vocabulary**
- **Daily Phonics: Words With /ô/ *all*, *aw***
- **Study Skills: Graphic Aids: Diagrams**

RESOURCES

Practice Book, pp. 24, 26
Spelling Resource Book, p. 161

Name WRITING

Get Ready to Write

▶ Look at the pictures.
Write a description of each thing.

To the Teacher: This is the prewriting organizer referenced in the lesson on writing a description.

24 Unit 5 • Information Finders • I'm a Caterpillar

PRACTICE BOOK p. 24

SHARED WRITING

Description

SELECTION CONNECTION Using *I'm a Caterpillar* as a model, children will write a description of something.

THINK ABOUT WRITING Ask children why they might want to describe something to someone. Discuss with children how *I'm a Caterpillar* describes how a caterpillar turns into a butterfly. Help them to understand that in stories and selections, descriptions often:

- help readers to picture things in their minds.
- help readers understand what is in a story or selection.

INTRODUCE THE WRITING EVENT Tell children that they are going to write their own descriptions for a class book.

TEACH/MODEL

PUT IT IN CONTEXT Invite children to look back at *I'm a Caterpillar*. Talk about the descriptions in the selection. Ask the following questions to help children think about these descriptions.

> **What does the caterpillar do?**

> **How is the caterpillar's eating described?**

> **How does the caterpillar become a pupa?**

Ask children to think about something they want to describe. It can be something they have seen outside, such as an animal or insect.

MODIFY Instruction

ESL/ELD

▲ Have children listen to and act out the song "Hokey Pokey." ("*I put my right hand in, I put my right hand out . . .*") Next, children choose one part of the body and write or dictate the steps for that part of the song. Children should listen to the song as often as necessary. **(RECORD)**

EXTRA HELP

■ If children have difficulty thinking of something to describe, suggest that they work with partners to list animals and insects that might be of interest to them. **(BRAINSTORM)**

GRAMMAR CONNECTION Encourage children to use the word *I* as they write their descriptions.

WRITE

WRITE A DESCRIPTION

- Have children write their descriptions. Encourage them to use the word *I* as they write.
- Have children draw pictures to illustrate their descriptions.
- Gather children's pages into a class book of descriptions.

ASSESS

PERFORMANCE-BASED ASSESSMENT The following questions will help children assess their work:

✔ **What did I describe?**

✔ **Did my writing help readers to picture or understand what I was describing?**

Children may wish to develop this piece through the writing process described on **pages T286–T289.**

DAILY LANGUAGE PRACTICE

SPELLING

DAY 4:

Review Words With /ô/ *all, aw.* **See page R13.**

GRAMMAR, USAGE, MECHANICS

DAY 4:

Apply Capitalizing *I.* **See page R15.**

ORAL LANGUAGE

This is what i like to dra.

(This is what I like to draw.)

TECHNOLOGY

Writing Skills
Encourage children to use the Unit Writer to develop their story. Suggest that they use the Record tool, the Paint tools, and stamp art.

Extend Vocabulary

Review High-Frequency Words

Write the high-frequency words ***next*** and ***all*** on note cards. For each word write a lowercase and uppercase version **(*next/Next*).** Then write the following incomplete sentences on the chalkboard:

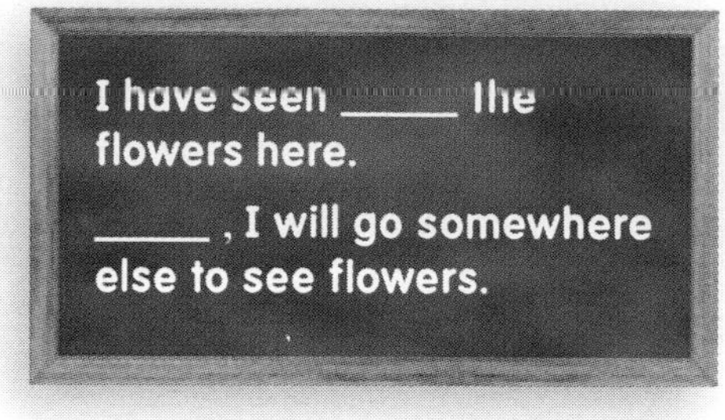

I have seen ____ the flowers here.
____, I will go somewhere else to see flowers.

Read aloud each incomplete sentence and have children place the appropriate high-frequency word note card in the blank space. Then help children to chorally read the sentences.

Review Story Words

Write the story words ***munch, wait, grow, wet, dry,*** and ***straw*** on note cards. Then write the following incomplete sentences on sentence strips:

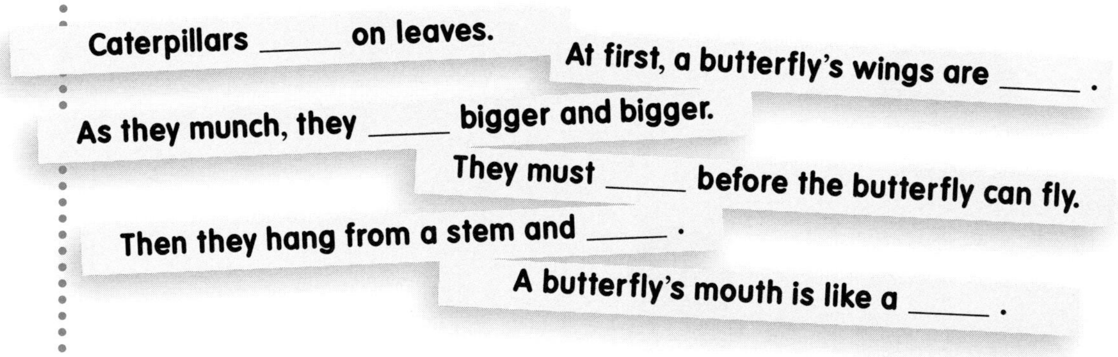

Caterpillars ____ on leaves.
At first, a butterfly's wings are ____ .
As they munch, they ____ bigger and bigger.
They must ____ before the butterfly can fly.
Then they hang from a stem and ____ .
A butterfly's mouth is like a ____ .

Read aloud the incomplete sentences and have children place the appropriate story-word note cards in the appropriate blank spaces. Then help children chorally read the sentences.

DESCRIBE THE LIFE OF A BUTTERFLY

Have children draw pictures to describe the four stages in a butterfly's life. The chart on page 66 of the selection will help children define these stages. Have children write sentences using the high-frequency words and the story words to go with their pictures. Encourage children to display their sentences and pictures and describe each stage.

Building Fluency

Phonics Reader

Guide children through a reading of **Phonics Reader #49,** *The Frog Trail* or **#50,** *A Rain Forest Day.* For a detailed lesson plan, see **Phonics Reader Teacher's Guide Part B, pages 40–43.** While children read, note how well they:

- **blend words,**
- **recognize high-frequency words,**
- **read with speed, accuracy, and expression.**

You may wish to have children reread the story with a partner.

★ See Phonics Readers Take-Home Books 37–72 for reproducible format.

More Support Materials . . .

Trade Book Library

For additional leveled reading practice, have children read one of the following:

Animal Tracks
CHALLENGE

Owl at Home
AVERAGE

Lost!
EASY

Phonics Chapter Book

For additional practice with long ***a (ai, ay)***, have children read Chapter 1, "Charlie and Kate on the Trail" in **Phonics Chapter Book 5,** *Let's Go on a Museum Hunt.*

Home-School Connection

Send home *The Frog Trail* and *A Rain Forest Day.* Have children read the books to a family member.

My Book

For additional practice with high-frequency words and words with long ***a***, have children read *Waiting for Suzy* or *Anna Jane, the Pain.* The My Books are also available on **WiggleWorks Plus.**

SKILLS TRACE

Graphic Aids: Diagrams TESTED

Introduce . . . . . pp. T124–T125
Review . . . . p. R53
Reteach . . . . .p. R62

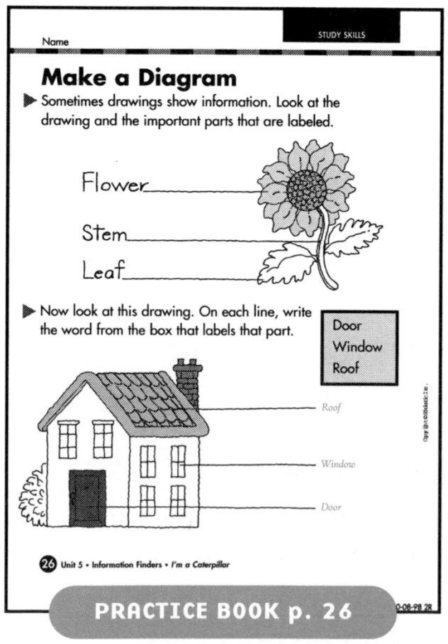
STUDY SKILLS

Name

Make a Diagram

▶ Sometimes drawings show information. Look at the drawing and the important parts that are labeled.

Flower

Stem

Leaf

▶ Now look at this drawing. On each line, write the word from the box that labels that part.

Door
Window
Roof

Roof

Window

Door

26 Unit 5 • Information Finders • I'm a Caterpillar

PRACTICE BOOK p. 26

STUDY SKILLS

Graphic Aids: Diagrams

Ⓐ TEACH/MODEL

DEFINE DIAGRAMS Talk about diagrams with children. Tell them that a diagram presents information with pictures and just a few words. Diagrams organize information to make it easier to understand.

PUT IT IN CONTEXT Point out that the picture chart on page 66 of *I'm a Caterpillar,* which shows the stages in the life of a butterfly, is a kind of diagram. It presents and summarizes the important information using pictures and just a few words.

PRESENT A DIAGRAM Copy the following diagram on the chalkboard or on chart paper.

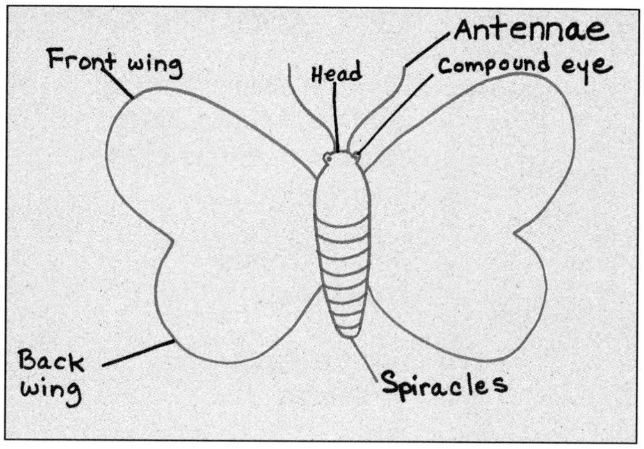

Encourage children to talk about what the diagram shows. Ask:

> **What is this diagram about?**

> **What do the words on the diagram tell you?**

THINK ALOUD *Suppose I wanted to share information about the parts of a butterfly. I could write a description or I could draw a picture and label the parts, the way this diagram does.*

B PRACTICE/APPLY

USE THE DIAGRAM TO FIND INFORMATION

Ask children to use the diagram to answer the following questions:

> **What is a butterfly's body like?**

> **What is a butterfly's mouth like?**

> **How many wings does a butterfly have?**

INFORMAL ASSESSMENT: PERFORMANCE-BASED

✔ Were children able to get information from the diagram?

✔ Did children use the diagram correctly?

✔ Did children understand that diagrams are made up of pictures and a few words?

TECHNOLOGY

Presentation Tools Have children use **WiggleWorks Plus** PlaceMaker or a familiar art program to make a poster of the caterpillar life cycle. Be sure they use the terms *egg, caterpillar, pupa, chrysalis,* and *butterfly.*

DAY 4 WRAP-UP

READ ALOUD *To develop children's ability to get information from diagrams, spend five to ten minutes sharing a nonfiction selection of your choice that includes diagrams and other graphic aids.*

GUIDED READING *Meet with the* ***green*** *and* ***yellow*** *reading groups and assign Independent Center activities.* ***See pages R10–R11.***

DAY 5 OBJECTIVES

CHILDREN WILL:

READ 30 MINUTES
- **Reading Assessment**
- **Daily Phonics: Words With /ô/ *all, aw* Vowel /ā/ *ai, ay***

WRITE 30 MINUTES
- **Writing Assessment**
- **Spelling: Words With /ô/ *all, aw***
- **Grammar, Usage, Mechanics: Capitalizing *I***
- **Oral Language**

EXTEND SKILLS 30 MINUTES
- **Integrated Language Arts**
- **Read Aloud**
- **Guided Reading**

RESOURCES
- **Selection Test**
- **Spelling Practice Book, p. 163**

TEACHER SELF-ASSESSMENT

✔ Did I frequently model how to blend words?

✔ Did I review high-frequency words on the Word Wall each day?

✔ Did I provide children with successful, daily reading and writing opportunities?

Reading Assessment

INFORMAL ASSESSMENT: OBSERVATION

PHONICS

Write the following spellings on note cards: ***all, aw, ay, ai.*** Display one card at a time and have the class state the sound(s) the spelling stands for. Note children who respond incorrectly or who wait for classmates to respond before providing an answer.

HIGH-FREQUENCY WORDS

Write the following high-frequency words on note cards: ***next, all.*** Display one card at a time and have the class read the word. Note children who have difficulty recognizing either word.

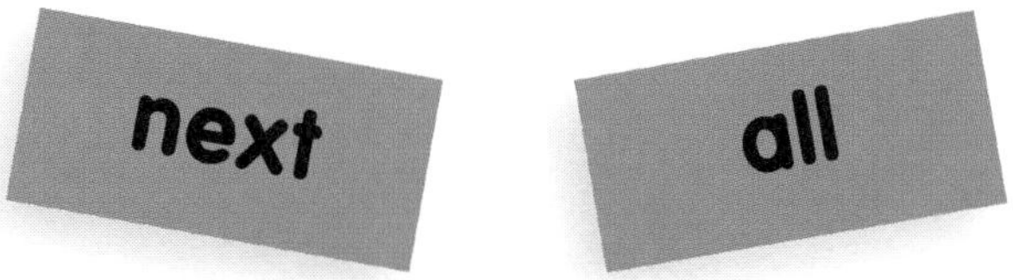

KEY SKILL: SEQUENCE

Choose a trade book whose story has a clear and simple sequence. Read the story with children. Then ask children to write a sentence or draw a picture to show what happened in the beginning, middle, and end of the story.

CONFERENCE

Have children reread *I'm a Caterpillar.* As they reread, select several children to conference with. Ask them to do the following:

- read aloud a few pages of the story.
- retell the story in their own words.
- explain what they do to figure out an unfamiliar word.

Keep anecdotal records of the conferences. Place your findings in each child's assessment folder. Use the information to determine which children need additional support.

I'm a Caterpillar

FORMAL ASSESSMENT

DECODING TEST

Make two copies of the assessment below. The assessment piece is designed to be used individually.

- Give one to the child and keep the other to record each child's errors.
- As the child reads aloud the words and sentences in the assessment boxes, record his or her attempts, corrections, errors, and passes.
- Once completed, keep each assessment piece in the child's portfolio as a running record of his or her emerging reading skills.

NAME: ______________________ **DATE:** __________

A Have children read the following word list:

straw	**chain**	**always**	**more**	**next**
fall	**wait**	**paw**	**belongs**	**were**
rain	**crawl**	**claw**	**all**	**way**
afraid	**ball**	**awful**	**make**	**look**
play	**gray**	**wall**	**which**	**about**

B Have children read the following sentences:

- **It may rain all day.**
- **I will draw a paw with claws.**

C On a separate sheet of paper, have children write the following words and sentences.

- **straw tall wait stay**
- **I play all day.**
- **I saw the rain fall.**

SELECTION TEST

Use the selection test to obtain a formal measure of children's mastery of the week's reading objectives.

SELF-SELECTION

Have children select one or two pieces of work from the week that they would like to place in their portfolios. Suggest that children write a sentence telling why they chose each piece. You may also wish to select a piece that best illustrates the child's work.

Periodically review the pieces in the portfolio and remove any that no longer seem appropriate.

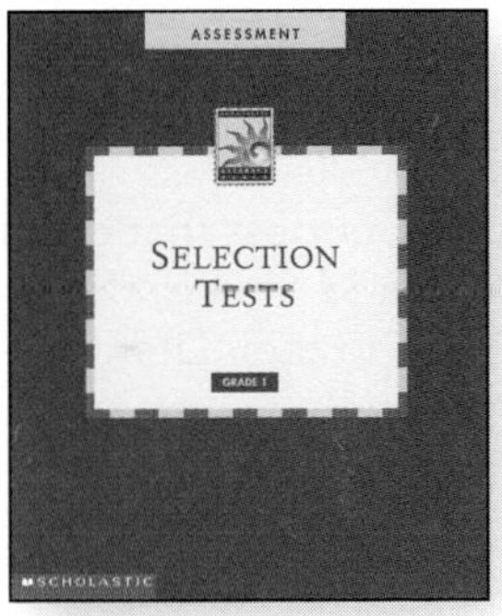

SELECTION TEST

DAILY LANGUAGE PRACTICE

SPELLING

DAY 5:
Administer Posttest for Words with /ô/ *all, aw.*
See page R13.

GRAMMAR, USAGE, MECHANICS

DAY 5:
Assess Capitalizing *I.*
See page R15.

ORAL LANGUAGE

May i have a starw?
(May I have a straw?)

PORTFOLIO

Suggest that children add their drafts and revisions to their Literacy Portfolios.

Writing Assessment

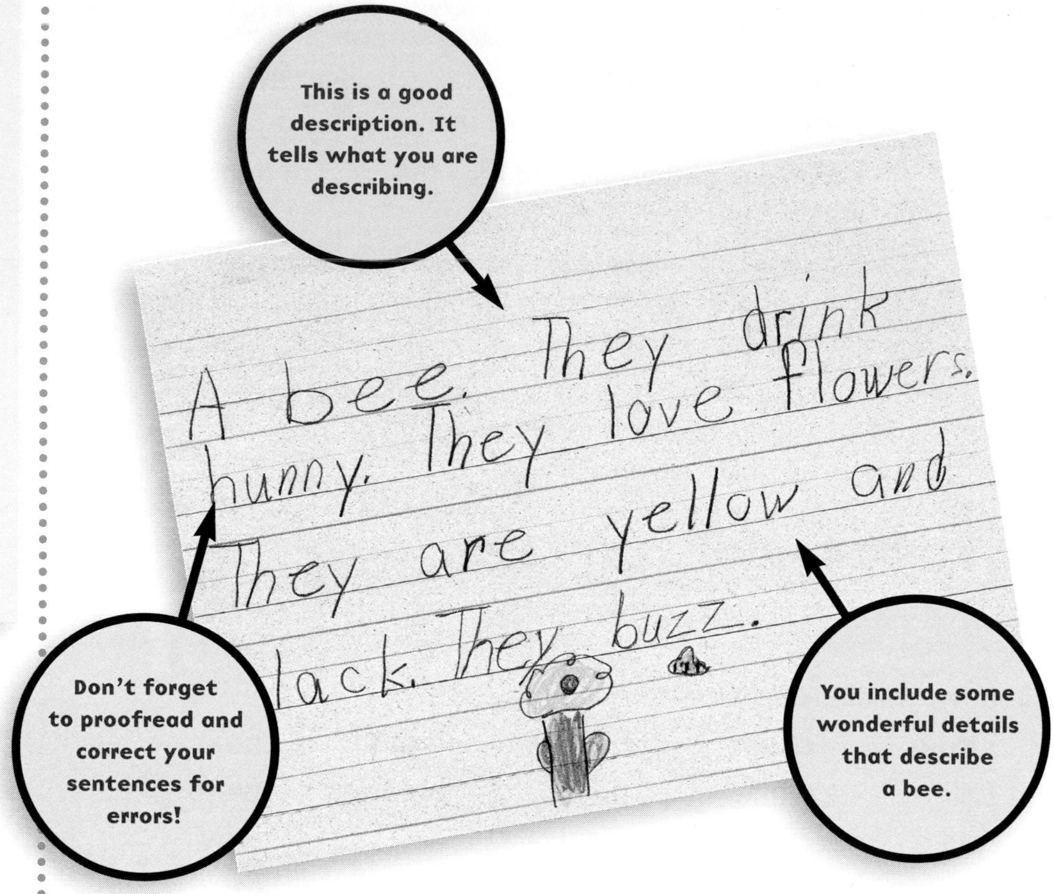

Apprentice

Use the rubric below to assess children's writing.

CHILDREN'S WRITING RUBRIC

Proficient	• What is being described is identified and defined. • The description includes identifying details.	• The description is proofread and corrected for errors.
Apprentice	• What is being described may be identified, but may not be defined. • The description may not include identifying details.	• The description may have been proofread but not completely corrected for errors.
Novice	• What is being described is unclear and cannot be identified. • The description does not include identifying details.	• The description has not been proofread or corrected for errors.

Integrated Language Arts

WRITING

Create a Word Butterfly

MATERIALS:
Paper
Pencil

SUGGESTED GROUPING:
Individuals

HAVE children write descriptions of butterflies in the shape of butterflies. Begin by providing a large pattern for a butterfly outline that the children can trace lightly with pencils on large sheets of paper.

ASK children to brainstorm words to describe butterflies. Make a list of these words on chart paper for children to use as a resource to create their butterfly descriptions.

INVITE children to write describing words on their butterfly outlines. Children should begin by writing the word ***Butterflies,*** then continue by writing describing words on the outlines.

Children may want to include their word butterflies in the Literacy Journals.

VIEWING/READING/WRITING

Make a Butterfly Book

MATERIALS:
Construction paper
Markers or crayons
Cardboard
Yarn
Stapler
Hole punch

SUGGESTED GROUPING:
Individuals

PROVIDE books about butterflies that include lots of colored photographs of different species of butterflies and moths. Encourage children to spend time with the books, looking at the pictures and deciding on their favorites.

HAVE children draw their own colored pictures of their favorite butterflies or copy the photographs they find in the butterfly books. Ask children to write the names and brief descriptions of the butterflies under the pictures.

ASSEMBLE the children's writing and pictures. Use the yarn to bind these pages together to create a class butterfly book.

Integrated Language Arts

READING/LISTENING/VOCABULARY

Explore Sounds

MATERIALS: None

SUGGESTED GROUPING: Whole class

REMIND children that the sounds of the caterpillar eating leaves are represented in *I'm a Caterpillar* by the words ***munch*** and ***crunch.*** Have children imagine other sounds the caterpillar, the butterfly, and other insects might make.

THEN have children play a sound guessing game. Ask children to make the caterpillar and insect sounds and challenge their classmates to guess what sounds they are imitating. When a sound has been identified, have children work together to come up with a way to write the word for that sound.

Onomatopoeia

TEACH/MODEL Discuss with children that words like ***munch*** and ***crunch*** imitate sounds and are called *onomatopoeia.*

PRACTICE/APPLY Challenge children to think of more words that sound like the sounds. You may wish to suggest words such as ***plunk, splash, gulp, yum.***

DAY 5 WRAP-UP

READ ALOUD *Spend five to ten minutes reading from a selection of your choice.*

GUIDED READING *Meet with the **red** and **blue** reading groups and assign Independent Center activities.* ***See pages R10–R11.***

SPEAKING/LISTENING

Interview the Caterpillar

MATERIALS: Audiocassette player and audiocassette (optional)

SUGGESTED GROUPING: Partners

HAVE children go back to page 66 and review the life cycle of a butterfly.

ASK one child to play the part of the caterpillar while his or her partner plays a news reporter or a talk-show host who will interview the caterpillar.

ENCOURAGE partners to shake hands and introduce themselves in their roles before the interviewer begins to ask questions about the caterpillar's life and habits. Some questions should be ones that can be answered with information from the selection. Some should require the "caterpillar" to use his or her imagination. Encourage children to use hand gestures and other movements as they speak.

> **How do you spend your time?**

> **Which do you like better—being a caterpillar or being a butterfly? Why?**

> **What is your favorite flower? Why?**

TECHNOLOGY

Speaking Skills Suggest that children tape-record their interviews and listen to them before rereading the story.

How to Keep an Observation Log

WHY DO THIS WORKSHOP?

Children often play outdoors, but may seldom take the time to stop and really observe the environment around them. Ask children what living things they see. How do those living things get their food?

This Workshop Card gives children an opportunity to observe more closely the sights and sounds of nature. They'll use their senses—particularly sight and hearing, and sometimes their sense of smell. They'll discover that the natural world around them is always changing. Children are encouraged to choose a convenient place to visit, preferably at two or three different times of day. Children will record the changes in plant or animal life that they notice. They'll learn that managing information by recording it in an organized way helps them compare natural changes.

GETTING STARTED

Use Observation

To focus children on the task at hand, you might discuss Side 1 of the Workshop Card with the whole class. Ask children where there might be some good places outside to see animals. You could also ask any of the following questions to focus children further on the task:

> **What animals might you see in a backyard or park?**

> **What are some things animals do in a backyard or park?**

> **What could writing or drawing in a nature log help you remember?**

WORKSHOP OBJECTIVES

CHILDREN LEARN TO:

- **Observe plants and animals in an outdoor environment**
- **Record their observations in an observation log**

MATERIALS

- **Paper and pencils**
- **An interesting environment to observe**

TECHNOLOGY

Organizing Information Children can use **WiggleWorks Plus** Unit Writer to design a recording sheet to answer the Getting Started questions. Type the questions, being sure to leave space for responses. Children can enter their ideas, save, and print the sheets to share with the class.

WORKSHOP

WORKSHOP 1

GRADE 1 MANAGING INFORMATION

How to Keep an Observation Log

An observation log is a place to write down the things you see in nature.

NAME: Andrea

My Ranger Notebook

Draw pictures or write about what you see in your backyard.

Date: May 2 **Time of the day:** 8:30 **Weather:** Sunny

Animals I Saw:

Pigeons

Signs of Animals I Saw:

Feathers

Ways I think Animals Use This "Backyard"

- ___ To look for food
- ___ To hide from enemies
- ✓ To rest
- ___ To raise young
- ___ For shelter
- ___ Other?________

THINK ABOUT IT: What if you looked in your "backyard" at a different time of the day? In different weather?

Observations stay organized when you record the day, time, and weather conditions.

This is an observation log about the animals you might find in your backyard or neighborhood.

Now Make Your Own

1 GATHER INFORMATION

Discuss with children some of the ways they use their senses to observe. For example, they use their eyes to see things, their ears to listen for sounds, and their noses to detect smells. For this activity, of course, children won't touch or taste things. Talk about how children can closely observe something. How close should they get? What kinds of things can they look for that show that animals have been around a place or that they live there? Ask children what they might see in trees and on the ground. Some signs of animals might be nests, a disturbed pile of dirt or leaves, holes around trees or shrubbery, pieces of acorns, or other nuts and fruit from trees. What about insects—where can children spot them? Let children suggest places they can go to observe nature.

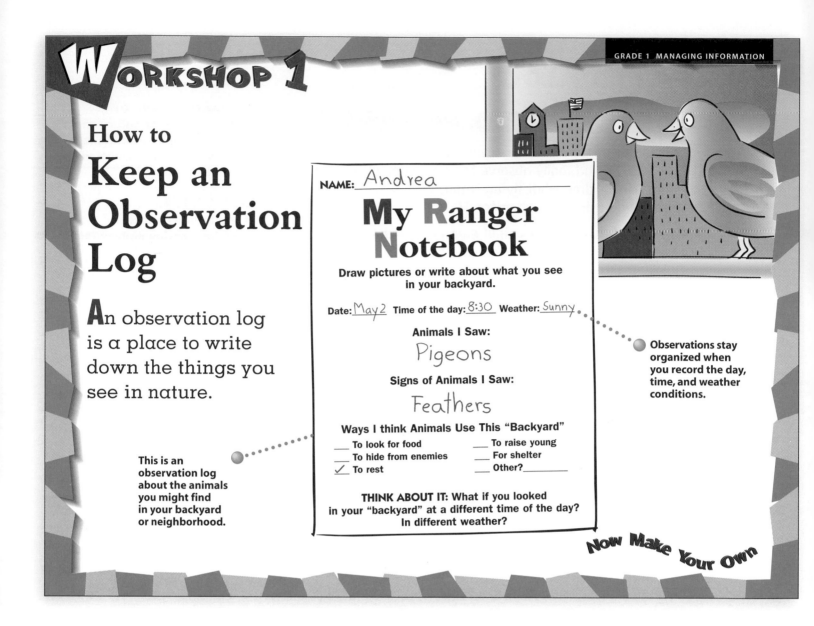

WORK

1 Gather Information

Think of an outdoor place nearby. Go there and look around carefully. What kinds of animals and plants do you see? What kinds of smells and sounds do you notice? The closer you look, the more you'll find.

2 Record What You Notice

Now it's time to record what you notice. Draw pictures and write about all the things you see, smell, and hear. Be sure to record the day and time of your observations.

Tools
paper ▶
◀ pencils
an interesting environment to observe
THINK
Why do you think patience is important to information finders?
Laela Sayigh ▶
Marine Biologist

2 Record What You Notice

Encourage children to work in pairs to draw as well as describe what they observe. They could use the Ranger Notebook shown on Side 1 of the Workshop Card as a model.

SELF-SELECTION

When children complete this Workshop Card, they may want to save their observation logs in their Literacy Portfolios as examples of work done well.

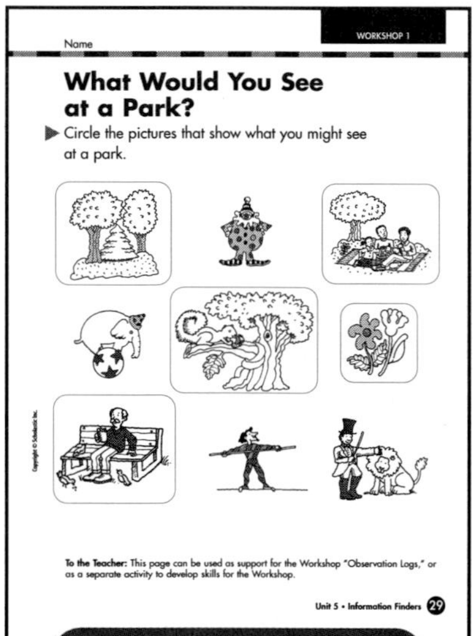

Name
WORKSHOP 1

What Would You See at a Park?

▶ Circle the pictures that show what you might see at a park.

Copyright © Scholastic Inc.

To the Teacher: This page can be used as support for the Workshop "Observation Logs," or as a separate activity to develop skills for the Workshop.

Unit 5 • Information Finders 29

PRACTICE BOOK p. 29

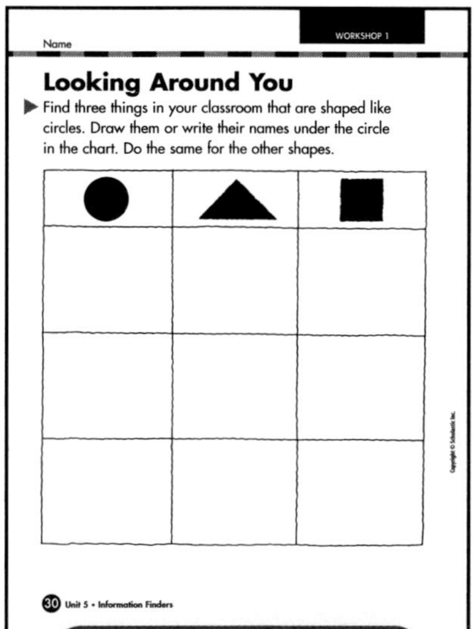

Name
WORKSHOP 1

Looking Around You

▶ Find three things in your classroom that are shaped like circles. Draw them or write their names under the circle in the chart. Do the same for the other shapes.

Copyright © Scholastic Inc.

30 Unit 5 • Information Finders

PRACTICE BOOK p. 30

Use **Practice Book pages 29 and 30** as practice for the Workshop or as a separate activity to strengthen children's skills.

ASSESSMENT

INFORMAL ASSESSMENT

OBSERVATION

Review children's work. Ask yourself:

- ✔ Did children record observations or draw pictures?
- ✔ Did children record the day and time?
- ✔ Did children record observations of the same spot at different times?

IF NOT, TRY THIS:

Have children look at nature books and magazines and make a log of the plants and animals they see.

CHILDREN'S SELF-ASSESSMENT

> What were two things I put in my log?

Use the rubric below to assess children's understanding of the Workshop.

CHILDREN'S WORKSHOP RUBRIC

Proficient	Children notice changes in the environment when they return to the same site at a different time. Children organize important details about plants and animals in their observation logs.
Apprentice	Children may not have completed a second observation for comparison, or the second observation may contain entirely different information. Some, but not necessarily all, of the details children recorded are important.
Novice	Children have difficulty observing closely and don't include important details about the site in their observation logs.

from *Frog and Toad Together* "The Garden"

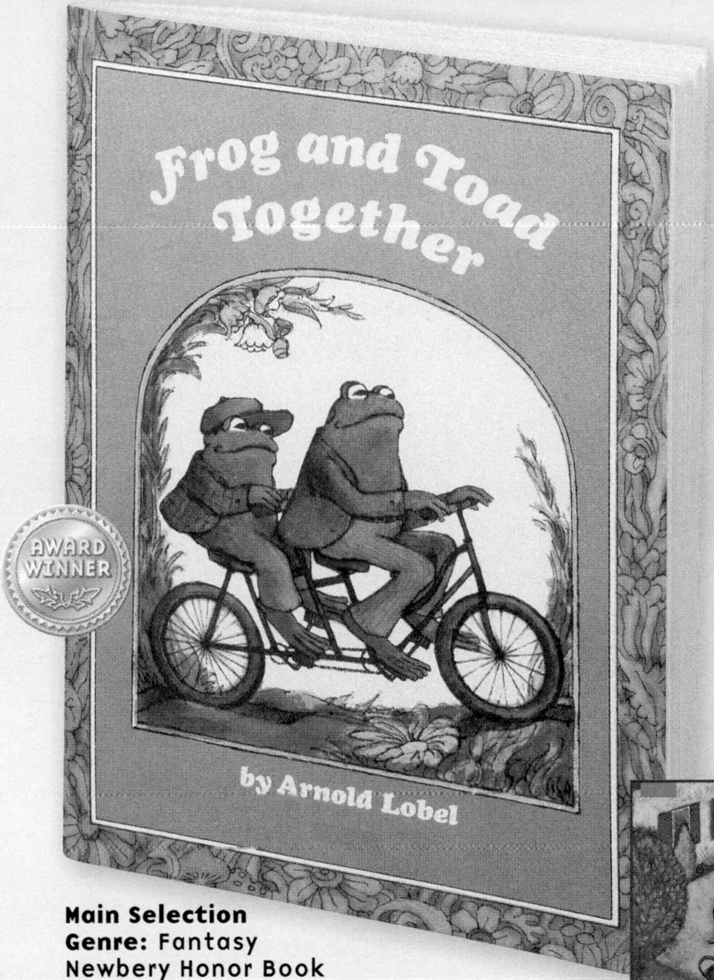

Main Selection
Genre: Fantasy
Newbery Honor Book
Caldecott Award–winning illustrator

Paired Selection
Genre: Poem and Rhyme
Pulitzer Prize-winning poet

WEEK 3 TESTED SKILLS

- **Key Comprehension Skill: Setting**
- **Vocabulary**
- **Daily Phonics: Vowel /ō/ *oa* Inflectional Ending *ed* (/t/,/d/)**
- **Spelling: Words With Vowel /ō/ *oa***
- **Grammar, Usage, Mechanics: Homophones**

Technology Connection

Build Background Get your spades and go cybergardening. Have children visit the web site **aggie-horticulture.tamu.edu** at Texas A&M University and click on kinderGARDEN to find fun gardening activities for kids, including tips on creating a school garden.

Selection Summary

Toad wants to have a nice garden like his friend Frog. When Frog gives Toad some seeds, Toad runs home to plant them. Toad expects quick results, but Frog explains that Toad must not rush the seeds. Toad tries to encourage the seeds by reading to them, singing to them, and playing the violin for them. Finally, the seeds sprout.

PAIRED SELECTION In the poem, Tommy plants seeds, just as Toad did. Like Toad, Tommy is anxious to see them grow.

Author/Illustrator

ARNOLD LOBEL credits the inspiration for his Frog and Toad series to his children's practice of catching frogs and toads. His children would keep the toads as pets and Lobel grew to love the creatures. Among his other books is *Mouse Soup*.

Weekly Organizer

Visit Our Web Site
www.scholastic.com

The Garden

	DAY 1	DAY 2
READ and Introduce Skills • VOCABULARY • PHONICS • COMPREHENSION • LISTENING • SPEAKING • VIEWING   	**BUILD BACKGROUND,** p. T141 ▲ ✓ **VOCABULARY,** p. T142 ▲ ✷ Practice Book, p. 31 ✓ **DAILY PHONICS:** ▲ ■ Words With /ō/*oa*, pp. T144–T145 Practice Book, pp. 32, 33 **PREVIEW AND PREDICT,** p. T146 **READ:** ▲ ✷ ■ "The Garden," pp. T146–T151 ✓ **COMPREHENSION:** Setting, p. T149	**READ:** ▲ ■ ✷ "The Garden," pp. T152–T157 ✓ **DAILY PHONICS:** Inflectional Ending *-ed* /d/, /t/, p. T153 Vowel /ō/*oa*, p. T155
WRITE and Respond • GRAMMAR • USAGE • MECHANICS • SPELLING • WRITING	**SHARED WRITING,** p. T141 **JOURNAL:** High-Frequency Words, p. T143 **QUICKWRITE:** Predict, p. T151 ✓ **SPELLING:** Pretest: Words With Vowel /ō/*oa*, p. R20 Spelling Resource Book, p. 119 ✓ **GRAMMAR, USAGE, MECHANICS:** Teach/Model: Homophones, p. R22 **ORAL LANGUAGE,** p. T151	**SHARED WRITING:** Prewrite, p. T157 Practice Book, p. 39 ✓ **SPELLING:** Vocabulary Practice, p. R20 Spelling Resource Book, pp. 120–122 ✓ **GRAMMAR, USAGE, MECHANICS:** Practice, p. R22 **ORAL LANGUAGE,** p. T157
EXTEND SKILLS and Apply to Literature • SKILLS • INTEGRATED LANGUAGE ARTS • INTEGRATED CURRICULUM • GUIDED READING • INDEPENDENT READING	**READ ALOUD,** p. T151 **GUIDED READING,** pp. R18–R19 **INTEGRATED CURRICULUM:** Science, p. R24 **TRADE BOOKS** • *Lost!* • *Animal Tracks* • *Owl at Home*  	**READ ALOUD,** p. T157 **GUIDED READING,** pp. R18–R19 **INTEGRATED CURRICULUM:** The Arts, p. R25 Math, p. R24

TECHNOLOGY and **REAL-WORLD SKILLS**	**WIGGLEWORKS PLUS CD-ROM** Magnet Board, pp. T142, T144 **WIGGLEWORKS PLUS CD-ROM** Expanding Vocabulary, p. T149	**WIGGLEWORKS PLUS CD-ROM** Comprehension Skills, p. T153

MODIFY INSTRUCTION

● INTERVENTION ▲ ESL/ELD ■ EXTRA HELP
✳ GIFTED & TALENTED ✓ = TESTED SKILL

DAY 3	DAY 4	DAY 5
✓ **READ:** ▲ ■ "Tommy," pp. T158–T159 ✓ **COMPREHENSION:** ▲ ✳ Setting, pp. T162–T163 Practice Book, pp. 35, 36 ✓ **DAILY PHONICS:** ▲ ✳ Inflectional Ending *-ed* /d/, /t/, pp. T164–T165 Practice Book, pp. 37, 38 **BUILDING FLUENCY,** p. T166 **FOCUS ON HIGH-FREQUENCY WORDS,** p. T167 **FOCUS ON PHONICS,** p. T167	**VOCABULARY REVIEW,** p. T170 ✓ **DAILY PHONICS:** Words With /ō/*oa,* p. T171 **BUILDING FLUENCY,** p. T171	**READING ASSESSMENT,** p. T174 Selection Test, p. T175 Conference Decoding Test, p. T175
RESPOND: ▲ ■ Think About Reading, p. T160 Practice Book, p. 34 **WRITE A HEADLINE,** p. T161 ✓ **SPELLING:** Write/Proofread, p. R21 Spelling Resource Book, p. 123 ✓ **GRAMMAR, USAGE, MECHANICS:** Practice, p. R23 **ORAL LANGUAGE,** p. T161	**SHARED WRITING:** ▲ ■ Poem, p. T168 Practice Book, p. 39 ✓ **SPELLING:** Study/Review, p. R21 Spelling Resource Book, p. 161 ✓ **GRAMMAR, USAGE, MECHANICS:** Apply, p. R23 **ORAL LANGUAGE,** p. T169	**WRITING ASSESSMENT,** p. T176 Child Model Children's Writing Rubric ✓ **SPELLING:** Posttest, p. R21 Spelling Resource Book, p. 163 ✓ **GRAMMAR, USAGE, MECHANICS:** Assess, p. R23 **ORAL LANGUAGE,** p. T176
READ ALOUD, p. T167 **GUIDED READING,** pp. R18–R19 **INTEGRATED CURRICULUM:** Social Studies, p. R25 **OPTIONAL MATERIALS,** p. T166 Phonics Reader #59: *The Hungry Toad* Phonics Reader #60: *Goat's Book*	**READ ALOUD,** p. T173 **GUIDED READING,** pp. R18–R19 **EXTEND VOCABULARY:** Review High-Frequency Words, p. T170 Review Story Words, p. T170 **OPTIONAL MATERIALS,** p. T171 Phonics Reader #53: *Small Animals with Big Names* Phonics Reader #54: *See the Sea* **STUDY SKILLS:** Follow Directions, p. T172	**READ ALOUD,** p. T178 **GUIDED READING,** pp. R18–R19 **INTEGRATED LANGUAGE ARTS:** Write About Your Senses, p. T177 Put Sounds in a Setting, p. T177 Toad Says . . ., p. T178 Make a Frog and Toad Book, p. T178
WIGGLEWORKS PLUS CD-ROM Presentation Tools, p. T161 **WIGGLEWORKS PLUS CD-ROM** Magnet Board, p. T164	**WIGGLEWORKS PLUS CD-ROM** Study Skills, p. T173	**WORD PROCESSING** Language Development, p. T177

Weekly Assessment

ASSESSMENT PLANNING

USE THIS CHART TO PLAN YOUR ASSESSMENT OF THE WEEKLY READING OBJECTIVES.

- **Informal Assessment is ongoing and should be used before, during and after reading.**
- **Formal Assessment occurs at the end of the week on the selection test.**
- **Note that intervention activities occur throughout the lesson to support children who need extra help with skills.**

YOU MAY CHOOSE AMONG THE FOLLOWING PAGES IN THE ASSESSMENT HANDBOOK:

- **Informal Assessment**
- **Anecdotal Record**
- **Portfolio Checklist and Evaluation Forms**
- **Self-Assessment**
- **English Language Learners**
- **Using Technology to Assess**
- **Test Preparations**

SKILLS AND STRATEGIES	Informal Assessment
COMPREHENSION Setting	OBSERVATION **p. T149** • Can children recognize the time and place? QUICKCHECK **p. T162** • Can children recognize time and place as components of setting? CHECK PRACTICE BOOK **p. 35** CONFERENCE **p. T174**
DAILY PHONICS Vowel /ō/*oa* Inflectional Ending *-ed* /d/, /t/	OBSERVATION **pp. T153, T155** • Did children identify the long *o* sound with the letters *oa*? • Did children identify words with the inflectional ending *-ed*? CHECK PRACTICE BOOK **pp. 32, 37** DICTATION **pp. T145, T165**
VOCABULARY Story Words **frog** **garden** **work** **plant** **flower** **seeds** High-Frequency **was** **grow**	OBSERVATION **p. T148** • Did children identify story words? • Did children identify high-frequency words? CHECK PRACTICE BOOK **p. 31**

Formal Assessment	**INTERVENTION** and Instructional Alternatives	Planning Notes
SELECTION TEST • Questions 1–3 check children's mastery of the key skill, setting. **UNIT TEST**	**If children need help with setting, then go to:** • **Instructional Alternatives, p. T163** • **Review, p. R45** • **Reteach, p. R56**	
DECODING TEST • See p. T175 **SELECTION TEST** • Questions 4–7 check children's ability to recognize vowel /ō/*oa* and inflectional ending *-ed*. **UNIT TEST**	**If students need help identifying words with vowel /ō/*oa*, then go to:** • **Intervention Activity, p. T167** **If students need help identifying words with inflectional ending *-ed*, then go to:** • **Review, p. R52** • **Reteach, p. R59**	
SELECTION TEST • Questions 8–10 check children's recall of story words and high-frequency words. **UNIT TEST**	**If children need additional practice with the vocabulary words, then go to:** • **Intervention Activity, p. T167** • **Extend Vocabulary, p. T170** • **Integrated Language Arts Activity, p. T177**	

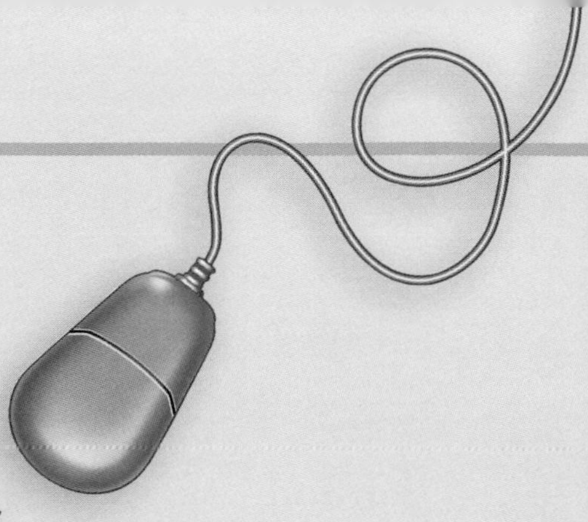

Technology

The technology in this lesson helps teachers and children develop the skills they need for the 21st century. Look for integrated technology activities on every day of instruction.

DAY 1 Expanding Vocabulary	• Children use **WiggleWorks Plus** PlaceMaker to draw a garden and label it using the story vocabulary.
DAY 2 Comprehension Skills	• Children create a table in **WiggleWorks Plus** Unit Writer and compare the needs of babies to the needs of gardens.
DAY 3 Presentation Tools	• Children create a headline banner using **WiggleWorks Plus** PlaceMaker.
DAY 4 Study Skills	• Children use the PlaceMaker poster format in **WiggleWorks Plus** and create a poster to show how plants germinate and grow.
DAY 5 Language Development	• Children use a word processor to write a rebus story about the senses.

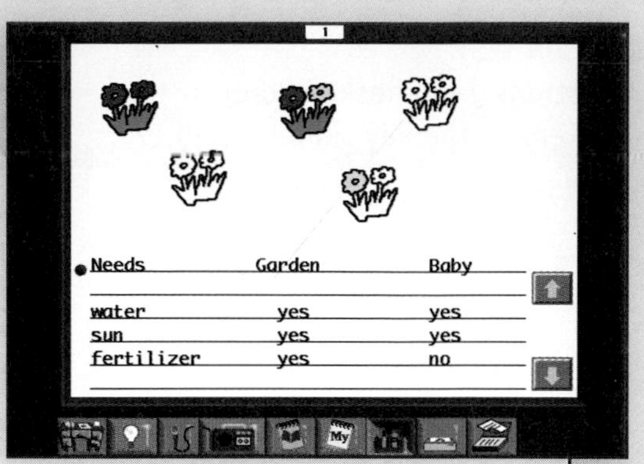

WiggleWorks Plus CD-ROM

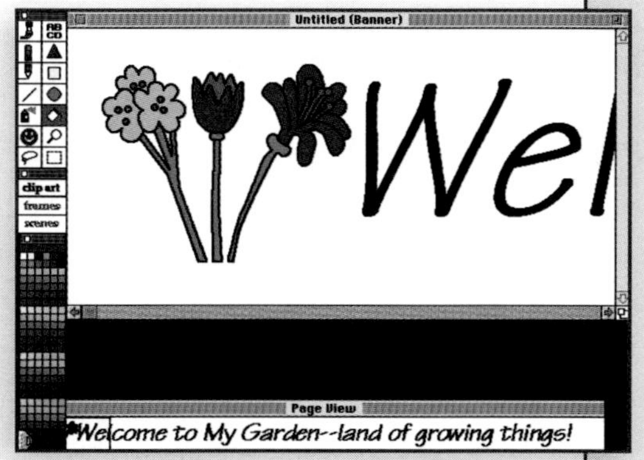

WiggleWorks Plus CD-ROM

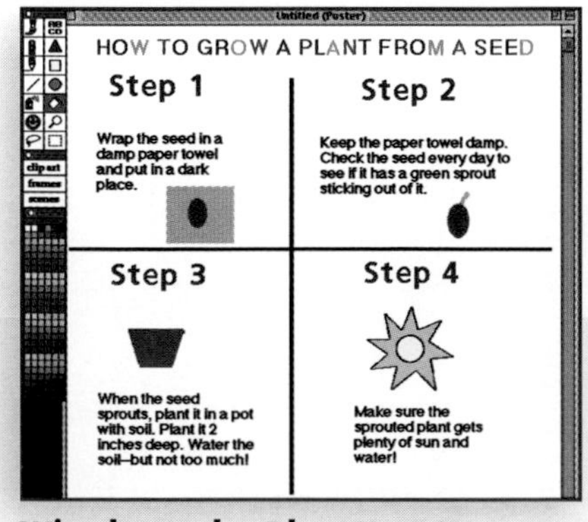

WiggleWorks Plus CD-ROM

Build Background

In I'm a Caterpillar, *children learned information about real-life creatures. Now as they read "The Garden," they will learn about planting seeds from two fantasy characters!*

Activate Prior Knowledge

DISCUSS FANTASY CHARACTERS Ask children if they have read or listened to stories about Frog and Toad. Point out that even though Frog and Toad are make-believe characters, they often learn about life as real people do.

DISCUSS GARDENS Explain to children that in this story, Frog gives Toad some seeds so that he can start his own garden. Ask children what they know about gardens.

> **What does a garden need to help it grow?**

> **What can you do to help a garden grow?**

SHARED WRITING *Poems*

INTRODUCE Suggest that a garden might be a good subject for a poem. Have children brainstorm titles for a poem and write them on chart paper.

DAY 1 OBJECTIVES

CHILDREN WILL:

READ 30 MINUTES

- **Build Background**
- **Vocabulary**
- **Daily Phonics: Vowel /ō/*oa***
- **"The Garden," pp. 70–75**
- **Key Comprehension Skill: Setting**

WRITE 30 MINUTES

- **Shared Writing: Introduce Writing a Poem**
- **Quickwrite: Predict**
- **Spelling: Words With Vowel /ō/*oa***
- **Grammar, Usage, Mechanics: Homophones**
- **Oral Language**

EXTEND SKILLS 30 MINUTES

- **Integrated Curriculum**
- **Read Aloud**
- **Guided Reading**

RESOURCES

- **Practice Book, pp. 31–33**
- **Spelling Resource Book, p. 119**

MODIFY Instruction

ESL/ELD

▲ Bring in seed packets and pictures of gardens to bolster understanding of the story's context. Talk with children about planting a garden. Help children brainstorm a list of plants and vegetables they would like to plant. Encourage them to share garden experiences. **(MAKE CONNECTIONS)**

VOCABULARY

HIGH-FREQUENCY

was grow

STORY WORDS

frog garden
work plant
flower seeds

TECHNOLOGY

Have children create a find-a-word puzzle using the Magnet Board.

- Give children the high-frequency and story words from this page, and then add them to the Magnet Board.
- They can fill in the remaining spaces with any letters.

VOCABULARY
High-Frequency Words

A TEACH/MODEL

INTRODUCE HIGH-FREQUENCY WORDS

Write the high-frequency words ***was*** and ***grow*** in sentences on the chalkboard. Read the sentences aloud, underline the high-frequency words, and ask children if they recognize them. You may wish to use the sentences shown.

Frog was Toad's friend.
Frog had seeds that would grow.

Ask volunteers to dictate sentences using the high-frequency words. Add these to the chalkboard.

B PRACTICE/APPLY

FOCUS ON SPELLING

Write each high-frequency word on a note card. Read each word aloud. Then do the following:

ROUTINE

1. **Display one card at a time, and ask children to state each word aloud.**
2. **Have children spell each word aloud.**
3. **Ask children to write each word in the air as they state aloud each letter. Then have them write each word on a sheet of paper or in their Journals.**

MAINTAIN VOCABULARY

Add the note cards to the **Word Wall**. Then review the following high-frequency words on the wall: ***next, all, more, belongs.***

MODIFY Instruction

ESL/ELD

▲ Help children create individual cards that contain a story word and a matching picture. Read aloud sentences: _____ and Toad are friends. *(Frog)* Toad wants the seeds to _____ *(grow)* quickly. Have children hold up the card with the correct word, and say the word aloud. **(CONTEXT CLUES)**

GIFTED & TALENTED

✷ Mix up the letters in the high-frequency words ***was*** and ***grow*** and write them on the chalkboard. Challenge children to unscramble each word and write it on paper. You may want to continue with other high-frequency words such as ***am, all, more,*** and ***belongs.*** **(USE VISUALS)**

Story Words

A TEACH/MODEL

INTRODUCE STORY WORDS

The story also contains the following story words—***frog, garden, work, plant, flower, seeds.***

- Write these words on the chalkboard, read them aloud, and discuss their meanings if necessary.
- Point out previously taught sound-spelling correspondences such as ***l***-blends, ***r***-blends, and **long *e* (ea, ee).**
- Have children mimic your actions as you act out working in a garden and planting flower seeds. Then have them hop like a frog.

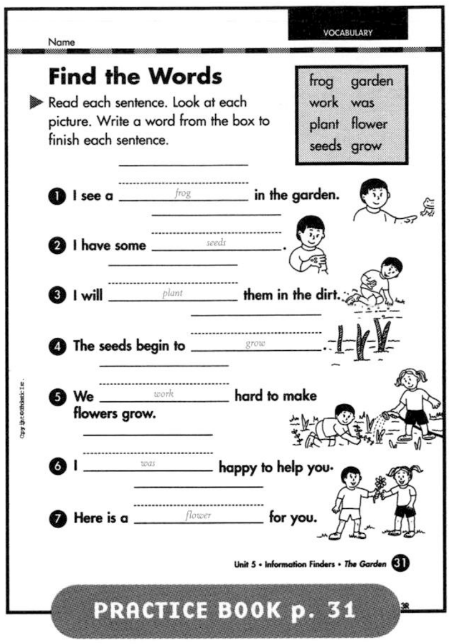

Name VOCABULARY

Find the Words

▶ Read each sentence. Look at each picture. Write a word from the box to finish each sentence.

frog	garden
work	was
plant	flower
seeds	grow

1. I see a frog in the garden.
2. I have some seeds.
3. I will plant them in the dirt.
4. The seeds begin to grow.
5. We work hard to make flowers grow.
6. I was happy to help you.
7. Here is a flower for you.

Unit 5 • Information Finders • The Garden 31

PRACTICE BOOK p. 31

B PRACTICE/APPLY

BUILD STORY BACKGROUND

Discuss gardens with children.

- Have children describe things that might grow in a garden.
- Have children close their eyes and imagine a garden. Ask them to picture the colors and pretend they can smell the plants and flowers that grow there.
- Have children draw a picture of the garden they imagined.

WRITE TO READ

- When completed, have children write a sentence about their picture using one or more of the story words.

LEAPFROG

Have pairs of children play leapfrog while they spell out story words. To begin, have two children crouch down as frogs. Tell them that they will jump over each other while spelling a story word such as ***frog***. Have each child say a letter of the spelling while jumping over his or her partner. Then have children spell the word together. Continue with other story words.

JOURNAL

Ask children to write a sentence using each **high-frequency word** in their Journals. You might suggest the following sentence starters:

The frog was _____.

I can grow _____.

SELECTION WORD With /ō/oa

Toad

SKILLS TRACE

VOWEL /ō/oa TESTED

Introduce	pp. T144–T145
Practice	pp. T155, T167
Reteach	p. R59

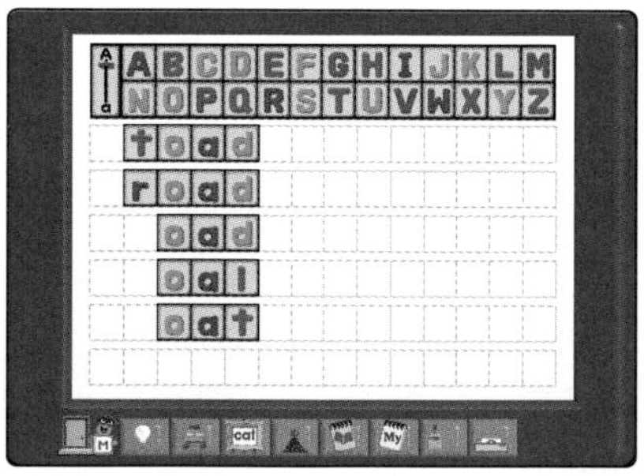

TECHNOLOGY

Have children build words with long *o (oa)* on the Magnet Board.

- Begin with the word **boat** or write rows of phonograms ***(oad, oal, oat)*** to which children will add initial consonants.

DAILY PHONICS

Vowel /ō/ oa

A PHONOLOGICAL AWARENESS

RHYME Read aloud the poem "Miss Lucy" from the *Big Book of Rhymes and Rhythms 1B*, pages 22–23. As you read, stress the long ***o*** sound in the words ***soap*** and ***throat***.

- When children are familiar with the rhyme, have them read along with you.
- Isolate the words ***soap*** and ***throat*** and have children repeat them.

Miss Lucy
Miss Lucy had a baby.
She named him Tiny Tim.
She put him in the bathtub
To see if he could swim.
He drank up all the water.
He ate up all the soap.
He tried to eat the bathtub,
But it wouldn't go down his throat.
soap

Big Book of Rhymes and Rhythms 1B, pp. 22–23.

ORAL BLENDING Say the following word parts, and have children blend them. Provide corrective feedback and modeling as needed.

- **/t/ . . . oad**
- **/r/ . . . oad**
- **/g/ . . . oal**
- **/k/ . . . oal**
- **/g/ . . . oat**
- **/b/ . . . oat**

B CONNECT SOUND-SPELLING

INTRODUCE VOWEL /ō/oa Explain to children that the letters ***oa*** can stand for the long ***o*** sound as in ***boat.*** Write the word ***boat*** on the chalkboard and have a volunteer circle the letters ***oa.***

THINK ALOUD *I can put the letters* ***b, oa,*** *and* ***t*** *together to make the word* ***boat.*** *Let's say the sounds slowly as I move my finger under the letters. Listen to the sound that* ***oa*** *stands for in the word* ***boat.*** *The sound of* ***oa*** *is* **/ō/.**

MODIFY Instruction

ESL/ELD

▲ Have children work in pairs to make an *oa* word collage. Brainstorm *oa* words, such as *toad,* and make sure they know their meanings before having them look for pictures. Have them label each picture, writing the *oa* part of the word in color. Display children's work. **(COLOR CODE)**

EXTRA HELP

■ Before children build words, give them cards on which you have written the initial consonants *r, c, t, g* and the phonograms *oad, oal, oat.* Have children put the initial consonant cards together with the phonogram cards to make words with long *o (oa).* Ask children to read each word they made. **(STEP-BY-STEP)**

- Ask children to suggest other words that have the long ***o*** sound spelled ***oa***. You might begin by having children suggest words that rhyme with ***toad***.

toad	coal	goat
load	goal	coat
road	foal	boat

- List the words on chart paper as they are given. Have volunteers circle the letters ***oa*** or the common phonogram in each word.

PHONICS MAINTENANCE Review the following sound-spellings: /ō/***oa;*** /ô/ ***all, aw;*** /ā/ ***ay, ai.*** Say one of these sounds. Have a volunteer write on the chalkboard the spelling or spellings that stand for the sound. Continue with all the sounds.

Name

PHONICS: Vowel /ō/ oa

Rhymes With Boat

▶ Write two oa words that rhyme with the word inside each boat.

oat — boat, coat

load — toad, road

▶ Finish the following oa words. Write a sentence for one of the words you made.

___ oap ___ oak

Answers will vary.

32 Unit 5 • Information Finders • The Garden

PRACTICE BOOK p. 32

C PRACTICE/APPLY

BLEND WORDS To practice using the sound-spelling and review previous sound-spellings, list the words and sentences on the chalkboard. Have children read each chorally. Model blending as needed.

foam	soak	loaf
loan	train	straw

Toad has a thick coat.

The coat is in the boat.

DICTATION Dictate the following words for children to spell: ***float, crawl, hay.***

BUILD WORDS Distribute the following letter cards, or have children use their own sets: ***oa, c, f, g, l, t.*** Allow children time to build words using the letter cards. Children can write their words on paper. **(INDEPENDENT WORK)**

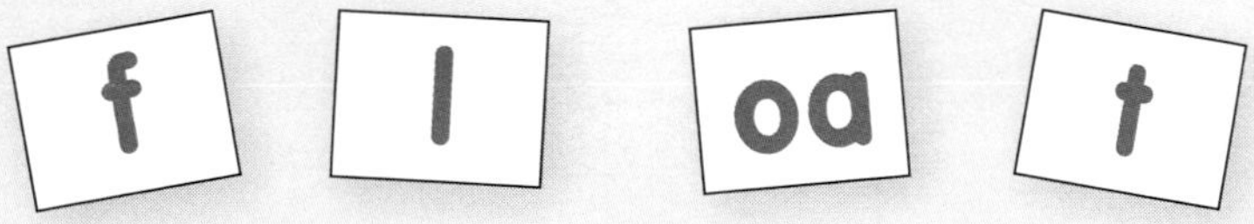

Name

PHONICS: Vowel /ō/ oa

Yes or No?

▶ Read each sentence. If the sentence tells about the picture, write yes on the line. If it does not tell about the picture, write no on the line.

1. The toad hops on the road. — yes
2. The goat eats oatmeal and toast. — no
3. The boat floats in the lake. — yes
4. The coat is as black as coal. — yes

Unit 5 • Information Finders • The Garden 33

PRACTICE BOOK p. 33

DECODABLE TEXT

For practice reading decodable text, see ***Scholastic Decodable Reader #61.***

For additional phonics instruction and review, see ***Scholastic Phonics A, pp. 235–236.***

BOAT SHOW

Have children make boats out of shoeboxes and collage materials. Ask them to fill their boats with pictures and small items whose names have the long o sound spelled ***oa***. You may wish to have a "boat" show where children display their boats and recite the names of the pictures and items that have the long ***o (oa)*** sound.

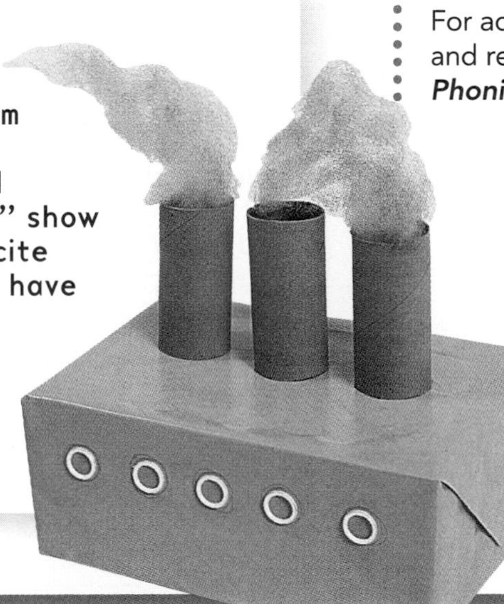

COMPREHENSION

Preview and Predict

Remind children that "The Garden" is a story that comes from the book *Frog and Toad Together*. Have children preview the first few pages of the story.

- **What does the title tell you about the story?**
- **Will Frog and Toad act like a real frog and toad in this story? Why do you think so?**

Help children make predictions before they read by asking a question:

- **What do you think Frog and Toad will do in this story?**

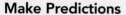

JOURNAL

Make Predictions

Ask children to write their predictions in their Journals. Encourage children to write about what both characters might do together as well as what each character might do separately.

Set a Purpose

Ask children to think about a purpose for reading. They may want to read to find out why Frog and Toad are good friends. Then have children read page 71 of the story.

70

FANTASY

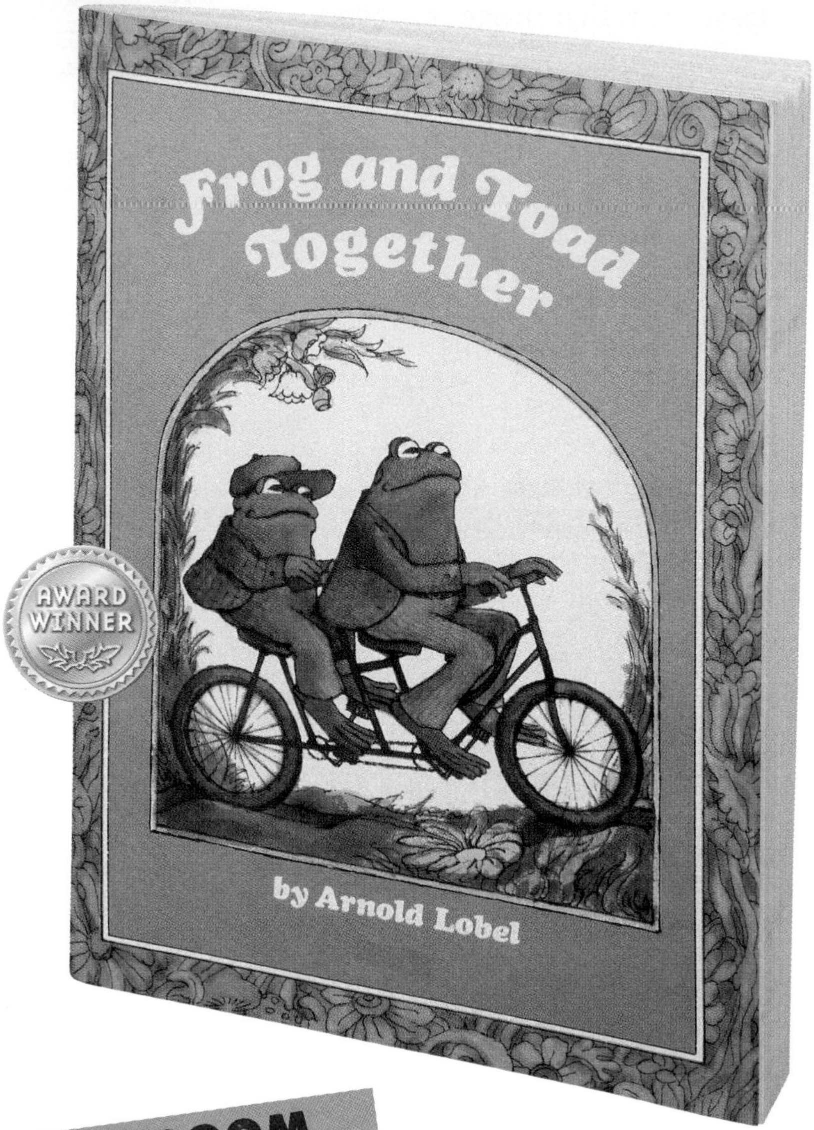

70

CLASSROOM Management

WHOLE CLASS

On-Level Use the questions, think alouds, and the skills and strategies lessons to guide children through a reading of the story.

Below-Level Help children prepare for reading the story by looking through the illustrations with them while discussing the pictures.

COOPERATIVE

Above-Level Children can work in groups of three to read aloud the story. One child can be narrator while the others can read aloud the parts of Frog and Toad. Have children tape-record their reading for the rest of the class.

71

The Garden

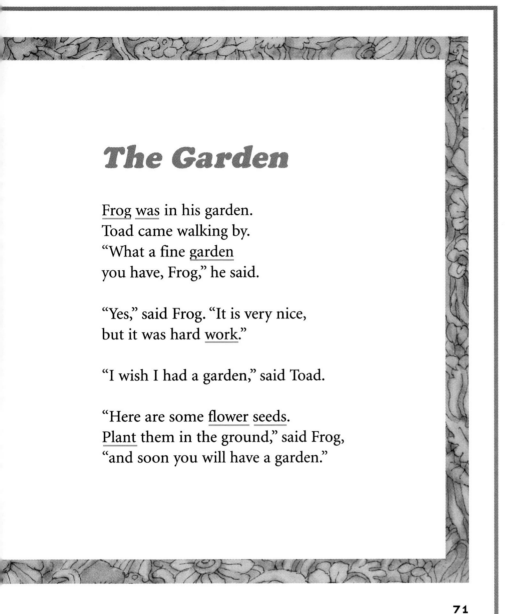

Frog was in his garden.
Toad came walking by.
"What a fine garden
you have, Frog," he said.

"Yes," said Frog. "It is very nice,
but it was hard work."

"I wish I had a garden," said Toad.

"Here are some flower seeds.
Plant them in the ground," said Frog,
"and soon you will have a garden."

71

SKILLS AND STRATEGIES

Revisit the selection for skills instruction.

✓ = Tested Skill

COMPREHENSION
Setting T149

DAILY PHONICS
✓ **Inflectional Ending *-ed* (/t/, /d/)** T153
✓ **Vowel /ō/ *oa*** T155

GENRE
✓ **Poem and Rhyme** T159

SMALL GROUP TO WHOLE CLASS

ESL/ELD Have children who need extra help or who are acquiring English listen to the story on the audiocassette prior to the class reading. This will help them to become familiar with the story sequence and vocabulary. Have children do the pre- and post-listening activities. **(AUDIO CLUES)**

COMPREHENSION

1 SETTING

> **Let's think about where and when this part of the story takes place. Where is Toad? What time of year is it? Why do you think so?** *(Possible answers: Toad is home, in his own garden. It is summer or late spring. I think so because the text tells me Toad went home. I also see plants already growing.)*

2 MAKE INFERENCES

> **When the seeds do not start growing right away, Toad talks loudly to them, telling them to grow. What does this tell you about Toad?** *(Possible answer: Toad thinks the seeds need to be told to grow; Toad does not understand how seeds grow.)*

3 COMPARE/CONTRAST

> **How is Toad's garden different from Frog's?** *(Toad's garden is bare. There are no flowers growing yet.)*

INFORMAL ASSESSMENT
OBSERVATION

VOCABULARY Assess children's recognition and understanding of the vocabulary words *was* and *grow*. Did children:

- ✔ recognize the high-frequency words *was* and *grow*?
- ✔ use picture and context clues to figure out the words?
- ✔ pronounce the words correctly?

72

"How soon?" asked Toad.

"Quite soon," said Frog.

72

MODIFY Instruction

ESL/ELD

▲ Talk with children about Toad's garden: *Are the seeds growing? Is Toad happy or sad?* Make sure children realize that Toad is talking to the seeds. Ask: *What is Toad saying? Who is Toad talking to?* Guide children to see that Toad wants his garden to grow quickly. **(GUIDED QUESTIONS)**

GIFTED & TALENTED

✷ Have children take turns acting out the role of Toad as he plants his seeds, paces up and down, and speaks to the seeds. Remind children to consider how Toad says loudly, "Now seeds, start growing!" **(ROLE-PLAY)**

73

1

Toad ran home.
He planted the flower seeds.
"Now seeds," said Toad,
"start growing."
Toad walked up and down
a few times.
The seeds did not start to grow.

3

Toad put his head
close to the ground
and said loudly,
"Now seeds, start growing!" 2
Toad looked at the ground again.
The seeds did not start to grow.

73

TECHNOLOGY

Expanding Vocabulary Guide children in the use of **WiggleWorks Plus** PlaceMaker to draw a garden scene that contains the story words. They can use clip art and the drawing tools and then type the story words next to their pictures.

CONNECT TO THEME

Have children suggest gardening questions for which Toad might need answers. Then have them brainstorm a list of sources from which Toad might find answers. Examples might include: books, magazines, television shows, garden centers.

SKILLS AND STRATEGIES

COMPREHENSION

Setting

TEACH/MODEL

Explain to children that setting is where and when a story takes place. Point out that it is important to read the story and look at the pictures in order to determine the setting. Talk about how the setting can change within a story.

THINK ALOUD *When I read, it helps me to think about where the story takes place. As I look at Toad, I see he is in a bare garden. The first sentence tells me that he is home now. I see some plants growing, so it must be summer or late spring because that's when plants grow.*

PRACTICE/APPLY

Have children talk about the setting and how it has changed.

> **Where and when did the story begin?**

> **Where is Toad on pages 72 and 73? How do you know?**

> **How has the setting changed from page 71 to pages 72–73?**

INFORMAL ASSESSMENT

OBSERVATION

As children read, can they:

✔ recognize the time and place?

✔ distinguish when the setting changes?

See pages T162–T163 for a full skills lesson on setting.

COMPREHENSION

4 FANTASY/REALITY

> **How are Frog and Toad different from real frogs? What does this tell you about the story?** *(Possible answers: Frog and Toad wear clothes and speak. They act like people. Because Frog and Toad are make-believe, the story is a fantasy.)*

5 CRITICAL THINKING: ANALYZE

> **What facts about seeds does Frog have wrong? What facts are correct?** *(Possible answers: Seeds do not become afraid to grow. Seeds do need sunshine and rain to help them grow.)*

INTERVENTION TIP

Using Type for Emphasis

Point out the words *NOW SEEDS, START GROWING!* on page 74. Guide children to recognize that the words are set in all capital letters. Explain that the capital letters tell readers that Toad is saying the words in a very loud voice. Point out the exclamation mark at the end of the sentence. Explain that the exclamation mark tells readers that Toad is saying the words in an excited way. Have children say the words with expression as Toad might say them.

74

Toad put his head
very close to the ground and shouted,
"NOW SEEDS, START GROWING!"

Frog came running up the path.
"What is all this noise?" he asked.

"My seeds will not grow," said Toad.

"You are shouting too much,"
said Frog. "These poor seeds
are afraid to grow."

"My seeds are afraid to grow?"
asked Toad.

74

MODIFY Instruction

ESL/ELD

▲ Ask children to look back through the story so far. Ask: *Is this story real or make-believe? How do you know?* Ask volunteers to show or tell one thing on each page that could happen in real life and one which is make-believe. Ask: *Do you think the seeds are afraid to grow?* **(PICTURE CLUES)**

EXTRA HELP

■ Give children extra help in reading dialogue. Point out examples of dialogue in the paragraphs on page 74. Help children recognize that the words that are said aloud by the characters are set off by quotation marks. Ask volunteers to point to the words in each paragraph spoken by characters. **(DIALOGUE)**

75

"Of course," said Frog.
"Leave them alone for a few days.
Let the sun shine on them,
5 let the rain fall on them.
Soon your seeds will start to grow."

75

SCIENCE

Have children complete the **Frogs and Toads** activity on **page R24.** Children will use a variety of resources to chart the differences between frogs and toads. Children can work with a partner to collect data.

CULTURAL CONNECTION

Many of our favorite flowers come from different countries. Marigolds come from Mexico. Geraniums are natives of South Africa. Tulips, which are thought to be Dutch flowers, originally came from central Asia. Invite children to draw their own favorite flower.

Quickwrite

PREDICT

Ask children to write about the ways in which Frog and Toad are friends. Children may also refine the predictions they made before reading and predict what will happen next.

DAILY LANGUAGE PRACTICE

SPELLING

DAY 1:
Administer the Pretest for Words With Vowel /ō/*oa*.
See page R20.

GRAMMAR, USAGE, MECHANICS

DAY 1:
Teach and Model Homophones.
See page R22.

ORAL LANGUAGE

He planted a lode of seeds in the son.
(He planted a load of seeds in the sun.)

DAY 1 WRAP-UP

READ ALOUD *To develop children's oral vocabularies, spend five to ten minutes reading from a selection of your choice.*

GUIDED READING *To extend reading, meet with the **red** and **blue** reading groups and assign Independent Center activities. **See pages R18–R19.***

COMPREHENSION

DAY 2 OBJECTIVES

CHILDREN WILL:

READ 30 MINUTES

- ***The Garden***, pp. 76–81
- **Daily Phonics: Inflectional Ending *-ed* /t/, /d/**
- **Vowel /ō/*oa***

WRITE 40 MINUTES

- **Shared Writing: Prewrite**
- **Spelling: Words With Vowel /ō/*oa***
- **Grammar, Usage, Mechanics: Homophones**
- **Oral Language**

EXTEND SKILLS 20 MINUTES

- **Integrated Curriculum**
- **Read Aloud**
- **Guided Reading**

RESOURCES

- **Spelling Resource Book, pp. 120–122**

Reread

You may wish to have children independently reread the first part of the story before beginning Day 2 reading.

6 SUMMARIZE

> **What has happened so far in "The Garden"?** *(Frog has given Toad seeds and he has planted them. Toad talks loudly to the seeds, but they do not grow. Frog tells him that the seeds are afraid and that Toad should leave them alone.)*

76

6

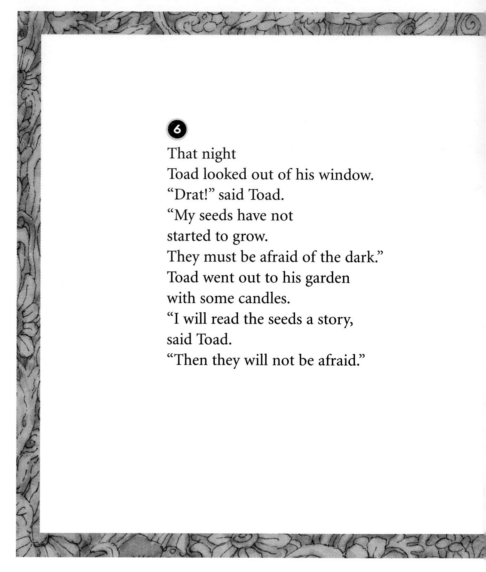

That night
Toad looked out of his window.
"Drat!" said Toad.
"My seeds have not
started to grow.
They must be afraid of the dark."
Toad went out to his garden
with some candles.
"I will read the seeds a story,
said Toad.
"Then they will not be afraid."

76

MODIFY Instruction

ESL/ELD

▲ Help English language learners summarize the story by teaching ordinal numbers: *first, second, third, fourth,* and so on. Ask them to list what happened in sequence. (For example: *First, frog gave Toad seeds. Second, Toad planted the seeds.*) **(SEQUENCE)**

GIFTED & TALENTED

✳ Challenge children to name homophones for words on pages 76 and 77. Point out the words *night, not, some,* and *read*. Have children give the definitions of words that sound like these words but have different spellings. (*knight, knot, sum, red*) **(HOMOPHONES)**

77

Toad read a long story
to his seeds.

77

WORD STUDY

High-Frequency Word Point out the word *grow* and ask children to say it with you. Write *grow* on the board and discuss the sound they hear at the end. Have children name some things that can grow. Write each suggestion in front of *grow* and have children read the sentence, for example: *Children grow.*

TECHNOLOGY

Comprehension Skills Have children create a three-column table in **WiggleWorks Plus** Unit Writer with the headings Needs, Garden, and Baby. Help them brainstorm a list of needs for the first column, and let them decide which needs apply to gardens, babies, or both.

DAILY PHONICS

Inflectional Ending *-ed* /d/, /t/

CONNECT SOUND-SPELLING

TEACH/MODEL Explain to children that when ***-ed*** is added to words, it changes the sound and meaning of the words. The ending can stand for either the **/d/** or **/t/** sound. Invite children to find words with ***-ed*** on page 76.

PHONICS MAINTENANCE Review the following sound-spellings: ***-ed* /d/, /t/; /ō/ *oa*;** digraphs ***sh, th.***

PRACTICE/APPLY

BLEND WORDS Point out ***started*** on page 76. Write ***start*** on the chalkboard. Have children say the word.

- Add the ending ***-ed*** and have children say it again. Ask if the ending ***-ed*** stands for **/d/** or **/t/.**
- As children continue to read, have them find other words that end with ***-ed.*** Ask them whether each of these words ends with **/d/** or **/t/.**

INFORMAL ASSESSMENT
OBSERVATION

As children read, can they:

✔ identify words with the inflectional ending ***-ed***?

✔ differentiate between **/d/** and **/t/** in the inflectional ending ***-ed***?

See pages T164–T165 for a full skills lesson on Inflectional Ending ***-ed* /d/, /t/.**

COMPREHENSION

7 SETTING

> **How was the setting different on the day that Toad sang to the seeds?** *(It rained in the garden that day.)*

8 SEQUENCE

> **Toad does a lot of things to help his seeds on page 78. What does he do first, next, and last?** *(First he sings to the seeds. Next he reads poems to them. Last of all he plays music for them.)*

9 MAKE PREDICTIONS

> **What do you think Toad will find when he wakes up? Why do you think this?** *(Possible answer: His seeds have grown. Enough time has passed for them to grow.)*

78

All the next day
Toad sang songs
to his seeds.

7

And all the next day
Toad read poems
to his seeds.

And all the next day
Toad played music
for his seeds.

8

78

MODIFY Instruction

ESL/ELD

▲ Point out that there are four pictures on these pages showing what Toad did during the next 3 days. Have children act out each action as volunteers guess which one they are acting: singing, reading, playing music, sleeping. Ask: *Why do you think Toad is doing all of these things?* **(ACT IT OUT)**

EXTRA HELP

■ Help children recognize sequence of events. Have them point to the pictures on pages 77–78 in turn as they say the words *first, next, then, last*. Then have them read the text that appears next to each picture. Point out that the text and pictures show the order of what Toad is doing. **(STEP-BY-STEP)**

79

Toad looked at the ground.
The seeds still did not
start to grow.
"What shall I do?" cried Toad.
"These must be
the most frightened seeds
in the whole world!"

Then Toad felt very tired,
and he fell asleep. 9

79

THE ARTS

Have children complete the **Music for Seeds** activity on **page R25**. Children will work in groups to brainstorm a song for Toad's seeds. They will then perform the song for the class.

WORD ATTACK

Discuss with children how they figured out the word *frightened.* Ask what small words they can find inside the word *frightened.* (Possible answers: *right, ten, fright)* Then help children conclude that they can sometimes figure out a long word by looking for small words they can read and putting them together.

DAILY PHONICS

Vowel /ō/*oa*

CONNECT SOUND-SPELLING

TEACH/MODEL Review with children that the letters ***oa*** can stand for the long ***o*** sound in ***Toad.***

PHONICS MAINTENANCE Review the following sound-spellings: **/ō/ *oa***; digraphs ***sh, th***; **/ô/ *all, aw***; **/ā/ *ai, ay.***

PRACTICE/APPLY

BLEND WORDS Have children practice making other words with long ***o (oa).***

- Write the phonograms ***oak, oal, oam, oan*** on the chalkboard.
- Have children take turns adding initial consonants to the phonograms. Children can write the new words on the chalkboard, then read them aloud.

INFORMAL ASSESSMENT

OBSERVATION

As children read, note if they can:

✔ identify the long ***o*** sound with the letters ***oa.***

✔ recognize and reproduce the long vowel sound represented by ***oa.***

COMPREHENSION

10 CRITICAL THINKING: EVALUATE

> **Do you think Frog is a good friend to Toad? What events from the story show your answer is true?** *(Possible answer: Frog gave Toad seeds. Frog helped Toad understand how gardens grow. Frog made sure Toad saw his new seeds as soon as possible.)*

11 DRAW CONCLUSIONS

> **Why does Toad think that gardening is hard work?** *(Possible answer: He thinks he has to read, sing, and play music in order for seeds to grow.)*

12 MAKE INFERENCES

> **How do you think Toad feels when he finds that the seeds have finally grown?** *(Possible answer: He is happy that he no longer has to worry about the seeds growing.)*

JOURNAL

Revisit Predictions

Ask children to look back at their predictions and record how they were or were not confirmed by the story.

80

"Toad, Toad, wake up," said Frog.
"Look at your garden!"
Toad looked at his garden.
Little green plants were coming up out of the ground.

80

MODIFY Instruction

ESL/ELD

▲ Discuss with children what Toad thinks about gardening. Ask: *What did Toad do to make the seeds grow?* List children's answers. Then ask: *What **really** made the seeds grow?* Write children's answers on the board. Ask: *Is Toad right or wrong?* (both) **(GUIDED QUESTIONS)**

EXTRA HELP

■ Some children may not have direct experience with watching seeds grow. Help them understand the cycle by showing pictures of new seeds, sprouting seeds, seedlings, and full-grown plants from an encyclopedia or gardening book. Explain that different seeds have different sprouting times. **(USE VISUALS)**

81

"At last," shouted Toad,
"my seeds have stopped
being afraid to grow!"

"And now you will have
a nice garden too," said Frog.

"Yes," said Toad,
"but you were right, Frog.
It was very hard work." 12

81

Poem
SHARED WRITING

PREWRITE Explain that children will write a poem about a garden based on their experiences with this story as well as the poem that follows. Then have children complete the prewriting organizer on **Practice Book page 39.**

DAILY LANGUAGE PRACTICE

SPELLING
DAY 2:
Practice Words With Vowel /ō/*oa*. See page R20.

GRAMMAR, USAGE, MECHANICS
DAY 2:
Practice Homophones.
See page R22.

ORAL LANGUAGE
Tode red to his plants.
(Toad read to his plants.)

DAY 2 WRAP-UP

READ ALOUD *To develop children's oral vocabularies, spend five to ten minutes reading from a selection of your choice.*

GUIDED READING *To extend reading, meet with the* ***green*** *and* ***yellow*** *reading groups and assign Independent Center activities.* ***See pages R18–R19.***

MATH
Have children complete the **Days of Toad's Life** activity on **page R24** in which they will work independently to create a time line for Toad's seeds.

WORKSHOP
You may wish to introduce the Workshop on this day. Set aside specific times over the next two weeks for children to work on this ongoing activity.

COMPREHENSION

DAY 3 OBJECTIVES

CHILDREN WILL:

READ 30 MINUTES

- **"Tommy," pp. 82–83**
- **Assess Comprehension**
- **Key Comprehension Skill: Setting**
- **Genre: Poem and Rhyme**
- **Daily Phonics: Inflectional Ending *-ed* /t/, /d/ Long /ō/*oa***

WRITE 30 MINUTES

- **Respond: Write a Headline**
- **Spelling: Words With Vowel /ō/*oa***
- **Grammar, Usage, Mechanics: Homophones**
- **Oral Language**

EXTEND SKILLS 30 MINUTES

- **Integrated Curriculum**
- **Read Aloud**
- **Guided Reading**

RESOURCES

- **Practice Book, pp. 34–38**
- **Spelling Resource Book, p. 123**

Preview

Invite children to preview the poem by reading the title and studying the picture. Then read the poem with children.

1 SETTING

> **What is the setting for this poem?** *(The poem is set in a backyard garden in spring or summer.)*

2 SUMMARIZE

> **What does this poem tell you about the way seeds grow?** *(Seeds need water and care.)*

82

MODIFY Instruction

ESL/ELD

▲ Help children summarize the basic content of the poem. Ask: *What happens first? Then what happens? What happens at the end?* Then encourage children to act out the poem, putting lots of energy into the "popping out" at the end. **(ACT IT OUT)**

EXTRA HELP

■ Help children identify rhythm and rhyme in the poem. Read aloud the poem once, emphasizing the rhyming words. Then have children join in with you, clapping out the rhythm of the poem as they read it aloud. **(READ ALOUD)**

83

Tommy

by Gwendolyn Brooks

I put a seed into the ground.
And said, "I'll watch it grow."
I watered it and cared for it
As well as I could know.

One day I walked in my back yard,
And oh, what did I see!
My seed had popped itself right out,
Without consulting me. ❷

83

SKILLS AND STRATEGIES

GENRE

Poem and Rhyme

TEACH/MODEL

Explain to children that poems often include words that rhyme. The rhyming words usually are found at the end of lines in the poem.

THINK ALOUD *As I read the first four lines of "Tommy," I listen for words that rhyme. As I listen, I notice that the word* ***grow*** *rhymes with the word* ***know.*** *Then I look for other rhyming words as I continue to read the poem.*

PRACTICE/APPLY

- Reread the last four lines of the poem with children. Have them identify the words that rhyme.
- Write the word pairs ***grow/know*** and ***see/me*** on the chalkboard.
- Have children name other words that rhyme with ***grow, know*** and ***see, me.***

SOCIAL STUDIES

Have children complete the **Gardens in Our Town** activity on **page R25.** Children can work as a class to describe local gardens. They will plan and execute a mural that shows a garden they would like to have.

FAMILY LITERACY

Family members who have access to the Internet may wish to log on to **www.scholastic.com** and choose "At Home." Here adult family members will find monthly fun activities for their child as well as help in choosing books and web sites for children.

COMPREHENSION

Think About Reading

Below are the **answers** to the *Think About Reading* questions.

1. *Toad wishes he had a nice garden of his own.*
2. *He wants them to grow quickly.*
3. *Possible response: He feels impatient for them to grow.*
4. *Possible response: The seeds would probably have come up at the same time.*
5. *Possible response: Both Toad and Tommy plant seeds. Both have to wait for the seeds to grow.*

Name

COMPREHENSION CHECK

Toad in His Garden

Draw a picture of Toad enjoying his garden. Then write what Toad might say about his garden.

Answers will vary.

34 Unit 5 • Information Finders • The Garden

PRACTICE BOOK p. 34

84

RESPOND

Think About Reading

1. What does Toad wish?
2. Why does Toad shout at his seeds?
3. How do you think Toad feels while he waits for his seeds to grow?
4. What if Toad had not read and made music for his seeds? What do you think would have happened?
5. How are Toad and Tommy alike?

84

MODIFY Instruction

ESL/ELD

▲ Have English language learners work in small groups. Discuss each question with the group. Have them come up with one group answer for each question. Encourage children to talk about each question before they decide on their group answer. **(WORK IN GROUPS)**

EXTRA HELP

■ Show children examples of headlines from local newspapers. Point out the way in which the headlines tell as much information as possible in as few words as possible. You may wish to have children work in small groups to brainstorm possible headlines. **(MAKE CONNECTIONS)**

85

rite a Headline

d thinks his garden is big
s! He wants to write a story
the newspaper about how
tart a nice garden. Write a
dline for Toad's news story.
r headline should be short
say something about the
s story.

terature Circle

you think "The Garden" was
ny? Which parts of the story
you find funny? How did
d's attitude toward the plants
ce the story funnier?

Author Arnold Lobel

Arnold Lobel believed artists and writers should use their own lives in their work. Lobel even used a picture of himself in one of his books. Don't look for a drawing of a man, though. Lobel drew himself as a pig—a pig with glasses and a mustache, working hard to draw a good picture.

More Books by Arnold Lobel

- Days With Frog and Toad
- Grasshopper on the Road
- Owl at Home

85

TECHNOLOGY

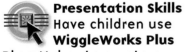

Presentation Skills Have children use **WiggleWorks Plus** PlaceMaker to create a banner for the newspaper headline for Toad. Explain to children that headlines are brief, creative, and catchy. Brainstorm a few ideas and discuss what type of clip art might be used to illustrate the idea.

VISUAL LITERACY

Have children look back at the story to find visual clues to Frog and Toad's friendship. Help them notice details such as Frog and Toad talking over the garden fence on page 72, Frog's arm around Toad's shoulder on page 75, and Frog's concern on page 80.

RESPOND

Write a Headline

Before children begin to write, have them think about these questions:

> **What is the most important thing that happens in Toad's garden?**

> **How can you describe that event in only a few words?**

> **How can you make those few words exciting and eye-catching for readers?**

Literature Circle

Encourage children to participate in a conversation about their personal responses to the story.

DAILY LANGUAGE PRACTICE

SPELLING

DAY 3:
Write Words With Vowel /ō/*oa*. See p. R21.

GRAMMAR, USAGE, MECHANICS

DAY 3:
Practice homophones. See p. R23.

ORAL LANGUAGE

The be wants to bee in Tode's garden.
(The bee wants to be in Toad's garden.)

COMPREHENSION
Setting

SKILLS TRACE

SETTING TESTED

Introduce	pp. T162–T163
Practice	p. T149
Review	p. R45
Reteach	p. R56

CONNECT TO TRADE BOOKS

Select one of the unit trade books. Read aloud the title, and discuss the cover illustration.

- Have children make predictions about what might happen in the story.
- Read a few pages at a time and pause to discuss the setting and any changes that occur in setting.
- Record children's observations about setting. Continue until the book is completed.

QUICKCHECK

Can children:

✔ recognize time and place as components of setting?

✔ realize that the setting may change during the course of a story?

If YES, go on to Practice/Apply.

If NO, start at Teach/Model.

A TEACH/MODEL

USE ORAL LANGUAGE

Encourage children to name a favorite story and talk about its setting, or when and where the story takes place. You may wish to prompt discussion by asking children to give as many details as they can about when and where the story takes place.

Explain to children that setting is **the place and time in which a story takes place.** Point out that knowing the story setting will help children better understand what is happening in the story. To identify setting, children should:

1. Use text and picture clues to decide where the story takes place.
2. Use text and picture clues to decide when the story takes place.
3. Remember that the setting can change during the story.

MODIFY Instruction

ESL/ELD

▲ To help children focus on the setting, brainstorm a list of words that can describe when and where the story takes place. List the words in columns. For example:

WHEN	WHERE
daytime	garden
night time	yard
spring	outdoors

(CATEGORIZE)

GIFTED & TALENTED

✳ As a follow-up activity, encourage children to draw a setting they especially like or know well. Then have them think of a story to go with the setting and share it with the class. **(USE VISUALS)**

LITERATURE CONNECTION

THINK ALOUD *I know from the pictures and words in "The Garden" that the story begins in Frog's garden. Then the story moves to Toad's garden. The pictures and words also tell me about the time of the year. There are a lot of plants growing and a lot of gardening being done. That tells me that the time of the year is summer or late spring. In some places in the story, I can also tell whether it is daytime or nighttime and whether the day is sunny or rainy.*

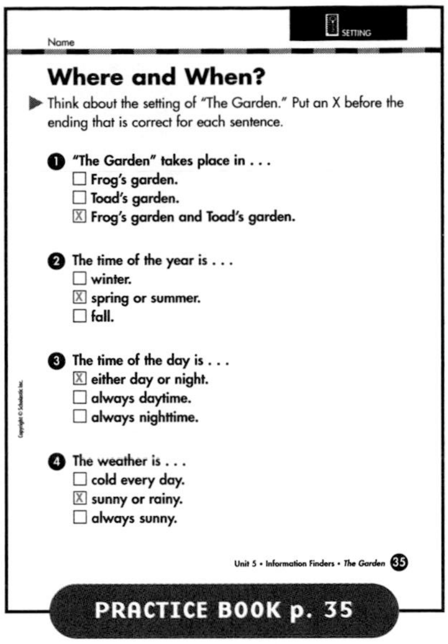
Name
SETTING

Where and When?

▶ Think about the setting of "The Garden." Put an X before the ending that is correct for each sentence.

1. "The Garden" takes place in . . .
   - ☐ Frog's garden.
   - ☐ Toad's garden.
   - ☒ Frog's garden and Toad's garden.
2. The time of the year is . . .
   - ☐ winter.
   - ☒ spring or summer.
   - ☐ fall.
3. The time of the day is . . .
   - ☒ either day or night.
   - ☐ always daytime.
   - ☐ always nighttime.
4. The weather is . . .
   - ☐ cold every day.
   - ☒ sunny or rainy.
   - ☐ always sunny.

Unit 5 • Information Finders • *The Garden* 35

PRACTICE BOOK p. 35

B PRACTICE/APPLY

USE PRACTICE BOOK

Have children practice what they learned about setting by completing **Practice Book page 35.** (individuals)

C ASSESS

APPLY INSTRUCTIONAL ALTERNATIVES

Based on children's completion of **Practice Book page 35,** determine their ability to identify setting. The instructional alternatives below will aid you in pinpointing children's level of proficiency. Consider the appropriate instructional alternatives to promote further skill development.

To reinforce skills, distribute **page 36** of the **Practice Book.**

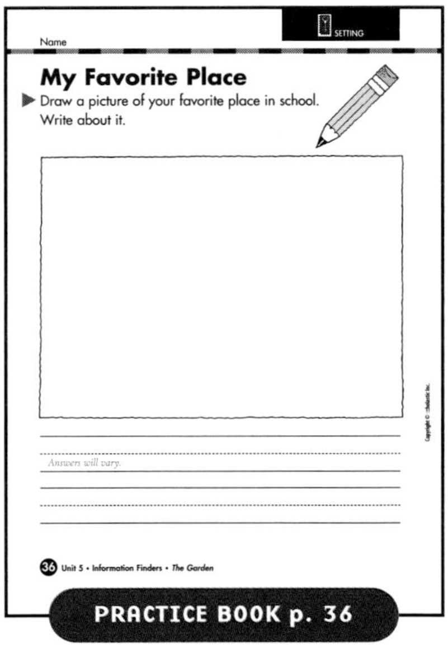
Name
SETTING

My Favorite Place

▶ Draw a picture of your favorite place in school. Write about it.

Answers will vary.

36 Unit 5 • Information Finders • *The Garden*

PRACTICE BOOK p. 36

INSTRUCTIONAL ALTERNATIVES

	If the child . . .	Then
Proficient	Correctly identifies setting	• Have the child apply this skill to a more challenging story. • Have the child draw a scene that shows a specific setting, then describe it.
Apprentice	Identifies either place or time, but not both elements of setting	• Have the child work with a partner to identify setting in a familiar fairy tale or folk tale.
Novice	Recognizes neither place or time when trying to identify setting	• Provide the child with a simple description of a setting and work with the child to identify elements of setting. • Complete the Reteach lesson on page R56.

SELECTION WORDS With *-ed* /d/, /t/

asked	frightened
looked	planted
played	shouted
walked	

SKILLS TRACE

INFLECTIONAL ENDING *-ed* /t/, /d/ TESTED

Introduce	pp. T164–T165
Practice	pp. T153, T171
Review	p. R52
Reteach	p. R59

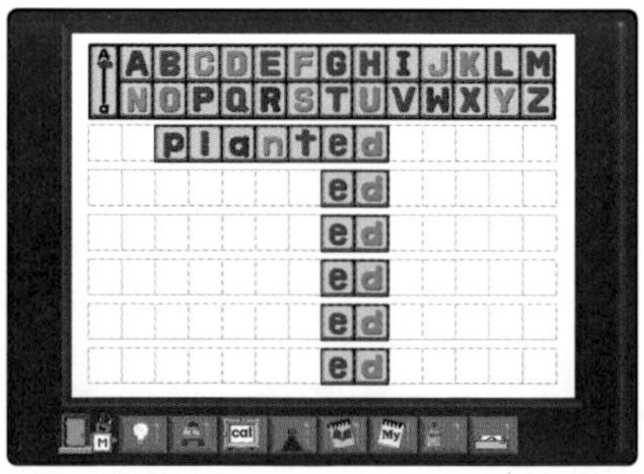

TECHNOLOGY

- Have children build words with *-ed* on the Magnet Board.

DAILY PHONICS

Inflectional Ending -ed /d/, /t/

A PHONOLOGICAL AWARENESS

RHYME Read aloud the poem "A Mouse in Her Room" from the *Big Book of Rhymes and Rhythms 1B,* page 18. As you read, stress the **/d/** sound of the ending ***-ed.***

- Isolate the words ***frightened, screamed,*** and ***meowed.*** Say the words and stress the ending consonant sound. Point out that it is the same ending sound that can be heard in the word ***red.***

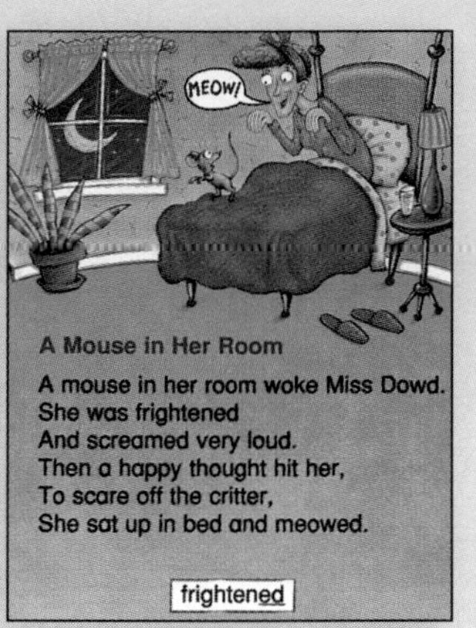

***Big Book of Rhymes and Rhythms 1B,* p. 18**

ORAL BLENDING Say the following words and the sound represented by the ***-ed*** ending. Have children blend them.

- **jump . . . /t/**
- **lock . . . /t/**
- **smell . . . /d/**
- **fill . . . /d/**

B CONNECT SOUND-SPELLING

INTRODUCE INFLECTIONAL ENDING *-ed* /d/, /t/ Explain that the letters ***-ed*** at the end of a word can stand for the sound **/d/** or **/t/.** Point out that when the ending is added to a word, the meaning of the word changes, as does the pronunciation.

MODIFY Instruction

ESL/ELD

▲ Make sure English language learners realize that these endings signal the past. Have children write the /t/ sound on one index card and the /d/ sound on another. As you read words from the list, have them hold up the appropriate card and make sure they understand the words. **(AUDITORY)**

GIFTED & TALENTED

✱ Following the lesson, challenge children to use the *-ed* ending. Write the following base words on the chalkboard: *run, make, pour, buy, watch, kiss.* Then invite children to determine which words can be used with the *-ed* ending. **(IRREGULAR VERBS)**

THINK ALOUD *I can add the ending* ***-ed*** *to words to change their sound and meaning. If I add* ***-ed*** *to* ***walk,*** *I make a new word* ***walked.*** *Let's say the sounds slowly. Listen to the sound* ***-ed*** *stands for in* ***walked.***

bored	hatched
rained	raced
climbed	bumped
played	kicked

- Ask children to suggest other words that end with ***-ed.*** List them on chart paper. Read all the words with children and have them tell which words end with **/t/** and which end with **/d/.**

PHONICS MAINTENANCE Review the following sound-spellings: inflectional ending ***-ed; /ô/ all, aw; /ā/ ay, ai; /ō/ o, oa.*** Say one of these sounds. Have a volunteer write on the chalkboard the spelling or spellings that stand for the sound. Continue with all the sounds.

C PRACTICE/APPLY

BLEND WORDS List the following words and sentences on the chalkboard. Have children read each chorally. Model blending as needed.

show	showed	clawed
loaded	soap	rain

Frog loaned a rake to Toad.

Toad roamed around his garden.

DICTATION Dictate the following words for children to spell: ***played, ball, boat.***

BUILD WORDS On individual cards, write words to which ***-ed*** can be added. Write ***-ed*** on several cards. Have children build words with ***-ed.*** Children can write their words. **(INDEPENDENT WORK)**

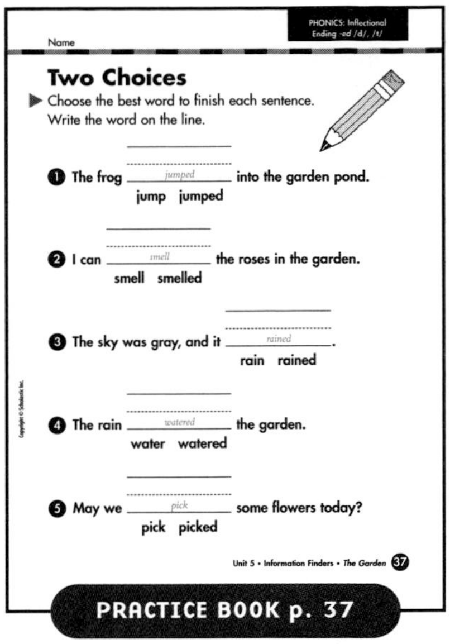
Name

PHONICS: Inflectional Ending -ed /d/, /t/

Two Choices

▶ Choose the best word to finish each sentence. Write the word on the line.

1. The frog jumped into the garden pond. jump jumped
2. I can smell the roses in the garden. smell smelled
3. The sky was gray, and it rained. rain rained
4. The rain watered the garden. water watered
5. May we pick some flowers today? pick picked

Unit 5 • Information Finders • The Garden 37

PRACTICE BOOK p. 37

Name

PHONICS: Inflectional Ending -ed /d/, /t/

A Letter to Frog

▶ Finish the letter from Toad to Frog. Use words from the box. Write the words on the lines.

stopped
planted
yelled
waited

Dear Frog,

Thank you for the seeds! I planted them today. I waited to see if they would grow. I even yelled at them. The seeds did not grow. They stopped being afraid when I read to them.

Your friend,

Toad

38 Unit 5 • Information Finders • The Garden

PRACTICE BOOK p. 38

DECODABLE TEXT

For practice reading decodable text, see ***Scholastic Decodable Reader #62.***

For additional phonics instruction and review, see ***Scholastic Phonics A, pp. 221–222.***

WORD SORT

Write these base words on index cards: ***lean, rain, play, clean, fill, jump, help, work, walk,*** and ***dump.*** Label two containers *Sounds Like /d/* and *Sounds Like /t/.* Have children pick a card, add ***-ed*** to the end, and decide in which container it belongs.

Building Fluency

PHONICS READER

Guide children through a reading of **Phonics Reader #59** *The Hungry Toad* or **#60** *Goat's Book*. For a detailed lesson plan, see **Phonics Reader Teacher's Guide Part B, pages 60–63.** While children read, note how well they:

- **blend words,**
- **recognize high-frequency words,**
- **read with speed, accuracy, and expression.**

You may wish to have children reread the story with a partner.

★ See Phonics Readers Take-Home Books 37–72 for reproducible format.

More Support Materials . . .

TRADE BOOK LIBRARY

For additional leveled reading practice, have children read one of the following:

Animal Tracks
CHALLENGE

Owl At Home
AVERAGE

Lost!
EASY

PHONICS CHAPTER BOOK

For additional practice reading words with **/ō/*oa*,** have children read Chapter 6, "The Goal," in **Phonics Chapter Book 5,** *Let's Go on a Museum Hunt.*

HOME-SCHOOL CONNECTION

Send home *The Hungry Toad, Goat's Book,* and *Rabbit's New Coat.* Have children read the books to a family member.

MY BOOK

For additional practice reading words with **long *o* (*oa*),** have children read *Rabbit's New Coat.* The My Book is also available on **WiggleWorks Plus.**

Intervention

For children who need extra help . . .

FOCUS ON HIGH-FREQUENCY WORDS

Write the words ***was*** and ***grow*** on note cards. Then follow this procedure:

- State each word aloud as children repeat it.
- Have children spell the word aloud as you point to each letter.
- Have children write each word in their Journals.
- Provide children with simple sentences containing each word. Help them to read the sentences. Allow ample time for them to practice reading the words and the sentences before rereading "The Garden."

FOCUS ON PHONICS

- Provide time for children to play with the decodable words that they encountered in the story, such as ***toad***.
- Make each word, using magnetic letters or letter cards as children observe.
- Have children trace the letters in each word with their fingers as you say the sound for which each stands.
- Then mix the letters and have children reform the words.
- Model blending as needed.

PROFESSIONAL DEVELOPMENT

GAY SU PINNELL

Repeated Readings

Children need to reread stories many times to develop fluency, gain automaticity with high-frequency words, have additional blending practice, and develop a sense of comfort in and control over their reading progress. Begin each lesson with a quick rereading of yesterday's story or the portion of the story previously read. Circulate as children read and take note of those who need additional help.

DAY 3 WRAP-UP

READ ALOUD *To conclude each reading session and develop children's oral vocabularies, read aloud a book of your choice. If the book contains chapters, you might choose to read only one chapter a day.*

GUIDED READING *Meet with the **red** and **blue** reading groups and assign Independent Center activities.* ***See pages R18–R19.***

DAY 4 OBJECTIVES

CHILDREN WILL:

READ 30 MINUTES

- **Reread the poem "Tommy" on pages 82–83**

WRITE 35 MINUTES

- **Shared Writing: Poem and Rhyme**
- **Spelling: Words With Vowel /ō/*oa***
- **Grammar, Usage, Mechanics: Homophones**
- **Oral Language**

EXTEND SKILLS 25 MINUTES

- **Vocabulary**
- **Daily Phonics: Inflectional Ending *-ed*/d/, /t/**
- **Study Skills: Follow Directions**

RESOURCES

- **Practice Book, p. 39**
- **Spelling Resource Book, p. 161**

Name
PREWRITING ORGANIZER

Get Ready to Write

▶ Think of pairs of words that rhyme. Write them on the cards.

Answers will vary.

frog
log

To the Teacher: This is the prewriting organizer referenced in the lesson on how to write a poem.

Unit 5 • Information Finders • The Garden 39

PRACTICE BOOK p. 39

SHARED WRITING

Poem

SELECTION CONNECTION Using the poem "Tommy" as a model, children will write their own poem with rhyming lines.

THINK ABOUT WRITING Encourage children to talk about why they like poems that rhyme. Help children understand that in some poems:

- two words that end in the same sound are used to make a rhyme.
- two or more lines can end with words that rhyme.

INTRODUCE WRITING Tell children that they are going to write their own rhyming poem.

TEACH/MODEL

PUT IT IN CONTEXT Reread the poem "Tommy" with children. Then ask:

> **What are the rhyming words?**

> **What sound is the same in each pair of rhyming words?**

Invite children to make a list of their own rhyming words.

- Help children use the rhyming words to develop pairs of rhyming sentences about the same idea.
- Record the sentences on the chalkboard and point out the rhyming words.

MODIFY Instruction

ESL/ELD

▲ Work with small groups to make lists of rhyming words. Make sure they know the meaning of the words. Then provide a poetry frame for them to complete with meaningful rhyming words. For example, use the frame: I have _____ *(a boat)*. You have _____ *(a goat)*. **(STEP-BY-STEP)**

EXTRA HELP

■ Write pairs of rhyming words on the chalkboard. Encourage children to suggest other words that rhyme with each pair. Write children's suggestions beside the appropriate word pairs. Children can then select a rhyming pair and use it to compose their poems. **(HANDS-ON LEARNING)**

GRAMMAR CONNECTION

- If any words in the sentences have homophones, point them out.

WRITE

WRITE RHYMING POEMS

- Have each child work independently to write a two-line poem that rhymes.
- Ask children to underline the words that rhyme in their poems.
- Encourage children to draw pictures to go with their poems. Display the finished poems on a class bulletin board.

ASSESS

PERFORMANCE-BASED ASSESSMENT

The following questions will help children assess their work:

> **Is my poem two lines long?**

> **Did I end the lines of my poem with rhyming words?**

Children may wish to carry this piece through the writing process described on **pages T286–T289.**

DAILY LANGUAGE PRACTICE

Spelling

DAY 4:

Apply Words With Vowel /ō/*oa*. **See page R21.**

Have children proofread sentences. **See page R21.**

Grammar, Usage, Mechanics

DAY 4:

Apply writing homophones. **See page R23.**

Oral Language

Tod went down the rode with Frog.

(Toad went down the road with Frog.)

Extend Vocabulary

was

grow

TEACHER TIP

Make and distribute copies of the vocabulary words on pages R70–R71. Have children use these cards for additional practice.

Review High-Frequency Words

Write the high-frequency words ***was*** and ***grow*** on note cards. Then write the following incomplete sentences on the chalkboard:

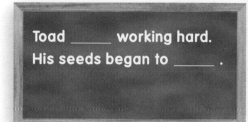

Toad ____ working hard.
His seeds began to ____ .

Read aloud each incomplete sentence and have children place the appropriate high-frequency word note card in the blank space. Then help children read aloud the sentences together.

Review Story Words

Write the story words ***Frog, garden, work, plant, flower,*** and ***seeds*** on note cards. Then write the following incomplete sentences on sentence strips:

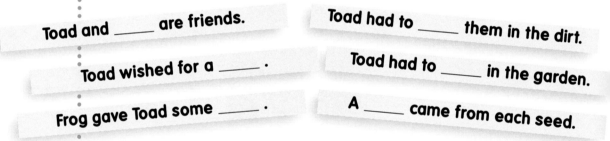

Toad and ____ are friends.

Toad wished for a ____ .

Frog gave Toad some ____ .

Toad had to ____ them in the dirt.

Toad had to ____ in the garden.

A ____ came from each seed.

Read aloud the incomplete sentences, and have children place the appropriate story word note card in the blank space. Then help children chorally read the sentences.

was	grow	Frog
garden	work	plant
flower	seeds	
was	grow	

ACT IT OUT

Write each of the high-frequency and story words on the chalkboard. Invite partners to pretend that they are Frog and Toad. Have them act out a scene in which Frog and Toad talk about their gardens. Encourage children to use as many words from the chalkboard as possible.

Building Fluency

Phonics Reader

Guide children through a reading of **Phonics Reader #53** *Small Animals with Big Names* or **#54** *See the Sea*. For a detailed lesson plan, see **Phonics Reader Teacher's Guide Part B, pages 48–51.** While children read, note how well they:

- **blend words,**
- **recognize high-frequency words,**
- **read with speed, accuracy, and expression.**

You may wish to have children reread the story with a partner.

* See Phonics Readers Take-Home Books 37–72 for reproducible format.

More Support Materials . . .

Trade Book Library

For additional leveled reading practice, have children read one of the following:

Animal Tracks
CHALLENGE

Owl at Home
AVERAGE

Lost!
EASY

Phonics Chapter Book

For additional practice reading words with */ō/oa,* have children read Chapter 3, "What They Looked at in Creep and Crawl Hall," in **Phonics Chapter Book 5,** *Let's Go on a Museum Hunt.*

Home-School Connection

Send home *Small Animals with Big Names, See the Sea,* and *Don't Be Bored.* Have children read the books to a family member.

My Book

For additional practice with inflectional ending *-ed* /d/, /t/, have children read *Don't Be Bored.* This Book is also available on **WiggleWorks Plus.**

SKILLS TRACE

FOLLOWING DIRECTIONS TESTED

RESEARCH IDEA

Have children choose books from the library that give directions for how to do a project or an activity. Have them read the books with a partner or in small groups.

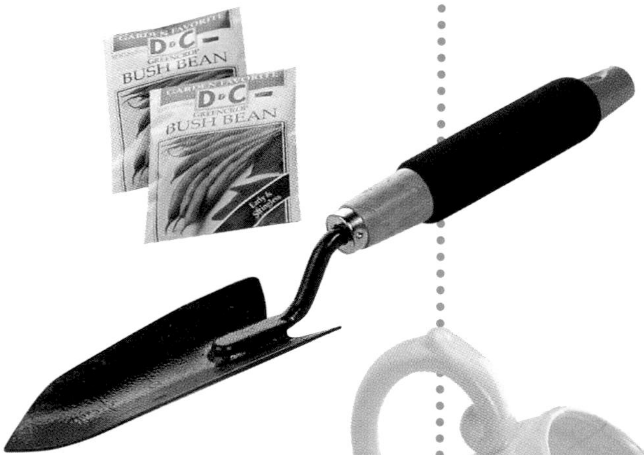

STUDY SKILLS
Follow Directions

A TEACH/MODEL

DISCUSS THE IMPORTANCE OF FOLLOWING DIRECTIONS Have children name a few of their favorite games and give directions for playing each one. Talk with them about what might happen if the players did not follow the directions for the game. Encourage children to share any experiences they have had with the importance of following directions. Point out to children that following directions is very important.

PUT FOLLOWING DIRECTIONS IN CONTEXT Ask children to picture the garden that Frog grew. Have them brainstorm possible directions that Frog could give Toad for planting such a garden.

> **What might Frog tell Toad to do first?**

> **What might Frog tell Toad to do next?**

> **What might Frog tell Toad to do last?**

WRITE DIRECTIONS On the chalkboard or on chart paper, write the children's suggestions for the gardening directions. List the directions in numerical order. Encourage children to use signal words in their directions. For example:

1. First, plant the seeds.
2. Next, water the seeds.
3. Then, wait patiently.
4. Last, enjoy the flowers.

Talk with children about what might have happened if Toad did the steps in the wrong order or if he skipped a step.

> **Why does Toad have to do Step 4 last?**

> **Why is it important for Toad to follow these directions?**

Ⓑ PRACTICE/APPLY

Write directions for playing Tic-Tac-Toe on the chalkboard or on chart paper:

1. First, draw a Tic-Tac-Toe grid.
2. Next, one player draws an *X* in the grid.
3. Then, a second player draws an *O* in the grid.
4. Next, the player who is *X* draws another *X* on the grid.
5. The game continues until a player gets three *X*'s or three *O*'s in a row.

Ask pairs of children to try to play Tic-Tac-Toe by skipping the first direction, then by skipping the third direction, and finally by skipping the third and fourth directions.

> **How does not following directions affect the game you are trying to play?**

> **What happens when the directions are not followed correctly?**

INFORMAL ASSESSMENT: PERFORMANCE-BASED

✔ Did children understand the importance of following directions?

✔ Did children understand what happens when directions are not followed correctly or in order?

✔ Did children identify instances when directions are and are not being followed?

Name

STUDY SKILLS: Follow Directions

Follow the Directions

▶ Look at each row of pictures. Which person is following the directions? Circle that person.

1. Plant seeds in rows. — Plant seeds in rows.
2. Water the plants. — Water the plants.
3. Weed every day. — Weed every day.
4. Put cut flowers in water. — Put cut flowers in water.

Unit 5 • Information Finders • The Garden 41

PRACTICE BOOK p. 41

TECHNOLOGY

Study Skills Have children use **WiggleWorks Plus** PlaceMaker to create an instructional poster on growing a plant from a seed. Ask them to divide the poster into the steps necessary to germinate a seed and then care for the growing plant.

DAY 4 WRAP-UP

READ ALOUD *Spend five to ten minutes reading from a selection of your choice.*

GUIDED READING *Meet with the* ***green*** *and* ***yellow*** *reading groups and assign children work in the Independent Centers.* ***See pages T18–T19.***

DAY 5 OBJECTIVES

CHILDREN WILL:

READ 30 MINUTES

- **Reading Assessment**
- **Daily Phonics: Vowel /ō/*oa* Inflectional Ending *-ed* /t/, /d/**

WRITE 30 MINUTES

- **Writing Assessment**
- **Spelling: Words With Vowel /ō/*oa***
- **Grammar, Usage, Mechanics: Homophones**
- **Oral Language**

EXTEND SKILLS 30 MINUTES

- **Integrated Language Arts**
- **Read Aloud**
- **Guided Reading**

RESOURCES

- **Selection Test**
- **Spelling Resource Book, p. 163**

TEACHER SELF-ASSESSMENT

✔ Did I frequently model how to blend words?

✔ Did I regroup children according to skill needs and reading level?

✔ Did I provide children with successful, daily reading and writing opportunities?

Reading Assessment

INFORMAL ASSESSMENT: OBSERVATION

PHONICS

Write the following spellings on note cards: ***oa, ed.*** Display one card at a time and have the class state aloud the sound for which the spelling stands, and give a word that contains the sound. Continue with all the spellings. Note children who respond incorrectly or wait for classmates to respond before providing an answer.

HIGH-FREQUENCY WORDS

Write the following words on note cards: ***was, grow.*** Display one card at a time and have the class read the word. Continue with all the words. Note children who have difficulty recognizing either word.

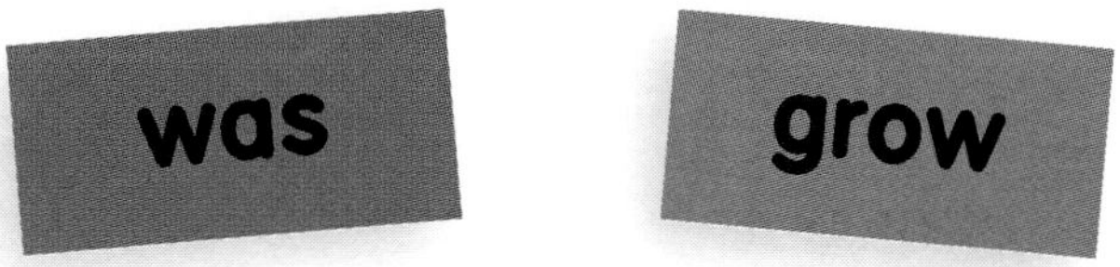

KEY SKILL: SETTING

Display a book children haven't read yet. Have them browse through the pictures and read the first few pages of the book. Have children write a sentence or draw a picture to identify the setting of the story.

CONFERENCE

Have children reread "The Garden." As they reread, select several children to conference with. Ask them to do the following:

- read aloud a few pages of the story.
- retell the story in their own words.
- explain what they do to figure out an unfamiliar word.

Keep anecdotal records of the conferences. Place your findings in each child's assessment folder. Use the information to determine which children need additional support.

"The Garden" from *Frog and Toad Together*

FORMAL ASSESSMENT

DECODING TEST

Make two copies of the assessment below. The assessment piece is designed to be used individually.

- Give one to the child and keep the other to record each child's errors.
- As the child reads aloud the words and sentences in the assessment boxes, record his or her attempts, corrections, errors, and passes.
- Once complete, keep each assessment piece in the child's portfolio as a running record of his or her emerging reading skills.

NAME: ______________________ **DATE:** ____________

A Have children read the following word list:

road	**looked**	**oak**	**which**	**make**
loan	**coat**	**played**	**were**	**way**
ball	**say**	**paw**	**more**	**belong**
paid	**foam**	**wished**	**am**	**all**
then	**roam**	**sheet**	**was**	**grow**

B Have children read the following sentences:

- **Toad was happy.**
- **All the seeds he planted will grow.**

C On a separate sheet of paper, have children write the following words and sentences:

- **boat played need fall**
- **A toad hopped up the road.**
- **The goat ate the seeds.**

SELECTION TEST

Use the selection test to obtain a formal measure of children's mastery of the week's reading objectives.

SELF-SELECTION

Have children select one or two pieces of work from the week that they would like to place in their Portfolios.

Suggest that children write a sentence telling why they chose each piece. You may also wish to select a piece that best illustrates the child's work.

Periodically review the pieces in the Portfolio and remove any that no longer seem appropriate.

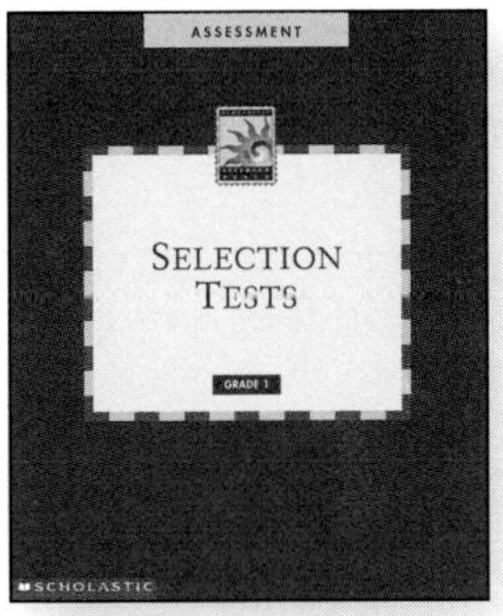

SELECTION TEST

DAILY LANGUAGE PRACTICE

SPELLING

DAY 5:

Administer the Posttest for Words With Vowel /ō/*oa*. **See page R21.**

GRAMMAR, USAGE, MECHANICS

DAY 5:

Assess Homophones. **See page R23.**

ORAL LANGUAGE

Tod red poems to the seeds all day.

(Toad read poems to the seeds all day.)

PORTFOLIO

Suggest that children add their drafts and revisions to their Literary Portfolios.

Writing Assessment

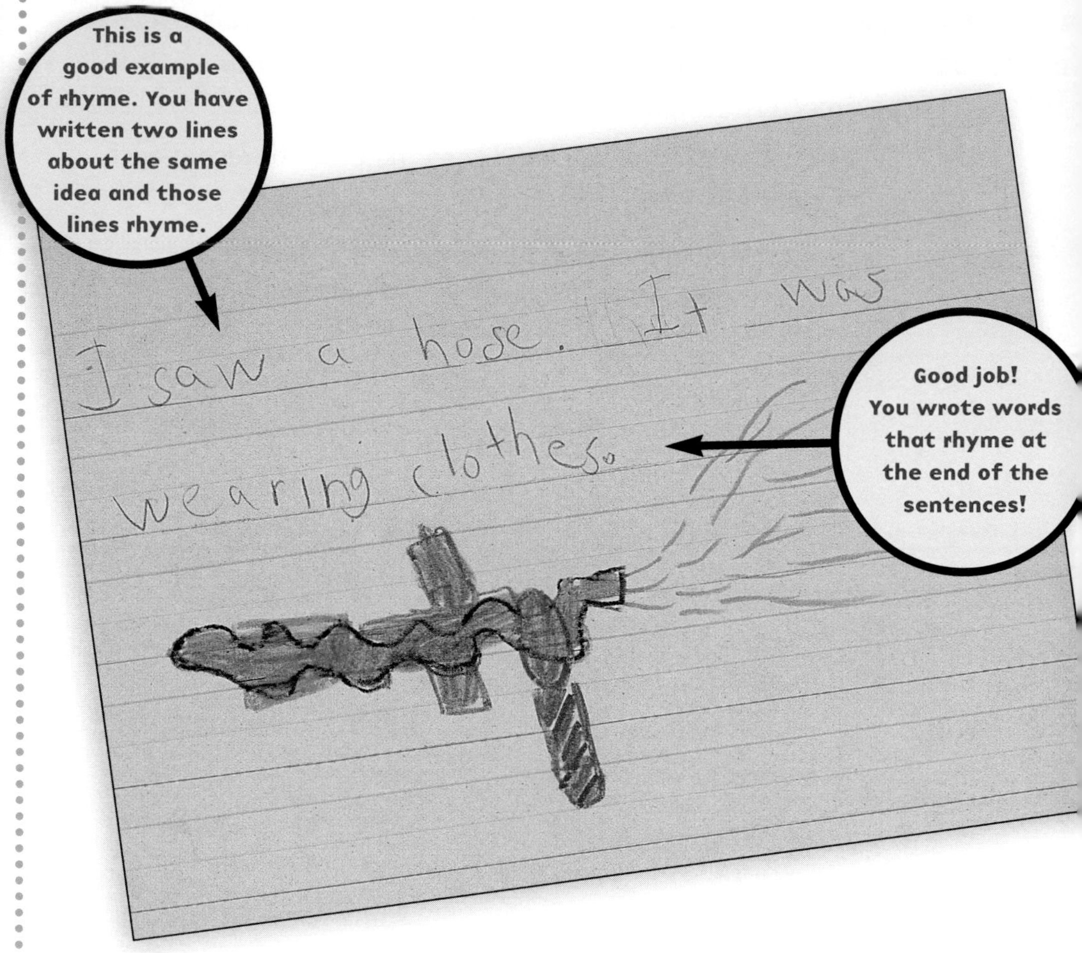

Proficient

Use the rubric below to assess children's writing.

CHILDREN'S WRITING RUBRIC

Proficient	• There are two lines about the same idea. • The rhyming words have the same sound and come at the end of the lines.	• The writing is proofread and corrected for grammar, usage, and mechanics.
Apprentice	• There may or may not be two lines about the same idea. • The rhyming words do not come at the end of lines.	• The writing is proofread but not completely corrected for errors.
Novice	• There are not two lines about the same idea. • There is no rhyme in the poem.	• The poem has not been corrected for grammar, usage, mechanics, and spelling errors.

Integrated Language Arts

WRITING/VIEWING

Write About Your Senses

MATERIALS:
Anthology pp. 70–81
Collage supplies

SUGGESTED GROUPING:
Individuals

ASK children to turn to the picture of Frog's garden on page 71 of the Anthology.

HAVE children imagine that they are standing in Frog's garden. What would they experience with their senses? Have children think about the answers to these questions:

> **What would you see and hear in Frog's garden?**

> **What would you smell?**

> **What things might you touch? How would they feel?**

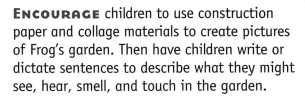

ENCOURAGE children to use construction paper and collage materials to create pictures of Frog's garden. Then have children write or dictate sentences to describe what they might see, hear, smell, and touch in the garden.

TECHNOLOGY

Language Development Guide children in using a word processor or page layout program to create rebus sentences. Tell children to pretend they are in a garden and report what they see, hear, smell, etc. Have them replace some of the words with clip art and drawings. For example, in the sentence, "I see yellow flowers," the word *see* could be replaced with an eye and *flowers* could be replaced with flower art.

WRITING/LISTENING

Put Sounds in a Setting

MATERIALS:
Anthology pp. 70–81

SUGGESTED GROUPING:
Cooperative Groups

ASK cooperative groups to think of a familiar setting. Remind children that setting includes place, time of year, and time of day. Then ask children what three sounds might be found in that setting.

HAVE children in each group work together to write or dictate sounds that they might hear in their setting.

ENCOURAGE groups to take turns sharing their setting and its sounds. Invite listeners to identify the things that made the sounds. Be sure to have children explain their guesses.

Children may wish to include their sounds in their Literacy Place Portfolios.

Sound/Letter Relationships

TEACH/MODEL Talk about how sounds help you write unknown words. Say the word ***croak.*** Explain that ***croak*** has the long ***o*** sound in the middle and that the long ***o*** sound can be spelled ***oa***. Write ***croak*** on the chalkboard and circle the ***oa*** as you say ***croak,*** emphasizing the middle vowel sound.

PRACTICE/APPLY Ask children to talk about and identify the vowel sounds in the other sounds they listed. You may wish to begin a rhyming word-chart.

Integrated Language Arts

ORAL LANGUAGE

Toad Says...

SUGGESTED GROUPING: Whole Class

TELL children that they will be playing the game "Toad Says." In the game, they must listen closely, follow directions, and act out gardening activities. Explain that the game is similar to "Simon Says," but Toad has been substituted for Simon.

START the game by giving gardening directions that involve more than one action. Some of the directions should begin with the words "Toad says. . ." and others should not, for example:

- Toad says rake the garden.
- Pick the flowers.
- Toad says plant the seeds.

WHEN children are familiar with the game, invite them to take turns being Toad and giving the commands. Encourage as many children as possible to take a turn being the leader of the game.

WRITING/READING

Make a Frog and Toad Book

MATERIALS:
Construction paper
Markers or crayons
Yarn
Stapler
Hole punch

SUGGESTED GROUPING:
Partners

ASK partners to talk about the friendship that Frog and Toad enjoyed together. Invite children to create their own book about Frog and Toad.

BEGIN by having partners write sentences and draw pictures to make a book that describes:

- a place that Frog and Toad visit together.
- a problem that happens at that place.
- how Frog and Toad use their friendship to solve the problem.

SUGGEST that partners put one picture on each page and describe the picture with one or more sentences. Children can create a title and a cover for their book, then bind the pages together with yarn.

Frog and toad make a Snowfrog.

DAY 5 WRAP-UP

READ ALOUD *Spend five to ten minutes reading from a selection of your choice.*

GUIDED READING *Meet with the **red** and **blue** reading groups and assign Independent Center activities.* ***See pages R18–R19.***

Daniel's Dinosaurs

Main Selection
Genre: Fantasy

Paired Selection
Genre: Rhyme
Caldecott Award-winning illustrator

WEEK 4 TESTED SKILLS

- **Vocabulary**
- **Daily Phonics: Vowel /ē/ *y, ey* Compound Words**
- **Key Comprehension Skill: Fantasy/Reality**
- **Spelling: Compound Words**
- **Grammar, Usage, Mechanics: Verbs (Past Tense)**

Technology Connection

VIEWING SKILLS If dinosaur stories are a big hit with the children, they might enjoy the Weston Woods video, *Danny and the Dinosaur*. In this video, Danny strikes up a friendship with a dinosaur or two.

Selection Summary

Daniel loves dinosaurs. They're all he reads about, writes about, and draws. He imagines them as his neighbors, traffic director, and teacher. To get Daniel's mind off of dinosaurs, his mother takes him to the aquarium. There, Daniel becomes fascinated with sharks. As he leaves the aquarium, he imagines the ticket booth attendant as a shark!

PAIRED SELECTION This Dr. Seuss rhyme reinforces the idea that the more children read and learn, the more they know.

Author

MARY CARMINE credits her ambition to be a writer to her mother. When Carmine was a child, her mother encouraged her to read. Her mother also wrote poetry, so Carmine had a writer in the house as a role model.

Weekly Organizer

Visit Our Web Site
www.scholastic.com

Daniel's Dinosaurs

	DAY 1	DAY 2
READ and Introduce Skills • VOCABULARY • PHONICS • COMPREHENSION • LISTENING • SPEAKING • VIEWING 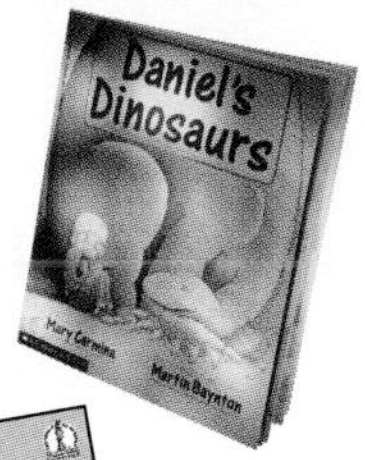  	**BUILD BACKGROUND,** p. T185 ▲ **VOCABULARY,** p. T186 ▲ ■ Practice Book, p. 45 **DAILY PHONICS:** ▲ ■ Vowel /ē/y, *ey*, pp. T188–T189 Practice Book, pp. 46, 47 **PREVIEW AND PREDICT,** p. T190 **READ:** ▲ ✱ ■ *Daniel's Dinosaurs*, pp. T190–T203 **GENRE:** Fantasy, p. T191 **COMPREHENSION:** Fantasy/Reality, p. T193	**READ:** ▲ ■ ✱ *Daniel's Dinosaurs*, pp. T204–T213 **DAILY PHONICS:** Digraphs *sh* and *th*, p. T205 Vowel /ē/y, *ey*, p. T207 *s*-Blends, p. T209 **COMPREHENSION:** Plot, p. T211
WRITE and Respond • GRAMMAR • USAGE • MECHANICS • SPELLING • WRITING	**SHARED WRITING,** p. T185 **JOURNAL:** High-Frequency Words, p. T187 **QUICKWRITE:** Predict, p. T203 **SPELLING:** Pretest: Compound Words, p. R28 Spelling Resource Book, p. 124 **GRAMMAR, USAGE, MECHANICS:** Teach/Model: Past Tense Verbs, p. R30 **ORAL LANGUAGE,** p. T203	**SHARED WRITING:** Prewrite, p. T213 Practice Book, p. 153 **SPELLING:** Vocabulary Practice, p. R28 Spelling Resource Book, p. 125–127 **GRAMMAR, USAGE, MECHANICS:** Practice, p. R30 **ORAL LANGUAGE,** p. T213
EXTEND SKILLS and Apply to Literature • SKILLS • INTEGRATED LANGUAGE ARTS • INTEGRATED CURRICULUM • GUIDED READING • INDEPENDENT READING	**READ ALOUD,** p. T203 **GUIDED READING,** pp. R26–R27 **INTEGRATED CURRICULUM:** Science, p. R32 Social Studies, p. R33 The Arts, p. R33 **TRADE BOOKS** • *Lost!* • *Owl at Home* • *Animal Tracks*  	**READ ALOUD,** p. T213 **GUIDED READING,** pp. R26–R27 **INTEGRATED CURRICULUM:** Math, p. R32
TECHNOLOGY and **REAL-WORLD SKILLS**	**WIGGLEWORKS PLUS CD-ROM** **Magnet Board, pp. T186, T188** **SCHOLASTIC NETWORK** **Finding The Facts, p. T201** **WORKSHOP 2, pp. T235–T238**	**WIGGLEWORKS PLUS CD-ROM** **Speaking Skills, p. T211** **WORKSHOP 2, pp. T235–T238**

MODIFY INSTRUCTION

● INTERVENTION ▲ ESL/ELD ■ EXTRA HELP
✷ GIFTED & TALENTED ✓ = TESTED SKILL

DAY 3	DAY 4	DAY 5
READ: ▲ ✷ "I Can Read With My Eyes Shut," pp. T214–T215 **COMPREHENSION:** ▲ ■ Fantasy/Reality, pp. T218–T219 Practice Book, pp. 49, 50 ✓ **DAILY PHONICS:** ▲ ✷ Compound Words, p. T220 Practice Book, pp. 51, 52 **BUILDING FLUENCY,** p. T222 **FOCUS ON HIGH-FREQUENCY WORDS,** p. T223 **FOCUS ON PHONICS,** p. T223	**VOCABULARY REVIEW,** T226 ✓ **DAILY PHONICS:** Compound Words, p. T227	**READING ASSESSMENT,** p. T230 Selection Test Conference Decoding Test
RESPOND: ▲ ■ Think About Reading, p. T216 Practice Book, p. 48 **WRITE A JOURNAL ENTRY,** p. T217 ✓ **SPELLING:** Write/Proofread, p. R29 Spelling Resource Book, p. 128 ✓ **GRAMMAR, USAGE, MECHANICS:** Practice, p. R31 **ORAL LANGUAGE,** p. T217	**SHARED WRITING:** ▲ ■ Fantasy, p. T224 Practice Book, p. 53 ✓ **SPELLING:** Study/Review, p. R29 Spelling Resource Book, p. 161 ✓ **GRAMMAR, USAGE, MECHANICS:** Apply, p. R31 **ORAL LANGUAGE,** p. T225	**WRITING ASSESSMENT,** p. T232 Child Model Children's Writing Rubric ✓ **SPELLING:** Posttest, p. R29 Spelling Practice Book, p. 163 ✓ **GRAMMAR, USAGE, MECHANICS:** Assess, p. R31 **ORAL LANGUAGE,** p. T232
READ ALOUD, p. T223 **GUIDED READING,** pp. R26–R27 **OPTIONAL MATERIALS,** p. T222 Phonics Reader #57: *Baby Pig at School*	**READ ALOUD,** p. T229 **GUIDED READING,** pp. R26–R27 **EXTEND VOCABULARY:** Review High-Frequency Words, p. T226 Review Story Words, p. T226 **OPTIONAL MATERIALS,** p. T227 Phonics Reader #58: *Donkey and Monkey* **READ ALOUD:** An Alphabet of Dinosaurs, p. T228	**READ ALOUD,** p. T234 **GUIDED READING,** p. R26–R27 **INTEGRATED LANGUAGE ARTS:** Compare Sharks and Dinosaurs, p. T233 Write About Daniel's Sharks, p. T233 Interview Daniel's Dinosaur, p. T234 Create a Shark Exhibit, p. T234
WIGGLEWORKS PLUS CD-ROM Language Development, p. T217 **WIGGLEWORKS PLUS CD-ROM Magnet Board, p. T220** **WORKSHOP 2, pp. T235–T238**	**WIGGLEWORKS PLUS CD-ROM Study Skills, p. T228** **WORKSHOP 2, pp. T235–T238**	**WIGGLEWORKS PLUS CD-ROM Speaking Skills, p. T234** **WORKSHOP 2, pp. T235–T238**

Weekly Assessment

ASSESSMENT PLANNING

USE THIS CHART TO PLAN YOUR ASSESSMENT OF THE WEEKLY READING OBJECTIVES.

- **Informal Assessment is ongoing and should be used before, during and after reading.**
- **Formal Assessment occurs at the end of the week on the selection test.**
- **Note that intervention activities occur throughout the lesson to support children who need extra help with skills.**

YOU MAY CHOOSE AMONG THE FOLLOWING PAGES IN THE ASSESSMENT HANDBOOK.

- **Informal Assessment**
- **Anecdotal Record**
- **Portfolio Checklist and Evaluation Forms**
- **Self-Assessment**
- **English Language Learners**
- **Using Technology to Assess**
- **Test Preparations**

SKILLS AND STRATEGIES	Informal Assessment
COMPREHENSION Fantasy/Reality	**OBSERVATION p. T193** • Did children identify realistic and make-believe elements of a story? **QUICKCHECK p. T218** • Can children identify realistic and make-believe elements of a story? **CHECK PRACTICE BOOK p. 49** **CONFERENCE p. T230**
DAILY PHONICS Vowel /ē/*y, ey* Compound Words	**OBSERVATION pp. T201, T207** • Can children recognize words with /e/*y, ey*? • Can children identify compound words? **CHECK PRACTICE BOOK pp. 46, 51** **DICTATION pp. T189, T221**
VOCABULARY Story Words **library, office, supermarket, teacher, city, shark** High-Frequency **school, their**	**OBSERVATION p. T226** • Did children identify story words? • Did children identify high-frequency words? **CHECK PRACTICE BOOK p. 44**

Formal Assessment	INTERVENTION and Instructional Alternatives	Planning Notes
SELECTION TEST • Questions 1–3 check children's mastery of the key strategy, fantasy/reality. **UNIT TEST**	**If children need help with fantasy/reality, then go to:** • **Instructional Alternatives, p. T219**	
DECODING TEST • See p. T231 **SELECTION TEST** • Questions 4–7 check children's ability to recognize vowel /ē/*y, ey* and compound words. **UNIT TEST**	**If children need help identifying words with vowel /ē/*y, ey*, then go to:** • **Intervention, p. T223** • **Reteach, p. R60** **If children need help identifying compound words, then go to:** • **Reteach, p. R60**	
SELECTION TEST • Questions 8–10 check children's recall of high-frequency and story words. **UNIT TEST**	**If children need additional practice with the vocabulary words, then go to:** • **Intervention Activity, p. T223** • **Extend Vocabulary, p. T226** • **Integrated Language Arts Activity, p. T233**	

Technology

Exploring WiggleWorks Plus

Children can interact with an electronic version of the literature selection in this lesson. Use this activity to direct children as they explore the WiggleWorks Plus CD-ROM.

STEP 1 Read	Have children read *Daniel's Dinosaurs* on the **WiggleWorks Plus** CD-ROM. By choosing the Read Aloud mode, they can hear the story read and make special note of the dinosaur words.
STEP 2 Write	As the story goes along, have children copy the names of the dinosaurs onto their My Words list.
STEP 3 Write	Next, ask the children to open the Magnet Board and their My Words list. Have them add a couple of dinosaur names from the list onto the Magnet Board. Then have them create some make-believe dinosaur names—for example, *babyosaurus, dogosaurus,* and *Tommyosaurus.*
STEP 4 Illustrate	Conclude the activity by having children illustrate their fantasy dinosaurs using the clip art and drawing tools in **WiggleWorks Plus** PlaceMaker. For more activity suggestions, see the **WiggleWorks Plus** Teaching Guide.

WiggleWorks Plus CD-ROM

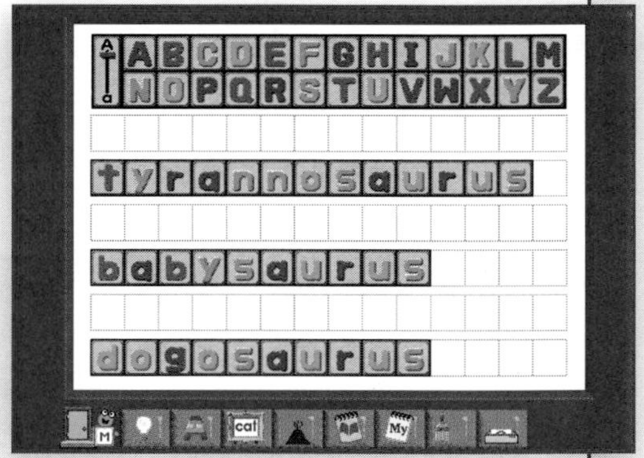

WiggleWorks Plus CD-ROM

WiggleWorks Plus CD-ROM

Build Background

Children often have a favorite interest and want to read about it, watch programs about it, and play with related toys and games. The boy in this story has this kind of interest in dinosaurs.

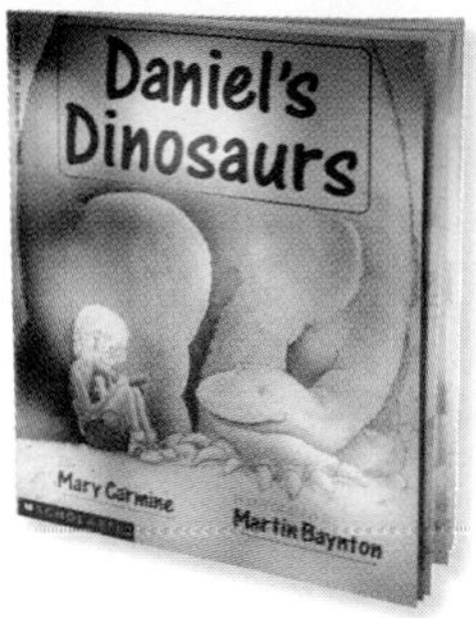

Activate Prior Knowledge

DISCUSS SPECIAL INTERESTS Ask children to talk about their special interests. Invite children to tell how they learn about the things they are curious about. Then ask:

> **What do you like to learn about?**

> **What is the most interesting thing you have learned?**

> **Where did you find your information?**

SHARED WRITING *Fantasy*

INTRODUCE Explain to children that a fantasy story has some parts that are make-believe. A story about a fantastic toy in a real setting is an example of a fantasy. Encourage children to suggest examples of fantasy toys. Then ask children to write a sentence telling about one of the toys.

DAY 1 OBJECTIVES

CHILDREN WILL:

READ 30 MINUTES

- **Build Background**
- **Vocabulary**
- **Daily Phonics: Vowel /ē/y, ey**
- ***Daniel's Dinosaurs*, pp. 86–99**
- **Key Comprehension Skill: Fantasy/Reality**

WRITE 30 MINUTES

- **Shared Writing: Introduce Writing a Fantasy**
- **Quickwrite: Predict**
- **Spelling: Compound Words**
- **Grammar, Usage, Mechanics: Verbs: Past Tense**

EXTEND SKILLS 30 MINUTES

- **Integrated Curriculum**
- **Read Aloud**
- **Guided Reading**

RESOURCES

- **Practice Book, pp. 45–47**
- **Spelling Resource Book, p. 124**

MODIFY Instruction

ESL/ELD

▲ Help children participate in the discussion by showing pictures of animals, rocks, stars, and other objects of nature. Make sure children have the vocabulary they need. Then ask: *Do you have any pets? Who likes to look at the stars? Do you collect rocks? Shells?* **(MAKE CONNECTIONS)**

VOCABULARY

HIGH-FREQUENCY

school their

STORY WORDS

library city
office teacher
shark
supermarket

VOCABULARY
High-Frequency Words

A TEACH/MODEL

INTRODUCE HIGH-FREQUENCY WORDS Write the high-frequency words ***school*** and ***their*** in sentences on the chalkboard. Read the sentences aloud, underline the high-frequency words, and ask children if they recognize them. You may wish to use these sentences:

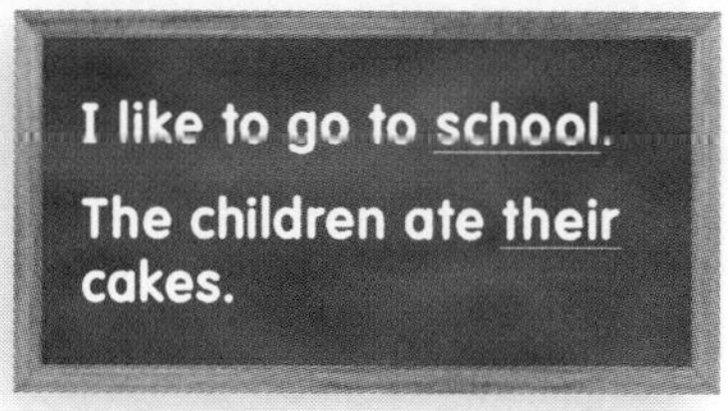

I like to go to school.
The children ate their cakes.

Ask volunteers to dictate sentences using the high-frequency words. Add these to the chalkboard.

B PRACTICE/APPLY

FOCUS ON SPELLING Write each high-frequency word on a note card. Read each aloud. Then do the following:

ROUTINE

1. **Display one card at a time, and ask children to state each word aloud.**
2. **Have children spell each word aloud.**
3. **Ask children to write each word in the air as they state aloud each letter. Then have them write each word on a sheet of paper or in their Journals.**

MAINTAIN VOCABULARY Add the note cards to the **Word Wall.** Then review the following high-frequency words on the wall: ***was, grow, am, all, more, belongs.***

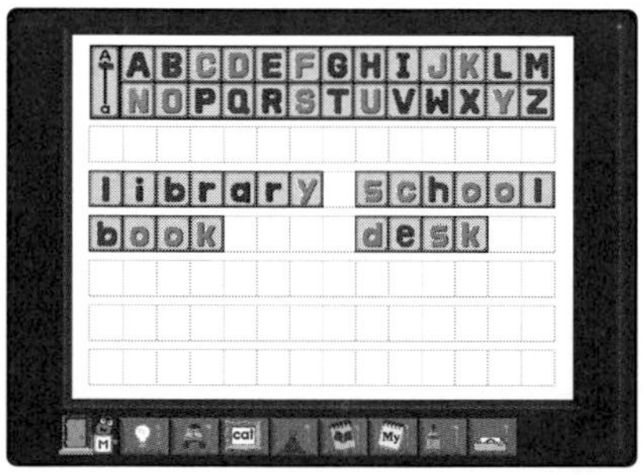

TECHNOLOGY

Have children spell vocabulary words on the Magnet Board and think of things related to those words. Begin with the words ***library*** and ***school.*** Under those, have them spell the names of related items, such as ***book*** and ***desk.***

MODIFY Instruction

ESL/ELD

▲ Have children work in groups to create vocabulary collages. Assign each group one or two "city" words: *library, supermarket, city, office,* or *school.* Discuss the meaning of each word. Have them cut and paste pictures, dictate labels, and share their collages with the other groups. **(MULTISENSORY TECHNIQUES)**

EXTRA HELP

■ Provide additional support during the discussion of *Daniel's Dinosaurs* by assembling and displaying a collection of books and posters that deal with dinosaurs. Seeing the pictures with dinosaur names may help children understand how Daniel can name the different kinds of dinosaurs. **(USE VISUALS)**

Story Words

Ⓐ TEACH/MODEL

INTRODUCE STORY WORDS

The story also contains the following story words—***library, supermarket, city, office, teacher, shark.***

- Write these words on the chalkboard, read them aloud, and discuss their meanings, if necessary.
- Point out previously-taught sound-spelling correspondences, such as digraphs ***ch, sh,*** or long ***e.***
- If possible, have children group the related words and explain how they are related. For example, ***library, supermarket,*** and ***office*** are all buildings.

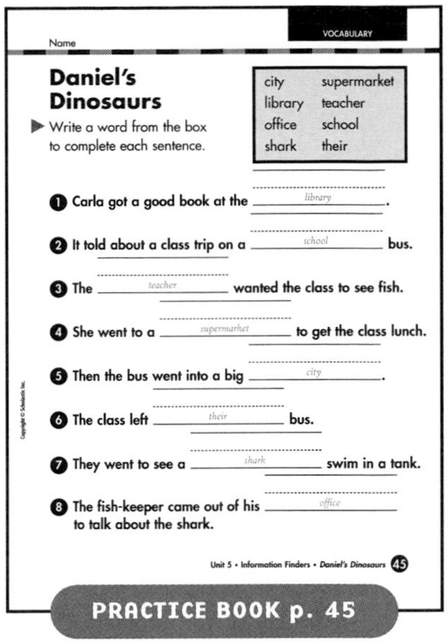

Name VOCABULARY

Daniel's Dinosaurs

▶ Write a word from the box to complete each sentence.

city	supermarket
library	teacher
office	school
shark	their

1. Carla got a good book at the library.
2. It told about a class trip on a school bus.
3. The teacher wanted the class to see fish.
4. She went to a supermarket to get the class lunch.
5. Then the bus went into a big city.
6. The class left their bus.
7. They went to see a shark swim in a tank.
8. The fish-keeper came out of his office to talk about the shark.

Unit 5 • Information Finders • Daniel's Dinosaurs 45

PRACTICE BOOK p. 45

Ⓑ PRACTICE/APPLY

BUILD STORY BACKGROUND

Discuss a city with children.

- Invite them to tell about places they might visit in a city.
- Invite them to close their eyes and visualize a busy, noisy city with tall buildings.
- Then have children draw a picture of a city scene and include many different objects or buildings they might see.

WRITE TO READ

- When completed, have each child write a sentence about his or her picture using one or more of the story words.

I can visit mom's office in the city

MATCH-UP

Write the story words and high-frequency words on note cards. On a second set of cards, draw or paste a picture for each word. Place each set of cards in a box.

- Partners take turns taking a card from each box and reading the word. If the word and the picture match, the child keeps them. If the word and picture do not match, the cards are returned to the boxes.
- Play continues until all the pairs are matched.

supermarket
SALE

JOURNAL

Ask children to write a sentence using each **high-frequency word** in their Journals. You might suggest the following sentence starters:

The school is _____ .

They lost their _____ .

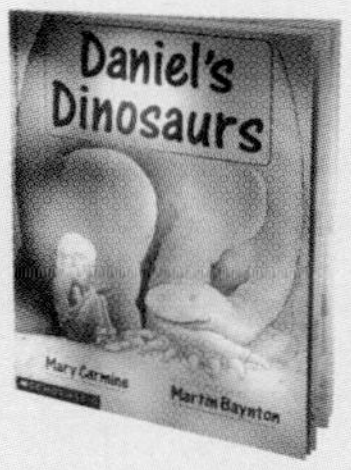

SELECTION WORDS With /ē/y, ey

city	every
friendly	library
money	variety
everywhere	

SKILLS TRACE

WORDS WITH /ē/y, ey TESTED

Introduce . . . . . pp. T188–T189
Practice . . . pp. T207, T222–T223
Reteach . . . . p. R60

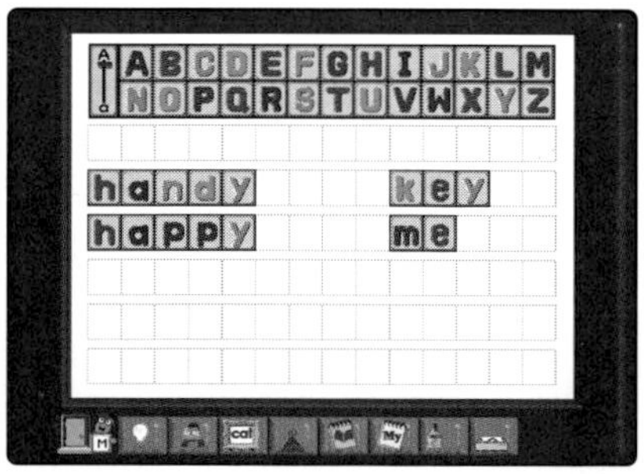

TECHNOLOGY

Have children build words with /ē/y, *ey* on the Magnet Board.

- Begin with the words *handy* and *key*.
- Have children search for /ē/y, *ey* words to add to the list.

DAILY PHONICS

Vowel /ē/y, ey

A PHONOLOGICAL AWARENESS

RHYME Read aloud the rhyme "Three Little Monkeys" from the *Big Book of Rhymes and Rhythms 1B,* pages 20–21. As you read, stress the words that contain long ***e*** spelled ***y*** and ***ey,*** such as ***monkeys, Jenny.***

- Ask children to read along with you.
- Isolate the words ***monkeys*** and ***Jenny*** and point out the long ***e*** sound at the end of each word.

Three Little Monkeys
Three little monkeys jumping on the bed,
One fell off and bumped his head.

***Big Book of Rhymes and Rhythms 1B,* pp. 20–21**

ORAL BLENDING Say the following word parts, and ask children to blend them. Provide modeling and corrective feedback when needed.

- **snow . . . y**
- **sand . . . y**
- **mon . . . ey**
- **sleep . . . y**
- **han . . . dy**
- **mon . . . key**

B CONNECT SOUND-SPELLING

INTRODUCE /ē/y, ey Explain to children that the letters ***y*** and ***ey*** can stand for the **/ē/** sound at the end of words. Write the words ***lumpy*** and ***honey*** on the chalkboard and say each word. Circle the letter or letters that stand for **/ē/**.

THINK ALOUD *I can string together the sounds of these letters to read the word. Let's say the word slowly as I run my finger under each letter. What letter or letters stand for* **/ē/**?

MODIFY Instruction

ESL/ELD

▲ Write long **e** words that end in *y* or *ey* in three columns: 1) Sammy, Jenny, Tommy; 2) funny, happy, pretty; 3) monkey, bunny, turkey. Read the words aloud, stressing the long **e** sound. Model a sentence: ***Tommy** is a **funny turkey**.* Invite children to make up and chant similar sentences. **(WORD PLAY)**

EXTRA HELP

■ Have children say and clap words that end with *y* or *ey*, such as *happy, silly,* and *monkey*. Point out that the words have two parts. When a word has two parts and ends with a long *e* sound, the sound is usually spelled with *y* or *ey*. **(MULTISENSORY TECHNIQUES)**

- Have children suggest words that end with **/ē/**.
- List the words on the chalkboard. Have volunteers circle the ***y*** or ***ey*** at the end of each word.

PHONICS MAINTENANCE Review the following sound-spellings: ***/ē/y, ey; /ō/oa; /ā/ay; /ô/all, aw; /sh/sh; /th/th.*** Say one of the sounds and have a volunteer write the spelling(s) that stand(s) for the sound on the chalkboard. Continue with all the sounds.

C PRACTICE/APPLY

BLEND WORDS To practice using the sound-spelling and to review previous sound-spellings, list the following words and sentences on the chalkboard. Have children read each chorally. Model blending as needed.

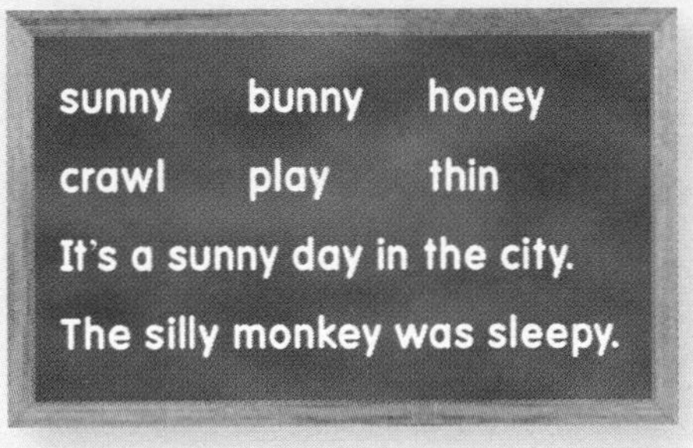

DICTATION Dictate the following words for children to spell: ***monkey, toad, day, ball.***

BUILD WORDS Distribute letter cards for ***y***, or have children use their own sets. Write these words on the chalkboard: ***sleep, speed, rust, hand, sand, leak, creep, snow,*** and ***rain.*** Invite children to place a ***y*** at the end of each word and to read the new word. Children can write the new words on paper. **(INDEPENDENT WORK)**

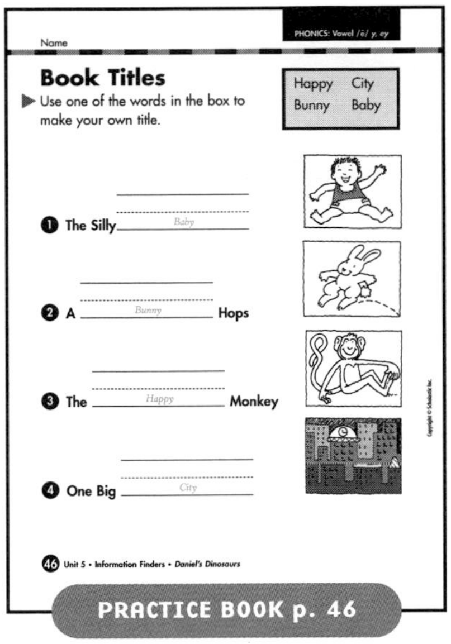
Name
PHONICS: Vowel /ē/ y, ey
Book Titles
▶ Use one of the words in the box to make your own title.
Happy City
Bunny Baby
1 The Silly Baby
2 A Bunny Hops
3 The Happy Monkey
4 One Big City
46 Unit 5 • Information Finders • Daniel's Dinosaurs

PRACTICE BOOK p. 46

Name
PHONICS: Vowel /ē/ y, ey
Mix and Match
▶ Unscramble the words to make a sentence that tells about each picture. Write the sentence on the line. Then circle the words that end in the long e sound as in funny.
1 It is day. a sunny — It is a sunny day.
2 her money. Peggy saves — Peggy saves her money.
3 made bees The honey. — The bees made honey.
4 silly. The is baby — The baby is silly.
Unit 5 • Information Finders • Daniel's Dinosaurs 47

PRACTICE BOOK p. 47

DECODABLE TEXT

For practice reading decodable text, see ***Scholastic Decodable Reader #63.***

For additional phonics instruction and review, see ***Scholastic Phonics A, pp. 231–232.***

BUNNY AND BEE

Using two sheets of paper, draw and label a bunny and a bee. Provide index cards with words having a long ***e*** sound, some spelled ***ee*** or ***ea***, and others spelled with final ***y*** or ***ey***. Pairs of children read the words and sort the cards into the bee stack if the word has long ***e*** spelled ***ee*** or ***ea***, or the bunny stack if the word has long ***e*** spelled ***y*** or ***ey***.

COMPREHENSION

Preview and Predict

Ask children to read the title and the author's and illustrator's names. Ask them to look at the pictures on the first few pages of the story.

> **What kind of book do you think the boy is reading?**

> **Do you think the dinosaurs in this story are real? Why or why not?**

Help children make predictions before they read by asking:

> **What do you want to learn or find out in this story?**

JOURNAL

Make Predictions

Invite children to write their predictions in their Journals. Encourage them to record the parts of the story that they like the best.

Set a Purpose

Discuss with children a purpose for reading. They may want to find out what the boy learns about dinosaurs. Then have them read page 87.

86

FANTASY

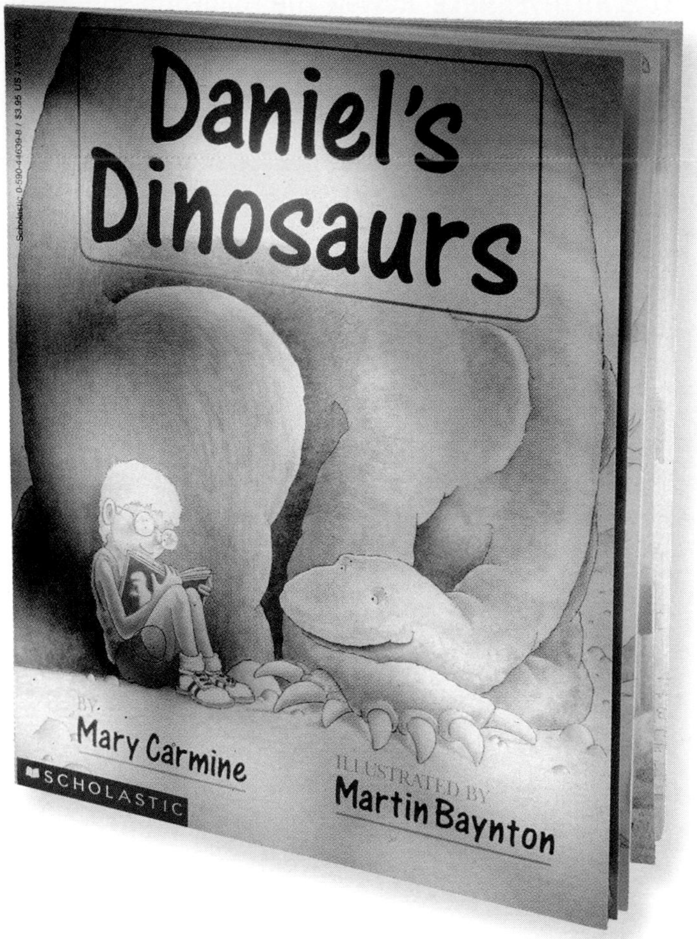

86

CLASSROOM Management

WHOLE CLASS

On-Level Use the questions, Think-Alouds, and Skills and Strategies lessons to guide children through a reading of the story.

Below-Level Have children listen to the selection on audiocassette prior to the whole class reading to familiarize themselves with the story.

PARTNER

Above-Level Above-level children may read the story independently and discuss their favorite parts of the story with a partner. When completed, have these children rejoin the group to participate in the story discussion.

87

Daniel loved dinosaurs.
He loved big dinosaurs
and he loved little dinosaurs.

87

SKILLS AND STRATEGIES

Revisit the selection for skills instruction.

✓ = Tested Skill

GENRE	
Fantasy	T191
COMPREHENSION	
Fantasy/Reality	T193
Sequence	T197
DAILY PHONICS	
✓ Vowel /ē/ *y, ey*	T207
✓ Compound Words	T201

GENRE

Fantasy

TEACH/MODEL

Discuss with children the key elements of a fantasy.

> **A fantasy is a story that has make-believe characters or places.**

> **A fantasy could never really happen.**

THINK ALOUD *I know that dinosaurs haven't existed for a long time. But I see pictures of dinosaurs together with people, so this story must be fantasy.*

PRACTICE/APPLY

Ask children to identify elements of fantasy in parts of the story they have previewed.

> **How do the pictures tell us that this story could not happen in real life?**

> **What in this story could not really happen?**

SMALL GROUP TO WHOLE CLASS

ESL/ELD Have children listen to the story on audiocassette prior to the class reading. This will help them to become familiar with the story sequence and vocabulary. Have children pay attention to the pre- and post-listening activities. **(AUDIO CLUES)**

COMPREHENSION

1 **Make Inferences**

> **Why do you think Daniel likes dinosaurs so much?** *(Answers will vary.)*

88

At the library,
he read books about dinosaurs.
When he drew pictures,
he drew pictures of dinosaurs. 1

88

MODIFY Instruction

ESL/ELD

▲ To help children with the inference question, say: *Show me three things Daniel does because he likes dinosaurs.* To be sure English language learners recognize the past tense verb forms on these pages, start a board list that shows both present and past tense forms of key words. **(LINGUISTIC CLUES)**

EXTRA HELP

■ Point out that the word ***library*** ends with a long ***e*** sound but is spelled with a ***y***. Invite children to say ***library*** aloud with you. Ask them what letter stands for the last sound in ***library***. As children read the story, have them look for other words that end with the letter ***y*** that stands for the sound of long ***e***. **(KEY POINTS)**

89

When he wrote stories,
he wrote stories about dinosaurs.

89

SKILLS AND STRATEGIES

COMPREHENSION
Fantasy/Reality

TEACH/MODEL
Explain to children that in order to decide whether a story is realistic or make-believe, they should think about what they know and then ask themselves if this is something that could happen in real life.

THINK ALOUD *I know that some stories like* Daniel's Dinosaurs *include both fantasy and reality. To tell the difference between what is fantasy and what is real in* Daniel's Dinosaurs, *I think about what I know. For example, I know that dinosaurs don't exist anymore. So Daniel couldn't have seen them in his neighborhood. That part of the story is fantasy, or make-believe.*

PRACTICE/APPLY
Ask children to look at the pictures on this page and make a list of what is real and what is make-believe. Display the list in the classroom and have children add to it as they continue to read the story.

INFORMAL ASSESSMENT
OBSERVATION
Did children
- ✔ identify realistic and make-believe elements of a story?
- ✔ ask themselves if the story events could or could not happen in real life?

See pp. T218–T219 for a full skills lesson on Fantasy/Reality.

CULTURAL CONNECTION
Children can make dinosaurs using a patch style from the San Blas islands off the Panama coast, called *mola*. Have children cut out a dinosaur outline, then trace it onto colored paper. Have them cut out their dinosaurs, and tape them to their shirts.

FAMILY LITERACY RESOURCES
Encourage family members to discuss children's special interests with them. Ask them to share books, magazines, or other materials from home or from the library that tell about something the child finds interesting.

COMPREHENSION

2 FANTASY/REALITY

> **Do two Plateosaurs really live next door to Daniel? If Daniel didn't think of dinosaurs all the time and see them everywhere, what do you think might be in this picture?** *(Children will probably say that Daniel's neighbors should be in the picture because Plateosaurs do not really live next door.)*

3 CHARACTER

> **Think of what we've learned about Daniel so far and the things we've seen him doing in the pictures. How would you describe Daniel? Do you think he'd be fun to know? Why do you think so?** *(Possible answers: Daniel is always talking about dinosaurs and playing games about them. He likes to read books and learn about things. Yes, it would be fun to know Daniel because he knows a lot and can make up good stories about dinosaurs.)*

90

Daniel's dinosaurs were everywhere.
Two Plateosaurs lived next door.
2
3
90

MODIFY Instruction

ESL/ELD

▲ Help children understand the phrase "really." Explain that this word means that something can happen in real life. Then help children make inferences about Daniel's dinosaurs: *Are they real? Do they **really** play sports? Do they **really** live next door?* **(MAKE CONNECTIONS)**

EXTRA HELP

■ During the discussion of question 2, encourage children to view the pictures on pages 90–91. Ask questions such as: *Do you think dinosaurs could really live next door? Would dinosaurs play badminton?* Help children distinguish fantasy from reality. **(GUIDED QUESTIONS)**

91

DAILY PHONICS

Plurals

TEACH/MODEL
Ask how many dinosaurs Daniel sees next door.

THINK ALOUD *I see more than one dinosaur. In English, when we talk about more than one thing, we usually add an* **s** *to the word. So I can say one dinosaur and two dinosaurs. Ask children to find another word on page 90 that means more than one.* (Plateosaurs)

PRACTICE/APPLY
Write the following words on the chalkboard: ***cat, bug, friend, star, book.*** Ask children to read each word, then to change each one to mean "more than one." Have children read each new word and use each one in a sentence.

- Ask children to look back through the story so far to find other words that name more than one thing.

IF children need more support with Plurals,

THEN see the review lesson on page R50.

SOCIAL STUDIES

Ask children to do the **A Dinosaur in My Neighborhood** activity on **page R33** where they will imagine what life would be like if dinosaurs were still alive today. Children will analyze how things might be different today.

CONNECTING TO SCIENCE

Point out to children that the Plateosaurus was a plant-eating dinosaur. It stood about 25 feet tall and walked either on two legs or on all four. Lead a discussion about why the author might have chosen this particular dinosaur for the badminton scene on these pages.

COMPREHENSION

4 FANTASY/REALITY

> **If Daniel didn't think of dinosaurs all the time, whom might we see in this picture instead of the Segnosauruses?**
(We would see people behind the checkout counters.)

SELF-MONITORING STRATEGY

Decoding

THINK ALOUD *When I see a long word like* ***Segnosaurus,*** *I stop and look for little words or word parts I may already know. I see* s, e, g *that sounds like* seg, *then I see* no, *and then at the end I see* us. *Saur is in* dinosaur. *Now, when I put all the parts together I get seg-no-saur-us,* Segnosaurus. *That's one way to figure out how to read a long word.*

92

MODIFY Instruction

ESL/ELD

▲ Study the pictures and encourage children to name as many objects as they can. As they name the objects and people, focus on whether they would see them in real life or not. Point out that the customers are real, but the cashiers are not real. They are make-believe. **(PICTURE CLUES)**

GIFTED & TALENTED

✷ Children may share Daniel's interest in dinosaurs. Invite them to name the real dinosaurs that they recognize in the story. **(INNOVATE)**

93

A Segnosaurus sat behind each check-out at the supermarket.

VISUAL LITERACY

Have children complete a Venn diagram to compare and contrast two of the dinosaurs in the story.

ORAL LANGUAGE

Ask children to compare and contrast a library and a supermarket. Have them tell how they are alike and how they are different. (*They both have shelves and they both have people to help you. They are different because you borrow things at a library and you buy them at a supermarket.*)

SKILLS AND STRATEGIES

COMPREHENSION

Sequence

TEACH/MODEL

Remind children that when they think about the sequence of events, they should ask themselves: What happened first? What happened next? What happened last?

THINK ALOUD *There is a certain order to the way things happen in* Daniel's Dinosaurs. *If I ask myself what happened* first, next, *and* last, *I can figure out the sequence of events. First, Daniel thinks about dinosaurs at home. Next, he imagines them next door. Then he sees dinosaurs at the supermarket. When I talk about what happens in order, I use the words* **first, next,** *and* **last** *to help me.*

PRACTICE/APPLY

Ask children to use the pictures to retell the story so far. Encourage them to use the words *first, next,* and *last.*

IF children need more support with Sequence,

THEN see the review lesson on page R44.

COMPREHENSION

5 FANTASY/REALITY

> **If there were no dinosaurs in this picture, what might there be instead? What might the Allosaurus be? What might the dinosaur behind the fence be? What does this tell you about what is real and what is make-believe?** *(The allosaurus might be a crossing guard. The dinosaur behind the fence might be a dog. This shows that Daniel is imagining dinosaurs where real people and animals should be.)*

6 MAKE INFERENCES

> **Do you think the other children in the picture see the dinosaurs? Why or why not?** *(Possible answer: Only Daniel sees the dinosaurs because he thinks about them all the time.)*

94

MODIFY Instruction

ESL/ELD

▲ Focus on picture clues in discussing what is real and what is make-believe. For example: "Every morning Daniel sees dinosaurs." Ask: *Does he really see dinosaurs?* **(PARAPHRASE)**

GIFTED & TALENTED

✴ Invite children to find out more about one of the dinosaurs mentioned in the story. Have them draw a picture of the dinosaur and write three or four facts about it. Encourage them to share their work with the class. **(RESEARCH)**

95

An Allosaurus directed traffic,
and one unknown variety barked at him 5
from behind a high fence every morning
as Daniel passed by on his way to school. 6

WORD STUDY

Ask children to find the **high-frequency word** *school* on this page. Write *school* on the chalkboard. Ask children to spell the word aloud with you as you point to each letter. Then have them use the word in sentences.

SCIENCE

Ask children to do the **Dinosaur Facts** activity on **page R32**, where they'll collect data about dinosaurs and illustrate what they have learned.

DAILY PHONICS

Ending -ed /t/, /d/

TEACH/MODEL

Review with children that the letters ***-ed*** at the end of a word can stand for **/t/** or **/d/.**

- Write the sentence ***A dinosaur barked when he passed*** on the chalkboard and call on a volunteer to read it aloud.
- Underline ***barked*** and ***passed*** and point out the ***-ed*** ending in each word.
- Pronounce each word slowly, moving your hand under the letters. Emphasize the sound represented by ***-ed*** at the end of each word.
- Tell children that the letters ***-ed*** can stand for **/t/** or **/d/** at the end of some words.

PRACTICE/APPLY

Write ***race, walk, puff, rain, place, lock, follow,*** and ***sail*** on the chalkboard. Have volunteers read each word, add an ***-ed*** ending, and read the new word formed. Discuss the sound ***-ed*** stands for at the end of each word. Tell children to look for words that end in ***-ed*** as they read the rest of the story.

COMPREHENSION

7 FANTASY/REALITY

> **Look at this classroom. What is real and what is make-believe?** *(Children are reading, sitting at desks, working, and writing on the chalkboard the way real children might. The dinosaur in the classroom, the children swinging from the dinosaur's neck, and a child sliding down the dinosaur's tail are make-believe.)*

96

Daniel's teacher
was a nice, friendly, plant-eating Diplodocus,
but sometimes . . .

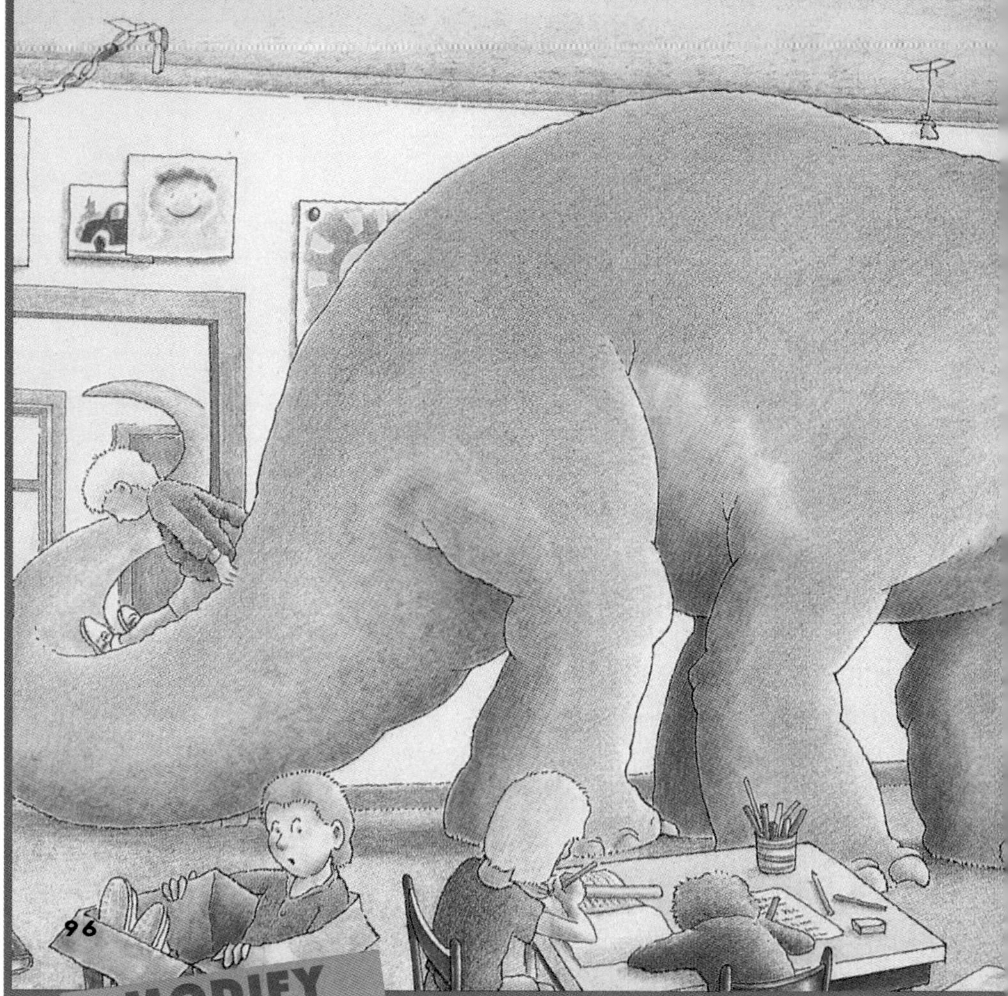

MODIFY Instruction

ESL/ELD

▲ Help children describe what is real and what is make-believe in this classroom. Have children practice oral language—ask multi-level questions: *Is the girl on the desk singing or reading? Who and what is real? Who and what is make-believe?* **(PICTURE CLUES)**

EXTRA HELP

■ Ask partners to draw pictures that use both realistic and make-believe elements. When they finish their pictures, children can trade them with a partner. Then ask them to identify as many real and make-believe things as they can in their partners' drawings. **(ANALYZE)**

97 ▼

DAILY PHONICS

Compound Words

TEACH/MODEL

Explain that some words are made of two smaller words.

- Write ***footprint*** on the chalkboard and read it aloud. Ask what two words make up the word ***footprint.***
- Have a child draw a line to separate the two words in ***footprint.***

PRACTICE/APPLY

Blend Words Ask children to find the compound word on page 96. When they identify ***sometimes,*** write it on the chalkboard.

- Have volunteers identify the two words in ***sometimes.*** Write each word, ***some*** and ***time*** on an index card.
- Write ***thing, lone, bed, day, spring, where*** on index cards. Give each word card to a child and have children stand in front of the class. Ask the children to match up the words to see what compound words they can make. *(something, lonesome, bedtime, daytime, springtime, somewhere)*

INFORMAL ASSESSMENT
OBSERVATION

As children read, note if they can:

✔ identify compound words.

✔ identify the two words that make up a compound word.

See pages T220–T221 for a full skills lesson on Compound Words.

TECHNOLOGY

Finding the Facts Have children visit **www.scholasticnetwork.com** and meet Dr. Don Lessem, a dinosaur expert, in the Scientists Online area. Also, have children visit the site at **www.ZoomDinosaurs.com**—a great source of dino facts and activities. Ask children to find Daniel's favorites there.

CONNECTING TO MATH

Diplodocus was one of the longest dinosaurs. It measured about 85 feet long and walked on four legs. Have children use yardsticks, or a measuring tape, and measure 85 feet. Ask children if they think this dinosaur would fit in their school.

COMPREHENSION

8 SEQUENCE

> **Daniel sees dinosaurs wherever he goes. What did he see first? What did he see next? What did he see after that?** *(First, Daniel went to see his neighbors, then he went to the supermarket, after that he went to school.)*

9 MAKE INFERENCES

> **What did Daniel mean when he said his teacher was a big, fierce Tyrannosaurus?** *(Possible answer: The teacher sometimes scolds the children to get to work.)*

OPTION You may end the first day's reading here or have children continue reading the entire selection.

98

MODIFY Instruction

ESL/ELD

▲ Help children understand why Daniel calls his teacher a "big, fierce Tyrannosaurus." Brainstorm other words that are similar in meaning to "fierce," such as *mean.* Have children make the fiercest face they can. Then have them describe others in the picture. **(BRAINSTORM)**

EXTRA HELP

■ Help children figure out the word *fierce.* Point out that the children in the picture look afraid. Encourage children to think of a word that begins with *f* and describes a mean dinosaur. Tell children that the word is *fierce.* **(CONTEXT CLUES)**

99

she turned into
a big, fierce Tyrannosaurus! 9

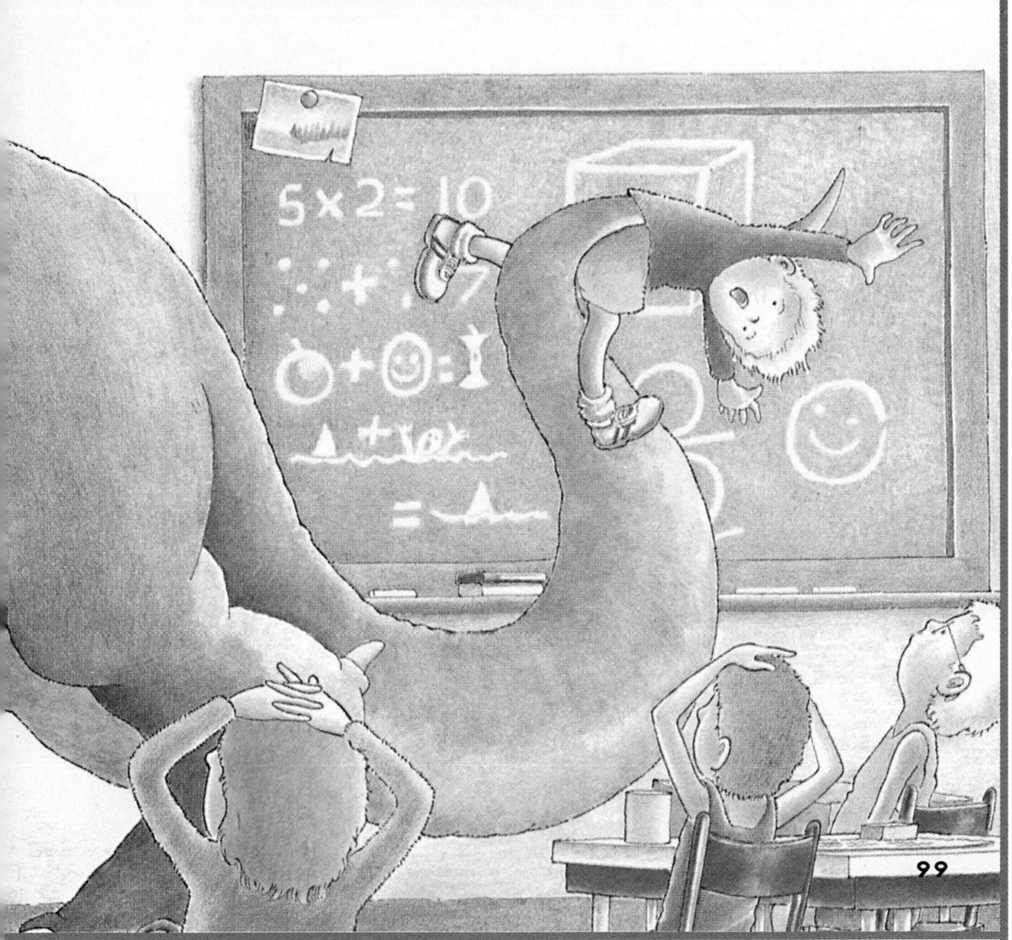

VISUAL LITERACY

Point out that the boy being tossed about on the Tyrannosaurus's tail is the same boy who was sliding on the dinosaur's tail on page 96. Ask children to compare the two pictures to find other details that appear in both.

THE ARTS

Ask children to complete the **Make a Model of a Fossil** activity on **page R33.** They will use modeling clay to make their own fossil-like molds and discuss how scientists learn about dinosaurs.

QuickWrite

PREDICT
Ask children to write what they think about Daniel and his dinosaurs so far. You may also wish to have children refine the predictions they made before reading and predict what will happen next.

DAILY LANGUAGE PRACTICE

SPELLING

DAY 1:
Administer the Pretest for Compound Words. **See page R28.**

GRAMMAR, USAGE, MECHANICS

DAY 1:
Teach and Model Past Tense Verbs. **See page R30.**

ORAL LANGUAGE

Peter look for some one to play baseball with.
(Peter looked for someone to play baseball with.)

DAY 1 WRAP-UP

READ ALOUD *To develop children's oral vocabularies, spend five to ten minutes reading from a selection of your choice.*

GUIDED READING *To extend reading, meet with the **green** and **yellow** reading groups and assign Independent Center activities. **See pages R26–R27.***

COMPREHENSION

DAY 2 OBJECTIVES

CHILDREN WILL:

READ 30 MINUTES
- **Daniel's Dinosaurs, pp. 100–109**
- **Daily Phonics: Vowel /ē/y, *ey*, p. T207**

WRITE 30 MINUTES
- **Shared Writing: Prewrite Fantasy**
- **Spelling: Compound Words**
- **Grammar, Usage, Mechanics: Past Tense Verbs**
- **Oral Language**

EXTEND SKILLS 30 MINUTES
- **Integrated Curriculum**
- **Read Aloud**
- **Guided Reading**

RESOURCES
- **Practice Book, pp. 46–47**
- **Spelling Resource Book, pp. 125–127**

Reread

You may wish to have children independently reread the first part of the story before beginning Day 2 reading.

10 SUMMARIZE

> **What has happened so far?** *(Daniel thinks about dinosaurs all the time. He imagines that he sees dinosaurs everywhere.)*

11 CRITICAL THINKING

> **Why do you think Daniel's mother wants to take him to the Aquarium?** *(Possible answer: Daniel's mother wants him to think about something other than dinosaurs.)*

100

"I wish you'd think of something else sometimes," said Daniel's mother.
"Why don't we go to the city and visit the Aquarium?"

"That's a good idea," said Daniel. **10**
"I like fish . . .
but not as much as dinosaurs." **11**

100

MODIFY Instruction

ESL/ELD

▲ Ask children to look on each page and tell you one thing that happened in order to summarize the story so far. Write what they mention on the chalkboard. Be sure children know what an aquarium is. Then say: *Daniel is going to the Aquarium now. Will he see more dinosaurs?* **(GUIDED QUESTIONS)**

EXTRA HELP

■ To help children understand what has happened in the story so far, encourage them to use the pictures to list the events in the correct order. **(SUMMARIZE)**

101

It was a long drive to the city.
All the way there,
Daniel drew pictures of dinosaurs.

101

MATH

Ask children to do the **Dinosaur Footprints** activity on **page R32.** They will estimate the footprint sizes of dinosaurs pictured in the story and compare the dimensions.

CONNECTING TO THEME

Ask children if they have ever visited an aquarium and what they saw there. Have children name places they might visit to learn more about dinosaurs. Then children can compare an aquarium and a museum and discuss how they are alike and how they are different.

DAILY PHONICS

Digraphs *sh* and *th*

CONNECT SOUND-SPELLING

TEACH/MODEL Review with children that sometimes two letters together can stand for one sound.

- Write the words ***she*** and ***with*** on the chalkboard and have the words read aloud.
- Cover the ***e*** on ***she*** and ask children what sound the ***sh*** stands for. Ask children to give some words that have the **/sh/** sound.
- Cover the ***wi*** in ***with*** and ask what sound the ***th*** stands for. Ask children to give some words that have the **/th/** sound.

PRACTICE/APPLY

Ask children to find words with ***sh*** and ***th*** on pages 100 and 101. *(wish, think, something, mother, that's, fish, the, there)*

- Have children identify the letters that stand for the **/sh/** or **/th/** sound in each word.
- Encourage children to look for other words in the story with the **/sh/** or **/th/** sound.

IF children need more support with consonant digraphs *sh, th,*

THEN see the review activity on page R57.

COMPREHENSION

12 FANTASY/REALITY

> There's a dinosaur at the aquarium to take the money from Daniel and his mother. What is real and what is make-believe in this part of the story? *(Children may identify the ticket booth, the souvenirs, and the fish as real and the Ceratosaurus as make-believe.)*

102

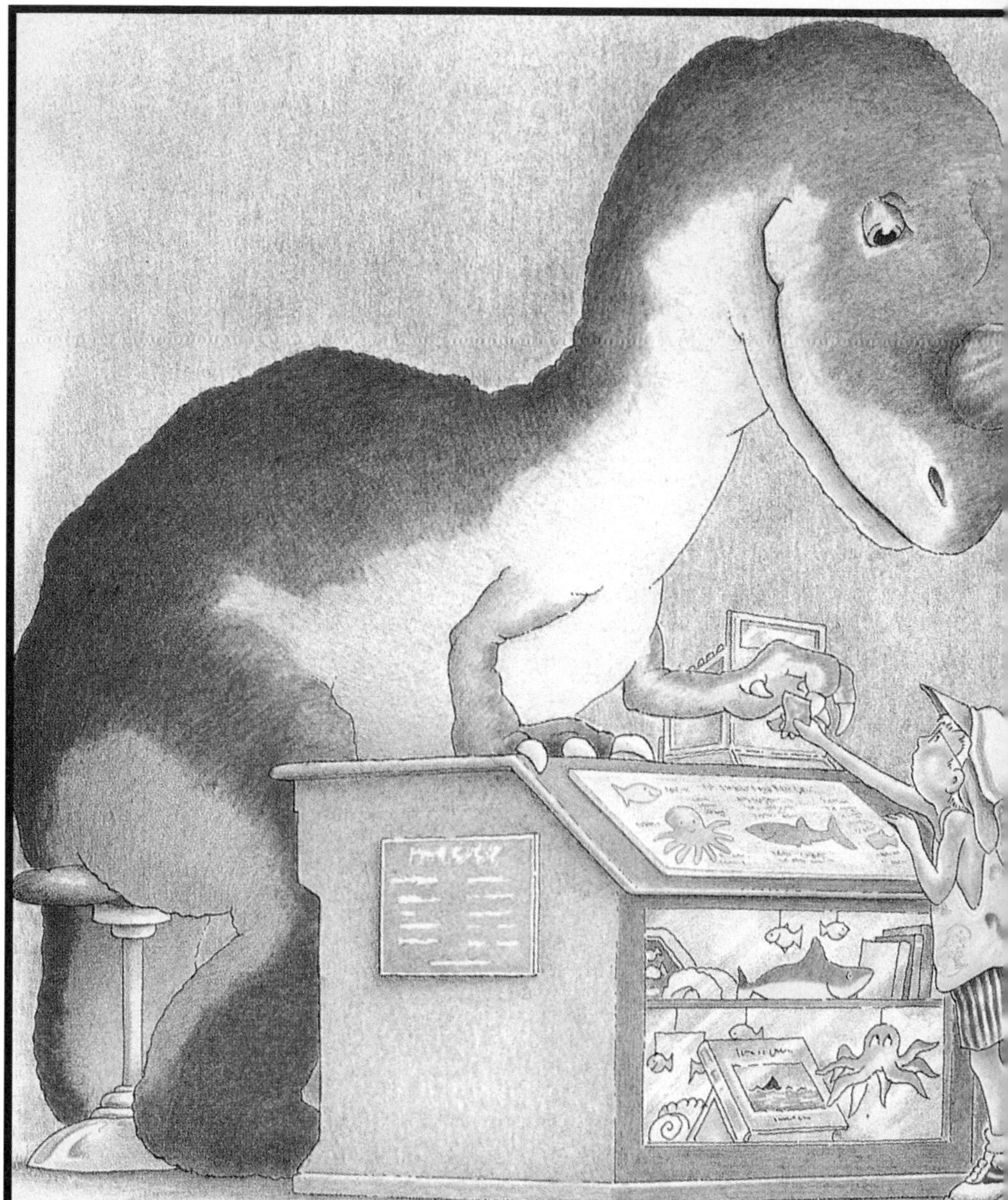

102

MODIFY Instruction

ESL/ELD

▲ Explain to children that the dinosaur taking the money at the ticket office is called a *cashier.* Challenge children to find another picture where Daniel saw a dinosaur who was a cashier. Ask: *Is this cashier real or make-believe?* **(COMPARE AND CONTRAST)**

GIFTED & TALENTED

✷ Children may enjoy working in pairs to produce a pronunciation guide for the dinosaur names in the selection. They can use rhyming words rather than dictionary markings. For example, *ceratosaurus* might become *sir-rat-o-soar-us.* **(DECODING)**

103

A smiling Ceratosaurus took their money at the ticket office.

Daniel and his mother looked at the rock pools, the sea horses, and the little fish.

12

103

WORD STUDY

Have children find the **high-frequency word** *their* on page 103. Ask what the word means. Help children make a connection between the possessive pronoun *their* and the pronoun *they*, and Daniel and his mother. Write the word *their* on the chalkboard. Invite children to use the word *their* in sentences.

DAILY PHONICS

Vowel /ē/ *y, ey*

CONNECT SOUND-SPELLING

TEACH/MODEL Review with children that the letters ***y*** and ***ey*** can stand for the **/ē/** sound at the end of words.

- Write the words ***funny monkey*** on the chalkboard and have them read aloud.
- Ask children to circle the letters that stand for the **/ē/** sound at the end of each word.

PRACTICE/APPLY

BLEND WORDS Ask children to find words that end with the **/ē/** sound on page 103. *(money)*

- Have children identify the letters that stand for the long ***e*** sound. *(ey)*
- Encourage children to look for other words in the story with ***y*** or ***ey*** at the end. *(very on page 107)*

INFORMAL ASSESSMENT
OBSERVATION

As children read, can they:

- recognize words with **/ē/*y, ey***?
- blend words with **/ē/*y, ey***?

COMPREHENSION

13 SEQUENCE

> **Let's think about what Daniel and his mother have done together. First they drove to the aquarium. What did they do next? What did they do after that?** *(They bought tickets, they looked at little fish, they looked at stingrays, and, finally, they looked at octopuses.)*

104

They looked at the stingrays . . .

and stayed for a long time.

104

MODIFY Instruction

ESL/ELD

▲ Have children take turns telling what has happened on the trip to the aquarium. Let each child stand up to tell one thing. Take notes on the chalkboard. Then go back over the notes, inserting the words *first*, *next*, and *then* to help children keep track of the sequence of events. **(SEQUENCE)**

EXTRA HELP

■ To help children understand that the fish in this part of the story are real, not imaginary, have them use what they learned about fish from reading *Fish Faces*. **(MAKE CONNECTIONS)**

105 ▼

They looked at the octopuses . . .

and stayed even longer.

105

s-Blends

DAILY PHONICS

CONNECT SOUND-SPELLING

TEACH/MODEL Remind children that usually, when consonants come together in a word, the sound of each consonant is pronounced.

- Say the words ***slip, skip,*** and ***stop*** and have children repeat them.
- Write ***slip, skip,*** and ***stop*** on the chalkboard. Read each word slowly, emphasizing the pronunciation of the consonant blend at the beginning of the word. Ask children to circle the consonant blends. *(sl, sk, st)*

PRACTICE/APPLY

BLEND WORDS Ask children to find words that begin with an **s**-blend on page 107. *(stayed)*

- Have children identify the letters in the **s**-blend. *(st)*
- Encourage children to look through the story for other words that begin with **s**-blends. *(smiling on p. 103, school on p. 95, stories on p. 89)*

MENTOR CONNECTION

Ask children if they think Daniel might like to talk to the mentor, Laela Sayigh. Suggest that children brainstorm what Daniel might ask her about.

CONNECTING TO NATURE

Not all of the creatures at the aquarium are fish. Challenge children to find out why octopuses are not considered fish. Encourage them to share what they learn with the class.

COMPREHENSION

14 FANTASY/REALITY

> **Do you think this picture is an example of fantasy or reality? Why do you think so?**
> *(This is an example of reality because Daniel and his mother could look at fish in real life.)*

15 MAKE INFERENCES

> **Look at Daniel's face. What do you think he's thinking?**
> *(Possible answer: Daniel likes watching fish. He is very interested in them.)*

106

Then they looked at the sharks . . . 14 15

106

MODIFY Instruction

ESL/ELD

▲ Have pairs of children take turns pretending they are Daniel and his mother. Have them role-play what Daniel and his mother might be saying as they watch the sharks on this page. The role-play will help children understand why Daniel stays so long to look at the sharks. **(ROLE-PLAY)**

EXTRA HELP

■ Some children may have difficulty identifying who is telling the story. Remind children that words like *they* and *them* will help them recognize third-person narrative. In third-person narrative, the story is told by a narrator, or someone who is not in the story. **(ANALYZE)**

107

and stayed for a very long time indeed.

107

SKILLS AND STRATEGIES

COMPREHENSION

Plot

TEACH/MODEL
Share with children that the plot is the plan of the story. It is made up of events, characters, and a central problem or series of problems.

THINK ALOUD *Let's think about the plot of* Daniel's Dinosaurs. *In the first part of the story, we learn about Daniel. The problem is that he only thinks of dinosaurs. Then he goes to the aquarium. What happens there? What happens to Daniel's problem at the end of the story?*

PRACTICE/APPLY
Encourage children to participate in a conversation about the plot of *Daniel's Dinosaurs*. You may wish to ask them to talk about their favorite part of the plot.

ORAL LANGUAGE

Invite pairs of children to play the parts of Daniel and his mother. Children can act out what the characters might have said to each other while at the aquarium.

TECHNOLOGY

Speaking Skills Have children read *Daniel's Dinosaurs* in **WiggleWorks Plus** and use the audio buttons to hear the sentences read aloud. Encourage them to record themselves reading each page after they've heard it read aloud.

COMPREHENSION

16 MAKE INFERENCES

> **Why do you think a shark is at the ticket office now?**
> *(Possible answer: Daniel is so interested in sharks now that he sees sharks everywhere.)*

108

MODIFY Instruction

ESL/ELD

▲ Focus on the picture that shows Daniel's new favorite animal as a cashier. Have children draw a picture of a make-believe cashier that is their favorite animal. Children can then talk about and share their pictures with each other. **(MAKE CONNECTIONS)**

EXTRA HELP

■ Have children compare the pictures at the beginning of the story to the pictures at the end. Help them understand that Daniel's interests have changed; now he sees sharks everywhere. **(COMPARE/CONTRAST)**

109

As they left, Daniel said goodbye
to the smiling, grey nurse shark
in the ticket office . . .
109

VISUAL LITERACY

If children don't understand the significance of the shark replacing the dinosaur at the ticket office, remind them that Daniel loved dinosaurs so much that he saw them wherever he looked. Now he's seeing sharks, which means that sharks are his new interest.

ORAL LANGUAGE

Challenge children to try their hand at fantasy by drawing a picture of a real place, some real people and objects, and an imaginary character. Invite them to make up stories to tell their classmates about their picture.

Fantasy

SHARED WRITING

PREWRITE Using *Daniel's Dinosaurs* as a model, discuss fantasy. Tell children that later they will be developing a story about a fantastic toy in a real setting. Ask children to think of a setting for their story. Make sure they complete the prewriting organizer on **Practice Book page 53.**

DAILY LANGUAGE PRACTICE

SPELLING

DAY 2:
Practice Spelling Compound Words. **See page R28.**

GRAMMAR, USAGE, MECHANICS

DAY 2:
Practice Past Tense Verbs. **See page R30.**

ORAL LANGUAGE

Did anywun saw my book?
(Did anyone see my book?)

DAY 2 WRAP-UP

READ ALOUD *Spend five to ten minutes reading from a selection of your choice.*

GUIDED READING *To extend reading, meet with the* ***red*** *and* ***blue*** *reading groups and assign Independent Center activities.* ***See pages R26–R27.***

COMPREHENSION

DAY 3 OBJECTIVES

CHILDREN WILL:

READ 30 MINUTES

- **"I Can Read With My Eyes Shut!" pp. 110–111**
- **Assess Comprehension**
- **Key Comprehension Skill: Fantasy/Reality**
  Genre: Rhyme
- **Daily Phonics: Compound Words**
  Vowel /ē/y, *ey*

WRITE 30 MINUTES

- **Respond: Journal Entry**
- **Spelling: Compound Words**
- **Grammar, Usage, Mechanics: Past Tense Verbs**
- **Oral Language**

EXTEND SKILLS 30 MINUTES

- **Read Aloud**
- **Guided Reading**

RESOURCES

- **Practice Book, pp. 48–50**
- **Spelling Resource Book, p. 128**

Preview

Invite children to preview the poem by reading the title and looking at the pictures. Discuss any characters they may recognize and what children may know about books by Dr. Seuss.

1 SUMMARIZE

> **What is this poem about? What does it say will happen the more you read?** *(The poem tells about reading. It says that the more you read, the more you will learn.)*

2 DRAW CONCLUSIONS

> **Why do you think the elephant is carrying a book on his head?** *(The elephant is carrying a book on his head so the Cat in the Hat can read it.)*

110

MODIFY Instruction

ESL/ELD

▲ Provide English language learners with an audiocassette of the poem that they can listen to until they are able to read along with it. This will give children confidence when they read the poem aloud with the rest of the class. **(USE AUDIO)**

GIFTED & TALENTED

✳ Encourage independent readers to read the whole book *I Can Read with My Eyes Shut*. Invite them to read aloud favorite pages to the class. **(READ ALOUD)**

111

om
Can Read with My Eyes Shut!
By Dr. Seuss

The more that you read,
the more things you will know.
The more that you learn,
the more places you'll go. 1

SKILLS AND STRATEGIES

GENRE
Rhyme

TEACH/MODEL
Remind children that rhyming words have the same middle and ending sounds.

THINK ALOUD *When I read this poem, I notice that the words* **know** *and* **go** *rhyme. These words sound alike at the end, but they do not look alike. Sometimes rhyming words are spelled the same way, and sometimes they are not.*

PRACTICE/APPLY
Have children read the poem aloud. Ask them to say the rhyming words. Then encourage them to suggest other words that rhyme with ***know.***

- Write children's suggestions on the chalkboard.
- Ask children to circle the words that are spelled like ***know.***
- Have children write the words in two lists, words that are spelled like ***know*** and words that are spelled like ***go.***

FAMILY READING

Make a copy of the poem. Then invite a family member of a second-language learner to read the poem aloud with his or her child. This will boost children's confidence and support them when they read the poem aloud with their classmates.

VISUAL LITERACY

Ask children to find *The Cat in the Hat* and tell what he is doing. Discuss whether or not he looks happy. Would children be happy to ride an elephant and read?

COMPREHENSION

Think About Reading

Below are the **answers** to the *Think About Reading* questions.

1. *In the beginning, Daniel saw dinosaurs everywhere.*
2. *He saw two Plateosaurs, a Segnosaurus, an Allosaurus, and a Diplodocus (or other dinosaurs named in the story).*
3. *Then Daniel and his mother went to the Aquarium.*
4. *At the end, Daniel saw a shark in the ticket office.*

Name

COMPREHENSION CHECK

Daniel's Book

Draw a picture of a book about what Daniel loves. Then write about the book.

48 Unit 5 • Information Finders • Daniel's Dinosaurs

PRACTICE BOOK p. 48

112

RESPOND

Think About Reading

Think about Daniel's Dinosaurs. Finish the story map by writing each sentence on another piece of paper.

In the beginning, Daniel saw ______ everywhere.

↓

He saw two ______, a ______, an ______, and a ______.

↓

Then Daniel and his mother went to the ______.

↓

At the end, Daniel saw a ______ in the ticket office.

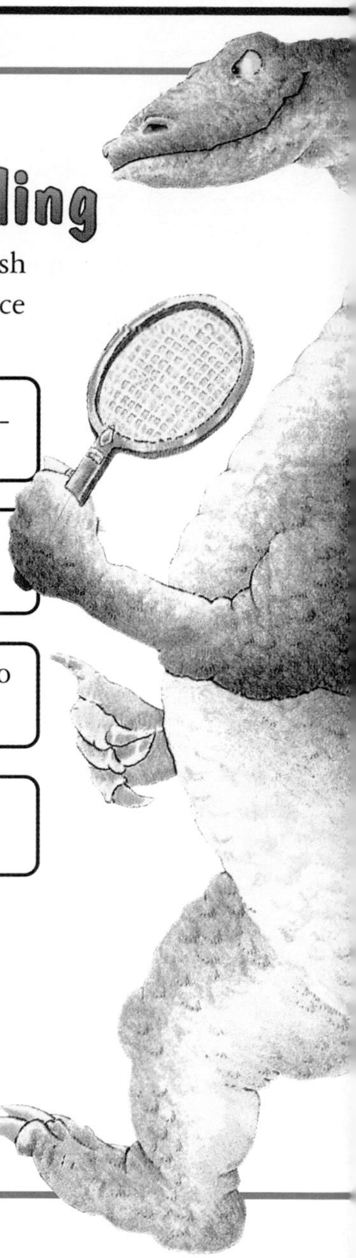

112

MODIFY Instruction

ESL/ELD

▲ Before children work on the story map, help them understand sequencing by having them tell about the previous day. Write these phrases on the chalkboard, and have children complete each by telling what they did that day: First I ______ . Then I ______ . Finally I ______ . **(RELATE TO REAL LIFE)**

EXTRA HELP

■ For the writing activity, children may work with partners. Have partners take turns portraying Daniel, telling about what he saw at the aquarium. The partners can keep a list of some of the words they use to tell what Daniel saw. **(WORK IN PAIRS)**

113

Write a Journal Entry

Maybe Daniel keeps a journal. He writes about the special things he sees and does. What do you think Daniel will add to his journal on the day he goes to the aquarium? Write Daniel's journal entry for this day.

Literature Circle

How would you describe Daniel to someone who hasn't read the story? Would you want to be like Daniel? Why or why not?

Author Mary Carmine

Almost all children like to know about dinosaurs! Some parents check out dinosaur books from the library or look for dinosaur shows on TV. That's not what Mary Carmine did. When her son asked about dinosaurs, she wrote a book for him. That's right—Danicl's Dinosaurs!

113

RESPOND

Write a Journal Entry

Before children begin writing, have them think about these questions:

> **What did Daniel see?**

> **What do you think Daniel will write in his journal after his visit to the aquarium?**

> **What did Daniel do?**

Literature Circle

Ask children to take turns describing Daniel. Encourage children to participate in a conversation about why they would or would not want to be like him.

DAILY LANGUAGE PRACTICE

SPELLING

DAY 3:
Write Compound Words.
See page R29.

GRAMMAR, USAGE, MECHANICS

DAY 3:
Practice Past Tense Verbs.
See page R31.

ORAL LANGUAGE

I wantd to read sumthing about dinosaurs.
(I wanted to read something about dinosaurs.)

TECHNOLOGY

Language Development Have children compose the journal entry using Unit Writer in **WiggleWorks Plus.** Have them describe and illustrate what Daniel saw and heard at the aquarium. Encourage children to write about one realistic thing and one fantastic thing that Daniel did that day.

TEACHER TIP

"Children are fascinated by dinosaurs. I use this fascination to spark interest in writing activities by keeping a supply of dinosaur illustrations, such as posters and coloring-book pictures, in our writing center. When children are stumped for something to write about, I suggest that they select a picture and write about it."

CONNECT TO TRADE BOOKS

Select one of the unit trade books. Read aloud the title, and discuss the cover illustration.

Have children make predictions about what might happen in the story. Record their predictions on chart paper or the chalkboard.

Then read a few pages at a time, stopping to have children identify what parts of the story could happen in real life and what parts could not happen in real life.

Record children's observations. Continue this procedure until the book is completed.

COMPREHENSION

Fantasy/Reality

QUICKCHECK

Can children:

- ✔ identify realistic and make-believe elements of a story?
- ✔ understand that, although parts of a story may seem real, any make-believe element makes the story a fantasy?

If YES, go on to Practice/Apply.

If NO, start at Teach/Model.

A TEACH MODEL

USE ORAL LANGUAGE

Ask children if they could expect to find a bear wearing clothing and eating with a knife and fork in a restaurant. Discuss reasons why real animals could not do that.

Share with children that deciding whether a story is realistic or fantastic means deciding whether the elements and events in the story could happen in real life. To distinguish between fantasy and reality, have children:

- read the text and think about what they know.
- ask themselves if the story events could or could not occur in real life.
- ask themselves whether the story is fantasy or reality, based on the answers to Steps 1 and 2.

MODIFY Instruction

ESL/ELD

▲ Have children go through the pictures one page at a time and point to real and make-believe things. As they point to each picture have them say, "Real" or "Make Believe." Be sure they are aware that not all pages have make-believe elements. **(PICTURE CLUES)**

EXTRA HELP

■ Many children have difficulty distinguishing between make-believe and real characters and events. If children insist that some make-believe characters are real, ask them to name some of the characteristics of the character. Ask: *Could any person/animal you know really do that?* **(ANALYZE)**

LITERATURE CONNECTION

Use the following Think Aloud to model the strategy:

THINK ALOUD *As I read* Daniel's Dinosaurs, *I could see in the pictures that dinosaurs were doing things people usually do. I know that there are no more dinosaurs alive. I also know that they could not work in stores or play games. That is how I knew that this story would be a fantasy.*

B PRACTICE/APPLY

USE PRACTICE BOOK

Have children practice distinguishing fantasy from reality by completing **page 49** of the **Practice Book.**

C ASSESS

APPLY INSTRUCTIONAL ALTERNATIVES

Based on children's completion of **Practice Book page 49,** determine if they were able to distinguish between fantasy and reality. The instructional alternatives below will aid you in pinpointing children's levels of proficiency. Consider the appropriate instructional alternative to promote further skill development.

To reinforce the skills, have children complete **page 50** of the **Practice Book.**

INSTRUCTIONAL ALTERNATIVES

	If the child . . .	Then
Proficient	Distinguishes make-believe characters and events from real characters and events.	• Have the child apply the skill independently to a more challenging story. • Present a new situation and have the child explain what parts are real and what parts are make-believe.
Apprentice	Is not sure whether a character or event is real or is make-believe.	• Have the child work with a partner or a cooperative group to look for and list real qualities and make-believe qualities of characters and events. Point out that having *any* make-believe qualities makes the story make-believe.
Novice	Determines that all characters and events are real.	• Work with the child to determine which qualities are make-believe and why.

DISTINGUISH BETWEEN FANTASY/REALITY

Name

Could It Happen?

▶ Think about Daniel's Dinosaurs. Write what is real from the story.

Daniel loved dinosaurs.

1

2

▶ Now write what is make-believe from the story.
Answers will vary.

3

4

Unit 5 • Information Finders • Daniel's Dinosaurs 49

PRACTICE BOOK p. 49

DISTINGUISH BETWEEN FANTASY/REALITY

Name

Real or Make-Believe?

▶ Read the sentences. Underline the sentence that tells what is make-believe.

1. The boy reads a book about dogs.
The dog reads to the boy.
The boy reads to the dog.

2. A bunny can swim like a fish.
A bunny likes to eat vegetables.
A bunny can hop.

3. I ride my bicycle to school.
I fly on my bicycle to school.
I ride my bicycle to the library.

4. The girl took the bus to school.
The girl sat with a bear on the bus.
The girl was on time for the bus.

50 Unit 5 • Information Finders • Daniel's Dinosaurs

PRACTICE BOOK p. 50

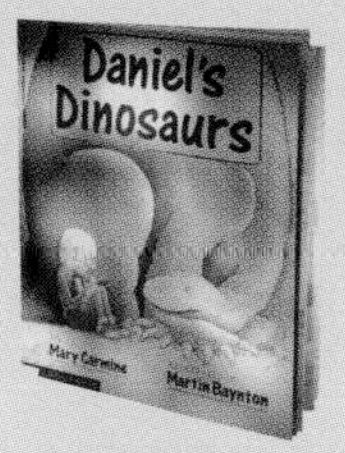

SELECTION WORDS: COMPOUNDS

everywhere

something

sometimes

stingrays

supermarket

SKILLS TRACE

COMPOUND WORDS TESTED

Introduce . . . . . pp. T220–T221
Practice . . . . . . pp. T201, T227
Reteach. . . . . p. R60

TECHNOLOGY

Have children build compound words using the Magnet Board. Start with the word ***everywhere.*** Have children add words using both parts of the compound, such as ***everyone*** and ***nowhere.***

DAILY PHONICS

Compound Words

Ⓐ PHONOLOGICAL AWARENESS

Say the following word parts and ask children to blend them.

- **flash . . . light**
- **lunch . . . box**
- **dog . . . house**
- **sting . . . ray**
- **button . . . hole**
- **butter . . . fly**

Ⓑ TEACH/MODEL

INTRODUCE COMPOUND WORDS Write the following sentence on the chalkboard:

Everyone saw the grasshopper and butterfly.

- Read the sentence with children.
- Point out the word ***grasshopper.***
- Frame the words ***grass*** and ***hopper*** in the word and explain that ***grasshopper*** is a compound word because it is made up of two small words put together.
- Tell children that a reader can sometimes look for small words in a big word. Reading the small words helps to read the big word.
- Have children find other compound words in the sentence and identify the two small words in each. ***(everyone, butterfly)***

PHONICS MAINTENANCE Review the following sound-spellings: ***/ē/y, ey; /ō/oa; /ô/all, aw; /sh/sh.***

MODIFY Instruction

ESL/ELD

▲ Use realia to help children understand compound words. For example, display a lunchbox, and write the word. Draw a line between the two parts of the word. Point to first one and then the other. Have children repeat the separate word parts and then the whole compound word. **(USE REALIA)**

GIFTED & TALENTED

✳ Ask children to make pages for a compound word book. Children can draw two pictures on the front of a page, then write the compound word on the back. For example, one page could show pictures of a cup and a cake, with the compound word *cupcake* on the back. Gather the pages into a book. **(WORK IN GROUPS)**

C PRACTICE/APPLY

BLEND WORDS To practice reading compound words, list the following words and sentences on the chalkboard. Have children read each chorally and identify the two small words in each compound. Model blending as needed.

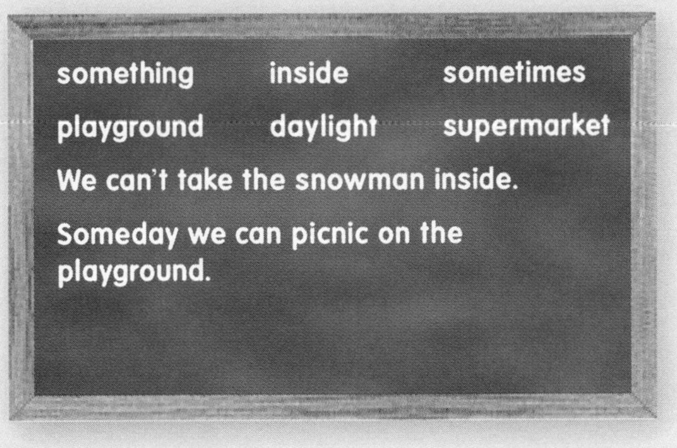

DICTATION Dictate the following words for children to spell: ***sometimes, daytime, mailbox.***

BUILD WORDS Display the following word cards on the chalkboard: ***bird, house, dog, box, lunch, mail.*** Allow children time to build as many compound words as possible using the word cards. Children can write their words on paper. **(INDEPENDENT WORK)**

SLAP IT

Make word cards for the following: *somewhere, butterfly, playground, doghouse, catfish, lighthouse, flashlight, rainbow, sleeping, pretty, under, camper, winter.*

- Pairs of children place the cards in a pile face down.
- The players take turns, turning over one card at a time. Both players read the word and try to slap the card if it is a compound word.
- The first player to *slap* the card gets to keep it. Words that are not compounds are left exposed and a new card is placed on top. The first to slap the next compound word keeps both cards.

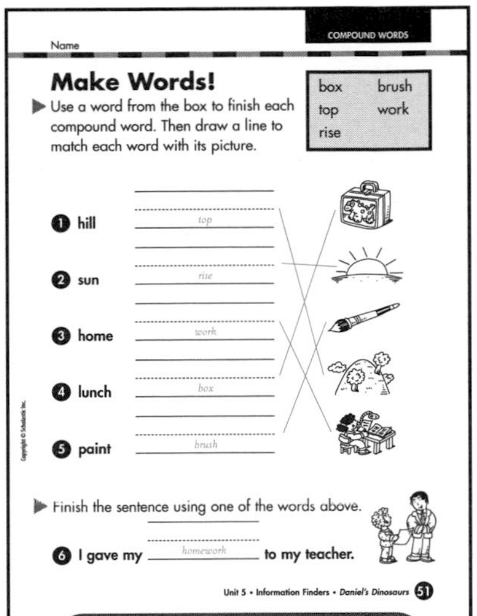

Name

COMPOUND WORDS

Make Words!

Use a word from the box to finish each compound word. Then draw a line to match each word with its picture.

box brush top work rise

1. hill top
2. sun rise
3. home work
4. lunch box
5. paint brush

Finish the sentence using one of the words above.

6. I gave my homework to my teacher.

Unit 5 • Information Finders • *Daniel's Dinosaurs* 51

Copyright © Scholastic Inc.

PRACTICE BOOK p. 51

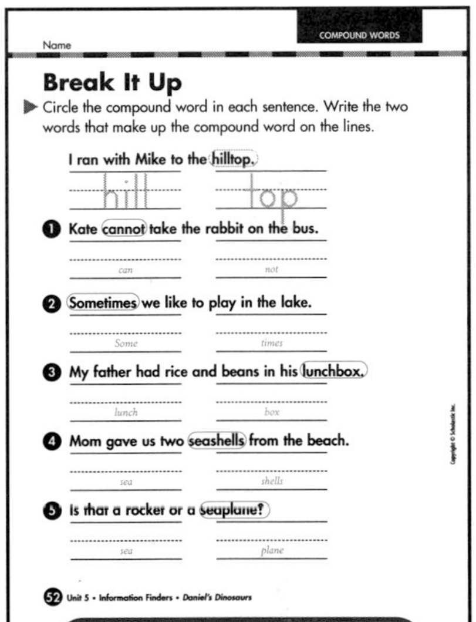

Name

COMPOUND WORDS

Break It Up

Circle the compound word in each sentence. Write the two words that make up the compound word on the lines.

I ran with Mike to the hilltop. — hill top

1. Kate cannot take the rabbit on the bus. — can not
2. Sometimes we like to play in the lake. — Some times
3. My father had rice and beans in his lunchbox. — lunch box
4. Mom gave us two seashells from the beach. — sea shells
5. Is that a rocket or a seaplane? — sea plane

52 Unit 5 • Information Finders • *Daniel's Dinosaurs*

Copyright © Scholastic Inc.

PRACTICE BOOK p. 52

DECODABLE TEXT

For practice reading decodable text, see ***Scholastic Decodable Reader #64.***

For additional phonics instruction and review, see ***Scholastic Phonics A, p. 237.***

Building Fluency

PHONICS READER

Guide children through a reading of **Phonics Reade**
#57, *Baby Pig at School*. For a detailed lesson plan, **Phonics Reader Teacher's Guide Part B, pages 56–57.** While children read, note how well they:

- **blend words,**
- **recognize high-frequency words,**
- **read with speed, accuracy, and expression.**

You may wish to have children reread the story with

★ See Phonics Readers Take-Home Books 37–72 for reproducible format.

More Support Materials . . .

TRADE BOOK LIBRARY

For additional leveled reading practice, have children read one of the following:

Animal Tracks
CHALLENGE

Owl at Home
AVERAGE

Lost!
EASY

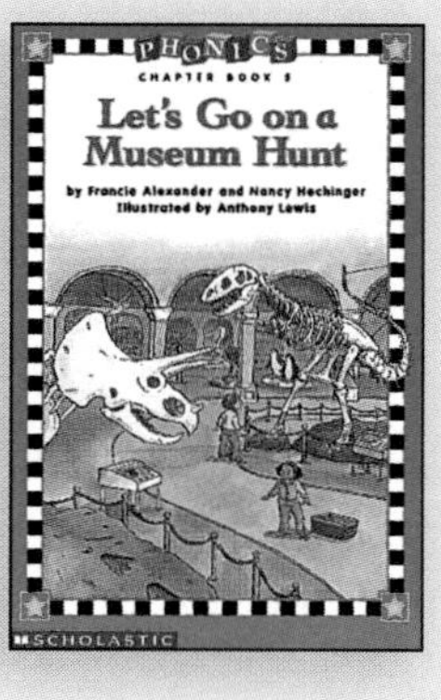

PHONICS CHAPTER BOOK

For additional practice with **/ē/*y, ey,*** have children read Chapter 5, "A Claw, a Straw, and a Key" in **Phonics Chapter Book 5, *Let's Go on a Museum Hunt.***

HOME-SCHOOL CONNECTION

Send home *Baby Pig at School* and *Monkey See, Monkey Do.* Have children read the books to a family member.

MY BOOK

For additional practice with **/ē/*y, ey,*** have children read *Monkey See, Monkey Do.* The My Book is also available on **WiggleWorks Plus.**

Intervention

For children who need extra help . . .

FOCUS ON HIGH-FREQUENCY WORDS

Write the words ***school*** and ***their*** on note cards. Then follow this procedure:

- State each word aloud as children repeat it.
- Have children spell the word aloud as you point to each letter.
- Provide children with simple sentences containing each word. Help them to read the sentences. Allow time for them to practice reading the words and sentences before rereading *Daniel's Dinosaurs*.

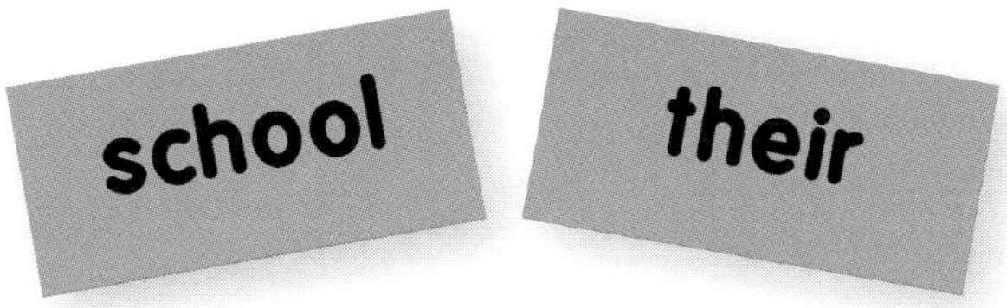

FOCUS ON PHONICS

Provide time for children to play with words they encountered in the story such as ***money*** and ***city.***

- Make each word using magnetic letters or letter cards as children observe.
- Have children trace the letters in each word with their fingers, as you say the sound each letter stands for.
- Mix the letters and have children respell the words.
- Model blending as needed.

PROFESSIONAL DEVELOPMENT

GAY SU PINNELL

The Importance of Thinking Aloud

Model for children daily how to use their developing repertoire of skills and strategies. For example, children might have difficulties choosing which sound associated with the letter y *to use when decoding words such as* yes, fly, *and* happy. *Model use of each sound until a known word can be blended. If the word is in the child's speaking or listening vocabularies, this strategy will be effective.*

DAY 3 WRAP-UP

READ ALOUD *To conclude each reading session and to develop children's oral vocabularies, read aloud a book of your choice. If the book contains chapters, you might choose to read one chapter each day.*

GUIDED READING *To extend reading, meet with the **yellow** and **green** reading groups and assign Independent Center activities.* ***See pages R26–R27.***

SHARED WRITING
Fantasy

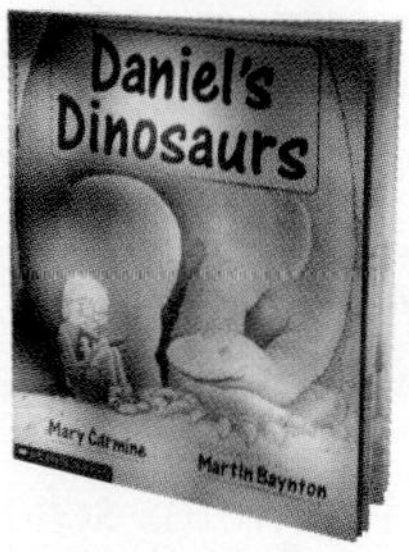

SELECTION CONNECTION Using *Daniel's Dinosaurs* as a model, children will write a story about a fantastic toy in a real setting.

THINK ABOUT WRITING Ask children to tell what might make a story a fantasy. Help them discover that in a fantasy:

- some parts of the story might be realistic and some parts might be make-believe.
- the realistic part might be the setting, or the place where the story happens.

INTRODUCE THE WRITING EVENT Let children know that they will be writing about a make-believe toy in a real setting.

TEACH/MODEL

PUT IT IN CONTEXT Discuss what makes *Daniel's Dinosaurs* a fantasy. Ask:

- What parts of *Daniel's Dinosaurs* are make-believe?
- What parts could happen in real life?
- What settings are used in the story? Are these places real?

Have children think about their story.

- Help children decide how their make-believe toys might be different from real toys.
- Help children create settings for their stories.
- List children's suggestions on the chalkboard.

DAY 4 OBJECTIVES

CHILDREN WILL:

READ 20 MINUTES
- **Reread *Daniel's Dinosaurs***

WRITE 30 MINUTES
- **Shared Writing: Fantasy**
- **Spelling Compound Words**
- **Grammar, Usage, Mechanics: Past Tense Verbs**
- **Oral Language**

EXTEND SKILLS 40 MINUTES
- **Vocabulary**
- **Daily Phonics: Compound Words**
- **Read Aloud**
- **Guided Reading**

RESOURCES
- **Practice Book, pp. 53–60**
- **Spelling Resource Book p. 161**

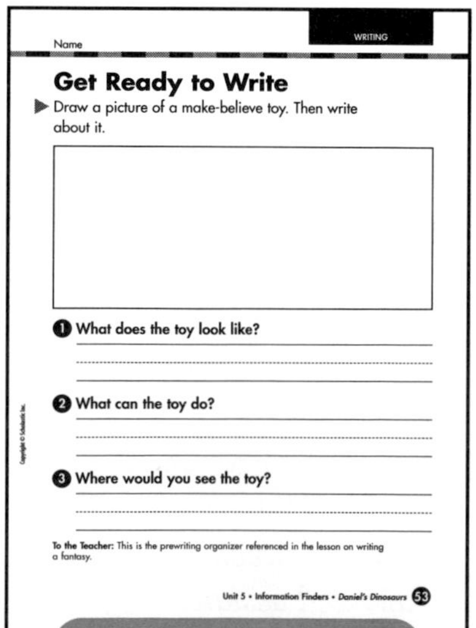
Name WRITING

Get Ready to Write

▶ Draw a picture of a make-believe toy. Then write about it.

1 What does the toy look like?

2 What can the toy do?

3 Where would you see the toy?

To the Teacher: This is the prewriting organizer referenced in the lesson on writing a fantasy.

Unit 5 • Information Finders • Daniel's Dinosaurs 53

PRACTICE BOOK p. 53

MODIFY Instruction

ESL/ELD

▲ Work together with children in a group. Help them work on a story about a toy animal in a real setting. Ask questions such as: *What does your make-believe animal look like? Where will this animal go? What will happen? How will your story end?* **(WORK IN A GROUP)**

EXTRA HELP

■ Some children may be better able to imagine a story if they can use real toys. Provide some stuffed animals or other toys for children to use to act out events for their story. **(USE REALIA)**

GRAMMAR CONNECTION

- Remind children that if they tell about what their toy did, they should use verbs in the past tense.

WRITE

CREATE GROUP STORIES

- Invite cooperative groups to write or dictate a story about a fantasy toy in a real setting.
- Give children time to draw pictures to go with their stories.
- Have groups take turns sharing their completed stories.

ASSESS

PERFORMANCE-BASED ASSESSMENT

The following questions will help children assess their work:

✔ **How was our toy a make-believe or fantasy toy?**

✔ **Was our setting real?**

Children may wish to carry this piece through the writing process described on **pages T286–T289.**

DAILY LANGUAGE PRACTICE

SPELLING

DAY 4:

Apply Compound Words.

Have children proofread sentences. **See page R29.**

GRAMMAR, USAGE, MECHANICS

DAY 4:

Apply Writing Past Tense Verbs. **See page R31.**

ORAL LANGUAGE

Did ennyone drop their mony at the museum?
(Did anyone drop their money at the museum?)

TECHNOLOGY

Writing Skills
Encourage children to use the Unit Writer to create their stories. Suggest that they use the Record tool, the Paint tools, and the stamp art.

Extend Vocabulary

Review High-Frequency Words

Write the high-frequency words ***their*** and ***school*** on note cards. Then write the following incomplete sentences on the chalkboard:

their

school

Pat and Sue read ______ dinosaur book.

We can play with ______ new ball.

Kim took her lunch to ______ .

Steve needs a new pencil for ______ .

Read aloud each incomplete sentence and have children place the appropriate high-frequency word card in the blank space. Then help children to chorally read the completed sentences.

TEACHER TIP

Make and distribute copies of the vocabulary cards on pages R72–R73. Have children use these cards for additional practice.

Review Story Words

Write the story words ***library, supermarket, city, office, teacher,*** and ***shark*** on the chalkboard.

Then write the following incomplete sentences on sentence strips:

We went to shop at the ______ .

Many skyscrapers are in the ______ .

Did you listen to your ______ ?

I borrowed a good book from the ______ .

A ______ swims all the time.

The principal has a desk in his ______ .

CHARACTER PORTRAITS

Have each child select a vocabulary word that names a place, and illustrate it. Then have each child add something fantastic to the setting. Suggest that children use some of the vocabulary words to write captions for their pictures.

Building Fluency

Phonics Reader

Guide children through a reading of **Phonics Reader #58 *Donkey and Monkey*.** For a detailed lesson plan, see **Phonics Reader Teacher's Guide Part B,** pp. 58–59. While children read, note how well they:

- **blend words,**
- **recognize high-frequency words,**
- **read with speed, accuracy, and expression.**

You may wish to have children reread the story with a partner.

* See Phonics Readers Take-Home Books 37–72 for reproducible format.

More Support Materials . . .

Trade Book Library

For additional leveled reading practice, have children read one of the following:

Animal Tracks
Challenge

Owl at Home
Average

Lost!
Easy

Scholastic Phonics A

For practice reading compounds, have children read "Bats at Home," **pp. 225–226** or "How to Make a Cake," **pp. 255–256.**

Home-School Connection

Send home *Donkey and Monkey, Father's Backpack,* and *Sunflowers.* Have children read the books to a family member.

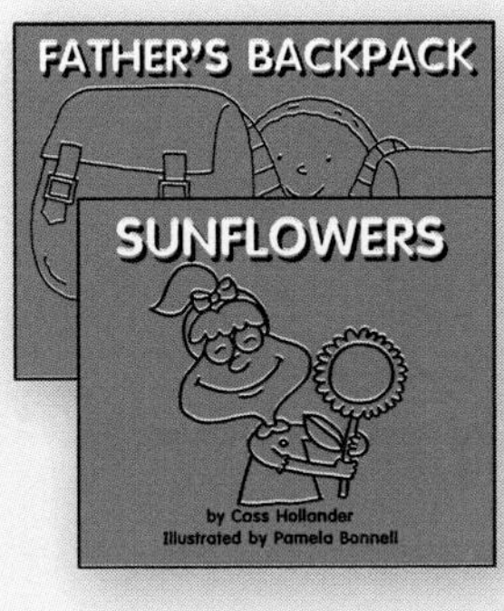

My Book

For additional practice with compound words, have children read *Father's Backpack* and *Sunflowers.* The My Books are also available on **WiggleWorks Plus.**

Listen to the Read Aloud

READ ALOUD BOOK
An Alphabet of Dinosaurs

TECHNOLOGY

Study Skills Have the children create a class dinosaur alphabet. They can use **WiggleWorks Plus** Place Maker to design alphabet posters and illustrate them with borders, drawings, and clip art. Ask them to include dinosaur names to match the alphabet letter. Any letters not represented by a dinosaur might show other items of the time period.

Introduce the Read Aloud

CREATE INTEREST

Display the book cover. Read the title and the names of the author and illustrator. Ask children to name any dinosaurs they can. Then discuss what they know about alphabet books and ask them to predict what they might find in this book. You might want to sing The Alphabet Song with children to review alphabetical order.

Share the Read Aloud

CHART IT

Make a chart similar to the one that follows on chart paper or on the chalkboard. Read *An Alphabet of Dinosaurs* aloud. As you read the description of each dinosaur, discuss whether or not children have heard of this dinosaur. Then record the dinosaur name in the correct column.

Dinosaur Names		
We Know	Some of Us Know	We Never Knew About

Think About the Read Aloud

DISCUSSION

Give children time to review the chart and respond to the information. You may wish to encourage discussion with questions such as:

> **What do you think about the different kinds of dinosaurs? What dinosaur do you think is the most interesting? Why?**

> **Do you know any other dinosaur names?**

> **What new dinosaur names did you learn?**

Focus on Language

DINOSAUR NAMES

Discuss with children some of the dinosaur names that they think are fun to say. Point out that these long words are often interesting ones to sound out. Explain that ***saurus*** means ***lizard.*** Then ask children to make up their own dinosaur names, such as ***laughasaurus*** (funny lizard) or ***porcusaurus*** (lizard with quills). Encourage children to draw pictures to illustrate their dinosaurs.

ACTIVITY: ORGANIZE BY ABC'S

Give children another opportunity to categorize information using alphabetical order. Challenge them to work together to place the first names of everyone in the class in alphabetical order.

Make Connections

ORAL LANGUAGE

To *Daniel's Dinosaurs*

DISCUSSION Remind children how Daniel felt about dinosaurs and discuss why people may be interested in dinosaurs.

To Children's Lives

DISCUSSION Ask children to tell what they enjoyed most about this book. Discuss other places, such as television, museums, or books, where people can learn more about dinosaurs.

LISTEN TO AND EXPAND VOCABULARY

TEACH/MODEL Help children understand that listening carefully can help them learn new words.

THINK ALOUD *When I first listened to this story, I learned many new words—especially the names of dinosaurs. Because I listened carefully, I now know these names, as well as other interesting things about dinosaurs.*

PRACTICE/APPLY Have partners share one or more new words or dinosaur names that they learned. Encourage children to use the names or words in sentences of their own.

DAY 4 WRAP-UP

READ ALOUD *Spend five to ten minutes reading from a selection of your choice. Try to read nonfiction selections each week.*

GUIDED READING *Meet with the **red** and **blue** reading groups and assign Independent Center activities.* ***See pages R26–R27.***

Reading Assessment

DAY 5 OBJECTIVES

CHILDREN WILL:

READ 30 MINUTES

- **Reading Assessment**
- **Daily Phonics: Vowel /ē/y, ey**

WRITE 30 MINUTES

- **Writing Assessment**
- **Spelling: Compound Words**
- **Grammar, Usage, Mechanics: Past Tense Verbs**
- **Oral Language**

EXTEND SKILLS 30 MINUTES

- **Integrated Language Arts**
- **Read Aloud**
- **Guided Reading**

RESOURCES

- **Selection Test**
- **Spelling Resource Book, p. 163**

TEACHER SELF-ASSESSMENT

✔ Did I frequently model how to blend words?

✔ Did I regroup children according to skill needs and reading level?

✔ Did I provide children with successful reading and writing opportunities each day?

INFORMAL ASSESSMENT: OBSERVATION

PHONICS

Write the following spellings on note cards: ***y, ey.*** Display one card at a time, and have the class state the sound the spelling stands for. Note children who respond incorrectly or who wait for classmates to respond before providing an answer.

HIGH-FREQUENCY WORDS

Write the following words on note cards: ***school, their.*** Display one card at a time, and have the class read the word. Note children who have difficulty recognizing either word.

KEY SKILL: FANTASY/ REALITY

Display a book children have not read yet. Have children browse the pictures and tell whether they think the story will be a fantasy or realistic fiction.

CONFERENCE

Have children reread *Daniel's Dinosaurs*. As they reread, select several children to conference with. Ask them to:

- read aloud a few pages of the story.
- retell the story in their own words.
- explain what they do to figure out an unfamiliar word.

Keep anecdotal records of the conferences. Take note of children's reading rate. Place your findings in each child's assessment folder. Use the information to determine which children need additional support.

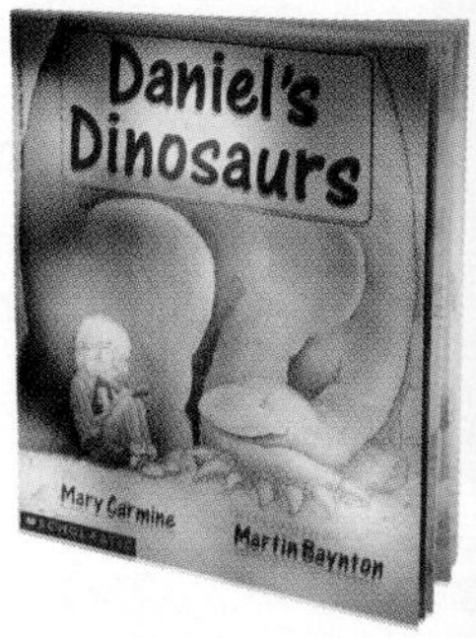

Daniel's Dinosaurs

FORMAL ASSESSMENT

DECODING TEST

Make two copies of the assessment below. The assessment piece is designed to be used individually.

- Give one to the child and keep the other to record each child's errors.
- As the child reads aloud the words and sentences in the assessment boxes, record his or her attempts, corrections, errors, and passes.
- Once completed, keep each assessment piece in the child's portfolio as a running record of his or her emerging reading skills.

NAME: ______________________________ **DATE:** ____________

A Have children read the following word list:

stay	**happy**	**with**	**school**	**all**
sunny	**somewhere**	**crunchy**	**their**	**more**
train	**shark**	**lunchbox**	**was**	**belongs**
monkey	**teacher**	**silly**	**grow**	**were**
stingray	**money**	**sandy**	**which**	**way**

B Have children read the following sentences:

- **They put their money in a piggy bank.**
- **We are very happy at school.**

C On a separate sheet of paper, have children write the following words and sentences.

- **leafy inside shake thin**
- **She saw a funny play.**
- **We went to a sandy beach.**

SELECTION TEST

Use the selection test to obtain a formal measure of children's mastery of the week's reading objectives.

TIME MANAGEMENT

Part C of the assessment can be administered whole class. Assess children throughout the entire day on Parts A and B. Each assessment should take no more than 2–3 minutes.

You may choose to assess children during independent reading time or Independent Center time. If you have a teacher's aide, allow him or her to give the assessment.

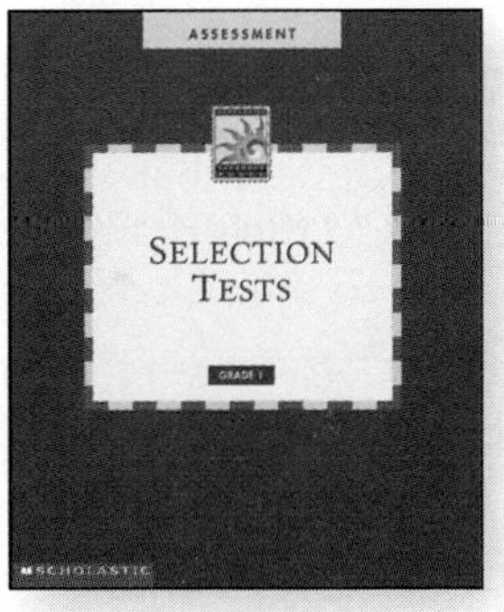

SELECTION TEST

DAILY LANGUAGE PRACTICE

Spelling

DAY 5:
Administer the Posttest for Compound Words. **See page R29.**

Grammar, Usage, Mechanics

DAY 5:
Assess Past Tense Verbs. **See page R31.**

Oral Language

Dan likeed the funy fish.
(Dan liked the funny fish.)

PORTFOLIO

Suggest that children add their drafts and revisions to their Literacy Portfolios.

Writing Assessment

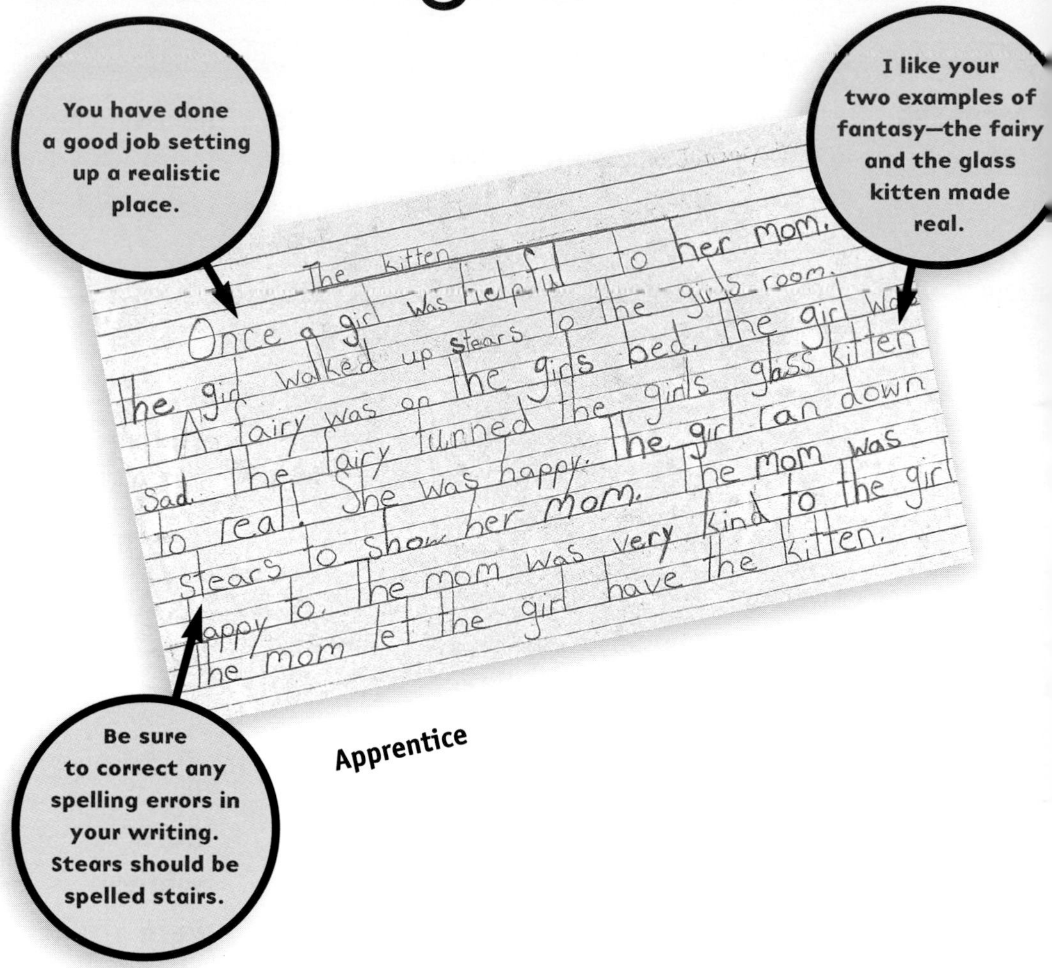
You have done a good job setting up a realistic place.
I like your two examples of fantasy—the fairy and the glass kitten made real.
Be sure to correct any spelling errors in your writing. Stears should be spelled stairs.
The kitten
Once a girl was helpful to her mom.
The girl walked up stears to the girls room.
A fairy was on the girls bed. The girl was
sad. The fairy turned the girls glass kitten
to real! She was happy. The girl ran down
stears to show her mom. The mom was
happy to. The mom was very kind to the girl
The mom let the girl have the kitten.

Apprentice

Use the rubric below to assess children's writing.

CHILDREN'S WRITING RUBRIC

Proficient	• The toy is make-believe. • The setting is realistic. • The setting stays realistic throughout the story.	• The story has been proofread and corrected for grammar, usage, and mechanics.
Apprentice	• The toy is make-believe. • The setting is generally realistic, but may at times become make-believe.	• The story may or may not have been proofread, but has not been completely corrected for errors.
Novice	• Both the setting and the toy are realistic. • There is nothing make-believe in the story, or there is nothing realistic in the story.	• The story has not been corrected for errors.

Integrated Language Arts

VIEWING/SPEAKING/LISTENING

Compare Sharks and Dinosaurs

MATERIALS:
paper, tinfoil, cardboard, and other recycled materials

SUGGESTED GROUPING:
Whole class and individuals

HAVE children discuss Daniel's love of dinosaurs and sharks. Encourage them to talk about how sharks and dinosaurs might act. Then ask children to think about how they could make shark and dinosaur costumes.

ASK children to discuss the different features of sharks or dinosaurs. Then challenge them to use a variety of materials—such as tinfoil, paper plates, crayons, and paper—to make paper fins, horns, cardboard tails, tinfoil claws, and other costume parts.

GIVE children an opportunity to wear their costumes and role-play sharks or dinosaurs. Remind them to use hand gestures and other movements to make their sharks or dinosaurs seem realistic. Encourage children to talk about how sharks and dinosaurs are the same and different.

VIEWING/WRITING/VOCABULARY

Write About Daniel's Sharks

MATERIALS:
Anthology Audiocassette player and audiocassette (optional)

SUGGESTED GROUPING:
Partners and individuals

CHALLENGE children to write a sequel to *Daniel's Dinosaurs*. Suggest that they title their stories "Daniel's Sharks."

HELP children organize their ideas by asking:

- Where will this story happen?
- Who will look like a shark to Daniel?
- What funny things might happen?
- What animal might Daniel be fascinated with next? How might he get the idea?

CHILDREN can work with partners or alone to write or dictate a new story. Encourage them to use as many of the story words as possible. Suggest that they illustrate their stories.

Children might want to include their sequels in their Literacy Portfolios.

Integrated Language Arts

WRITING/VIEWING

Interview Daniel's Dinosaur

Good For Grading

MATERIALS: Paper, pencil, cardboard tubes for microphones (optional)

SUGGESTED GROUPING: Partners and cooperative groups

HAVE partners or cooperative groups take turns interviewing dinosaurs. Have one child pretend to be one of Daniel's dinosaurs while other children pretend to be reporters.

CHILDREN can create a list of questions they would like to ask the dinosaur. Write the question words *who, what, when, where, why,* and *how* on the chalkboard so reporters can use them in writing their questions.

GRADE by looking for proper use of past tense verbs and relevance of the interview question.

TECHNOLOGY

Speaking Skills Children might use **WiggleWorks Plus** Unit Writer to compose two or three questions for a reporter to ask Daniel's Dinosaur friends. Record the interviews on audiocassettes.

WRITING/VIEWING

Create a Shark Exhibit

MATERIALS: Books about sharks and pictures of sharks, poster paper, pencils, markers

SUGGESTED GROUPING: Cooperative groups

CHALLENGE cooperative groups to research information on sharks. Then have children design a museum exhibit based on their research. They might:

- create a fact chart about sharks.
- display pictures, photographs, and realistic models of sharks.
- make clay models of different kinds of sharks.
- conduct tours of the museum, pointing to items of special interest.

CONTACT an aquarium to request a sample of shark skin or a shark's tooth, or gather information about sharks to display. Children can make labels identifying each object.

Singular and Plural Nouns

TEACH/MODEL Write the names of some possible museum items on a chart, such as *shark bones* and *model of a shark*. Identify with children the words that name more than one person, place, or thing.

PRACTICE/APPLY Children can look at the pictures and decide whether each naming word is singular or plural.

DAY 5 WRAP-UP

READ ALOUD *Spend five to ten minutes reading from a selection of your choice.*

GUIDED READING *Meet with the* ***green*** *and* ***yellow*** *reading groups and assign Independent Center activities.* ***See pages R26–R27.***

How to Make a Nature Poster

WHY DO THIS WORKSHOP?

As children's awareness of the world grows beyond their own immediate surroundings, they begin to realize that there are natural environments other than the ones most familiar to them. These other environments are also homes to many kinds of living things.

In this Workshop, children observe a poster that shows several natural environments. Then they choose a different environment and design a nature poster that presents information about it. Children will have to select resource materials that present information about plants and animals in the environment they've chosen. By doing this, children will practice sorting through information.

GETTING STARTED

Sort Information

To focus children on the task, you might read through Side 1 of the Workshop Card with the entire class. Invite children to tell you what they see and like about the "Home Sweet Home" poster. You could also ask any of these questions to focus them further on the Workshop:

> **What did you learn about the earth from this poster?**

> **What are some environments you know about? What do you know about the desert? the forest? other environments?**

> **How could you find out more about other environments?**

WORKSHOP OBJECTIVES

CHILDREN LEARN TO:

- **Look through nature books and magazines for ideas about living things in nature**
- **Sort information to plan and create a nature poster**

MATERIALS

- **Paper and pencil**
- **Markers or crayons**
- **Books and magazines about nature**

TECHNOLOGY

Presentation Tools Children can use **WiggleWorks Plus** PlaceMaker to create the nature posters. Using the clip art provided and the drawing tools, small groups should create posters representative of each environment discussed.

WORKSHOP

GRADE 1 MANAGING INFORMATION

WORKSHOP 2

How to Make a Nature Poster

Nature posters show places where plants, animals and people live.

This poster shows why it's important to take care of the environment.

Where does your favorite animal live?

Why do you think we should take care of plants?

Now Make Your Own

1 Choose an Environment

Encourage children to discuss animals they're curious about. Provide them with resources in which they can find information about those animals in their natural environments. You may want to suggest that children who have chosen a similar environment work together.

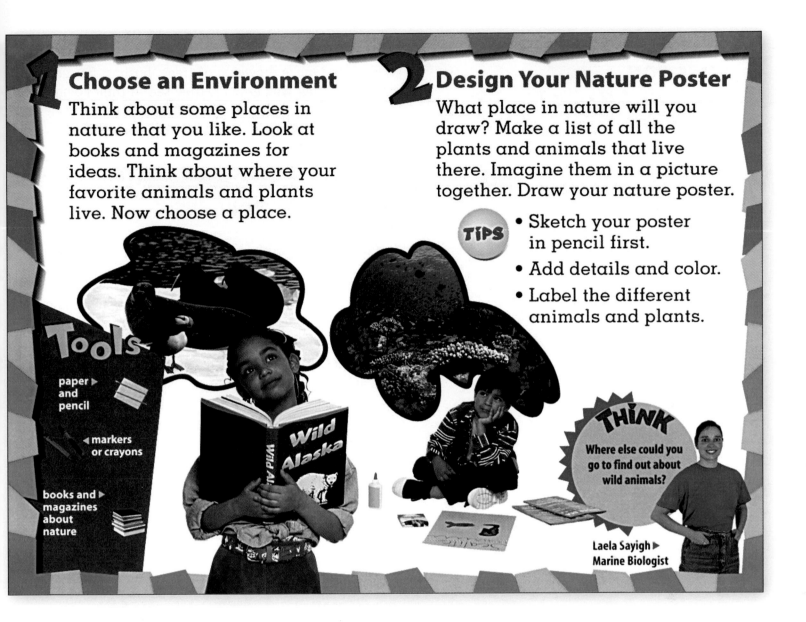

1 Choose an Environment

Think about some places in nature that you like. Look at books and magazines for ideas. Think about where your favorite animals and plants live. Now choose a place.

2 Design Your Nature Poster

What place in nature will you draw? Make a list of all the plants and animals that live there. Imagine them in a picture together. Draw your nature poster.

TIPS
- Sketch your poster in pencil first.
- Add details and color.
- Label the different animals and plants.

Tools

- paper and pencil
- markers or crayons
- books and magazines about nature

THINK

Where else could you go to find out about wild animals?

Laela Sayigh
Marine Biologist

2 DESIGN YOUR NATURE POSTER

You may want to demonstrate how people get and manage information. If you've written the names of some environments on the chalkboard, use those as headings. List some familiar plants and animals under each heading. When children select the environment for their poster, encourage them to begin their own list. Point out that the list is their guide to help them decide what to include in their poster.

SHOP

SELF-SELECTION

When children complete this Workshop Card, they may want to save their notes, lists, and posters. Reviewing what they learned will be helpful in the Project, where children create a big book of information.

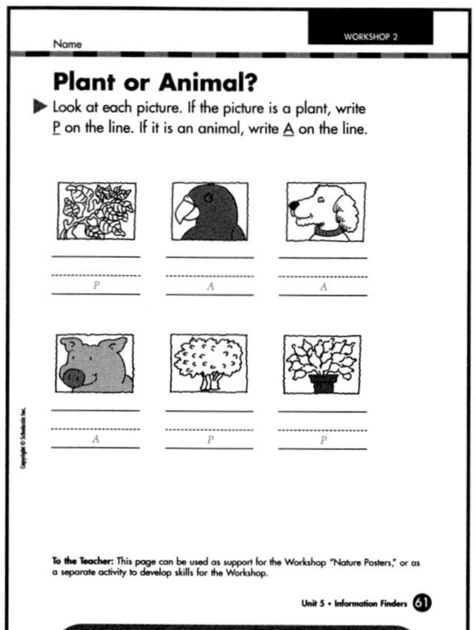
Name WORKSHOP 2

Plant or Animal?

Look at each picture. If the picture is a plant, write P on the line. If it is an animal, write A on the line.

P A A

A P P

To the Teacher: This page can be used as support for the Workshop "Nature Posters," or as a separate activity to develop skills for the Workshop.

Unit 5 • Information Finders 61

PRACTICE BOOK p. 61

Name WORKSHOP 2

What Doesn't Belong?

Put an X through each plant or animal that does not belong in the sea life nature poster. Then write sentences telling about the poster.

1

2

62 Unit 5 • Information Finders

PRACTICE BOOK p. 62

Use **Practice Book pages 61 and 62** as practice for the Workshop or as a separate activity to strengthen children's skills.

Connect to Home and Community

Children can make drawings of trees, bushes, flowers, birds, and other wild animals they see in their community for a classroom display. They can also bring in samples of plant life they see, such as different leaves and pods.

ASSESSMENT

INFORMAL ASSESSMENT

OBSERVATION

Review children's work. Ask yourself:

✔ Do children's posters show a natural environment?

✔ Do the plants and animals belong in the environment?

✔ How did children obtain and organize the information?

IF NOT, TRY THIS:

Have them focus on one environment with which they're familiar, such as the backyard or park where they made their Observation Log for the Workshop 1 Card. Have them list all the plants and animals they observed there.

CHILDREN'S SELF-ASSESSMENT

> **Does my poster show plants and animals that are in an environment?**

Use the rubric below to assess children's understanding of the Workshop.

CHILDREN'S WORKSHOP RUBRIC

Proficient	**Children are able to sort out information about plants and animals in one specific environment. Children's posters show important details in the environment.**
Apprentice	**Children may need help sorting information to list only plants and animals for one environment. Children's posters may show some incorrect details in an environment.**
Novice	**Children don't understand that all information should not be included; children may choose information that is unrelated or inappropriate to the environment.**

The Plant Castle

Main Selection
Genre: Realistic Fiction
Southwest Book Award-winning author

Paired Selection
Genre: Map

WEEK 5 TESTED SKILLS

- **Vocabulary**
- **Daily Phonics: Vowel /ō/ *o*, *ow***
  r*-Controlled Vowel /är/ *ar
- **Key Comprehension Skill: Compare/Contrast**
- **Spelling: Words With Vowel /ō/ *o*, *ow***
- **Grammar, Usage, Mechanics: Words That Compare**

Technology Connection

Build Background Try going on a garden tour at **commtechlab.msu.edu.** Look under Sites and then 4-H Children's Garden. Children will discover the beauty of gardens designed especially for young people. Have them compare the garden map included here to the map of the New York Botanical Garden found in the story.

Selection Summary

In this story, Carmen takes her friend Beth on a tour of the arboretum, or plant castle, where Carmen's mother works. The girls begin their tour in the desert room where they learn about plants such as the fishhook and pincushion cacti. In the orchid room, they spot a butterfly and follow it through the spring garden room, rain forest room, and tropical room.

PAIRED SELECTION This map introduces children to a different type of museum for plants: the Botanical Garden in the Bronx, New York.

Author

PAT MORA has been acknowledged as a leader in the contemporary movement to recognize and express the many voices of the Hispanic population in the United States. By portraying her native traditions as well as the physical surroundings of the desert southwest, Mora expresses her voice and those of her people.

Weekly Organizer

Visit Our Web Site
www.scholastic.com

The Plant Castle

	DAY 1	DAY 2
READ and Introduce Skills • VOCABULARY • PHONICS • COMPREHENSION • LISTENING • SPEAKING • VIEWING  	**BUILD BACKGROUND,** p. T245 ▲ **VOCABULARY,** p. T246 ▲ ■ Practice Book, p. 63 **DAILY PHONICS:** ▲ ✷ Vowel /ō/*o, ow*, pp. T248–T249 Practice Book, pp. 64, 65 **PREVIEW AND PREDICT,** p. T250 **READ:** ▲ ✷ ■ *The Plant Castle*, pp. T250–T255 **COMPREHENSION:** Compare/Contrast, p. T253	**READ:** ▲ ■ ✷ *The Plant Castle*, pp. T256–T264 "New York Botanical Garden," p. T265 **DAILY PHONICS:** *r*-Controlled Vowel /är/*ar*, p. T259 Vowel /ō/*o, ow*, p. T261 **GENRE:** Realistic Fiction, p. T263
WRITE and Respond • GRAMMAR • USAGE • MECHANICS • SPELLING • WRITING	**SHARED WRITING,** p. T245 **JOURNAL,** p. T247 **SPELLING:** Pretest: Words With Vowel /ō/*o, ow*, p. R36 Spelling Resource Book, p. 129 **GRAMMAR, USAGE, MECHANICS:** Teach/Model: Words That Compare, p. R38 **ORAL LANGUAGE,** p. T255	**SHARED WRITING:** Prewrite, p. T265 Practice Book, p. 71 **SPELLING:** Vocabulary Practice, p. R36 Spelling Resource Book, pp. 130–132 **GRAMMAR, USAGE, MECHANICS:** Practice, p. R38 **ORAL LANGUAGE,** p. T265
EXTEND SKILLS and Apply to Literature • SKILLS • INTEGRATED LANGUAGE ARTS • INTEGRATED CURRICULUM • GUIDED READING • INDEPENDENT READING	**READ ALOUD,** p. T255 **GUIDED READING,** pp. R34–R35 **TRADE BOOKS** • *Lost!* • *Owl at Home* • *Animal Tracks* 	**READ ALOUD,** p. T265 **GUIDED READING,** pp. R34–R35 **INTEGRATED CURRICULUM:** Science, p. R40 Math, p. R40 The Arts, p. R41 Social Studies, p. R41
TECHNOLOGY and **REAL-WORLD SKILLS**	**WIGGLEWORKS PLUS CD-ROM** Magnet Board, T246, T248 **FIRST THOUSAND WORDS CD-ROM** Expanding Vocabulary, T255	**CD-ROM ENCYCLOPEDIA** Finding the Facts, T263

MODIFY INSTRUCTION

● INTERVENTION ▲ ESL/ELD ■ EXTRA HELP
✷ GIFTED & TALENTED ✓ = TESTED SKILL

DAY 3	DAY 4	DAY 5
✓ **COMPREHENSION:** ▲ ■ Compare/Contrast, pp. T268–T269 Practice Book, pp. 67, 68 ✓ **DAILY PHONICS:** ▲ ✷ *r*-Controlled Vowel /är/*ar*, p. T270 Practice Book, pp. 69, 70 **BUILDING FLUENCY,** p. T272 **FOCUS ON HIGH-FREQUENCY WORDS,** p. T273 **FOCUS ON PHONICS,** p. T273	**VOCABULARY REVIEW,** p. T276 ✓ **DAILY PHONICS:** Vowel /ō/*o, ow,* p. T277	**READING ASSESSMENT,** pp. T280–T281 Selection Test, p. T281 Conference, p. T281 Decoding Test, p. T281
RESPOND: ▲ Think About Reading, p. T266 Practice Book, p. 66 **WRITE A THANK-YOU LETTER,** p. T267 ✓ **SPELLING:** Write/Proofread, p. R37 Spelling Resource Book, p. 133 ✓ **GRAMMAR, USAGE, MECHANICS:** Practice, p. R39 **ORAL LANGUAGE,** p. T267	**SHARED WRITING:** ▲ ✷ Personal Narrative, p. T274 Practice Book, p. 71 ✓ **SPELLING:** Study/Review, p. R37 Spelling Resource Book, p. 161 ✓ **GRAMMAR, USAGE, MECHANICS:** Apply, p. R39 **ORAL LANGUAGE,** p. T275	**WRITING ASSESSMENT,** p. T282 Child Model Children's Writing Rubric ✓ **SPELLING:** Posttest, p. R37 Spelling Resource Book, p. 163 ✓ **GRAMMAR, USAGE, MECHANICS:** Assess, p. R39 **ORAL LANGUAGE,** p. T282
READ ALOUD, p. T273 **GUIDED READING,** pp. R34–R35 **OPTIONAL MATERIALS,** p. T272 Phonics Reader #55: *Follow It!*	**READ ALOUD,** p. T279 **GUIDED READING,** pp. R34–R35 **EXTEND VOCABULARY:** Review High-Frequency Words, p. T276 Review Story Words, p. T276 **OPTIONAL MATERIALS,** p. T277 Phonics Reader #56: *Bo's Bows* ✓ **STUDY SKILLS:** Test-Taking Strategies, p. T278	**READ ALOUD,** p. T284 **GUIDED READING,** pp. R34–R35 **INTEGRATED LANGUAGE ARTS:** Grow a Plant, p. T283 Give a Tour, p. T283 Create Categories, p. T284 Make a Map, p. T284
WIGGLEWORKS PLUS CD-ROM Presentation Tools, T267 **WIGGLEWORKS PLUS CD-ROM** Magnet Board, T270	**WIGGLEWORKS PLUS CD-ROM** Writing Skills, T275 **WORD PROCESSING** Study Skills, T279	**WIGGLEWORKS PLUS CD-ROM** Presentation Tools, T284

Weekly Assessment

ASSESSMENT PLANNING

USE THIS CHART TO PLAN YOUR ASSESSMENT OF THE WEEKLY READING OBJECTIVES.

- **Informal Assessment is ongoing and should be used before, during, and after reading.**
- **Formal Assessment occurs at the end of the week on the selection test.**
- **Note that Intervention activities occur throughout the lesson to support children who need extra help with skills.**

YOU MAY CHOOSE AMONG THE FOLLOWING PAGES IN THE ASSESSMENT HANDBOOK.

- **Informal Assessment**
- **Anecdotal Record**
- **Portfolio Checklist and Evaluation Forms**
- **Self-Assessment**
- **English Language Learners**
- **Using Technology to Assess**
- **Test Preparations**

SKILLS AND STRATEGIES	Informal Assessment
COMPREHENSION Compare/Contrast	**OBSERVATION p. T253** • Can children use picture and story clues to compare and contrast? **QUICKCHECK p. T268** • Can children use text and picture clues to make comparisons? **CHECK PRACTICE BOOK p. 67** **CONFERENCE p. T280**
DAILY PHONICS Vowel /ō/*o, ow* *r*-Controlled Vowel /är/*ar*	**OBSERVATION pp. T259, T261** • Can children identify and blend words with /ō/*o, ow*? • Can children identify and blend words with *ar*? **CHECK PRACTICE BOOK p. 64** **DICTATION pp. T249, T271**
VOCABULARY Story Words **desert, forest, fruits, butterfly, leaves, trees** High-Frequency **mother, girl**	**OBSERVATION p. T276** • Did children identify story words? • Did children identify high-frequency words? **CHECK PRACTICE BOOK p. 63**

Formal Assessment	INTERVENTION and Instructional Alternatives	Planning Notes
SELECTION TEST • Questions 1–3 check children's mastery of the key strategy, compare/contrast. **UNIT TEST**	If children need help with compare/contrast, then go to: • **Instructional Alternatives, p. T269**	
DECODING TEST • See p. T281 **SELECTION TEST** • Questions 4–7 check children's ability to recognize words with vowel /ō/*o, ow* and /är/*ar.* **UNIT TEST**	If children need help identifying words with vowel /ō/*o, ow,* then go to: • **Intervention Activity, p. T273** • **Reteach, p. R61** If children need help identifying words with /är/*ar,* then go to: • **Intervention Activity, p. T273** • **Reteach, p. R61**	
SELECTION TEST • Questions 8–10 check children's recall of high-frequency words and story words. **UNIT TEST**	If children need additional practice with the vocabulary words, then go to: • **Intervention Activity, p. T273** • **Extend Vocabulary, p. T276** • **Integrated Language Arts Activity, p. T284**	

Technology

EXPLORING THE WIGGLEWORKS PLUS SELECTION

The children can interact with an electronic version of the literature selection in this lesson. Use this activity to direct the children as they explore the WiggleWorks Plus CD-ROM.

STEP 1 Read Aloud

Have children read the source book, *The Plant Castle,* on the **WiggleWorks Plus** CD-ROM. Direct them to choose Read Aloud and listen to the story for enjoyment, focusing on story sequence and plot.

WiggleWorks Plus CD-ROM

STEP 2 Collect Words

Next, have children read the story at their own pace, using the Read option. As they move through the story, have them collect plant words on a My Words list. The list should begin with *arboretum* and might include *cacti, succulents, thorns, fishhook,* and *pincushion.* Remind children to first select the word in the story and then use the + button to copy it from the story onto the list.

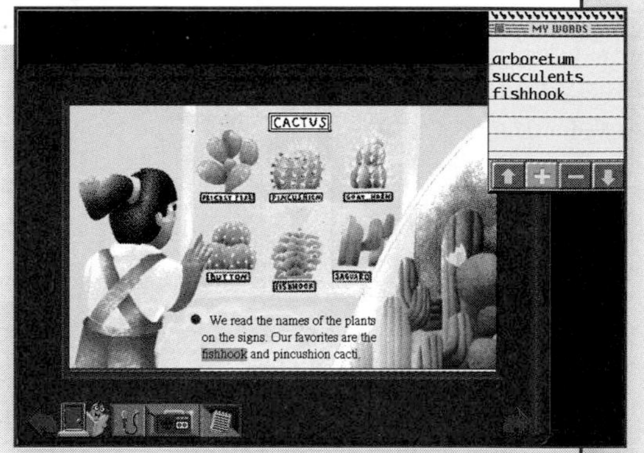

WiggleWorks Plus CD-ROM

STEP 3 Rewrite Story

Now, have children use the My Book version of the story. With the My Words list open, have them read through the story, stopping on the pages from which the words were taken. Direct them to rewrite the text on the page using the matching word from the My Words list.

STEP 4 Illustrate and Print

Finally, have children return to the title page and compose a new title for their version of the book. Encourage children to electronically paint their book using vibrant tropical or earthen desert colors as appropriate. Have them print the books to share with classmates and family.

For more activity suggestions, see the **WiggleWorks Plus** Teaching Guide.

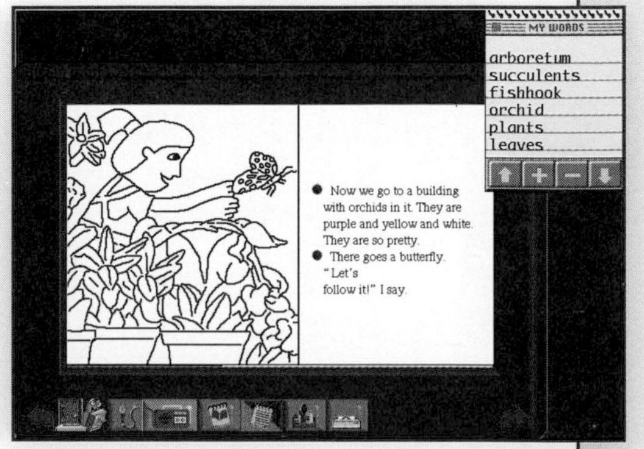

WiggleWorks Plus CD-ROM

Build Background

When children explore new places, they learn many new things. In The Plant Castle, *two children explore an unusual natural environment—an arboretum. Here they gather information about very different kinds of plants.*

Activate Prior Knowledge

DISCUSS PLACES Discuss with children how visiting new places can be an exciting way to learn. Some places to visit include museums, aquariums, or arboretums. Point out that an arboretum is like a museum of plants. It has a variety of plants from different places.

RECALL SPECIAL PLACES Invite children to talk about places they have seen or visited. You may wish to ask:

> **What places have you visited?**

> **What did you learn about?**

SHARED WRITING *Personal Narrative*

INTRODUCE Build background for writing a personal narrative by asking children to think about a place they like to visit. Have them close their eyes and imagine that place and what they would see there. Have them write a sentence or two about what they see.

DAY 1 OBJECTIVES

CHILDREN WILL:

READ 30 MINUTES
- **Build Background**
- **Vocabulary**
- **Daily Phonics: Vowel /ō/ *o, ow***
- ***The Plant Castle*, pp. 115–119**
- **Key Comprehension Skill: Compare/Contrast**

WRITE 30 MINUTES
- **Shared Writing: Introduce Personal Narrative**
- **Quickwrite: Predict**
- **Spelling: Words With Vowel /ō/ *o, ow***
- **Grammar, Usage, Mechanics: Words That Compare**
- **Oral Language**

EXTEND SKILLS 30 MINUTES
- **Read Aloud**
- **Guided Reading**

RESOURCES
- **Practice Book, pp. 63–65**
- **Spelling Resource Book, p. 129**

MODIFY Instruction

ESL/ELD

▲ Help English language learners develop their vocabulary by listing the places classmates suggest during the Recall Special Places discussion. Next to each place write words that name what children saw. Use pictures to clarify the meanings of the listed words. **(USE LISTS)**

VOCABULARY

HIGH-FREQUENCY

mother girl

STORY WORDS

desert	butterfly
forest	leaves
fruits	trees

TECHNOLOGY

For children needing additional practice with high-frequency words prior to reading the story, have them build, explode, and rebuild each high-frequency word on the **WiggleWorks Plus** Magnet Board.

VOCABULARY

High-Frequency Words

A TEACH/MODEL

INTRODUCE HIGH-FREQUENCY WORDS

Write the high-frequency words ***mother*** and ***girl*** in sentences on the chalkboard. Read the sentences aloud, underline the high-frequency words, and ask children if they recognize them. You may wish to use these sentences:

My mother likes plants.

Beth is a new girl at school.

Ask volunteers to dictate sentences using the high-frequency words. Add these to the chalkboard.

B PRACTICE/APPLY

FOCUS ON SPELLING

Write each high-frequency word on a note card. Read each word aloud. Then do the following:

mother

girl

ROUTINE

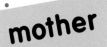

1. **Display one card at a time, and ask children to state each word aloud.**
2. **Have children spell each word aloud.**
3. **Ask children to write each word in the air as they state aloud each letter. Then have them write each word on a sheet of paper or in their journals.**

MAINTAIN VOCABULARY

Add the note cards to the **Word Wall.** Then review the following high-frequency words on the wall: **was, grow, school, their.**

MODIFY Instruction

ESL/ELD

▲ List both high-frequency words and story words on the chalkboard. Use visuals to make sure children understand the words. Then ask them to draw a picture that includes several of the vocabulary words. Have them label their pictures with the words, or dictate labels. **(MULTISENSORY TECHNIQUES)**

EXTRA HELP

■ Give each child two word cards on which you have written *mother* and *girl*, one word per card. Have children look through *The Plant Castle* to find those words. Ask volunteers to call out a word they find, identify the page number, and read the sentence that contains the word. **(USE WORD CARDS)**

Story Words

A TEACH/MODEL

INTRODUCE STORY WORDS

The story also contains the following story words—***desert, butterfly, forest, fruits, leaves, trees***.

- Write these words on the chalkboard, read them aloud, and discuss their meanings if necessary.
- Point out previously taught sound-spelling correspondences such as ***r-blends*** and ***long e (ee, ea)***.
- Provide visual clues for each of the story words. For example, show pictures of a desert and a forest. If possible, take a walk outside and have children find and identify different kinds of trees and their leaves.

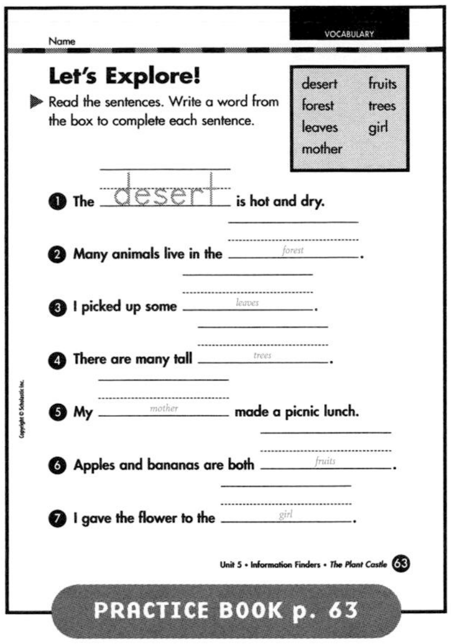

Name VOCABULARY

Let's Explore!

▶ Read the sentences. Write a word from the box to complete each sentence.

desert	fruits
forest	trees
leaves	girl
mother	

1. The desert is hot and dry.
2. Many animals live in the forest.
3. I picked up some leaves.
4. There are many tall trees.
5. My mother made a picnic lunch.
6. Apples and bananas are both fruits.
7. I gave the flower to the girl.

Copyright © Scholastic Inc.

Unit 5 • Information Finders • *The Plant Castle* 63

PRACTICE BOOK p. 63

B PRACTICE/APPLY

BUILD STORY BACKGROUND

Discuss forests and deserts with children.

- Have children talk about each environment and what kinds of plants they might see growing in each place.
- Have children close their eyes and imagine that they are in a forest or desert. What do they see there? What do they smell and feel?
- Encourage children to draw a picture of a forest or desert and to include the things they would see in either of these places.

WRITE TO READ

- When completed, have children use one or more of the story words to write sentences about their pictures.

It is hot at the desert.

FOREST PICTURES

Have children write the word ***forest*** horizontally on a large sheet of paper. Then invite them to draw a picture for each letter in the word. Explain that the pictures should show things that might be found in the forest, such as ferns, owls, rocks, eagles, seeds, and trees. If time permits, have children repeat the activity with ***fruits***.

f o r e s t

JOURNAL

Ask children to write a sentence using each **high-frequency word** in their Journals. You might suggest the following sentence starters:

My mother _____.

The girl _____.

SELECTION WORDS With Vowel /ō/ o, ow

go grow
no snow
show

SKILLS TRACE

VOWEL /ō/ o, ow TESTED

Introduce . . . . p. T248
Practice . . . pp. T249, T261, T273
Reteach . . . . p. R61

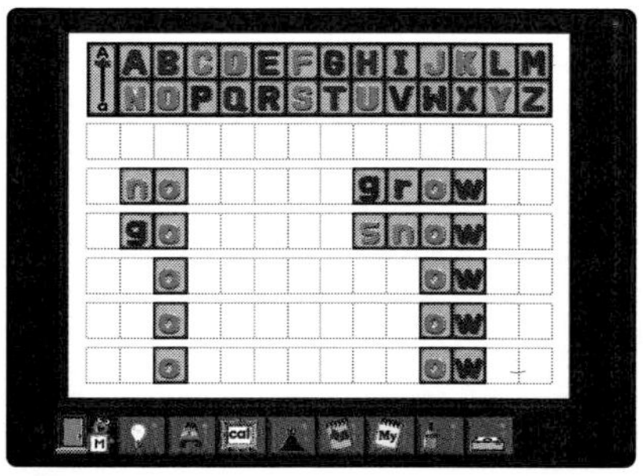

TECHNOLOGY

Have children build words with long o (o, ow) on the WiggleWorks Plus Magnet Board.

- Begin with the words *no* and *grow.*
- Have children change the initial consonant or consonant blend to make new words.

DAILY PHONICS

Vowel /ō/ o, ow

A PHONOLOGICAL AWARENESS

RHYME Read aloud "Mary Had a Little Lamb" from the *Big Book of Rhymes and Rhythms 1B,* page 19. As you read, stress the words that contain long ***o: snow, go.***

- When children are familiar with the poem, have them read along with you.
- Isolate the words ***snow*** and ***go*** and point out the /ō/ sound in each.

Mary Had a Little Lamb
Mary had a little lamb,
Its fleece was white as snow.
And everywhere that Mary went,
The lamb was sure to go.
snow go

Big Book of Rhymes and Rhythms 1B, p. 19

ORAL BLENDING Say the following word parts and have children blend them. Provide corrective feedback and modeling as needed.

- /g/ . . . /ō/
- /n/ . . . /ō/
- /s/ . . . /ō/
- /sl/ . . . /ō/
- /fl/ . . . /ō/
- /sn/ . . . /ō/

B CONNECT SOUND-SPELLING

INTRODUCE VOWEL /ō/ *o, ow* Explain to children that the letters ***o*** and ***ow*** can stand for **/ō/** as in ***go*** and ***snow.*** Write the words ***go*** and ***snow*** on the chalkboard, and have a volunteer underline the letters that stand for **/ō/.** Model how to blend each word.

THINK ALOUD *I can put the letters **s, n,** and **ow** together to make the word **snow.** Let's say the sounds slowly as I move my finger under the letters. Listen to the sound that **ow** stands for in **snow.** The sound of **ow** is **/ō/.***

MODIFY Instruction

ESL/ELD

▲ As children read the words with *o, ow* on the chalkboard, check that English language learners know what each word means. Then make word cards with the /ō/ sound. Let each child read a word sound by sound, then repeat the whole word, stressing the /ō/ sound. **(USE WORD CARDS)**

GIFTED & TALENTED

✷ Ask children to invent two-word combinations in which both words contain /ō/, such as *go slow* or *no snow.* Then have children pantomime their word combinations for their classmates to figure out. **(PANTOMIME)**

- Ask children to suggest other words that contain **/ō/.** List the words on chart paper. You might begin by having children suggest words that rhyme with ***blow.***

crow	go
glow	no
snow	so

PHONICS MAINTENANCE Review the following sound-spellings: ***/ē/ y, ey; /ā/ ai, ay; /ō/ o, ow, oa.*** Say one of these sounds. Have a volunteer write on the chalkboard the spelling or spellings that stand for the sound. Continue with all the sounds.

C PRACTICE/APPLY

BLEND WORDS To practice using the sound-spellings and review the previous sound-spellings, list the following words and sentences on the chalkboard. Have children read each chorally. Model blending as needed.

no	go	show
any	key	blow

This boat is so slow!

The girl will show you the garden.

DICTATION Dictate the following words: ***go, snow, pony, goat, train.***

BUILD WORDS Distribute the following letter cards, or have children use their own sets: ***o, ow, s, g, r, l.*** Allow children time to build as many words as possible using the cards. Children can write their words on paper. **(INDEPENDENT WORK)**

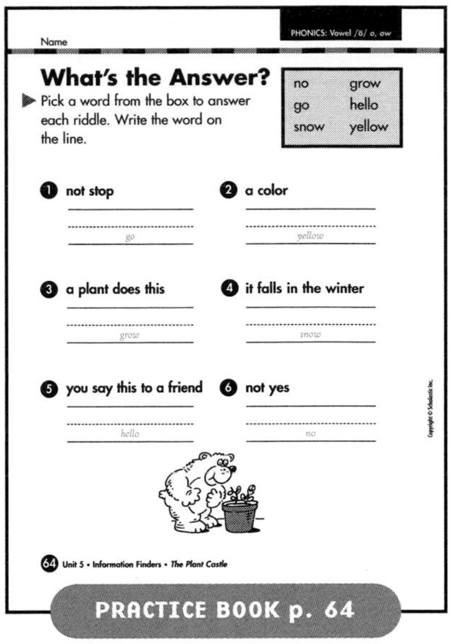

Name

PHONICS: Vowel /ō/ o, ow

What's the Answer?

Pick a word from the box to answer each riddle. Write the word on the line.

no	grow
go	hello
snow	yellow

1. not stop — *go*
2. a color — *yellow*
3. a plant does this — *grow*
4. it falls in the winter — *snow*
5. you say this to a friend — *hello*
6. not yes — *no*

64 Unit 5 • Information Finders • *The Plant Castle*

Copyright © Scholastic Inc.

PRACTICE BOOK p. 64

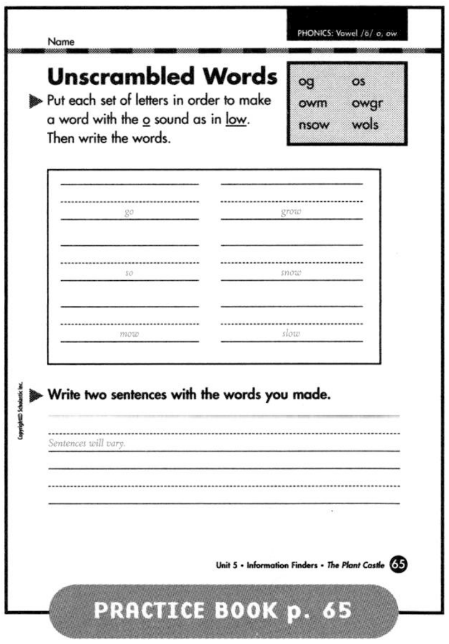

Name

PHONICS: Vowel /ō/ o, ow

Unscrambled Words

Put each set of letters in order to make a word with the o sound as in low. Then write the words.

og	os
owm	owgr
nsow	wols

go *grow*
so *snow*
mow *slow*

Write two sentences with the words you made.

Sentences will vary.

Unit 5 • Information Finders • *The Plant Castle* 65

Copyright © Scholastic Inc.

PRACTICE BOOK p. 65

DECODABLE TEXT

For practice reading decodable text, see ***Scholastic Decodable Reader #65.***

For additional phonics instruction and review, see ***Scholastic Phonics A, pp. 227–228.***

SHOW YOUR O'S

Have children look through magazines and cut out pictures whose names contain long ***o*** spelled with ***o*** or ***ow.*** They might cut out pictures of traffic signs that say ***SLOW*** or ***GO,*** or of a bow, crow, mow, or row. Have children label their pictures and display them on a bulletin board labeled: ***Show Your O's.***

COMPREHENSION

Preview and Predict

Tell children that *The Plant Castle* is about an arboretum, a museum of plants, trees, and flowers. Encourage children to preview the first few pages of the selection.

> **What kinds of plants will you see in the arboretum?**

> **Why do you think the title of this story is *The Plant Castle?***

Help children make predictions before they read by asking a question:

> **What do you think you will see when you visit the four rooms in the arboretum or *plant castle?***

JOURNAL

Make Predictions

Ask children to write their predictions in their Journals. Encourage them to write about what the characters see and do in the arboretum.

Set a Purpose

Ask children to think about a purpose for reading. They may want to find out why the story is called *The Plant Castle*. Then have them read page 115.

114

REALISTIC FICTION

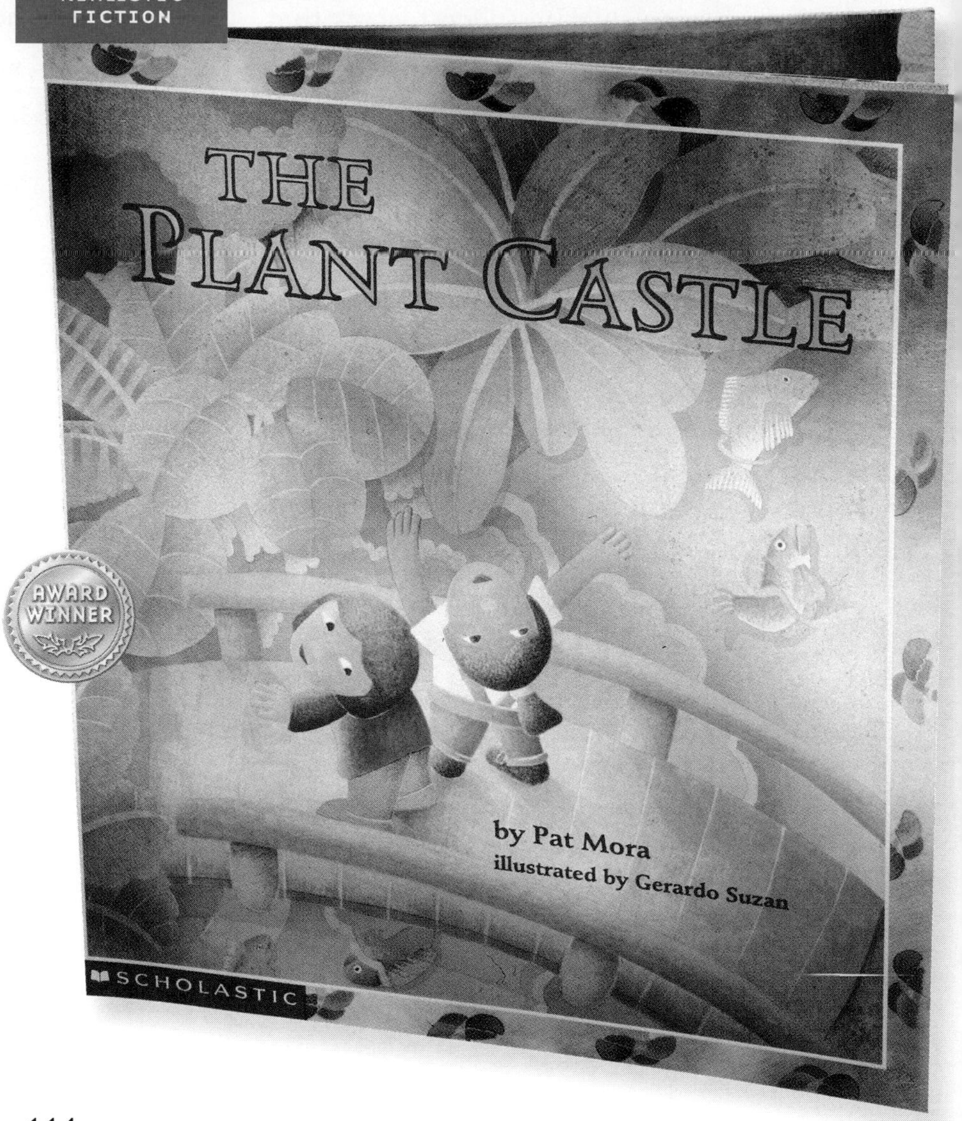

114

CLASSROOM Management

WHOLE CLASS

On-Level Use the questions, Think Alouds, and the Skills and Strategies lessons to guide children through a reading of the story.

Below-Level Have children preview the story by working with a partner to look at the pictures and talk about the different kinds of plants they see.

SMALL GROUP

Above-Level You might choose to have above-level children read the story independently or with a partner while you do a guided reading of the story with the rest of the class. When completed, have the above-level children work with a partner and answer the questions on the Respond page.

115

Every day after school, I go to the arboretum. People come from all around to see the plants and trees and flowers that grow inside. My mother works there, studying the plants.

Today Beth, a new girl at my school, comes with me.

115

SKILLS AND STRATEGIES

Revisit the selection for skills instruction.

✓ = Tested Skill

COMPREHENSION

✓ **Compare/Contrast** T253

DAILY PHONICS

✓ **r-Controlled Vowel /är/ *ar*** T259

Vowel /ō/ *o, ow* T261

GENRE

Realistic Fiction T263

SMALL GROUP TO WHOLE CLASS

ESL/ELD Have children who need extra help or who are acquiring English listen to the story on the audiocassette prior to the class reading. This will help them to become familiar with the story sequence and vocabulary. Have children do the pre- and post-listening activities. **(AUDIO CLUES)**

COMPREHENSION

1 MAIN IDEA/DETAILS

> **This place looks like fun. I think I would like to visit the desert, too! What is the main idea of this story? What details have you read about and seen so far?** *(The main idea of this story is a visit to the arboretum. There are two little girls visiting the arboretum and they are going to the desert room first.)*

2 COMPARE/CONTRAST

> **An arboretum is a kind of plant museum. How is an arboretum like an art museum? How are the two places different?** *(Possible answers: In both a museum and an arboretum there are things on display. In an arboretum, you see plants and trees. In an art museum there is art on display.)*

116

When we get to the arboretum, my mother meets us. She says, "¿Cómo estás, Carmen?" and gives me a hug. She says hello to Beth and Beth smiles. I think that Beth feels shy.

"Beth, let's go to the desert," I say.

"The desert?" asks Beth.

Even when it's snowing outside, this room is always dry and hot. It reminds me of the desert where my aunt Nina lives.

1 2

116

MODIFY Instruction

ESL/ELD

▲ Help English language learners discuss the main idea and details so far. Write Main Idea and Details on the chalkboard. Then ask questions and write the answers in the appropriate column: *Where are the girls? What can you see in the arboretum? What room will the girls visit first?* **(GUIDED QUESTIONS)**

GIFTED & TALENTED

✷ Challenge pairs of children to use the library or the Internet to find out about an arboretum in their area. Ask children to find out its location and what kinds of plants and trees it has. If there is not an arboretum in your area, have children research local parks or public gardens. **(RESEARCH)**

117

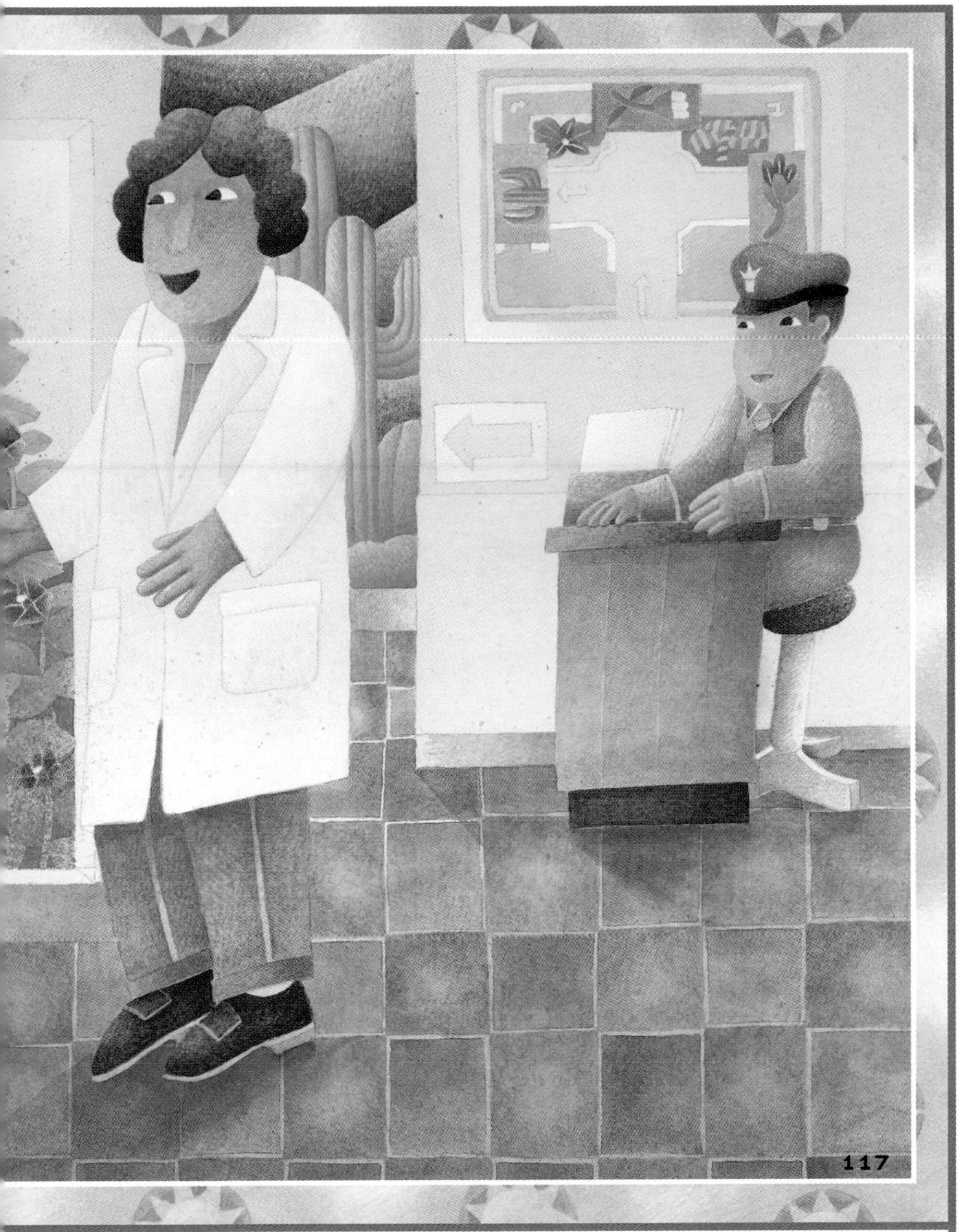

SKILLS AND STRATEGIES

COMPREHENSION
Compare/Contrast

TEACH/MODEL
Explain that to compare and contrast is to think about and decide how things are alike and different.

> **Look for picture and story clues that tell how things are alike and different.**

THINK ALOUD *When I read this part of the story, I realized that an arboretum is a lot like the aquarium in* Daniel's Dinosaurs. *You can learn new things at both places, but there are fish in an aquarium and plants in an arboretum.*

PRACTICE/APPLY
Ask children to complete a Venn diagram to compare and contrast these places.

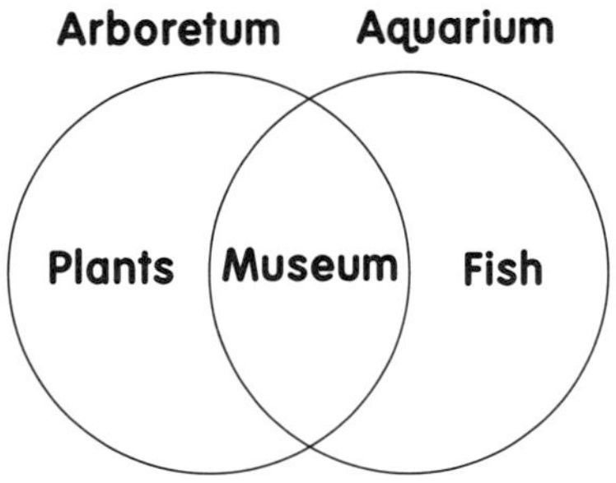

> **What is in an aquarium?**

> **What is in an arboretum?**

INFORMAL ASSESSMENT
OBSERVATION
As children read, note if they can:

✔ use picture and story clues to compare and contrast.

See **pages T268–T269** for a full skills lesson on Compare/Contrast.

WORD STUDY

Point out the word *arboretum* and explain that it is a place where you can see different trees and shrubs. Write *arboretum* on the chalkboard. Explain that *arbor* means "tree" and *-etum* means "place of." Explain how the two parts mean *arboretum.*

CULTURAL CONNECTION

Tell children that *¿Como estas?* means "How are you?" in Spanish. Invite children who speak other languages to teach the class how to ask "How are you?" For example:

- *Ni hao?*—Chinese
- *Kak dela?*—Russian

COMPREHENSION

❸ CATEGORIZE INFORMATION

> **Look at all the plants on the wall. Why do you think these plants are grouped together? What do they have in common?** *(Possible answer: The plants are all desert plants. They are all some type of cactus.)*

❹ USE PICTURE CLUES

> **Let's read this page together and then look at the picture. Which plant would you say is a pincushion? Which plant would you say is a fishhook?** *(Answers should indicate an understanding of the chart on page 118.)*

OPTION You may end the first day's reading here or have children continue reading the selection.

118

MODIFY Instruction

ESL/ELD

▲ Point to the pictures of individual plants on page 118 and read each name to children. Say: *This is a button cactus. This is a pincushion cactus.* Point to the word *cacti* on page 119 and make sure children understand that this is the plural form of the word *cactus.* **(PICTURE CLUES)**

EXTRA HELP

■ Help children organize information about cactus plants. Write *cactus* in the center of a poster. Have children suggest characteristics of a cactus. Write these characteristics around the word *cactus.* **(GRAPHIC DEVICES)**

119

I show Beth the cacti in the sunny desert room. These plants are called succulents because they store water in their leaves. Their sharp thorns keep away thirsty desert animals like mice and rabbits.

We read the names of the plants on the signs. Our favorites are the fishhook and pincushion cacti.

119

TECHNOLOGY

Expanding Vocabulary Have children use the **Usborne's Animated First Thousand Words** CD-ROM to look up story words. Direct them to focus on the Families, Park, and Yard sections. Since Carmen speaks Spanish, encourage children to look up the Spanish translations.

CONNECTING TO THEME

The girls in *The Plant Castle* gather information about plants and trees by seeing, smelling, and touching the plants. Ask children to suggest how the girls in the story could learn more about a specific plant.

Quickwrite

PREDICT

Ask children to write about what the girls have seen in the arboretum so far. Give children an opportunity to revise the predictions they made before reading. Have children predict what will happen next.

DAILY LANGUAGE PRACTICE

SPELLING

DAY 1:
Administer the Pretest for Words With Vowel /ō/ *o*, *ow*. **See page R36.**

GRAMMAR, USAGE, MECHANICS

DAY 1:
Teach and Model Words That Compare. **See page R38.**

ORAL LANGUAGE

Snoa is cold than rain.
(Snow is colder than rain.)

DAY 1 WRAP-UP

READ ALOUD *To develop children's oral vocabularies, spend five to ten minutes reading from a selection of your choice.*

GUIDED READING *To extend reading, meet with the* ***green*** *and* ***yellow*** *reading groups and assign Independent Center activities.* ***See pages R34–R35.***

COMPREHENSION

DAY 2 OBJECTIVES

CHILDREN WILL:

READ 30 MINUTES

- ***The Plant Castle*, pp. 120–128**
- **"New York Botanical Garden," p. 129**
- **Daily Phonics: *r*-Controlled Vowel /är/*ar***

WRITE 30 MINUTES

- **Shared Writing: Prewrite a Personal Narrative**
- **Spelling: Words With Vowel /ō/*o*, *ow***
- **Grammar, Usage, Mechanics: Words That Compare**
- **Oral Language**

EXTEND SKILLS 30 MINUTES

- **Integrated Curriculum**
- **Read Aloud**
- **Guided Reading**

RESOURCES

- **Practice Book, pp. 71, 73**
- **Spelling Resource Book, pp. 130–132**

▶ Reread

You may wish to have children independently reread the first part of the story before beginning Day 2 reading.

5 SUMMARIZE

› Where have the girls been so far? What have they seen?
(Possible answer: The girls have been to the desert room. They have seen different kinds of cacti.)

120

We go to the orchid house next. We see beautiful purple and yellow and white flowers blooming on tree branches.

We spot a butterfly. "Let's follow it!" I say.

The butterfly flies into the room where my friends Sonia and Mike are making a spring garden.

120

MODIFY Instruction

ESL/ELD

▲ Reread the text on these two pages aloud. Ask: *Where are Beth and Carmen now?* Write the words *desert room* and *spring garden* on the board. Ask: *What do the girls see in the desert room? What do they see in the spring garden?* Is anything the same? What is different? **(COMPARE/CONTRAST)**

EXTRA HELP

■ Help children understand the difference between a waterwheel and a windmill. Identify each in the picture on page 121. Write the two words on the chalkboard. Underline *water* in *waterwheel* and *wind* in *windmill*. Then discuss with children how the two structures work. **(PICTURE CLUES)**

121

SPRING GARDEN

Beth and I bend down and watch a waterwheel turning by a tiny windmill. Sonia lets us dip our fingertips in the brook. We see a cottage that is just the right size for mice. We peek inside the small windows. **5**

"There's the butterfly!" says Beth suddenly.

"Come on," I say. "It's going to the rain forest."

121

FAMILY TALK

Suggest to children that they visit a museum with a family member. Have children use maps and signs to find their way around the museum. Another alternative is to take a hike and try to identify different plants and trees. **(10-MINUTE LITERACY BYTE)**

SCIENCE

Ask children to complete the **How Trees Change** activity on **page R40** where they'll make drawings to show how trees change through the different seasons.

SKILLS AND STRATEGIES

LITERARY ELEMENT

Setting

TEACH/MODEL

Remind children that the setting is when and where a story takes place.

> **Use story and picture clues to find out where the story takes place.**

THINK ALOUD *There are a lot of different settings in* The Plant Castle. *I can tell that each setting is different by looking at the pictures and reading the words on the page. Each picture shows a different room in the arboretum.*

PRACTICE/APPLY

Have children use the following chart to record setting details.

SETTING
Cactus Room
Desert Room
Orchid Room
Spring Garden

> **What do I know about the story settings?**

> **What do the pictures tell me about the settings?**

Assign **Practice Book, page 73** for skill maintenance.

IF children need more support with setting,

THEN see the review lesson on page R45.

COMPREHENSION

6 DRAW CONCLUSIONS

> **What room have the children moved into now? How do you know?** *(The girls are in the rain forest room. There are big trees with large leaves everywhere. A sign on page 123 says RAIN FOREST.)*

INTERVENTION TIP

Identify a Setting Within a Setting

Some children may not see the changes in the artist's perspective on this page. Explain that the artist is showing the room from above. This is a change from the way the artist shows other rooms. Ask children how the picture is different from the others they have seen, and how it helps them learn about the room.

122

We follow the butterfly into a room filled with tall green trees. The air feels heavy and wet in the rain forest room. We smell the leaves and flowers and hear a waterfall.

We cross a bridge. Beth looks down and calls, "Fish!" Orange and white fish are swimming in the clear water below us.

I look way up high for the butterfly. Vines and large leaves brush against the glass ceiling. The tall trees are like giant umbrellas that protect the plants on the forest floor from the sun and the rain.

122

MODIFY Instruction

ESL/ELD

▲ Read each sentence aloud. Help children draw conclusions about the room by having them point to specific picture clues after each sentence. For example, they should point to the tall green trees after reading the first sentence. Follow this step-by-step procedure for both pages. **(STEP-BY-STEP)**

GIFTED & TALENTED

✳ Encourage children to reread page 122 and point out the sensory words, such as *smell* and *feel*. Have children work in small groups. Challenge them to describe what the characters feel, smell, see, and hear in the room with the tall green trees. **(WORK IN GROUPS)**

123

MATH

Ask children to complete the **Read a Garden Map** activity on **page R40** in which they'll use the map of the New York Botanical Garden to compare distances between places.

TEACHER TIP

"I try to take my class to at least one museum a year. I contact the museum well in advance to make a reservation and to request any materials prepared especially for children. As a class, we discuss which exhibits we would most like to see and which ones tie in what we are studying."

DAILY PHONICS

r-Controlled Vowel /är/ *ar*

CONNECT SOUND-SPELLING

TEACH/MODEL Hold up a toy car and ask children to say its name. Write the word ***car*** on the chalkboard. Tell children that the letters ***ar*** stand for /är/. Point out that when the letter ***r*** follows a vowel, it changes the vowel's sound.

PHONICS MAINTENANCE Review the following sound-spellings: /ō/ ***o, ow;*** digraphs ***ch, wh;*** /ō/ ***oa,*** /är/ ***ar.***

PRACTICE/APPLY

BLEND WORDS Ask children to find the word ***sharp*** on page 119.

- Write ***sharp*** on the chalkboard. Have a volunteer blend the word and underline ***ar.***
- Encourage children to look for other ***ar*** words in the story.

List the following words and sentence on the chalkboard. Have children read each chorally.

car	garden	sharp
asked	when	teach

Carmen is in the garden.

INFORMAL ASSESSMENT
OBSERVATION

As children read, can they:

✔ identify words with *ar*?

✔ blend words with *ar*?

See **pages T270–T271** for a full skills lesson on *r*-Controlled Vowel /är/ ***ar.***

COMPREHENSION

7 COMPARE/CONTRAST

> **How are the plants in the tropical room like the plants in the desert room? How are they different?** *(Possible answers: The plants in both rooms are green and have some kind of flower. The plants in the desert room are cacti. The plants in the tropical room are big and leafy, and have fruits on them.)*

8 MAKE INFERENCES

> **Why do you think this plant is named a shrimp plant?** *(Possible answer: The flower on the shrimp plant is pink and curved and looks like a shrimp.)*

124

MODIFY Instruction

ESL/ELD

▲ Show children other visuals of desert and tropical plants to assist in the comparing and contrasting discussion. Point out the colors, shapes, and fruits of the plants. Show children on a world map where they might find some of these plants. **(MAKE CONNECTIONS)**

EXTRA HELP

■ Help children create a chart of what is growing in the tropical room. Have children review the text and the pictures on pages 124 and 125. Then, using the column headings *Plants, Trees, Trees with Fruit,* help children list the plants, trees, and fruits that are growing there. **(VISUAL AID)**

125

Next we go to the tropical room. Beth looks at a plant alled elephant ears. She laughs and says, "Carmen, I see reen elephants."

I point to the shrimp plant and say, "I see pink shrimp!"

"Look! The butterfly!" says Beth very softly, and we watch it fly up into a palm tree.

"I'm getting hungry," I say. "Bananas, papayas, and other delicious fruits grow here."

Beth reads the label near the cacao tree. I tell Beth that chocolate comes from this tree. And the tree comes from Mexico, like my grandparents.

125

THE ARTS

Ask children to complete the **Fill a Greenhouse** activity on **page R41** where they'll make paper plants and flowers for a "greenhouse" display.

VISUAL LITERACY

Ask children to identify the drawings along the border of the page and then locate the plant in the picture. As they reread the story, children can look for the design in the border of the picture on each page. Encourage them to use self-sticking notes to label some of the items they see in the borders.

DAILY PHONICS

Vowel /ō/ *o, ow*

CONNECT SOUND-SPELLING

TEACH/MODEL Draw a gift bow on the chalkboard, label it, and ask children to pronounce the word. Remind children that the long ***o*** sound can be spelled ***o*** or ***ow***. Write the words ***no, hot, cow,*** and ***snow*** on the chalkboard. Pronounce each word as you write it. Ask:

> **In which words do the letters *ow* and *o* have the /ō/ sound?**

> **Circle the letters *ow* or *o* in those words.**

PHONICS MAINTENANCE Review the following sound-spellings: /ō/ *o, ow;* /ē/ *ea, ee;* *s*-blends.

PRACTICE/APPLY

BLEND WORDS List the following words and sentence on the chalkboard. Have children read each chorally. Model blending as needed.

no	know	grow
stand	bee	each

Let's go play in the snow.

INFORMAL ASSESSMENT
OBSERVATION

As children read, note if they can:

✔ identify words with /ō/ (*o, ow*).

✔ blend words with /ō/ (*o, ow*).

COMPREHENSION

9 CATEGORIZE INFORMATION

> **Name one thing from each room in the arboretum that Beth will tell her family about.** *(Answers should reflect an understanding of the unique characteristics of the plants in each room of the arboretum.)*

10 COMPARE/CONTRAST

> **Think about the rooms in the arboretum that Carmen and Beth visited. How are the rooms alike? How are they different?** *(Answers should reflect an understanding of the unique characteristics of each room of the arboretum.)*

11 DRAW CONCLUSIONS

> **Why do you think a plant has to reach for light?** *(A plant has to reach for the sun because it needs light to grow.)*

126

Just then the butterfly lands on Beth's shirt. She reaches for it, but it flies away. "It's shy like me," she says. 9 10

126

MODIFY Instruction

ESL/ELD

▲ Children can take turns pretending that they are Beth arriving home after her visit at the arboretum. Have them role-play what they think Beth will say to her family. Play the role of Beth's mother yourself so that you can ask specific questions about the various rooms. **(ROLE-PLAY)**

EXTRA HELP

■ Reinforce children's understanding of the story by having them use the pictures as a guide to summarize what has happened so far. Encourage children to talk about what the girls see in each part of the arboretum. **(SUMMARIZE)**

127

11

"It's time to go home now, girls," says Mother, joining us. "But I hope you'll come back soon, Beth!"

"Thank you, I will!" says Beth. "I can't wait to tell everybody at home about this place."

I don't think that Beth feels shy now.

127

WORD STUDY

Have children find the word *Mother* on page 127. Ask them to think about what the word means in the sentence. Then ask children to list other words for *Mother* that they know. Have children make up some sentences with the word *Mother*, and then read them aloud.

TECHNOLOGY

Finding the Facts Have children choose a cactus from the selection. Help them find facts about the cactus in a CD-ROM or Internet encyclopedia. Children might draw the cactus, or print the page from the **WiggleWorks Plus** version of the story, and write one fact near the illustration.

SKILLS AND STRATEGIES

GENRE

Realistic Fiction

TEACH/MODEL

Tell children that *The Plant Castle* uses elements of realistic fiction, since it is based on a real place—an arboretum in Ohio. Discuss with children the key elements of realistic fiction.

> **Realistic fiction tells about characters, events, and places that could exist in real life.**

THINK ALOUD *I know* The Plant Castle *is an example of realistic fiction because the characters, places, and events are just like those in real life.*

PRACTICE/APPLY

Ask children to list the things that are real in this story.

> **What are some of the real-life events in this story?**

Things that are real in *The Plant Castle*
Plants
Trees
Flowers

COMPREHENSION

12 Make Inferences

> **Why do you think Beth calls the arboretum a "castle"?** *(Possible answer: The arboretum is a special building that looks something like a castle.)*

JOURNAL

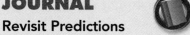

Revisit Predictions

Ask children to look back at their predictions and record how they were or were not confirmed by the end of the story.

Preview

Read the title of the map, point to the symbols, and read some of the labels on the page.

1 Make Inferences

> **Why do some of the same symbols appear in different places on the map?** *(Possible answer: The things the symbols stand for can be found in more than one place on the map.)*

2 Genre: Map

> **The symbols on the map stand for different things in the garden. Why do you think there are two question marks on the map?** *(There are two visitor centers in the Botanical Garden.)*

128

When we drive away, Beth looks back at the arboretum and says, "It's like a castle glowing in the night!"
I nod my head and smile.

128

MODIFY Instruction

ESL/ELD

▲ To help children understand maps, have them study the map and point out the various symbols as you help them interpret what each one means. Then have children run their fingers along the paths to help them visualize a walk through the Botanical Garden. **(MULTISENSORY TECHNIQUES)**

GIFTED & TALENTED

✳ Have children replace several symbols on the map with their own designs. For example, children may change the symbol for the cafe from a fork and spoon to a coffee cup. Invite children to share their new symbols with their classmates. **(INNOVATE)**

129

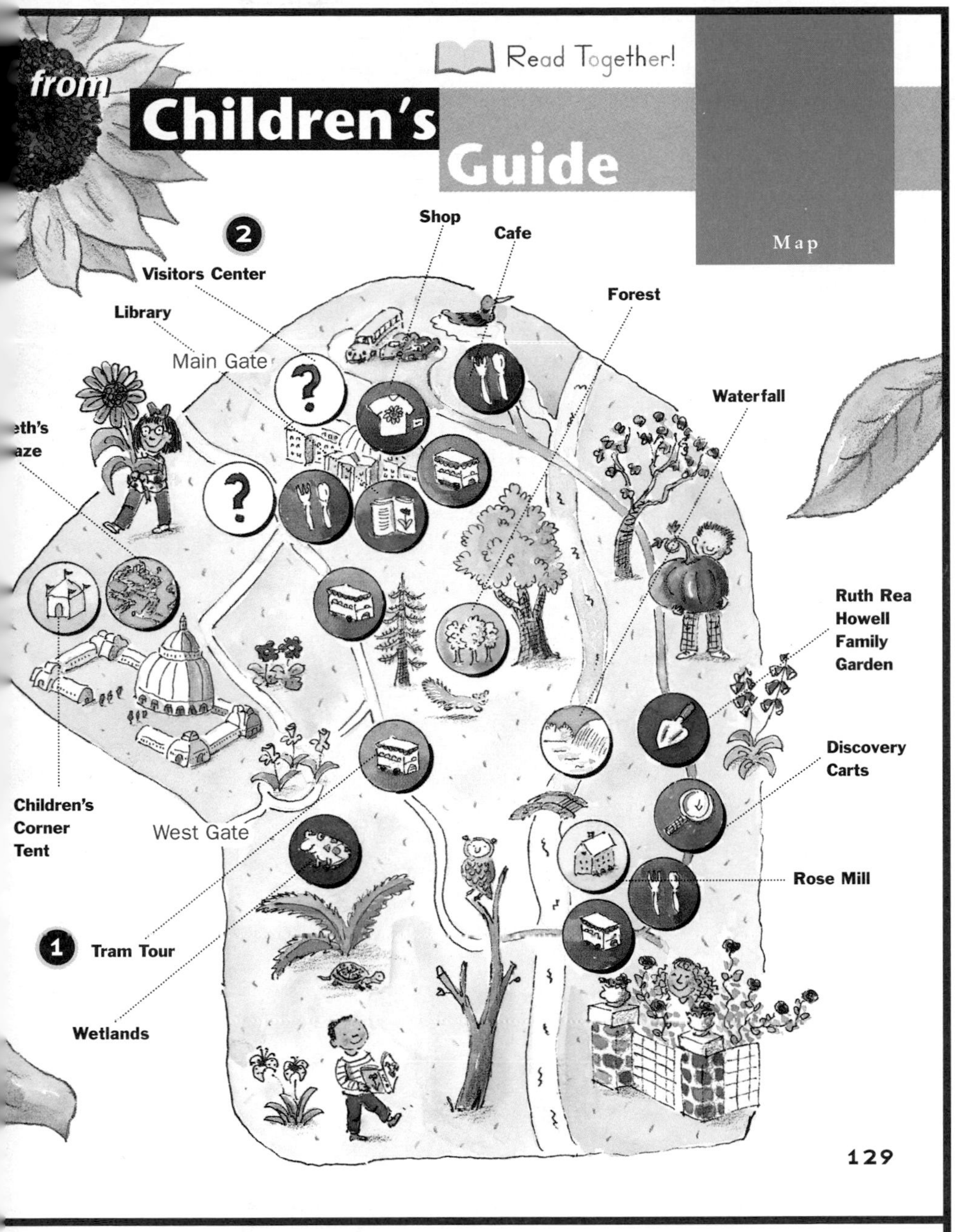

FAMILY LITERACY RESOURCES

Encourage family members to help children improve their literacy performance by identifying high-quality books. The American Library Association web site has lists such as "Good Books for Kids," and "Notable Books for Children" at **www.ala.org/parentspage/**

SOCIAL STUDIES

Have children complete the **Map the Neighborhood** activity on **page R41** where they'll use the map of the New York Botanical Garden as a guide to make maps of their school or neighborhood.

Personal Narrative

SHARED WRITING

PREWRITE Using *The Plant Castle* as a model, discuss how to write a personal narrative. Tell children that they will be writing a personal narrative about a visit to a favorite place. Have them think about a place they enjoyed visiting.

Use Practice Book, page 71.

DAILY LANGUAGE PRACTICE

SPELLING

DAY 2:

Practice Words With Vowel /ō/ *o, ow.* **See page R36.**

GRAMMAR, USAGE, MECHANICS

DAY 2:

Practice Words That Compare. **See page R38.**

ORAL LANGUAGE

The flowers in the garden are groeing more fast than the flowers inside.

(The flowers in the garden are growing faster than the flowers inside.)

DAY 2 WRAP-UP

READ ALOUD *To develop children's oral vocabularies, spend five to ten minutes reading from a selection of your choice.*

GUIDED READING *To extend reading, meet with the **red** and **blue** reading groups and assign Independent Center activities.* ***See pages R34–R35.***

COMPREHENSION

DAY 3 OBJECTIVES

CHILDREN WILL:

READ 30 MINUTES

- **Assess Comprehension**
- **Key Comprehension Skill: Compare/Contrast**
- **Daily Phonics: *r*-Controlled Vowel /är/ *ar***

WRITE 35 MINUTES

- **Respond: A Thank-You Letter**
- **Spelling: Words With Vowel /ō/ *o, ow***
- **Grammar, Usage, Mechanics: Words That Compare**
- **Oral Language**

EXTEND SKILLS 25 MINUTES

- **Read Aloud**
- **Guided Reading**

RESOURCES

- **Practice Book, pp. 66–70**
- **Spelling Resource Book, p. 133**

Think About Reading

Below are the **answers** to the *Think About Reading* questions.

1. *Carmen's mother works at the arboretum, studying plants.*
2. *Weather in the desert is hot and dry.*
3. *Possible response: The elephant ears plant has leaves like elephant's ears.*
4. *Possible response: Beth says that she will come back to the arboretum.*
5. *People can visit both places to see different plants.* **[PAIRED SELECTION]**

130

RESPOND

Think About Reading

1. What does Carmen's mother do at the arboretum?
2. What kind of weather does a desert have?
3. How do you think the elephant ears plant got its name?
4. How can you tell that Beth had a good time at the arboretum?
5. How is the arboretum in The Plant Castle like the botanical garden in "Children's Guide"?

130

Name

COMPREHENSION CHECK

What Did You See?

▶ What did you see in the plant castle? Draw a picture of a room you saw. Then write three things in that room.

1 *Answers will vary.*

2

3

66 Unit 5 • Information Finders • The Plant Castle

PRACTICE BOOK p. 66

MODIFY Instruction

ESL/ELD

▲ Work with English language learners in a group to help them prepare to write the thank-you letter. Brainstorm possible things Beth might say. Remind children they have role-played Beth. Some things she told her family might go into the thank-you letter. **(WORK IN GROUPS)**

131

Write a Thank-You Letter

:h had a great time at the
oretum! She would like to
te Carmen a thank-you letter.
her letter, she wants to tell
y she likes being at the
oretum. Write a thank-you
ter for Beth to send Carmen.

Literature Circle

hat if you could visit the New
rk Botanical Garden and the
oretum in The Plant Castle?
hat would you most want to
? Why? Talk about your ideas.

AUTHOR

Pat Mora

Author Pat Mora says, "I'm lucky!" She's lucky because she grew up speaking two languages—English and Spanish. She's also lucky because she is a writer. All her life she has liked reading books. "Now I get to write them, too," she explains.

More Books by Pat Mora

- A Birthday Basket for Tia
- Tomas and the Library Lady
- The Desert Is My Mother/ El Desierto Es Mi Madre

131

TECHNOLOGY

Presentation Tools Using **WiggleWorks Plus** PlaceMaker, have children create a thank-you card from Beth to Carmen and her mother. Show children how to use art tools, text tools, and clip art, and encourage them to use story words.

AUTHOR/ILLUSTRATOR STUDY

Pat Mora takes great pride in being a Hispanic writer. At the Scholastic web site **www.scholasticnetwork.com** children can turn to the "authors online" section to read about how many of Mora's writing ideas come from growing up on a desert.

RESPOND

Write a Thank-You Letter

Before children begin to write, have them think about these questions.

> **What were some of the things Beth liked at the arboretum?**

> **What were some of the unusual or surprising plants Beth saw there?**

Literature Circle

Encourage children to discuss the parts of the arboretum and the Botanical Garden that interested them the most. List children's responses on the chalkboard. You might take a vote to see which areas of the arboretum and the Botanical Gardens are the most popular with the class.

DAILY LANGUAGE PRACTICE

SPELLING
DAY 3:
Write Words With Vowel /ō/ *o, ow*. **See page R37.**

GRAMMAR, USAGE, MECHANICS
DAY 3:
Practice Words That Compare. **See page R39.**

ORAL LANGUAGE
are you more tall than yor sister? *(Are you taller than your sister?)*

COMPREHENSION

Compare/Contrast

SKILLS TRACE

COMPARE/ CONTRAST TESTED

Introduce . . . . p. T268
Practice . . . . . . pp. T253, T269
Reteach . . . . p. R56

CONNECT TO TRADE BOOKS

Select one of the unit trade books. Read aloud the title, and discuss the cover illustration.

- Have children make predictions about what might happen in the story. Record their predictions on chart paper or the chalkboard.
- Read a few pages at a time, stop, and have children compare and contrast some element of the story.
- Record children's ideas about the similarities and differences. Continue this procedure until the book is completed.

QUICKCHECK

Can children:

✔ use text and picture clues to make comparisons?

✔ distinguish between similarities and differences?

If YES, go on to Practice/Apply.

If NO, start at Teach/Model.

A TEACH/MODEL

USE ORAL LANGUAGE

Ask children how a pencil and a pen are alike and different. Encourage children to compare and contrast the pen and pencil by describing them.

To compare and contrast is to **think about and decide how things are alike and different.** Point out to children that they should compare and contrast characters, actions, and ideas to better understand what they read. In order to compare and contrast two or more things, tell children to:

1. Think about how the things are alike.
2. Think about how the things are different.
3. Look for picture clues of how the things are alike and different.

MODIFY Instruction

ESL/ELD

▲ Draw a chart on the chalkboard and work with children to fill in the details that compare a pencil to a crayon:

	Alike	Different
pencil	used for writing, drawing	has an eraser
crayon		has color

(GRAPHIC DEVICE)

EXTRA HELP

■ For additional practice with comparing and contrasting things, have children compare pairs of objects in the classroom. For example: glue and tape; a kickball and a soccer ball; a T-shirt and a sweatshirt. Ask children to talk about how the items are alike and how they are different. **(ANALYZE)**

LITERATURE CONNECTION

THINK ALOUD *When I read a story, I compare and contrast things to help me better understand what I am reading. As I read* The Plant Castle, *I notice that all the plants in the different exhibits are green and have flowers. They all need light and water to grow. Yet, they have very different shapes and sizes and grow in different climates.*

B PRACTICE/APPLY

USE PRACTICE BOOK

Have children practice what they learned about comparing and contrasting by completing **Practice Book, page 67. (INDIVIDUALS)**

C ASSESS

APPLY INSTRUCTIONAL ALTERNATIVES

Based on children's completion of **Practice Book, page 67,** determine if they were able to compare and contrast plants in *The Plant Castle*. The Instructional Alternatives below will aid you in pinpointing children's level of proficiency. Consider the appropriate Instructional Alternative to promote further skill development.

To reinforce the skills, distribute **Practice Book, page 68.**

INSTRUCTIONAL ALTERNATIVES

	If the child . . .	Then
Proficient	Is able to identify clear similarities and differences	• Have the child apply this skill independently to a more challenging story. • Present a story with diverse characters. Have the child list similarities and differences.
Apprentice	Can identify similarities but not differences	• Have the child work with others to brainstorm similarities and differences and find text and picture clues that support or negate their ideas.
Novice	Cannot identify similarities or differences	• Review with the child the steps to use when comparing and contrasting. • Complete the Reteach lesson on page R56.

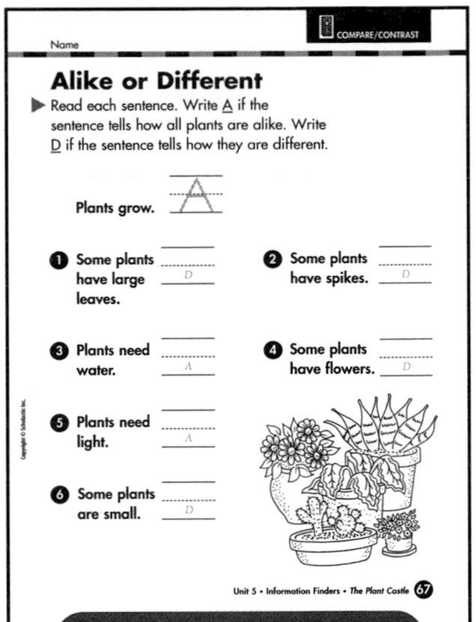
Name
COMPARE/CONTRAST
Alike or Different
Read each sentence. Write A if the sentence tells how all plants are alike. Write D if the sentence tells how they are different.
Plants grow. A
1 Some plants have large leaves. D
2 Some plants have spikes. D
3 Plants need water. A
4 Some plants have flowers. D
5 Plants need light. A
6 Some plants are small. D
Unit 5 • Information Finders • The Plant Castle 67

PRACTICE BOOK p. 67

Name
COMPARE/CONTRAST
Are We Alike?
Color the birds so they look alike. Then write about how they are alike. Responses will vary.
Color the birds so they look different. Then write about how they are different.
68 Unit 5 • Information Finders • The Plant Castle

PRACTICE BOOK p. 68

SELECTION WORDS With *r*-Controlled Vowel /är/*ar*

arboretum

Carmen

garden

large

SKILLS TRACE

r*-CONTROLLED VOWEL /är/*ar TESTED

Introduce. . . . . p. T259
Practice . . . pp. T270, T273, T277
Reteach. . . . . p. R61

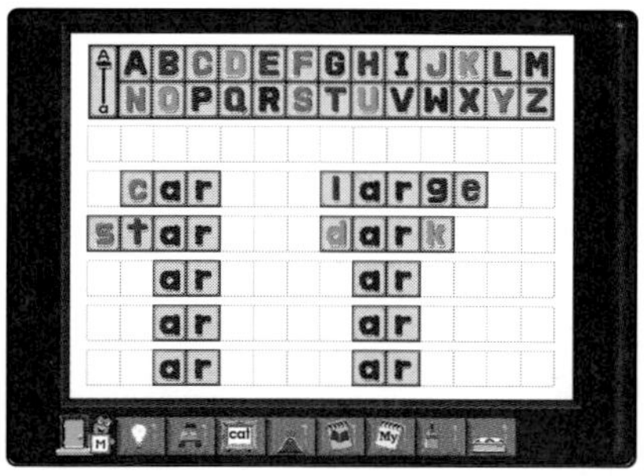

TECHNOLOGY

Have children build words with *ar* on the **WiggleWorks Plus** Magnet Board.

- Begin with the words *car* and *large*.
- Have children search classroom books for other words.

DAILY PHONICS

r-Controlled Vowel *ar*

A PHONOLOGICAL AWARENESS

RHYME Write the rhyme on chart paper and read it aloud. Stress the /är/ sounds in ***star.***

> **Star light, star bright,**
> **First star I see tonight,**
> **I wish I may, I wish I might,**
> **Have this wish I wish tonight.**

- On a second reading, ask children to read along with you.
- Frame the word ***star*** and point out the sounds the letters ***ar*** stand for.

ORAL BLENDING Say the following word parts, and ask children to blend them. Provide corrective feedback and modeling as needed.

/j/. . . /är/   /f/. . . /är/   /k/. . . /är/   /t/. . . /är/

B CONNECT SOUND-SPELLING

INTRODUCE *r*-CONTROLLED VOWEL /är/ *ar* Explain to children that the letters ***ar*** stand for /är/ as in the word ***star.*** Write the word ***star*** on the chalkboard, and have a volunteer underline the letters ***ar.***

THINK ALOUD *I can put the letters **c** and **ar** together to make the word **car.** Let's say the sounds slowly as I move my finger under the letters. Listen to the sounds that **ar** stand for in the word **car.** The sounds of **ar** are /är/.*

MODIFY Instruction

ESL/ELD

▲ Have English language learners make a picture book of words with *ar* endings. List common objects that end in the /är/ sounds, such as *star, car,* and *jar.* Have children cut and paste or draw the pictures, then label each picture and circle the letters *ar.* **(MULTISENSORY TECHNIQUES)**

GIFTED & TALENTED

✳ On index cards, write words with *ar* such as *yard, farm, yarn, sharp, dart, start, bark, jar, car,* and *scar.* Working in small groups, have children take turns giving clues for a word while others try to figure it out. To vary the game, players can act out words instead of giving verbal clues. **(WORK IN GROUPS)**

- Ask children to suggest other words that contain ***ar.*** You might suggest that children list words with the phonograms ***-ar, -ard, -ark, -arm,*** and ***-art.*** List the words in columns on a chart.

tar	card	bark
far	hard	dark
car	yard	park

PHONICS MAINTENANCE Review the following sound-spellings: /är/ ***ar;*** final ***e; -ing;*** /ō/ ***o, ow.***

C PRACTICE AND APPLY

BLEND WORDS To practice using the sound-spelling and review previous sound-spellings, list the following words and sentence on the chalkboard. Have children read each chorally. Model blending as needed.

dark star far
grow bake falling
Did your mother grow a large plant?

DICTATION Dictate the following words for children to spell: ***car, farm, cake, show, go.***

BUILD WORDS Distribute the following letter cards, or have children use their own sets: ***ar, r, s, t, c, f, m.*** Allow children time to build words using the letter cards. Children can write their words on paper. **(INDEPENDENT WORK)**

c ar

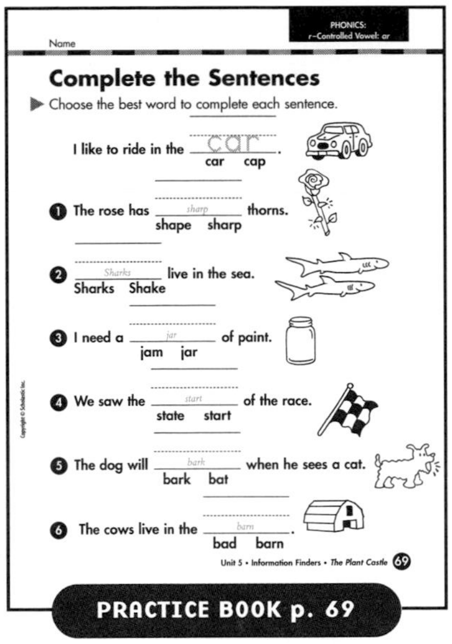
Name
PHONICS: r-Controlled Vowel: ar
Complete the Sentences
Choose the best word to complete each sentence.
I like to ride in the car. car cap
1 The rose has sharp thorns. shape sharp
2 Sharks live in the sea. Sharks Shake
3 I need a jar of paint. jam jar
4 We saw the start of the race. state start
5 The dog will bark when he sees a cat. bark bat
6 The cows live in the barn. bad barn
Unit 5 • Information Finders • The Plant Castle 69

PRACTICE BOOK p. 69

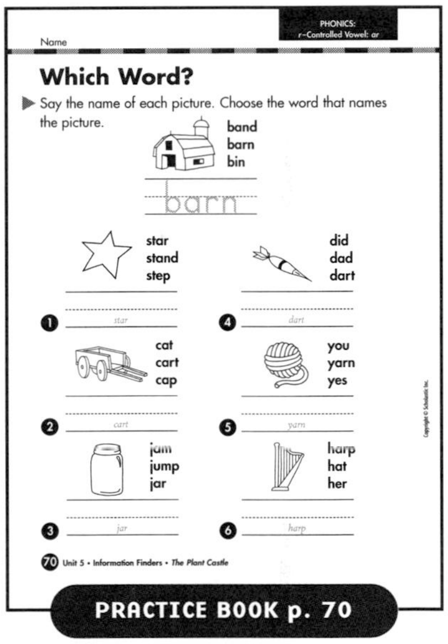
Name
PHONICS: r-Controlled Vowel: ar
Which Word?
Say the name of each picture. Choose the word that names the picture.
band barn bin — barn
1 star stand step — star
2 cat cart cap — cart
3 jam jump jar — jar
4 did dad dart — dart
5 you yarn yes — yarn
6 harp hat her — harp
70 Unit 5 • Information Finders • The Plant Castle

PRACTICE BOOK p. 70

DECODABLE TEXT

For practice reading decodable text, see ***Scholastic Decodable Reader #66.***

For additional phonics instruction and review, see ***Scholastic Phonics B, pp. 81–82.***

STAR CONCENTRATION

Duplicate and distribute star shapes. Ask children to make star pairs—one star with an ***ar*** word; the other star with a picture of the word. Children can use words such as ***car, star, barn, shark, jar, harp, yard, dark, cart, yarn.*** Children can then play Concentration with their star cards. Lay the cards face down on the table. The first player turns over two cards. Children get a match if they have a word card and a picture card that match.

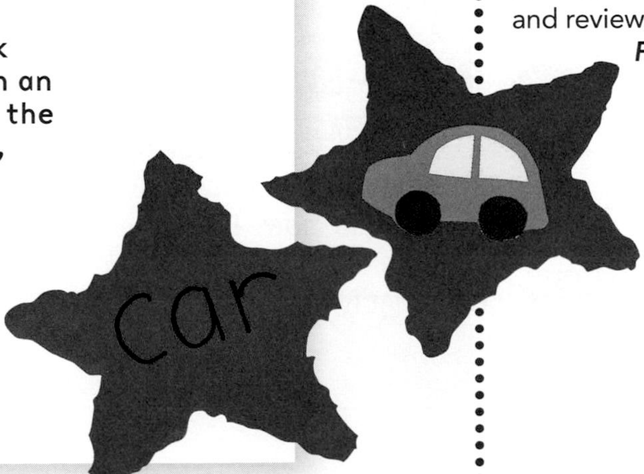

Building Fluency

PHONICS READER

Guide children through a reading of **Phonics Reader #55**, *Follow It!* For a detailed lesson plan, see **Phonics Reader Teacher's Guide Part B, pages 52–53.** While children read, note how well they:

- **blend words,**
- **recognize high-frequency words,**
- **read with speed, accuracy, and expression.**

You may wish to have children reread the story with a partner.

* See Phonics Readers Take-Home Books 37–72 for reproducible format.

More Support Materials . . .

TRADE BOOK LIBRARY

For additional leveled reading practice, have children read one of the following:

Animal Tracks
CHALLENGE

Owl at Home
AVERAGE

Lost!
EASY

PHONICS CHAPTER BOOK

For additional practice with Vowel **/ō/ *o, ow,*** have children read Chapter 4, "They Go to a Dinosaur Hall," in **Phonics Chapter Book 5,** *Let's Go on a Museum Hunt.*

HOME-SCHOOL CONNECTION

Send home *Follow It!* and *Don't Go So Slow!* Have children read the books to a family member.

MY BOOK

For additional practice with vowel **/ō/ *o, ow*** and high-frequency words, have children read *Don't Go So Slow!* The My Book is also available on **WiggleWorks Plus.**

Intervention

For children who need extra help . . .

FOCUS ON HIGH-FREQUENCY WORDS

Write the following sentences on sentence strips. Each sentence focuses on one or more of the high-frequency words.

My mother has a new car.

Your mother is in the garden.

That girl is playing in the yard.

The girl plays in the snow.

- Read aloud each sentence. Help children find or draw a picture to match each sentence. Attach the pictures to index cards.
- Then have children chorally read each sentence and match the sentence to the picture card.
- Continue by mixing the cards and strips for children to practice reading and matching.

FOCUS ON PHONICS

Write the words ***show, snow, slow, so, no, go, yard, garden, large,*** and ***car*** on index cards.

- Help children read the word on each card.
- Then mix the cards. Have children sort the cards according to vowel spelling pattern ***(o, ow, ar).***
- Ask children to read the words in each group.

go | no | so

PROFESSIONAL DEVELOPMENT

JOHN SHEFELBINE

Assessing Student Progress

When children appear to be having difficulty in beginning reading, three critical areas to assess are (a) sound-spelling knowledge, (b) blending, and (c) high-frequency (sight) word knowledge. Take a student aside and evaluate knowledge of the sound-spelling relationships and high-frequency words that have been covered. Assess blending by having children read 5–10 words with known sound-spelling relationships. The Day 5 Decoding Test can be used for these brief assessments.

DAY 3 WRAP-UP

READ ALOUD *To conclude each reading session and develop children's oral vocabularies, read aloud a book of your choice. Be sure to read at least two nonfiction books each week.*

GUIDED READING *To extend reading, meet with the **green** and **yellow** reading groups and assign Independent Center activities.* ***See pages R34–R35.***

DAY 4 OBJECTIVES

CHILDREN WILL:

READ 20 MINUTES

- **Reread *The Plant Castle***

WRITE 40 MINUTES

- **Shared Writing: Personal Narrative**
- **Spelling: Words With Vowel /ō/ *o, ow***
- **Grammar, Usage, Mechanics: Words That Compare**
- **Oral Language**

EXTEND SKILLS 30 MINUTES

- **Vocabulary**
- **Daily Phonics: *r*-Controlled Vowel /är/ *ar***
- **Study Skills: Test-Taking Strategies**

RESOURCES

- **Practice Book, p. 71**
- **Spelling Resource Book, p. 161**

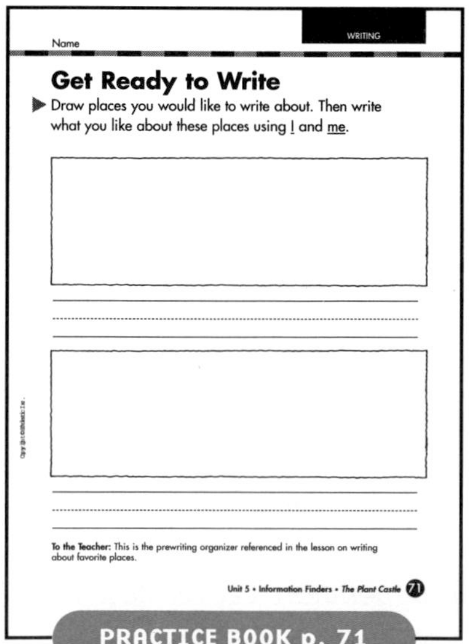
Name WRITING

Get Ready to Write

▶ Draw places you would like to write about. Then write what you like about these places using I and me.

To the Teacher: This is the prewriting organizer referenced in the lesson on writing about favorite places.

Unit 5 • Information Finders • The Plant Castle 71

PRACTICE BOOK p. 71

SHARED WRITING

Personal Narrative

SELECTION CONNECTION Using *The Plant Castle* as a model, children will write a personal narrative.

THINK ABOUT WRITING Ask children to think about how the main character in *The Plant Castle* tells the story. Help children see that in a personal narrative,

- the person telling the story is the main character.
- the main character uses words such as ***I*** and ***me.***
- the story might be about a place the main character likes to visit.

INTRODUCE THE WRITING EVENT Explain to children that they will write a story about a visit to a favorite place.

TEACH/MODEL

PUT IT IN CONTEXT Look back at *The Plant Castle* with children. Ask children to consider the following:

> **Who is the main character in the story?**

> **Who is telling the story?**

> **What place does the main character tell about?**

Help children note words like ***I*** and ***me*** in the story.

Invite children to make a list of places that they might like to write about.

MODIFY Instruction

ESL/ELD

▲ Help English language learners plan out their personal narratives. Remind them to use words like *I, me,* and *my*. Brainstorm words they might use to describe a place. Offer several sentence starters, such as: *I like to go* ______. *My favorite place is* ______. **(ASSIST IN PROCESS)**

GIFTED & TALENTED

✳ Encourage children to think about places that are special to them. Encourage them to look through family photographs to recall visits to the homes of relatives or to zoos, parks, lakes, seashores, or mountains. What have children done in these places? Why are the places special? **(RESEARCH/ANALYZE)**

- Have volunteers share some of the places on their list.
- Suggest some ways that children could begin their stories, such as: ***Last summer, I went to the lake again.*** or ***I really have fun at the zoo.***

GRAMMAR CONNECTION

- Have children use words that compare in their personal narratives.

WRITE

DESCRIBE A FAVORITE PLACE

- If they have not done so, have children choose the place they will write about in their personal narratives.
- Help children write their stories. Remind them to use pronouns such as ***I*** and ***me.***
- When their stories are complete, give children time to draw pictures to go with them.
- If each of their stories is more than one page long, staple the pages together to make a book.

ASSESS: PERFORMANCE-BASED

PERFORMANCE-BASED ASSESSMENT

The following questions will help children assess their work.

✔ **Is the person telling my story the same as the main character in my story?**

✔ **Did I use words such as *I* and *me* in the story?**

✔ **Is my story about a place?**

Children may wish to carry this piece through the writing process described on pages T286–T289.

DAILY LANGUAGE PRACTICE

SPELLING

DAY 4:

Review Words With Vowel /ō/ ***o, ow.*** Have children proofread sentences. **See page R37.**

GRAMMAR, USAGE, MECHANICS

DAY 4:

Apply Words That Compare. **See page R39.**

ORAL LANGUAGE

The tree will gro to be more large than the house. *(The tree will grow to be larger than the house.)*

TECHNOLOGY

Writing Skills Encourage children to use the **WiggleWorks Plus** Unit Writer to create their story. Suggest that they record themselves reading the story with the Record tool. Encourage them to use the Art tools to illustrate the story.

Extend Vocabulary

Review High-Frequency Words

Write the high-frequency words ***mother*** and ***girl*** on note cards. Then write the following incomplete sentences on sentence strips:

My _____ showed me the garden.

We saw a _____ water the plants.

Read aloud the incomplete sentences and have children place the appropriate high-frequency word in the blank space in each sentence. Then help children read aloud the sentences together.

Review Story Words

Write the story words ***desert, butterfly, forest, fruits, leaves,*** and ***trees*** on note cards. Then write the following incomplete sentences on the chalkboard:

It is hot in the _____ . (desert)
That plant has big, green _____. (leaves)
I saw birds in the tall _____. (trees)
Lemons and limes are sour _____. (fruits)
The _____ flew to the flower. (butterfly)
We got wet in the rain _____. (forest)

Read aloud the incomplete sentences and place the appropriate story word note card in the blank space. Then help children to chorally read the sentences.

PICTURE DICTIONARY

Have children make a small picture dictionary using the high-frequency and story words: *mother, girl, desert, butterfly, forest, fruits, leaves, trees*. Give each child a small blank book made with three pieces of paper folded and stapled together. Ask children to write a title on the first page. On each of the remaining pages, have children write a high-frequency or story word and illustrate it.

Building Fluency

Phonics Reader

Guide children through a reading of **Phonics Reader #56**, *Bo's Bows*. For a detailed lesson plan, see **Phonics Reader Teacher's Guide Part B, pages 54–55.** While children read, note how well they:

- **blend words,**
- **recognize high-frequency words,**
- **read with speed, accuracy, and expression.**

You may wish to have children reread the story with a partner.

★ See Phonics Readers Take-Home Books 37–72 for reproducible format.

More Support Materials . . .

Trade Book Library

For additional leveled reading practice, have children read one of the following:

Animal Tracks
CHALLENGE

Owl at Home
AVERAGE

Lost!
EASY

Phonics and Word Building Kit

To review words with *-ar*, select one of the Movement and Games or Building Words activities from the **Phonics and Word Building Kit Guide, pages 24–25.**

Home-School Connection

Send home *Bo's Bows* and *Sunflowers*. Have children read the books to a family member.

My Book

For additional practice with *r*-controlled vowel *ar*, have children read *Sunflowers*. The My Book is also available on **WiggleWorks Plus.**

STUDY SKILLS

Test-Taking Strategies

Ⓐ TEACH/MODEL

REVIEW STANDARDIZED TESTS

Remind children that a standardized test is a test that is taken by many children. It asks questions about a topic and it gives a choice of answers.

CHOOSING THE BEST ANSWER

Explain to children that when they take a standardized test they will read a question and then look at a number of choices to find the correct answer. Share with children that to make the best answer choice, good strategies to remember are:

- Read all of the choices carefully before picking the correct one.
- Narrow down the choices. Try to eliminate one answer choice right away.
- Pick the right answer from the choices that are left.
- If one item is taking too long, put a checkmark next to it and come back to it later.

MODEL THE SKILL

THINK ALOUD *Suppose I had to answer a question about spelling. First I would read the sentence with the missing spelling word. Next, I would read the answer choices and try to eliminate at least one that I know is wrong. Then I would read the other choices and try to decide which one best finishes the sentence.*

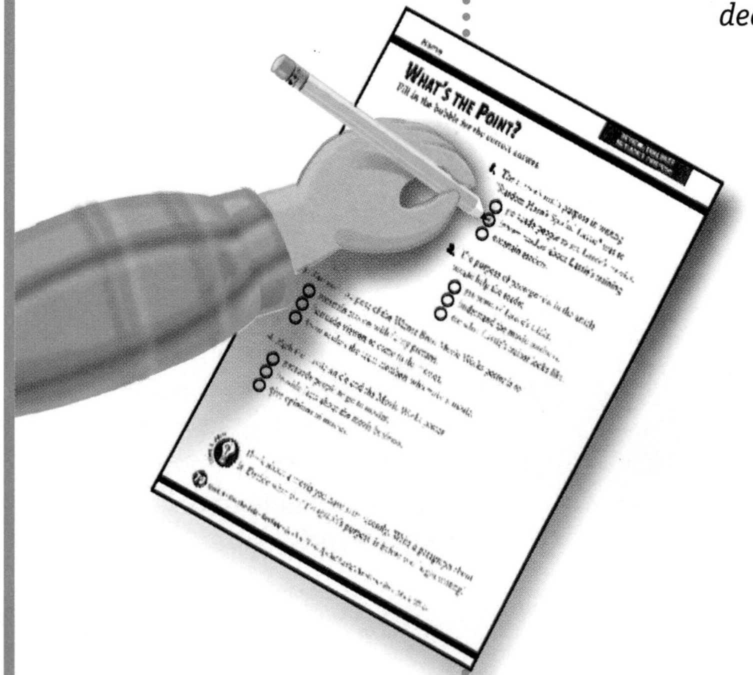

B PRACTICE/APPLY

PRACTICE TEST-TAKING STRATEGIES

Write the following sample test items on chart paper. You may want to duplicate and distrubute individual copies to children. Have children complete each practice test item by reading each incomplete sentence and all the answer choices, then narrowing down their choices before selecting the correct answer.

1. What is in the _______ ?
○ bg ○ bag ○ bage

2. I _______ help you.
○ wel ○ yl ○ will

When children have completed the sample items, discuss their strategies.

> **Did you read each incomplete sentence and the answer choices?**

> **Did you narrow down your choices by eliminating at least one answer?**

> **Were you able to choose an answer from the choices left?**

INFORMAL ASSESSMENT: PERFORMANCE-BASED

✔ Did children apply the test-taking strategies?

✔ Did children answer the questions correctly?

TECHNOLOGY

Study Skills Have children use a familiar word processor to write a short quiz based on *The Plant Castle*. Each question should have three or four answer choices, only one of which is correct. Show children how to insert check boxes or circles next to each answer choice.

DAY 4 WRAP-UP

READ ALOUD *Spend five to ten minutes reading from a selection of your choice.*

GUIDED READING *To extend reading, meet with the **red** and **blue** reading groups and assign Independent Center activities.* ***See pages R34–R35.***

Reading Assessment

DAY 5 OBJECTIVES

CHILDREN WILL:

READ 20 MINUTES

- **Reading Assessment**
- **Daily Phonics: Vowel /ō/o, ow, r-Controlled Vowel /är/ ar**

WRITE 30 MINUTES

- **Writing Assessment**
- **Spelling: Words With Vowel /ō/o, ow**
- **Grammar, Usage, Mechanics: Words That Compare**
- **Oral Language**

EXTEND SKILLS 40 MINUTES

- **Integrated Language Arts**
- **Read Aloud**
- **Guided Reading**

RESOURCES

- **Selection Test**
- **Spelling Resource Book, p. 163**

TEACHER SELF-ASSESSMENT

✔ Did I frequently model how to blend words?

✔ Did I regroup children according to skill needs and reading level?

✔ Did I provide children with successful, daily reading and writing opportunities?

INFORMAL ASSESSMENT: OBSERVATION

PHONICS

Write the following spellings on note cards: ***o, ow, ar.*** Display one card at a time and have the class state aloud the sound the spelling stands for. Note children who respond incorrectly or wait for classmates to respond before providing an answer.

HIGH-FREQUENCY WORDS

Write the following words on note cards: ***mother, girl.*** Display one card at a time and have the class read the word. Note children who have difficulty recognizing either word.

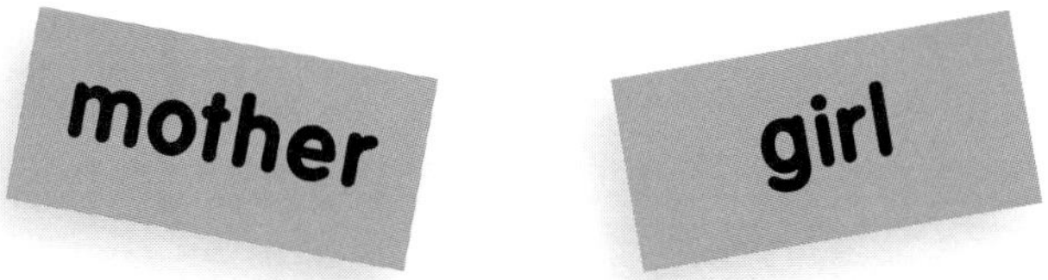

KEY SKILL: COMPARE/CONTRAST

Ask children to choose a nonfiction animal book. Have children look at the pictures and skim the text. Then ask each child to write or dictate sentences describing the similarities and differences between two animals featured in the book.

CONFERENCE

Have children reread *The Plant Castle.* As they reread, select several children to conference with. Ask them to do the following:

- read aloud a few pages of the story.
- retell the story in their own words.
- explain what they do to figure out an unfamiliar word.

Keep anecdotal records of the conferences. Place your findings in each child's assessment folder. Use the information to determine which children need additional support.

The Plant Castle

FORMAL ASSESSMENT

DECODING TEST

Make two copies of the assessment below. The assessment piece is designed to be used individually.

- Give one to the child and keep the other to record each child's errors.
- As the child reads aloud the words and sentences in the assessment boxes, record his or her attempts, corrections, errors, and passes.
- Once completed, keep each assessment piece in the child's portfolio as a running record of his or her emerging reading skills.

NAME: ______________________ **DATE:** ____________

A Have children read the following word list:

fish	**thin**	**sail**	**was**	**next**
may	**wait**	**say**	**mother**	**girl**
call	**paw**	**go**	**school**	**their**
tied	**toad**	**snow**	**which**	**more**
anyone	**far**	**grow**	**were**	**belongs**

B Have children read the following sentences:

- **Mother will water the plants.**
- **The tree will grow taller than the girl.**

C On a separate sheet of paper, have children write the following words and sentences:

- **boat slow far no**
- **The snow fell all day.**
- **We will go to the lake.**

SELECTION TEST

Use the selection test to obtain a formal measure of children's mastery of the week's reading objectives.

SELF-SELECTION

Have children select one or two pieces of work from the week that they would like to place in their portfolios.

Suggest that children write a sentence telling why they chose each piece. You may also wish to select a piece that best illustrates the child's work.

Periodically review the pieces in the portfolio and remove any that no longer seem appropriate.

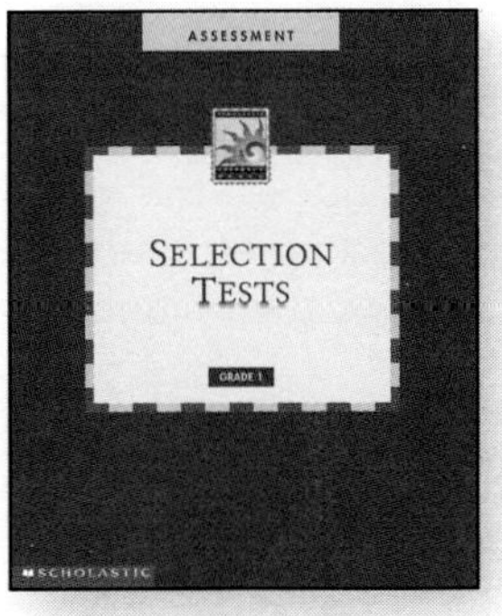

SELECTION TEST

DAILY LANGUAGE PRACTICE

SPELLING

DAY 5:
Administer the Posttest for Words With Vowel /ō/ *o, ow.* **See page R37.**

GRAMMAR, USAGE, MECHANICS

DAY 5:
Assess Words That Compare. **See page R39.**

ORAL LANGUAGE

Sho me a plant that is more big than you.
(Show me a plant that is bigger than you.)

PORTFOLIO

Suggest that children add their drafts and revisions to their Literacy Portfolios.

Writing Assessment

Good beginning! This question really gets the reader's attention.

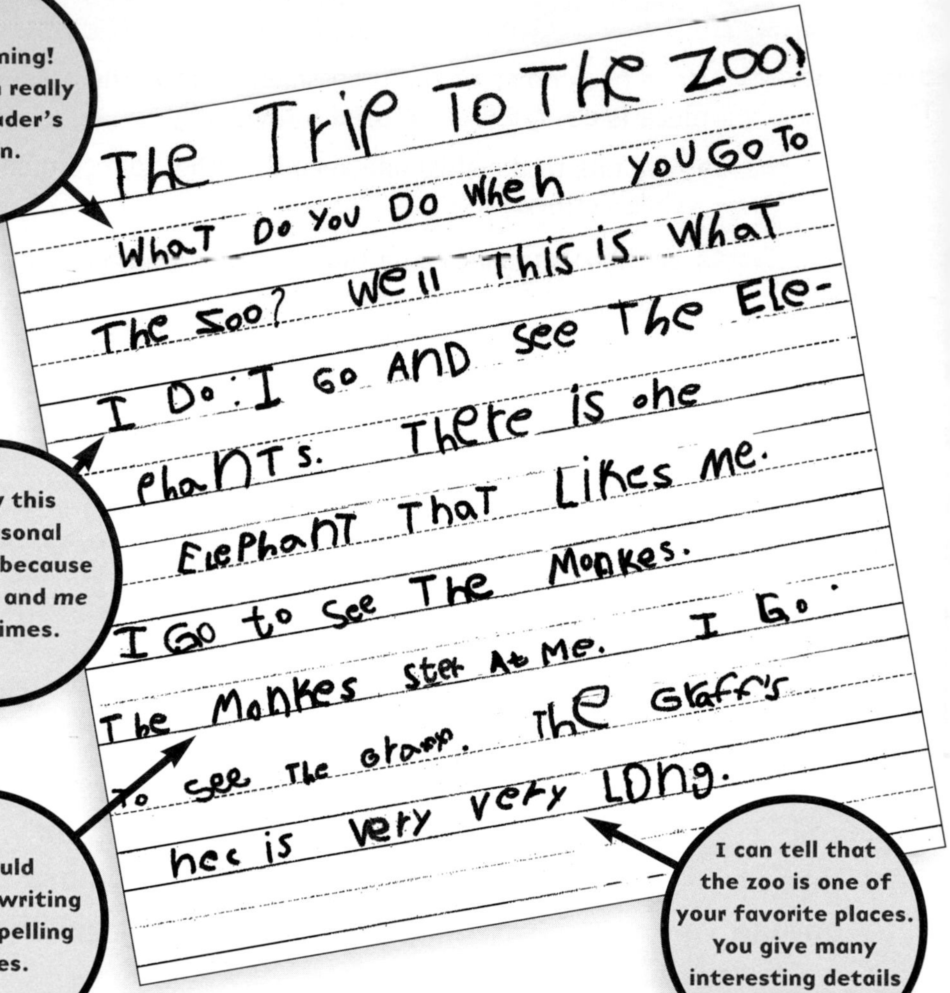
The Trip To The Zoo!
What Do You Do When You Go To The Soo? Well This is What I Do: I Go AND see The Ele-phanTs. There is one Elephant That Likes me. I Go to See The Monkes. The Monkes ster At Me. I Go. To see The Grafp. The Graff's nec is very very LOng.

I know this is a personal narrative because you use *I* and *me* many times.

You should check your writing again for spelling mistakes.

I can tell that the zoo is one of your favorite places. You give many interesting details about it.

Apprentice

Use the rubric below to assess children's writing.

CHILDREN'S WRITING RUBRIC

Proficient	• The person telling the story is the main character. • The story uses personal pronouns, such as *I* and *me*.	• The story is about a favorite place. • The story is proofread and corrected for grammar.
Apprentice	• The person telling the story is the main character. • The story uses personal pronouns, such as *I* and *me*.	• The story may not be about a favorite place. • The story is proofread but not completely corrected for errors.
Novice	• The person telling the story is not the main character. • The story is not a personal narrative that uses personal pronouns, such as *I* and *me*.	• The story may not be about a favorite place. • The story has not been corrected for errors.

Integrated Language Arts

VIEWING/WRITING/SPEAKING

Grow a Plant

MATERIALS:
Beans or other seeds
Potting soil
Paper cups or pots

SUGGESTED GROUPING:
Cooperative groups, partners, or individuals

LET children plant beans or other seeds in paper cups or pots. Children can place the cups in sunlight, water them, and watch the seeds grow.

ENCOURAGE children to plant different beans or seeds and to label the cups. Then they can start observation journals by drawing pictures of their seeds.

HAVE children record changes in their plants by drawing pictures and writing what happened in their observation journals.

ENCOURAGE children to share their observation journals. You may also wish to have them display their journals in a class library.

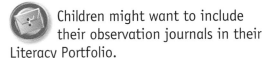

Children might want to include their observation journals in their Literacy Portfolio.

VIEWING/SPEAKING/LISTENING

Give a Tour

Good For Grading

MATERIALS:
Any already existing classroom display

SUGGESTED GROUPING:
Partners or individuals

CHILDREN can act as tour guides for centers or displays in the classroom. Have them prepare for the tour by writing notes.

HELP children organize their tours by suggesting that they:

- begin by explaining what the displays or centers are and how they are used.
- continue by pointing out two or three important items and telling about them.
- conclude with an invitation for listeners to look at the displays and ask questions.

GRADE their tours by looking for children's effort to communicate information clearly.

Select Information

TEACH/MODEL Explain to children that when they select information to share with others, they should choose the most important and interesting information. Point out a class poster or bulletin board. Model what you would say about it. Describe the main idea of the display.

APPLY Ask children to select and talk about the most important information on the tour.

Integrated Language Arts

WRITING/VIEWING/VOCABULARY

Create Categories

MATERIALS:
Anthology, pp. 114–128
Crayons
Drawing paper

SUGGESTED GROUPING:
Individual

INVITE children to make *Plant Castle* posters.

DIVIDE large pieces of paper into six sections. Have children label the sections *Desert, Orchid House, Spring Garden, Rain Forest Room,* and *Tropical Room.*

CHILDREN can draw and label pictures in each category. Encourage children to use the high-frequency and story words.

ENCOURAGE children to display their completed posters on the bulletin board. Invite children to compare and contrast the posters and to suggest plants and animals that weren't included on the posters.

TECHNOLOGY

Presentation Tools Have children create their category posters using **WiggleWorks Plus** PlaceMaker. Show them how to use clip art as well as freehand drawing tools, and how to stylize text.

Reference Sources Library

TEACH/MODEL Share with children that they can find information in books, magazines, and newspapers in the library.

APPLY Encourage children to visit the school library to research where different plants and animals live. Have them share their findings with classmates.

VIEWING/WRITING

Make a Map

MATERIALS:
Chart paper
Markers

SUGGESTED GROUPING:
Whole class

TAKE a class walk in the schoolyard or a park. Note major points of interest, such as playing fields, trees, or gym equipment.

WHEN you return to the classroom, have children work together to make a map of the area. They can list important things to be included.

THEN have children outline the general shape of the area on chart paper.

ASK volunteers to point to where they think the important features on the list should go. Then other children can mark these places.

INVITE children to add other important features to the map, based on their tour.

DISPLAY the map and have children take turns using it to describe the area and the tour.

DAY 5 WRAP-UP

READ ALOUD *Spend five to ten minutes reading from a selection of your choice.*

GUIDED READING *Meet with the* ***blue*** *and* ***green*** *reading groups and assign Independent Center activities.* ***See pages R34–R35.***

Unit 5 Wrap-Up

Children demonstrate independence and make meaningful connections to the real world.

WEEK 6 OBJECTIVES

WRITING PROCESS
Letter of Invitation
- write a letter inviting someone to a place

TRADE BOOK LIBRARY
- demonstrate independence

PROJECT
Make a Big Book of Information
- select information and use it to create a big book about a sea plant or animal

PRESENTATION SKILL
Listen to Learn
- practice listening as each Big Book is read aloud

HOME INVOLVEMENT
- plan a family literacy night

TECHNOLOGY
- write a nature story using **WiggleWorks Plus** CD-ROM

END OF UNIT ASSESSMENT
- follow-up on the baseline assessment and conduct formal and informal assessment

WEEKLY ORGANIZER

DAY 1	DAY 2	DAY 3	DAY 4	DAY 5
• WRITING PROCESS • TRADE BOOK LIBRARY • TECHNOLOGY	• WRITING PROCESS • TRADE BOOK LIBRARY • TECHNOLOGY	• WRITING PROCESS • TRADE BOOK LIBRARY • PROJECT	• TRADE BOOK LIBRARY • PROJECT • HOME INVOLVEMENT	• TRADE BOOK LIBRARY • PRESENTATION SKILL • END OF UNIT ASSESSMENT

WRAP-UP

WEEK 6 WRITING OBJECTIVES

CHILDREN WILL:
- write a letter of invitation
- include information that tells *who, what, when, where,* and *why*
- capitalize the word *I*

MATERIALS
- Anthology, pp. 114–128
- Practice Book p. 76

SUGGESTED GROUPING
- Pairs and individuals

A LETTER OF INVITATION

THINK ABOUT WRITING

Ask children if they have ever received a letter or invitation in the mail. Have them tell what kinds of letters or invitations they have received. Then ask children if they have ever written or sent a letter of invitation and for what purpose.

Discuss with children these key characteristics of a letter of invitation:

- A letter of invitation is written in letter format, including a greeting that tells who the letter is for and a closing telling who wrote the letter.
- A letter of invitation invites the reader to do something or go somewhere.
- A letter of invitation includes details such as what the invitation is for and when it is for.

Demonstrate letter format on the chalkboard. Invite children to suggest different words for the greeting such as ***Dear, Hello,*** or ***Greetings.*** Write one of the greetings followed by a name and a comma. Next, write a simple invitation such as ***Please come to my party on Monday. It will be at my house at four o'clock.*** Then ask for suggestions of ways to close the letter such as ***Love, From,*** or ***Your friend.*** Add one of these closings in the proper place followed by a comma and a person's name.

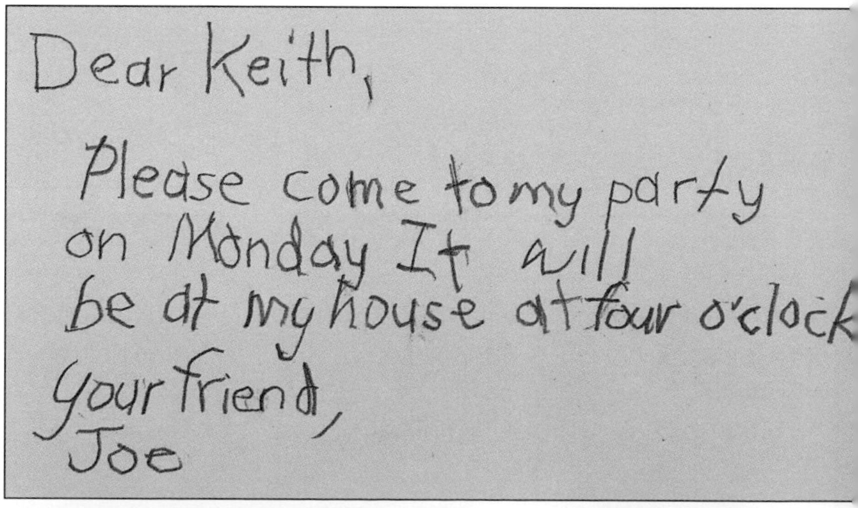
Dear Keith,
Please come to my party on Monday It will be at my house at four o'clock
Your friend,
Joe

WRI

LITERATURE CONNECTION

Remind children that in the story *The Plant Castle*, Carmen invites her friend Beth to visit the arboretum where her mother works. Have children imagine that Carmen writes Beth a letter of invitation. Work with children to create such a letter on chart paper or the chalkboard. Remind children that a letter of invitation is written in letter format, invites the reader to do something or go somewhere, and includes details such as what the invitation is for and when it is for. Also remind children to use a capital letter for ***I*** when appropriate. A sample letter might be:

Dear Beth,

Please come with me after school to visit the place where my mother works. It has lots of plants and flowers. Would this Monday, right after school, be good for you?

Your friend,

Carmen

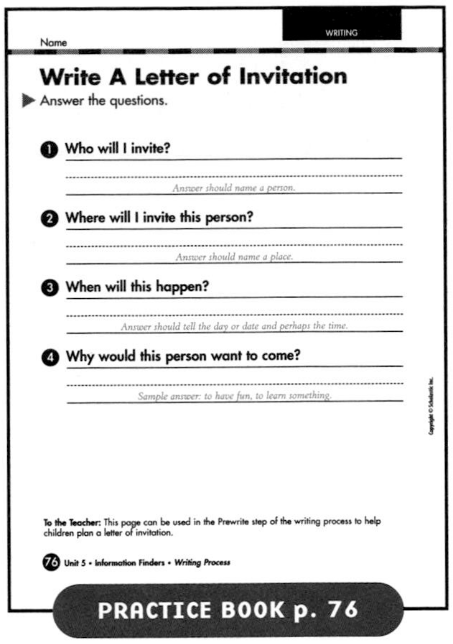
Name
WRITING
Write A Letter of Invitation
▶ Answer the questions.
1 Who will I invite?
Answer should name a person.
2 Where will I invite this person?
Answer should name a place.
3 When will this happen?
Answer should tell the day or date and perhaps the time.
4 Why would this person want to come?
Sample answer: to have fun, to learn something.
To the Teacher: This page can be used in the Prewrite step of the writing process to help children plan a letter of invitation.
76 Unit 5 • Information Finders • *Writing Process*

PRACTICE BOOK p. 76

PREWRITE

COMPLETE A PREWRITING ORGANIZER

Tell children they will be writing their own invitations. They should think about who they will invite, what place or activity the invitation is for, when it will happen, and why. You may wish to take this opportunity to discuss the distinguishing features of a paragraph, such as indenting the first line. Have children complete **Practice Book page 76** to plan their invitations.

After children have finished the Practice Book page, have them form pairs to share their ideas for writing an invitation. After they answer the questions, have children tell their partners what they will write in their invitations.

TECHNOLOGY

Matching Technology to Task Encourage children to use **WiggleWorks Plus** PlaceMaker to create their invitation. They can frame and illustrate the invitation with the program's clip art or with their own drawings.

TEACHER TIP

"I like to make ***Who? What? Where? When?*** *and* ***Why?*** *cards for each pair of children. Then I have partners read their invitations to each other. The reader holds up each card and the listener tells whether or not the answer to the question is in the invitation and what it is. In this way children can discover if their invitations are clear and give enough information."*

PROOFREADING MARKS

◯	Check spelling
∧	Add
—	Cross out

DRAFT

WRITE Based on their decisions in Prewrite, have children begin a draft. Remind them to begin with a greeting on a separate line that tells who the letter is to. After they write the invitation, they should end with a closing. Mention that the closing is often written on two lines with the writer's name on the last line. Point out where they would use commas.

Dear Jan, I would like you to come to my birthday party. It will be on Saturday, November 8, at 3 o'clock. From Anna ❶	❶ This is a good start to the letter, but the writer forgot to tell where the party is. Also, the writer should put the greeting and closing on separate lines.

REVISE/PROOFREAD

Have children ask themselves or a writing partner the following questions:

REVISE

- Does my letter of invitation start with a greeting and end with a closing?
- Does my letter of invitation include details such as what the invitation is for, where and when it is?

PROOFREAD

- Did I capitalize the letter *I*?
- Did I put a comma after the greeting and closing?
- Did I correct my misspellings?

Help children create a list of important features to include in their writing.

PUBLISH

ILLUSTRATING/ SHARING Suggest that children illustrate their invitations. Then they can read their invitations and display their pictures.

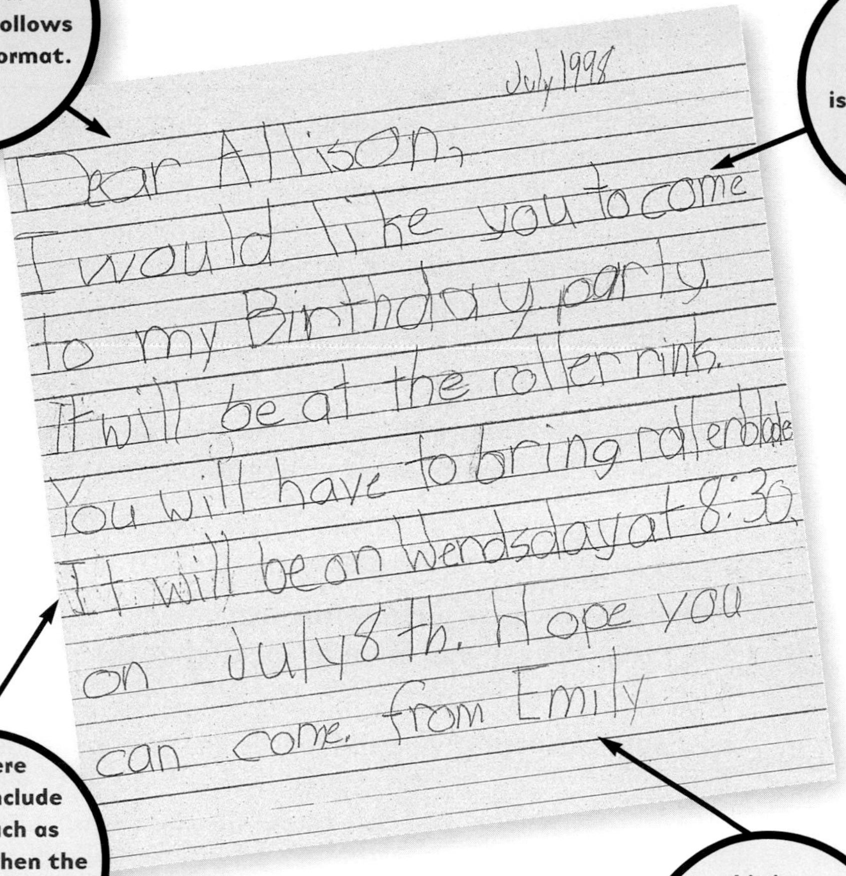
July 1998

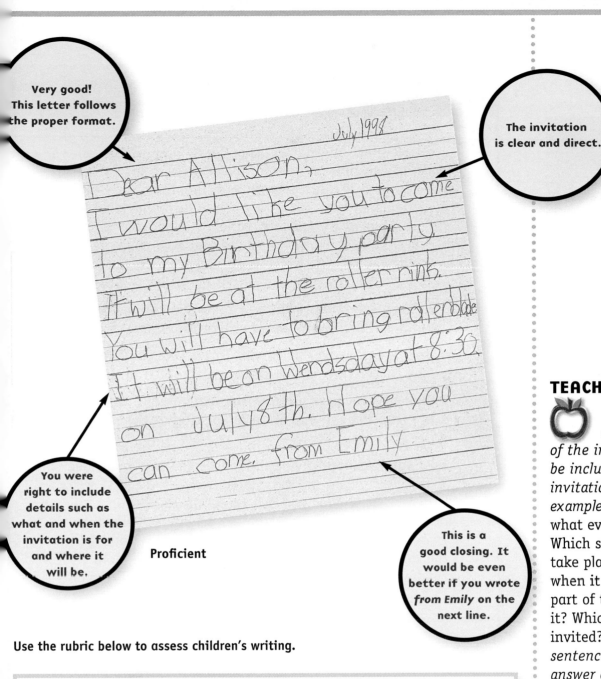

Dear Allison,
I would like you to come to my Birthday party. It will be at the roller rink. You will have to bring rollerblade. It will be on Wendsday at 8:30 on July 8th. Hope you can come. from Emily

Very good! This letter follows the proper format.

The invitation is clear and direct.

You were right to include details such as what and when the invitation is for and where it will be.

This is a good closing. It would be even better if you wrote *from Emily* on the next line.

Proficient

Use the rubric below to assess children's writing.

CHILDREN'S WRITING RUBRIC

Proficient	• The letter of invitation includes details such as *what, when,* and *where.* • The letter includes a greeting and a closing.	• The invitation clearly conveys the necessary information. • The letter is proofread and corrected for errors.
Apprentice	• The letter of invitation may include some details. • The letter includes a greeting and a closing that may not be correctly placed.	• The invitation may not be clearly stated. • The letter is proofread but not completely corrected for errors.
Novice	• The letter does not invite someone to do something. • The letter does not include details, a greeting, and a closing.	• The invitation does not include all the necessary information. • The letter has not been corrected for errors.

TEACHER TIP

"One way I check children's understanding of the information that should be included when writing an invitation is by asking, for example: 'Which sentence tells what event the invitation is to? Which sentence tells where it will take place? Which sentence tells when it will take place? Which part of the letter tells who wrote it? Which part tells who is being invited?' *Children point to the sentences in their invitations that answer each question I ask."*

▶ Challenge

Average

Easy

DECODABLE TEXT

For practice reading decodable text, see ***Scholastic Decodable Readers #67–69.***

THEME Connection

In the nonfiction books *Animal Tracks* and *Fish Faces*, children can find information on a given topic in both the text and in the illustrations or photographs. In *Fish Faces* children learn about the many different kinds of fish. In *Animal Tracks*, children learn about animal footprints, where they are found and how they are alike and different. Invite children to compare *Animal Tracks* and *Fish Faces* by exploring these questions:

> **In each selection, what new facts did you learn about animals that live in water or like to be near water?**

> **How is the beaver in *Animal Tracks* like the fish in *Fish Faces*? How is the beaver different from the fish?**

> **Choose a favorite picture from each book. What information can you learn by looking at the picture?**

Have children create two word webs, one for each selection. Have children help you decide the main idea of each selection. On the center circle of the first web, write the main idea for *Fish Faces;* on the center circle of the second web, write the main idea for *Animal Tracks*. Invite children to copy the word webs and fill in the details they have learned about each selection. Have children share their word webs in pairs or small groups.

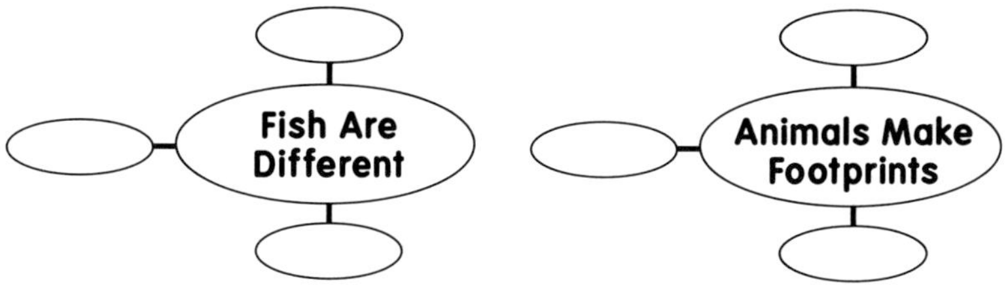

TRADE

AUTHOR Connection

Point out that the same author, Arnold Lobel, wrote both *Owl at Home* and *"The Garden"* from *Frog and Toad Together*. Ask: ***What kind of stories do you think Arnold Lobel likes to write? Why?*** *(funny stories, stories about animals that act like people, stories in which characters try to figure out a problem)*. Have children share examples of how these stories are alike and different by thinking about the characters, setting, and what happens in each story. Put more stories by Arnold Lobel on a special reading shelf in your classroom.

Challenge
▶ Average
Easy

KEY SKILL Connection

Compare/Contrast Help children compare and contrast the characters, setting, and plot of *Lost!* to *The Plant Castle* by filling in the chart below.

	LOST!	THE PLANT CASTLE
Main Characters	*a boy and a bear*	*two girls*
Setting	*a city and a forest*	*a place with plants and flowers*
What Characters Do	*look for bear's home*	*see all kinds of plants*

Invite children to share their answers and encourage further discussion with questions such as these:

> **Which story could have happened? Why?**

> **Which story probably didn't happen? Why?**

> **Imagine the boy had taken the bear to the arboretum. What might the bear have said about that?**

> **Which character would you like for a friend? Why?**

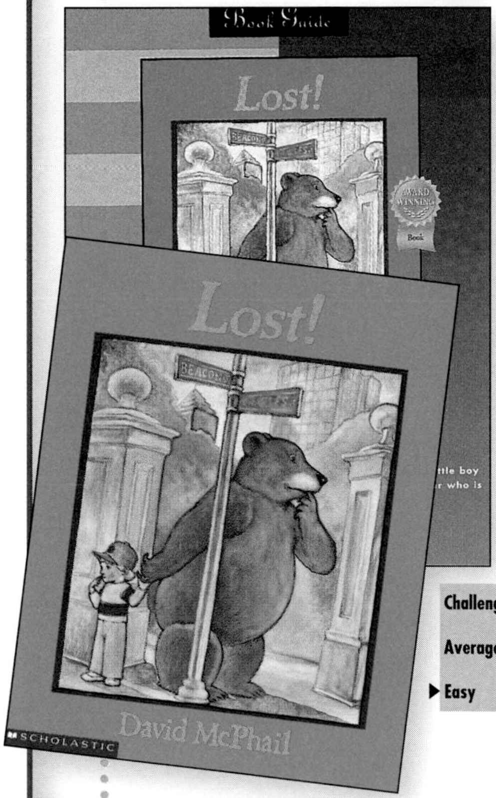

Challenge
Average
▶ Easy

PROJECT OBJECTIVES

CHILDREN WILL:
- **select information about a sea plant or animal from resource materials**
- **use the information to create a big book about the sea plant or animal**

MATERIALS
- **Big paper**
- **Pencils, markers**
- **Stapler**
- **Resource books**
- **Magazines or newspapers**
- **Glue**

MODIFY Instruction

EXTRA HELP

While discussing the project, consider peer sharing to help children who may be confused. Stop after part of the project discussion and ask children to turn to classmates and share questions they may have about the project. Then have children share what they know about something that lives in the sea. **(MAKE CONNECTIONS)**

TECHNOLOGY

Build Background You can take a field trip to the National Aquarium in Baltimore, Maryland, without leaving your classroom. Just visit **www.aqua.org** to learn about all sorts of sea life.

MAKE A BIG BOOK OF INFORMATION

GETTING STARTED

Select Information

To focus children on the project, spend some time discussing the information on Side 1 of the Project Card. You could also ask the following questions:

> **How is a storybook different from a book that gives information, such as a book about the ocean?**

> **If you read a nature book about seahorses, what things might you find out?**

> **Where do you think writers find information for their books?**

Home Involvement

To find out more about a sea animal or plant, children may enjoy having a family member or older friend take them to a local aquarium or pet store with a fish tank. Children can then incorporate information they learn in their Big Books.

Troubleshooting

You may want to have children look through available resources first and then choose an animal or plant to focus on. Otherwise, they may be disappointed to choose a topic first and not be able to find anything about it in your available resources. You may also want to help children staple their Big Book pages together or do it yourself.

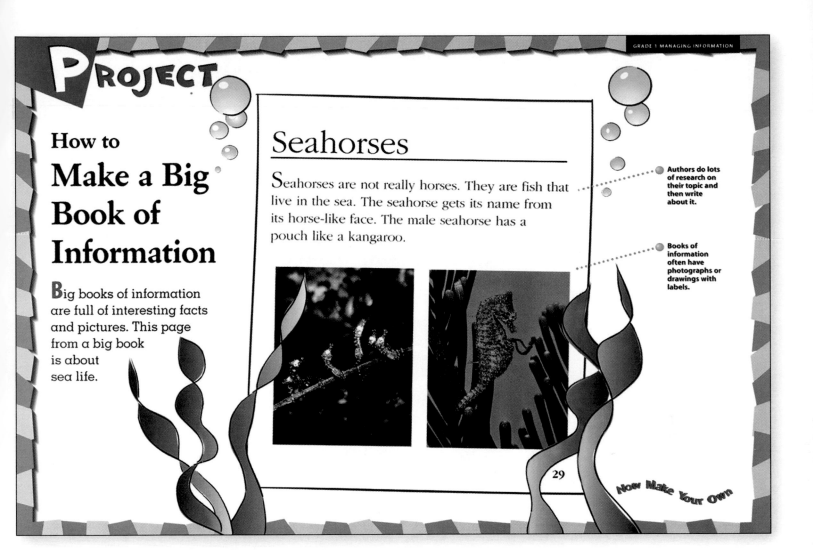

PRO

GRADE 1 MANAGING INFORMATION

PROJECT

How to Make a Big Book of Information

Big books of information are full of interesting facts and pictures. This page from a big book is about sea life.

Seahorses

Seahorses are not really horses. They are fish that live in the sea. The seahorse gets its name from its horse-like face. The male seahorse has a pouch like a kangaroo.

29

Authors do lots of research on their topic and then write about it.

Books of information often have photographs or drawings with labels.

Now Make Your Own

1 Get the Facts

Choose an animal or plant that lives in the sea that you'd like to learn more about. Use books and magazines to find out more about your topic. Make notes on what you find.

2 Make Your Big Book of Information

Use your notes to write a page about your topic. Draw pictures on your page with markers, or cut out pictures from magazines and newspapers to glue onto your page.

Gather your pages and staple them together.

TIP
- Draw BIG pictures so people can see them.
- Use bright colors so your book will stand out.
- Make sure you label your pictures.

Tools
big paper and pencils
markers
stapler
resource books and magazines about sea life
CONGRATULATIONS
You are now an information finder. You can be an expert on anything you choose!
Laela Sayigh
Marine Biologist

1 Get the Facts

With the whole class, discuss the kinds of things children would like to find out about a sea plant or animal. Remind them of what they observed about animals and plants when they made their Observation Log for Workshop Card 1 and the Nature Poster in Workshop Card 2. Then have children look through the available resources to choose their topics. Encourage them to help each other use the research resources and have them select only information related to their topics. Children can make their notes using words or pictures.

Have children work in cooperative groups to gather and assemble materials for their Big Book pages. Children can use the Project Planner on **Practice Book pages 74** and **75** to help organize ideas for their Big Book of Information.

PRO

2 Make Your Big Book of Information

Children can write the text part of their page on a piece of lined paper and then tape or paste it to their Big Book page. After they see how much room their text takes, they can plan their illustrations. Encourage children to use the Project Card to help them complete their pages.

Children may have fun presenting their Big Books of Information to the rest of the class. Use the Presentation Skill lesson on pages T296–T297 to support children in giving and viewing their presentations. The lesson will help children become attentive and active listeners.

Assessment

Informal Assessment

Observation

When children have finished making their Big Book pages, review their work. Ask yourself:

- ✔ Were they able to select information about a sea plant or animal from reference sources?
- ✔ Did children draw or cut out pictures to illustrate their Big Book pages? Did they label their pictures?
- ✔ How did children organize their information in their Big Books?

Children's Self-Assessment

> **Can I use books to find information? What could I learn from pictures of animals and plants?**

Use the rubric below to assess children's understanding of the Project.

Children's Project Rubric

Proficient	Children select information and material relevant to the topic. Their illustrations and labels give relevant support to the text.
Apprentice	Children have some difficulty selecting information that is only about the intended topic; some pictures may not be relevant to the text.
Novice	Children have difficulty selecting relevant information and selecting pictures that support the text.

Self-Selection

When children complete this project, they could include a page from their Big Book, or a copy of it, in their Literacy Portfolios as an example of work well done.

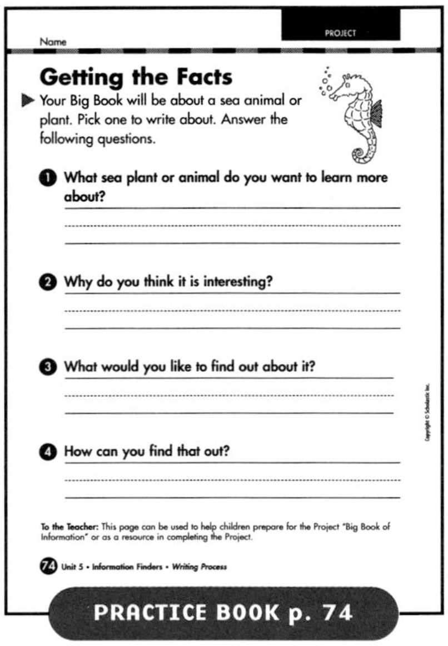
Name PROJECT

Getting the Facts

▶ Your Big Book will be about a sea animal or plant. Pick one to write about. Answer the following questions.

1. What sea plant or animal do you want to learn more about?
2. Why do you think it is interesting?
3. What would you like to find out about it?
4. How can you find that out?

To the Teacher: This page can be used to help children prepare for the Project "Big Book of Information" or as a resource in completing the Project.

74 Unit 5 • Information Finders • Writing Process

PRACTICE BOOK p. 74

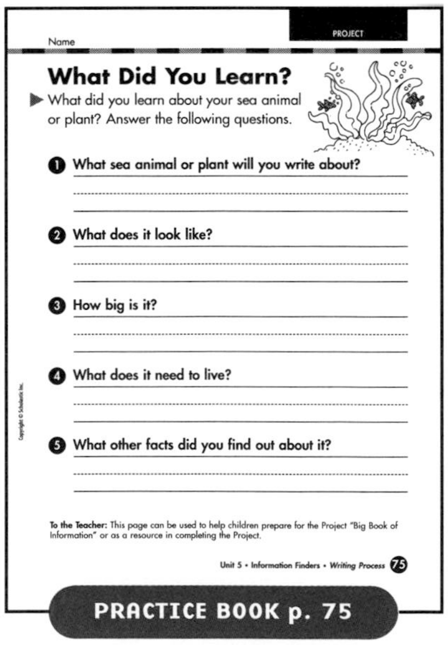
Name PROJECT

What Did You Learn?

▶ What did you learn about your sea animal or plant? Answer the following questions.

1. What sea animal or plant will you write about?
2. What does it look like?
3. How big is it?
4. What does it need to live?
5. What other facts did you find out about it?

To the Teacher: This page can be used to help children prepare for the Project "Big Book of Information" or as a resource in completing the Project.

Unit 5 • Information Finders • Writing Process 75

PRACTICE BOOK p. 75

PRESENTATION SKILL OBJECTIVE

CHILDREN WILL:
- **listen to get information from oral presentations**

MATERIALS
- **Children's Big Books**
- **Audiocassette recorder (optional)**
- **Blank audiotapes (optional)**

TECHNOLOGY

Presentation Tools Children can use the Poster format in **WiggleWorks Plus** PlaceMaker to create their Big Books. They might paste clip art, create drawings, or compose headlines and captions to use within the books.

LISTEN TO LEARN

A TEACH/MODEL

PUT IT IN CONTEXT

Point out to children that every day they learn a lot of things just by listening. At home, they learn how to do a job by listening to what someone, probably an adult, tells them. At school, they learn things by listening to their teacher and other adults. Discuss with children the different kinds of things you and other adults in the school tell them and what they learn from listening to such comments or instructions.

Next, point out that when children watch cartoons or television, or when they listen to a story being read to them, they probably listen carefully to what is being said. Doing so helps them understand what is happening. Explain that when children listen to you or anyone else, they should listen just as carefully. Point out that it's also very important for listeners to ask questions when they don't understand something, or when they're curious to know more about what's being said.

B PRACTICE/APPLY

LISTEN TO LEARN

Encourage the class to practice learning by listening as children take turns reading their Big Book page aloud. Before the presentations begin, tell them to think about these questions:

> **Do I understand everything the speaker is saying?**

> **Is there anything I don't understand or that I wonder about? What more do I want to know? What questions can I ask?**

Have volunteers present their pages of the Big Book to the class as an oral report. Encourage other children to ask questions about each page as they listen to the presentation, pointing out as necessary that asking good questions is part of good listening, too. Ask volunteers to tell what they learned by listening to each presentation.

Children could make an audiotape of the information on their pages of the Big Book of Information. They could then play each other's tapes and write information that they heard.

C ASSESS

INFORMAL ASSESSMENT: OBSERVATION

When children have finished listening to the oral presentations, review their ability to learn by listening, and answer any questions they might have about the strategy. Ask yourself:

✔ Did children listen quietly and attentively?

✔ Did they ask more after each presentation?

✔ How else did they show that they were learning as they listened?

CHILDREN'S SELF-ASSESSMENT

✔ What things did I learn by listening to the Big Book page presentations?

MODIFY Instruction

ESL/ELD

▲ Before presentations begin, explain that good listeners listen with their eyes as well as their ears. Then invite volunteers to demonstrate attentive listening posture and good eye contact. It might be helpful to form a listening team of one English learner and one native speaker. These children can coach each other as they listen to the presentations. **(WORK IN PAIRS)**

EXTRA HELP

■ If children need help listening attentively, you can provide support by encouraging them to use their bodies to stay tuned in and as a way to express understanding. For example, they could raise one finger if they understand very little, five fingers to show they understand a lot.

You might also give them more practice with listening. Before reading upcoming selections in the Anthology and Trade Books, give short oral introductions and explanations of them. Ask children to listen carefully. Then have volunteers recall what you said in the introduction. **(STEP-BY-STEP)**

JECT

Home Involvement

Family Literacy Night

Your classroom Aquarium can become the focus of a Literacy Event during which children share with family members their work completed during the *Information Finders* unit. You may use the following options for planning, organizing, and setting up the event.

- **A BANNER** Children can announce their Family Time at the Aquarium by making a banner using PlaceMaker. On the banner have them write the date and time and draw pictures of marine plants and animals. Hang the banner in the hallway.

- **TOUR OUR AQUARIUM** Have groups of children write a description of each exhibit in your Aquarium and record it for visitors.

Learning Stations

In the Aquarium, display children's work done during the unit. Have children help you set up active learning stations such as the following:

- **STORY CENTER** Place the trade books and Anthology in this area for family members to read together. Have groups of children present a dramatic reading of the class's favorite story.

- **WRITING CENTER** Use a shoebox to create a "fish" mailbox. Put out lined paper, pencils, and envelopes. Encourage parents to write a letter to their child telling what they like best about their visit to the Aquarium. Put the letters in the mailbox to be delivered tomorrow.

- **QUICKWRITE** Have children make lists of characters and places they visited in the unit. If possible, have a computer available in this center.

- **SCIENCE CENTER** Ask each child's family to bring in one of the following: things from the seashore, plants, dinosaur models, or insects to display for the evening. Discuss what story each relates to.

CONNE

Interactive Writing

Children can use the Unit Writer on the **WiggleWorks Plus** CD-ROM to compose a story about nature. The program's Story Starters, My Words list, and Paint Tools will help them manage the ideas and details presented in their story.

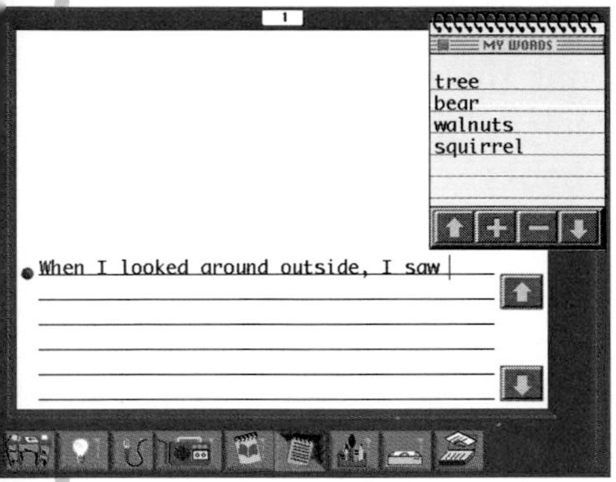

WiggleWorks Plus CD-ROM

- **WRITE** To begin their writing, ask children to click the lightbulb button to preview four Story Starters. Have them choose the Story Starter they like best to begin their story.

  When I looked around outside, I saw . . .

  On my nature poster, I want to show . . .

  One thing that I've learned about nature is . . .

  At an aquarium, you can find out about . . .

- **ORGANIZE** Encourage children to collect up to six nature words to use in their writing and store them on their My Words list. As they compose their story they can import these words into their writing until they have used all of them. This will help them organize information and make sure they don't leave out any important ideas.

WiggleWorks Plus CD-ROM

- **ILLUSTRATE** When they are happy with their writing, have children use the Paint Tools to illustrate their story. Encourage them to create images with a lot of detail and color.

- **DESCRIBE** Now, ask children to read their stories while looking at the illustrations they created. Is there any information missing from the stories? Ask children to look closely at the illustrations and then go back and add more detail to their stories based on what they saw. For example, they might put the finishing touch on their story by changing "bears" to "two brown bears."

For more activity suggestions, see the **WiggleWorks Plus** Teaching Guide.

SCHOLASTIC SOLUTIONS

Remember to visit the Scholastic Solutions area on www.scholastic.com to learn more about the variety of Scholastic's resources for teachers. Here you can find trade books, leveled libraries, phonics resources, magazines, videos, CD-ROMs, and professional books correlated to your content needs.

WEEK 6 ASSESSMENT

SEE THE ASSESSMENT HANDBOOK FOR:

- **Guidelines for Assessment Planning**
- **Methods of Assessment including Observation and Portfolio**
- **Tools for Assessment including Literacy Record and Literacy Log**
- **Oral Reading Assessment**
- **Rubrics for Evaluation**
- **Grading Guidelines**

CHILDREN'S ASSESSMENT

FOLLOW-UP ON BASELINE ASSESSMENT

The Baseline Assessment established the conceptual level at which each child began the unit. By repeating this task, children will demonstrate the growth they have accomplished over the course of this unit.

As you did before you taught the unit, have children draw pictures of various sources of information, such as television, newspapers, books, computers, and the library. Compare their pictures with those they completed before you taught the unit.

Refer to the unit and sectional concepts for *Information Finders* and ask yourself whether the child's present work reflects a greater understanding of these concepts and if these concepts have become part of their thinking. To determine this, you might ask: *If you were reading a book about snakes and it didn't have information about your favorite kind of snake, what would you do?*

K-W-L

Refer to the K-W-L chart you have been working on throughout this unit. Finish filling in the "What Did We Learn?" section. Have children write briefly about what they still want to learn about the many sources of information in the world.

CHILDREN'S SELF-ASSESSMENT

Children should complete the "What Did I Learn?" chart. Children can determine whether or not they had learned what they stated they wanted to learn. In either case you can confer with each child in order to suggest means for fulfilling their learning interests.

OBSERVATIONAL CHECKLIST

Use the Individual and Class Unit checklists for *Information Finders* in the Class Management Forms to record your end of unit evaluations and observations of each child in your class. You can complete and send home the Family Literacy Newsletter.

INFORMAL ASSESSMENT

Workshops, Projects, and writing activities are good opportunities for performance assessment. The rubrics mentioned in the Teacher's Edition, the rubrics in the Assessment Handbook, and child self-assessment pieces are all good assessment tools.

PORTFOLIO

Allow children time to sort through the material they've saved for their Portfolios. Distribute the Portfolio Checklist in the Assessment Handbook to help children decide what to keep in their *Information Finders* Portfolio.

FORMAL TESTING

- ✔ **See the Spelling Test Form in the Spelling Resource Book.**
- ✔ **To help prepare children for the *Information Finders* unit test, see the Teacher's Test Manual.**
- ✔ **Forms A and B of the test, and directions for administering, scoring, and using the tests, are in the Teacher's Test Manuals.**

Spelling Resource Book

Teacher's Test Manual

Unit Test Form A

Unit Test Form B

TEACHER SELF-ASSESSMENT

Ask yourself: Did I communicate the ideas that:

- ✔ Information comes from many sources?
- ✔ Our world is filled with information?
- ✔ There are many places to find information?
- ✔ We share information?

GLOSSARY

You will find all your vocabulary words in ABC order in the Glossary. This page shows you how to use it.

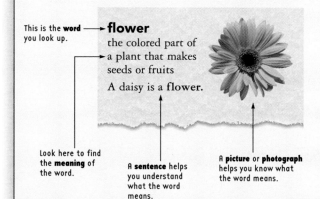

This is the **word** you look up. → **flower**

the colored part of a plant that makes seeds or fruits

A daisy is a **flower.**

Look here to find the **meaning** of the word.

A **sentence** helps you understand what the word means.

A **picture** or **photograph** helps you know what the word means.

132

butterfly
a flying insect with big wings, often in bright colors
The **butterfly** flew over the wall.

city
a large town where many people live and work
A **city** has tall buildings, lots of noise, and many busy people.

desert
a dry land with few plants
It is hot and dry in the **desert.**

desert

dry
to become free of wetness
Our wet clothes will **dry** in the sun.

eyes
the two parts of your face that you use to see with
I went to the doctor to have my **eyes** checked.

fins
small parts on a fish's body that flap to move it through water
Fins help a fish to swim.

fish
an animal with fins and scales that lives in water
A **fish** lives and breathes under water.

flower
the colored part of a plant that makes seeds or fruits
A daisy is a **flower.**

flower

forest
a big area full of trees and plants
We hiked on a trail through the **forest.**

133

GLOS

frog
a small green or brown animal with webbed feet and long back legs
I saw a **frog** jump into the pond.

fruits
the part of plants that are juicy, fleshy, and have seeds
Oranges and bananas are **fruits.**

garden
a piece of ground where flowers, vegetables, or trees grow
We grow carrots in our **garden.**

grow
to get bigger or to cause something to get bigger
The kitten will **grow** into a big cat.

leaves
the flat, usually green parts of plants or trees that grow from branches
Some **leaves** fall from trees in autumn.

library
a room or building where books are kept
People can borrow books from the **library** to read at home.

mouth
the opening in your face through which you take food
My teeth are in my **mouth.**

munch
to chew with a crunching sound
I heard my dog **munch** his hard food.

nose
the part of your face that you use to smell and to breathe
My **nose** is below my eyes and above my mouth.

office
a room or a building in which people work, usually at desks
Mom's computer is in her **office.**

plant
to put a plant or a seed in the ground and help it grow
Dad will **plant** grass in our yard.

seeds
small parts of plants from which new plants can grow
Tiny **seeds** can grow into trees.

shark
a kind of fish with sharp teeth that eats meat
I saw a large **shark** swimming in a huge tank.

straw
a hollow plastic or paper tube to drink through
Lee always drinks his juice through a **straw.**

supermarket
a large store that sells food and other things
My dad buys grapes, soap, and film at the **supermarket.**

supermarket

teacher
a person who shares knowledge and shows people how to do things
Our **teacher** told us how to add the numbers.

trees
large woody plants with trunks, roots, branches, and leaves
Apples grow on **trees.**

tree

wait
to stay or do nothing until something happens
We **wait** for the bus to come.

waves
curved, or up and down lines
Kerry used different colors to paint **waves** in her picture.

wet
covered with water or other liquid
The streets are **wet** on rainy days.

work
the effort to get something done
Moving rocks takes **work.**

134 135

SARY

ADDITIONAL SUPPORT

Information Finders

Information comes from many sources.

Instructional Support

WEEK 1 Guided Reading

CONDUCTING GUIDED READING GROUPS

Meet with at least two reading groups each day. Select a book on each group's instructional reading level from the *Scholastic Guided Reading Library* or a book in your classroom library. For more information on conducting guided reading groups, see *Scholastic Guided Reading Library,* Teacher's Guide.

SETTING UP INDEPENDENT CENTERS

While meeting with each reading group, have the rest of the class work in the Independent Centers listed below. Place the appropriate center cards in the pocket chart for student reference. Rotate the cards each day. Children may also use this time to do the following:

- revise or complete writing assignments,
- complete Practice Book pages,
- write in their Journals,
- read independently.

SAMPLE MANAGEMENT PLAN FOR CENTERS

RED GROUP	BLUE GROUP	GREEN GROUP	YELLOW GROUP
Listening	Independent	Poem Box	ABC Center
ABC Center	Listening	Independent	Poem Box
Poem Box	ABC Center	Listening	Independent

GROUPING AND REGROUPING

- **Assess and regroup children for guided reading every six weeks.**
- **Children progress at different rates, so ongoing assessment is essential. Use the results of your informal and formal assessments to regroup children as necessary. Remember, grouping should be dynamic. It should change according to children's needs.**
- **Form guided reading groups composed of children who are reading approximately the same level of text.**
- **Be sure children are in many different groups throughout the day. Children benefit from interactions with classmates at different levels. So both homogeneous small groups for guided reading and other small and large groups for literacy activities throughout the day are critical.**

TEACHER TIP

Remember, your goals and approaches should focus on:

- giving children many opportunities for reading and writing extended text.
- making sure that they have frequent opportunities to read and write whole texts.
- helping children understand the connections between the processes of reading and writing.
- teaching them how to use reading and writing strategies and match their thinking with written words.
- showing children how to use the visual information in print.

GAY SU PINNELL

Independent Centers

Children can work in these centers while you meet with guided reading groups.

LISTENING

Place three stories on tape, including the audiocassette version of *Fish Faces,* in the Listening Center. Ask children to select one story and follow along in the book as it is read aloud. To close the activity, suggest that children retell the story in their own words to a friend.

POEM BOX

Place poems that you have read to the children and that they can read on their own in the Poem Box. You can paste copies of the poems on tagboard. Decodable poems are available in *Scholastic Phonics A.* Have children select a poem they like and read it softly to themselves and then to a friend. Afterward, children can talk about what the poem means to them.

ABC CENTER

Set up several activities and games that focus on making words with a letter cluster at the beginning such as *r*-blends, *s*-blends, *l*-blends, and the digraphs *sh, th, ch, wh.* Have children work with partners on an activity that they select. You may want to ask children to use magnetic or tile letters to form the words.

INDEPENDENT READING

Collect several books to place in the Browsing Box for each reading group. Select books that children have read during guided reading or that match each group's independent reading level. Tell children to choose a book and read it independently. Afterward, children can retell the story to a classmate.

WEEK 1 Words With *sh* and *th*

Spelling

WEEK 1 RESOURCES

SPELLING RESOURCE BOOK
- **Word Sort,** p. 109
- **Extra Help,** p. 110
- **Vocabulary Practice,** p. 111
- **Challenge,** p. 112
- **Proofread,** p. 113
- **Student Test Form,** p. 161
- **Individual Progress Chart,** p. 162
- **Class Progress Chart,** p. 163
- **Word Sort Chart,** p. 164
- **My Words to Learn,** p. 165
- **Spelling Award Form,** p. 166
- **Family Newsletter,** p. 171★

ADDITIONAL RESOURCES
- **Spelling Strategy Poster**
- **Proofreading Marks Poster**

★You may wish to send home the Unit 5 Family Newsletter.

SPELLING LIST

Words With *sh* and *th*

fish	thin
wish	thick
dish	

High-Frequency

more	belongs

DAY 1 PRETEST/SELF-CHECK

ADMINISTER THE PRETEST

1. Do you have a pet **fish?**
2. I **wish** I had a pet.
3. Do not drop the **dish.**
4. I ate a **thin** piece of cake.
5. Dad wants a **thick** piece of cake.
6. Would you like **more** cake?
7. This book **belongs** to Julia.

SPELLING CONCEPT

Teach the spelling concept and present the spelling words. Point out that digraphs are two letters that stand for one sound.

WORD SORT

On the chalkboard, draw the word sort chart. Ask children to sort the spelling words under the corresponding digraph.

Digraphs	
sh	**th**
fish *wish* *dish*	*thick* *thin*

Have children complete **Spelling Resource Book, page 109.**

SPELLING RESOURCE BOOK p. 109

DAY 2 VOCABULARY PRACTICE

BUILD VOCABULARY: DESCRIPTIVE WORDS

- Review that adjectives are words that describe something or someone. Write on the chalkboard: *I put on my thick socks.* Ask children which word describes the socks. *(thick)*
- Children can make word webs for *thick* and *thin* by writing or drawing things that are described as being *thick* and *thin.*

WORD STUDY: BUILD WORDS

- Write *fish* on the chalkboard. Say the word, erase the *f,* and say *ish.* Ask children what other letter can come before *ish* to make a word. Have children blend *w* and then *d* with *ish* to say the new words. *(wish, dish)*
- Write on the chalkboard: *I closed my eyes and made a dish.* Ask children to replace the underlined word with a spelling word that makes sense in the sentence.

Have children complete **Spelling Resource Book, page 110, 111,** or **112.**

SPELLING RESOURCE BOOK pp. 110, 111, 112

DAY 3 **WRITE/PROOFREAD**

WRITE

- Tell children that they will write a description of a pet or another animal they have seen. Encourage children to include words that use the spelling concept.
- Using a word web will help children get started.

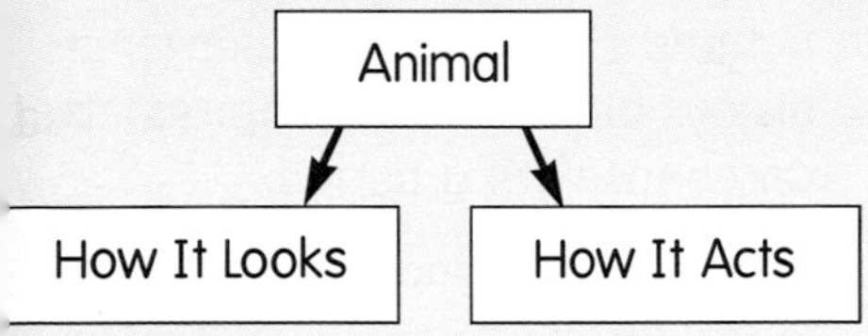

Children may:

- write a story and draw a picture of the animal they described.

PROOFREAD

PROOFREADING MARKS

- ◯ **Check spelling**
- ^ **Add**
- —— **Cross out**

- Review the proofreading marks, using the class Proofreading Chart for reference.
- Use the following sentence for proofreading practice:

Wish (above) / **you see** (above)
Wihs on the first star ~~see you~~.

Have children complete **Spelling Resource Book, page 113.**

Write and Proofread

Name

Make It Right

Sonya found one word she spelled wrong. Circle four more words she spelled wrong. Write them correctly above the lines.

Dear Grandma,
I got two mor fis. (more, fish)
One has fin stripes. The (thin)
other has thik stripes. (thick)
I wis you could see them. (wish)
Love, Sonya

PROOFREADING MARKS: Check spelling, Add, Cross out

SPELLING RESOURCE BOOK p. 113

DAY 4 **STUDY/REVIEW**

ABC ORDER

- Review the letters of the alphabet by naming two nonsequential letters and asking children to name a letter that appears between them in the alphabet.
- Write the following word groupings on the chalkboard. Ask children to put the words within each grouping in ABC order and to check their work by circling the first letter in each word.

wish	*dish*	**thick**	*dish*
thin	*thin*	**wish**	*fish*
dish	*wish*	**fish**	*thick*
		dish	*wish*

TEST YOURSELF

- Review the Spelling Strategy.
- Partners can take turns dictating a spelling word, and spelling it using magnetic letters or a dry-erase board.
- One child can choose a spelling word and put the letter cards for the word in a pocket chart in scrambled order. Then the partner can manipulate the letters to unscramble the word.

Children may practice for their spelling tests using the **Student Test Form, page 161.**

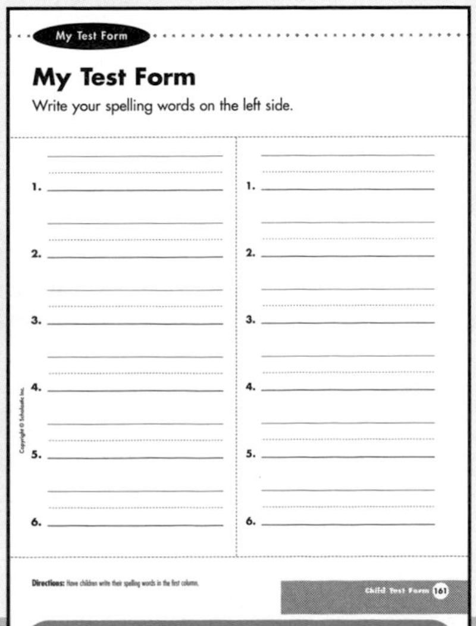
My Test Form

My Test Form

Write your spelling words on the left side.

1. ______ 1. ______
2. ______ 2. ______
3. ______ 3. ______
4. ______ 4. ______
5. ______ 5. ______
6. ______ 6. ______

SPELLING RESOURCE BOOK p. 161

DAY 5 **POSTTEST/SELF-CHECK**

ADMINISTER THE POSTTEST

For the Posttest, read aloud the sentences from Day 1. Have children write each spelling word.

Then have children:

- self-check.
- record the results of their Posttest on the **Individual Progress Chart.**
- keep a list of their misspelled words in their spelling journals.

ASSESSMENT

Record the results of children's Posttests on the **Class Progress Chart, Spelling Resource Book, page 163.**

See **Handwriting Practice, page 26** for practice writing the letters *K* and *X*.

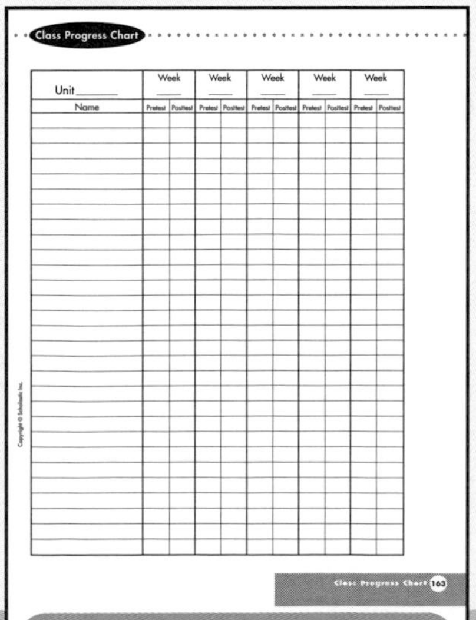
Class Progress Chart

Unit ____ Name | Week | Week | Week | Week | Week (Pretest / Posttest)

SPELLING RESOURCE BOOK p. 163

WEEK 1 Word Order

Grammar, Usage, Mechanics

OBJECTIVES

Children will explore word order in *Fish Faces* and in their writing.

RESOURCES

Practice Book, p. 15
Grammar, Usage, Mechanics Resource Book, pp. 84–87

Word Order

Words that are in order say something that makes sense.

Words that are out of order do not make sense.

MODIFY Instruction

ESL/ELD

▲ Make sentence strips for each of the practice sentences and read each one aloud in the correct order. Have pairs of children cut up the sentence strips. Have children take turns mixing up the order for the partner to rearrange correctly. Have each pair raise their hands when both children have successfully reordered their sentence. Then have them trade with another pair. **(KINESTHETIC)**

DAY 1 TEACH/MODEL

SELECTION LINK

- Write the following sentence from **Anthology page 27** on the chalkboard. Under it write the words out of order.

  Eyes stick up like periscopes.

  Eyes stick periscopes like up.

  Point out that the correct word order helps a sentence or group of words make sense. It tells who it is about and what is happening. Ask children to tell which group of words makes sense. Point out that although there are few complete sentences in the selection, *Fish Faces,* the word order is still important for us to understand the meaning.

- Write these scrambled sentences on the chalkboard and ask children to rearrange the words to make a sentence that tells or asks something. Read each aloud, pointing to the ending punctuation.

  glide on Fish fins.

  do How fish move?

- Have children choose a word group from **Anthology pages 24–26.** Then have them write their word group with the words in scrambled order. Ask volunteers to share their scrambled sentences and have the class reorder the words so they make sense. You may wish to record the scrambled and reordered sentences on a chart.

DAY 2 PRACTICE

REVIEW

- Review with children that words in order say something that makes sense. Words that are out of order do not make sense.
- Write the following mixed-up sentences on the chalkboard, and ask children to rearrange them so they tell or ask something. Remind children that a sentence always begins with a capital letter and ends with a period.

  fish Some have faces. friendly
  (Some fish have friendly faces.)

  fish look Other mean.
  (Other fish look mean.)

  fish is Which your favorite?
  (Which fish is your favorite?)

- Have children write a short scrambled sentence about fish. Have them place a capital letter on the first word of the sentence.

  Ask children to exchange papers and read each other's mixed-up word group. Then have each partner reorder the sentence so it makes sense.

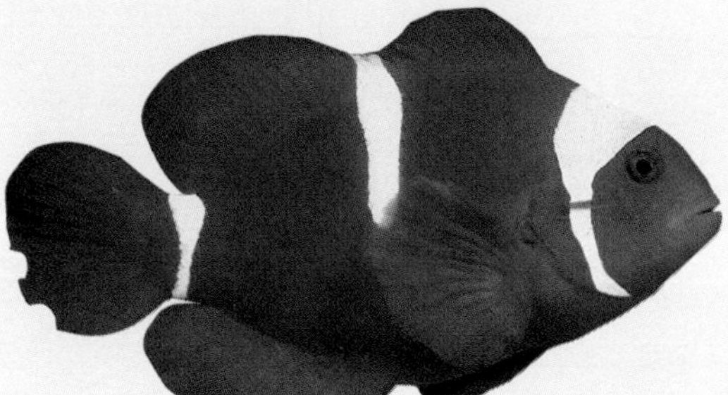

DAY 3 PRACTICE

RETEACH

- Review with children that words in order say something that makes sense. Words that are out of order do not make sense.
- Write the following groups of words on the chalkboard. Then ask children to read each group aloud and put the words in the order that makes sense. Ask children to write each sentence, including the correct punctuation.

fish at the Look
(Look at the fish.)

blue have spots Some
(Some have blue spots.)

black The lines are
(The lines are black.)

fish One has spikes
(One fish has spikes.)

Have children complete **Practice Book, page 15.**

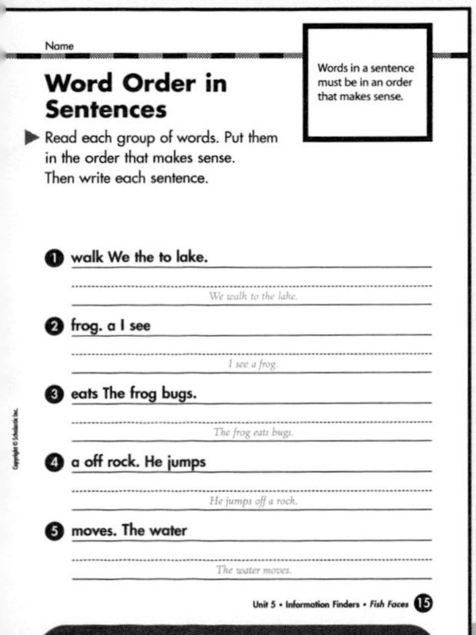
Name

Word Order in Sentences

Words in a sentence must be in an order that makes sense.

▶ Read each group of words. Put them in the order that makes sense. Then write each sentence.

1. walk We the to lake.
   We walk to the lake.
2. frog. a I see
   I see a frog.
3. eats The frog bugs.
   The frog eats bugs.
4. a off rock. He jumps
   He jumps off a rock.
5. moves. The water
   The water moves.

Unit 5 • Information Finders • *Fish Faces* 15

PRACTICE BOOK p. 15

DAY 4 APPLY

WRITING CONNECTION

- Review with children that words must be in an order that makes sense.
- Ask children to write two sentences about a water animal in which the word order makes sense. Then have them circle the beginning capital letter and end punctuation.

REVISE/PROOFREAD

- Have children search their *Book of Facts* for correct word order. Then ask children to select two sentences to place on a chart.

Word Order	Period or ?

DAY 5 ASSESS

QUICKCHECK

- Ask children to write a four-word sentence about a game they like, using a word order that makes sense.
- Write the following sentence on the chalkboard and have children identify the error.

My happy is friend

(My friend is happy.)

INFORMAL ASSESSMENT
OBSERVATION

✔ Did children begin each sentence with a capital letter?

✔ Did children place the words in an order that makes sense?

✔ Did children use the correct end punctuation?

✔ Did children identify an error in word order?

If children need additional support, use the **Reteach** lesson on **page R63.**

MATH

How Many Are Left?

OBJECTIVE: Note relevant details.

MATERIALS: Paper, Pencils

Activity

Children make up subtraction problems using animals in pictures that they draw. **(VISUAL LITERACY)**

Connect to the Anthology

Refer children to the first picture in the story.

Make New Discoveries

- Ask children how many fish are in the picture. Then ask how many fish there'd be if one fish swam away. Call on a volunteer to explain how he or she arrived at the answer.
- Use other story illustrations to use as a basis for subtraction problems.
- Children draw pictures and write or dictate sentences to describe subtraction problems in their pictures.

How to Assess

Were children able to use mathematical reasoning as they described their computations?

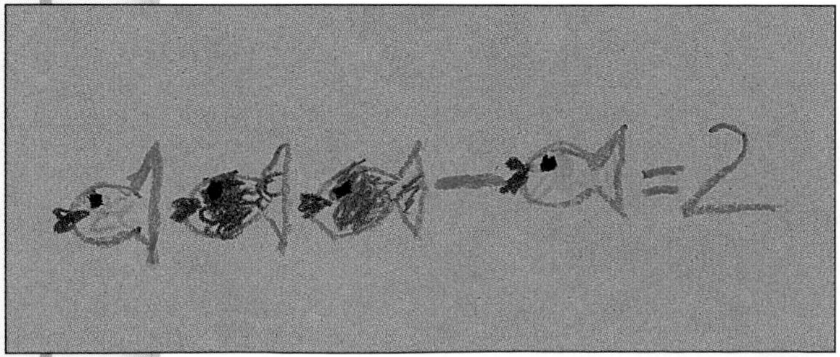

SCIENCE

From Mouth to Fin

OBJECTIVE: Analyze information.

MATERIALS: Paper, Pencils, crayons, or markers

Activity

Children draw a fish and label its body parts. **(VISUAL LITERACY)**

Connect to the Anthology

Draw attention to some of the many different fish in *Fish Faces*. Discuss body parts all fish have, such as eyes, mouth, fins, and tail.

Make New Discoveries

- Ask children to choose a favorite fish from *Fish Faces*. Tell them to look closely at its body and draw their fish carefully to show its body parts. Have them label the parts.
- When children have finished drawing and labeling their fish, ask questions to stimulate a discussion about what the parts are used for. Where are the fish's fins? Why are they important? Look at the fish's mouth. What do you think it eats?

How to Assess

Did children draw a fish and identify its body parts?

SOCIAL STUDIES

Where Fish Live

OBJECTIVE:
Use charts, graphs, and visual displays.

MATERIALS:
Local or state map showing bodies of water
Paper
Pencils

Activity

Children look at a map to determine different bodies of water in which fish live.

Connect to the Anthology

Point out that all the fish in *Fish Faces* live in the same kind of place. Ask children to name it. *(the ocean)*

Make New Discoveries

- Explain that not all fish live in the ocean. Invite children to name other bodies of water in which fish can live. Help children locate rivers and lakes on the map. Point out that they're different from oceans because they have fresh water, and oceans have salt water.
- Have children draw one of the environments in which fish live. They can label their pictures: "Fish live in [name of the environment]."

How to Assess

Were children able to identify and locate bodies of water on a map?

THE ARTS

Fish Shapes

OBJECTIVE:
Use observation.

MATERIALS:
Colored construction paper
Scissors
Glue or paste

Activity

Children combine various geometric forms to create original fish shapes. **(VISUAL LITERACY)**

Connect to the Anthology

Review that the fish in *Fish Faces* have many different kinds of shapes. Invite children to describe some of these shapes.

Make New Discoveries

- Have children cut out circles, ovals, and triangles from construction paper.
- They can combine various forms to create their own fish shapes. Challenge children to use their imaginations to make their fish as unique as possible.

How to Assess

Were children able to observe geometric forms in the fish and use these forms to create their own fish shapes?

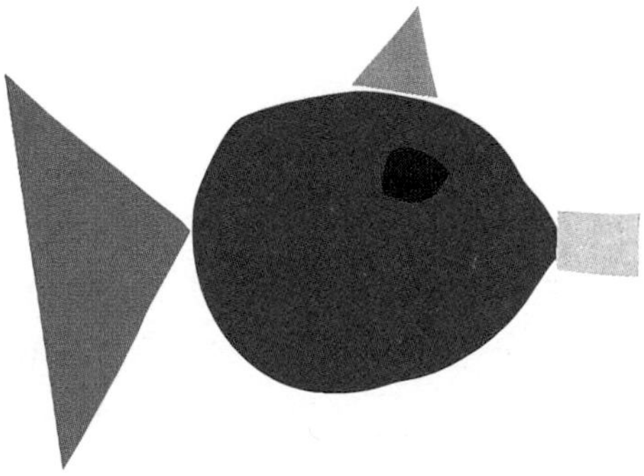

Conducting Guided Reading Groups

Meet with at least two reading groups each day. Select a book on each group's instructional reading level from the *Scholastic Guided Reading Library* or a book in your classroom library. For more information on conducting guided reading groups, see *Scholastic Guided Reading Library*, Teacher's Guide.

Setting Up Independent Centers

While meeting with each reading group, have the rest of the class work in the Independent Centers listed below. Place the appropriate center cards in the pocket chart for student reference. Rotate the cards each day. Children may also use this time to do the following:

- revise or complete writing assignments,
- complete Practice Book pages,
- write in their Journals,
- read independently.

SAMPLE MANAGEMENT PLAN FOR CENTERS

RED GROUP	BLUE GROUP	GREEN GROUP	YELLOW GROUP
ABC Center	Paired Reading	Art Center	Independent
Independent	ABC Center	Paired Reading	Art Center
Art Center	Independent	ABC Center	Paired Reading

ASSESSMENT

Select two children in each guided reading group to observe. Keep anecdotal records on each child's reading performance. Consider the following questions:

- ✔ **What cues does the child use to figure out words and make meaning while reading?**
- ✔ **How well does the child use strategies to solve problems?**
- ✔ **What sound-spellings or high-frequency words are causing the child difficulty?**

When completed, add the anecdotal records to the child's literacy folder for future use when grading or conferencing.

TEACHER TIP

After a guided reading session, remember to:

- share your own thoughts about the story.
- encourage children to talk about their personal responses.
- return to the text to take advantage of additional teaching opportunities.
- continue to evaluate children's comprehension of what they just read.
- involve children in activities that extend the story whenever time permits.

GAY SU PINNELL

Independent Centers

Children can work in these centers while you meet with guided reading groups.

ABC CENTER

Prepare sets of word cards for children to sort into categories. Categories can include words that have the same initial or final letter cluster, words that rhyme, and words that have the same number of syllables. Children can work independently or with partners. Encourage children to explain to a partner how they sorted the words into categories.

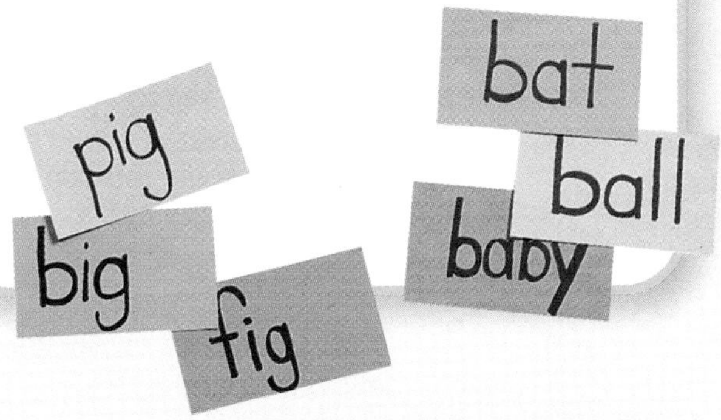

ART CENTER

Ask children to draw a picture about *I'm a Caterpillar* or another story that they like. The pictures they draw should capture their responses to the story. As an alternative activity, children can draw a picture of their favorite animal and tell a story about the animal to a friend.

INDEPENDENT READING

Choose several books for each reading group, and place them in the appropriate Browsing Box. The books can be a mix of previously read titles and ones that correspond to each group's independent reading level. Have children choose a book to read or reread independently. Afterward, children may enjoy drawing a picture of their favorite part of the story.

PAIRED READING

Have partners select and read a book together. Children can take turns reading the book to each other, or they can alternate reading one page at a time. If a child cannot find a partner, he or she can read the selection into a tape recorder and play it back.

WEEK 2 Words With *all* and *aw*

Spelling

WEEK 2 RESOURCES

SPELLING RESOURCE BOOK
- **Word Sort,** p. 114
- **Extra Help,** p. 115
- **Vocabulary Practice,** p. 116
- **Challenge,** p. 117
- **Proofread,** p.118
- **Student Test Form,** p. 161
- **Individual Progress Chart,** p. 162
- **Class Progress Chart,** p. 163
- **Word Sort Chart,** p. 164
- **My Words to Learn,** p. 165
- **Spelling Award Form,** p. 166

ADDITIONAL RESOURCES
- **Spelling Strategy Poster**
- **Proofreading Marks Poster**

SPELLING LIST

Words With *all* and *aw*

fall	straw
tall	draw
ball	

High-Frequency

next	all

DAY 1 PRETEST/SELF-CHECK

ADMINISTER THE PRETEST

1. Be careful not to **fall** down.
2. I want to grow to be very **tall**.
3. Throw me the **ball**.
4. I drank my milk with a **straw**.
5. Can you teach me how to **draw**?
6. I sit **next** to my friend.
7. She drank **all** her milk!

SPELLING CONCEPT

Teach the spelling concept and present the spelling words. Point out that words with the letters *all* or *aw* have the sound of /ô/ as in *ball*.

WORD SORT

On the chalkboard, draw the word sort chart. Ask children to sort the spelling words in the boxes.

all	aw
ball	*straw*
tall	*draw*
fall	

Have children complete **Spelling Resource Book, page 114.**

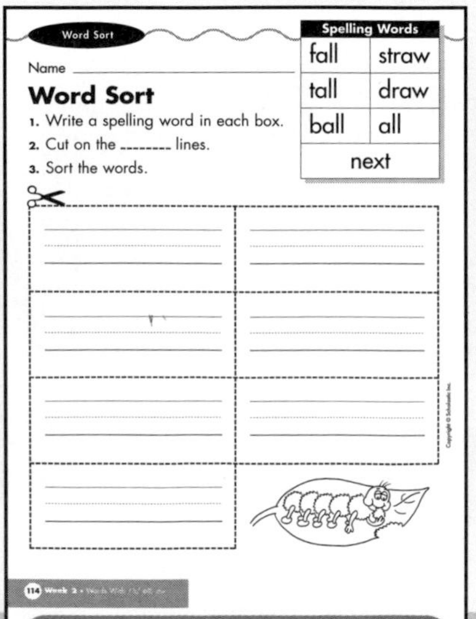

SPELLING RESOURCE BOOK p. 114

DAY 2 VOCABULARY PRACTICE

BUILD VOCABULARY: MULTIPLE-MEANING WORDS

- Review that some words have more than one meaning. Ask children what they think of when they hear the word *fall*. Elicit that it can mean "to tumble down" or "autumn." Remind children to look at the other words in the sentence to figure out which meaning to use.
- Discuss the different meanings of *straw* and *draw*. Then partners can take turns using these words in a sentence and telling which meaning is being used.

WORD STUDY: BUILDING WORDS

- Write *straw* on the chalkboard and say it. Erase *str* and say *aw*. Ask children what other spelling word has the same ending sound as *straw*. *(draw)* Write *dr*. Ask children to blend *dr* with *aw* to say the new word.
- Write the word *fall* on the chalkboard. Ask children to replace the initial consonant to build as many new words that rhyme with *fall* as they can. *(ball, call, hall, mall, tall, wall)*

Have children complete **Spelling Resource Book, page 115, 116,** or **117.**

SPELLING RESOURCE BOOK pp. 115, 116, 117

DAY 3 WRITE/PROOFREAD

WRITE

- Tell children that they will write about how an animal changes as it grows. They can choose an animal they've had as a pet or one they have seen on TV, at a zoo or aquarium, or read about in books.
- Suggest that children use a graphic organizer like the one below to organize their ideas.

Animal	
How It Looks When Grown	How It Looks When Young

Children may:

- draw pictures of their animal to show how it looks before and after it grows.
- write descriptive words to tell about the animal.

PROOFREAD

- Review the proofreading marks, using the class Proofreading Chart for reference.
- Use the following sentence for proofreading practice:

I   straw
~~i~~ **drink my milk with a (stra.)**

Have children complete **Spelling Resource Book, page 118.**

DAY 4 STUDY/REVIEW

GRAPHIC AIDS

- Review how pictures can help readers understand the meaning of a word.
- Draw a simple picture of leaves falling off a tree. Then write the word *fall* below the picture. Discuss with children how the drawing helps them understand what it is like during that season. Ask children to draw a picture of one of the spelling words below. Encourage them to include details that would help someone understand the meaning of the word.

tall **straw** **ball**

TEST YOURSELF

- Review the Spelling Strategy.
- In groups of four, children can have mini spelling bees. One child dictates one word at a time to group members who spell the word and use it in an oral sentence.
- Children can choose three spelling words and write them in scrambled order. Then partners can unscramble each other's words.

Children may practice for their spelling tests using the **Student Test Form, page 161.**

DAY 5 POSTTEST/SELF-CHECK

ADMINISTER THE POSTTEST

For the Posttest, read aloud the sentences from Day 1. Have children write each spelling word.

Then have children:

- self-check.
- record the results of their Posttest on the **Individual Progress Chart.**
- keep a list of their misspelled words in their spelling journals.

ASSESSMENT

Record the results of children's Posttests on the **Class Progress Chart, Spelling Resource Book, page 163.**

See **Handwriting Practice, page 27** for practice writing the letters *T* and *L*.

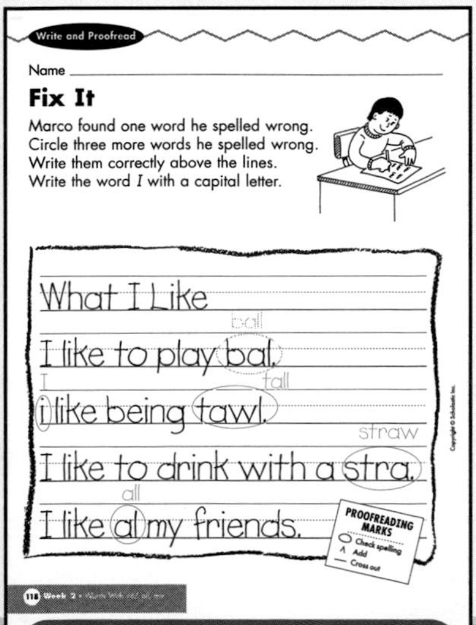
Write and Proofread

Name

Fix It

Marco found one word he spelled wrong. Circle three more words he spelled wrong. Write them correctly above the lines. Write the word *I* with a capital letter.

What I Like

I like to play bal. (ball)

i like being tawl. (I, tall)

I like to drink with a stra. (straw)

I like al my friends. (all)

PROOFREADING MARKS

SPELLING RESOURCE BOOK p. 118

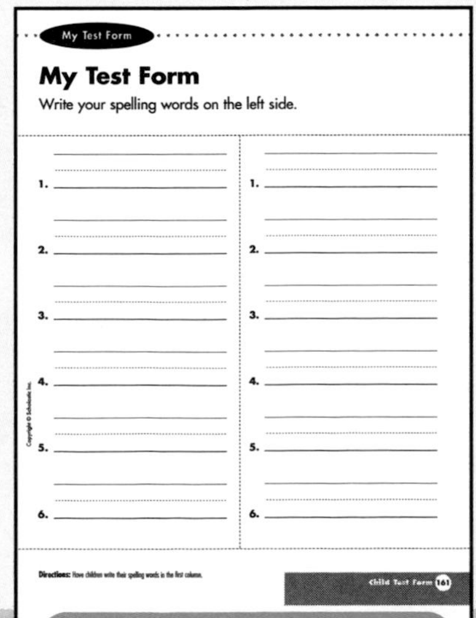
My Test Form

My Test Form

Write your spelling words on the left side.

1. 2. 3. 4. 5. 6.

STUDENT TEST FORM p. 161

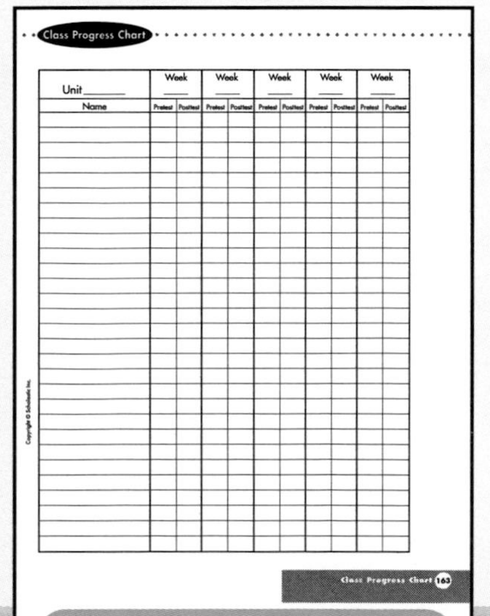
Class Progress Chart

Unit ____ Name | Week | Week | Week | Week | Week

SPELLING RESOURCE BOOK p. 163

Capitalizing the Word I

Grammar, Usage, Mechanics

OBJECTIVES

Children will explore capitalizing the word *I* in *I'm a Caterpillar* and in their writing.

RESOURCES

Practice Book, p. 25
Grammar, Usage, Mechanics Resource Book, pp. 88–91

The Word *I*

The word *I* is always capitalized.

MODIFY Instruction

ESL/ELD

▲ Offer English language learners more opportunities to practice capitalizing the word *I*. Create several little cloze stories on the chalkboard that follow the format of sentences in *I'm a Caterpillar*. For example:
______ am a puppy. Now ______ am little. Soon ______ will be a big dog!
Have children come to the chalkboard to fill in the word *I* in the blanks. More advanced language learners might like to create some sentences of their own. **(CLOZE)**

DAY 1 TEACH/MODEL

SELECTION LINK

- Write the following sentence from **Anthology page 63** on the chalkboard.

  Soon I will lay my eggs.

  Point out that the word *I* is always capitalized, whether or not it is at the beginning of a sentence.

  Elicit from children that *I* is in the middle of this sentence and is capitalized.
- Write these sentences on the chalkboard.

  I am a caterpillar.

  Soon I will be a butterfly.

  Ask a volunteer to circle the word *I* in each sentence. Have children tell whom the capital letter *I* stands for. Elicit from children that *I* is capitalized in the middle of the sentence as well as at the beginning.
- Ask children to find sentences with *I* from **Anthology pages 46–47.** Have children record these on a chart, underlining the word *I*.

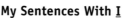

My Sentences With I
I am soft inside.
I am a pupa.
I am now a chrysalis.

DAY 2 PRACTICE

REVIEW

- Review with children that *I* is always capitalized no matter where it is in the sentence.
- Write the following sentences on the chalkboard and ask a volunteer to circle the word *I* in each sentence.

  Every day I visit flowers.

  I drink the nectar.

  My mate and I are not afraid.

  Have children tell the location of the word *I* in each sentence. Ask whom *I* stands for. Then elicit that *I* is always capitalized.
- Have children draw a picture about something they do in the spring. Then have them write a sentence using the word *I* under the picture. Ask volunteers to share their drawings and sentences.

DAY 3 PRACTICE

RETEACH

- Review with children that *I* is always capitalized.
- Write the following sentences on the chalkboard. Have children write each sentence putting the word *I* where it belongs. Ask children to check that they capitalized *I*.

My family and ______ went camping.

That day ______ saw a caterpillar.

______ see one on a tree.

Will ______ see a butterfly?

Have children complete **Practice Book, page 25.**

DAY 4 APPLY

WRITING CONNECTION

- Review with children that *I* is always capitalized.
- Write the word *I* on the chalkboard and have children write two short sentences using *I*. Ask children to write one in which the word *I* is in the middle of the sentence. Have children share their sentences with a partner and check for capitalization.

REVISE/PROOFREAD

- Have children search their descriptions for sentences with *I*, and have them list the sentences on the chart. Ask where they used the word *I* most often.

I at the Beginning
I in the Middle

DAY 5 ASSESS

QUICKCHECK

- Ask children to write a sentence about something they might see in the woods, using the word *I*.
- Write the following sentence on the chalkboard and have children identify the error.

My friends and i like
spiders

(My friends and I like spiders.)

INFORMAL ASSESSMENT
OBSERVATION

✔ Did children capitalize the word *I*?

✔ Did children identify an error in capitalizing the word *I*?

If children need additional support, use the **Reteach** lesson on page **R63.**

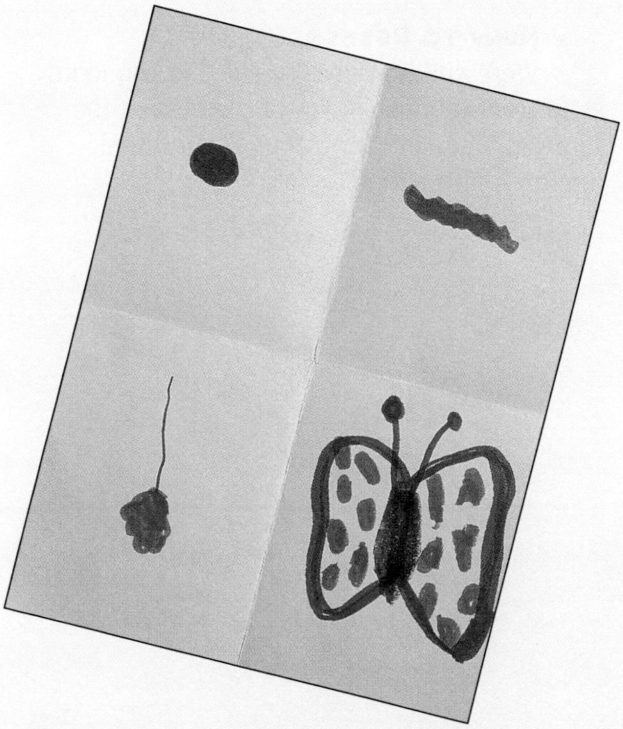

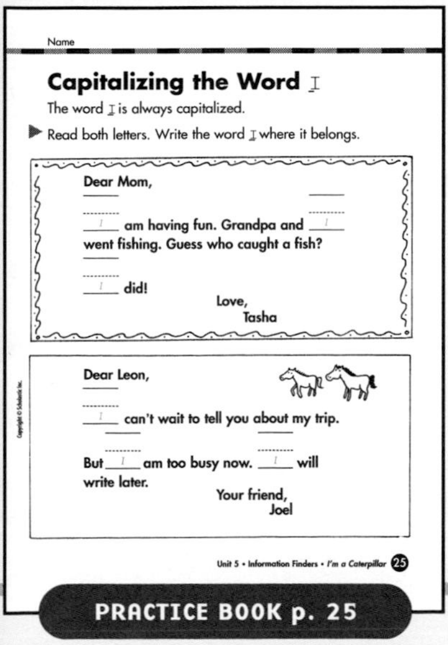

Name

Capitalizing the Word I

The word I is always capitalized.

▶ Read both letters. Write the word I where it belongs.

Dear Mom,

___I___ am having fun. Grandpa and ___I___ went fishing. Guess who caught a fish?

___I___ did!

Love,
Tasha

Dear Leon,

___I___ can't wait to tell you about my trip.

But ___I___ am too busy now. ___I___ will write later.

Your friend,
Joel

Unit 5 • Information Finders • I'm a Caterpillar 25

PRACTICE BOOK p. 25

MATH

Larger Than Life?

OBJECTIVE: Compare/contrast.

MATERIALS: Paper clips, 4-inch strips of tagboard

Activity

Children measure the wingspan of the butterflies in the story illustrations to find out if any of them is actual size. **(VISUAL LITERACY)**

Connect to the Anthology

Review the pictures of the butterflies in the *I'm a Caterpillar* pictures. Ask children if they think any of the pictures is the same size as a real monarch butterfly.

Make New Discoveries

- Distribute the four-inch tagboard strips to children. Explain that these strips are four inches long, exactly the width of the wingspan of a female monarch butterfly. Demonstrate how to use the strips to measure the butterflies in the story.
- Have children compare the length of the strip with the width of each butterfly's wingspan to see if any of the butterflies in the pictures are the same size as a real monarch butterfly.

How to Assess

Were children able to use the tagboard strip to determine if the butterflies in the pictures were smaller or larger than real monarch butterflies?

SCIENCE

From an Egg

OBJECTIVE: Categorize.

MATERIALS: Index cards, Markers

Activity

Children brainstorm creatures that are hatched from eggs and then group the creatures by type.

Connect to the Anthology

Remind children that caterpillars hatch from eggs.

Make New Discoveries

- Have children name creatures that hatch from eggs. Write each creature's name on an index card.
- Review all the creatures children have named and discuss how these creatures can be grouped together.
- Have children organize the creatures into groups by sorting the index cards. Then ask children to create labels for the categories. Some labels might include *Birds, Insects, Reptiles*, and so on.
- Keep the cards and labels, organized into groups, displayed in the classroom. Encourage children to research other creatures that hatch from eggs and add them to the appropriate categories.

INSECTS	REPTILES	BIRDS
caterpillars	dinosaurs	chickens
ants	turtles	geese
	lizards	ducks

How to Assess

Were children able to name specific creatures that were hatched from eggs? Were they able to group creatures by type?

SOCIAL STUDIES

Butterfly Territory

OBJECTIVE: Use charts, graphs, and visual displays.

MATERIALS: White butcher paper
Markers, pencils, or crayons

Activity

Children think about places around school or their homes that butterflies might enjoy. Children can show these areas on maps they create. **(VISUAL LITERACY)**

Connect to the Anthology

Review the selection to help children recall where butterflies spend their time and what they do. Help children recognize what kind of places butterflies like best.

Make New Discoveries

- Organize children into groups based on where they live. Encourage children who live near each other to work together.
- Have children think about the areas around their homes that butterflies might like.
- Then each group can map its neighborhood. Suggest that children divide the project by drawing their own home and the area around it.
- Children should use labels or butterfly shapes to indicate areas on the map that would be attractive to butterflies.

How to Assess

Did children's maps indicate gardens and other areas that butterflies might like?

THE ARTS

Paint a Butterfly

OBJECTIVE: Use graphs, charts, and visual displays.

MATERIALS: Construction paper
Pipe cleaners
Paints or markers
Butterfly picture books

Activity

Children create their own colorful butterfly patterns. **(VISUAL LITERACY)**

Connect to the Anthology

Have children review the pictures of the butterflies in *I'm a Caterpillar*. Point out that these butterflies have the characteristic markings of the Monarch butterfly.

Make New Discoveries

- Have children look through the butterfly books to see typical patterns and colors of butterfly markings.
- Help children cut out large butterfly shapes from sheets of folded paper. Children can sketch and paint colorful patterns on their butterfly's wings. They can reproduce the colors and pattern of an actual butterfly, or they can create their own butterflies with unique patterns and color combinations.
- Invite children to add construction paper heads and bodies to the butterfly wings, together with antennae made from pipe cleaners.
- You may wish to suspend the finished butterflies from the ceiling or arrange them into a bulletin board display.

How to Assess

Did children imitate patterns or create their own? Were their patterns symmetrical?

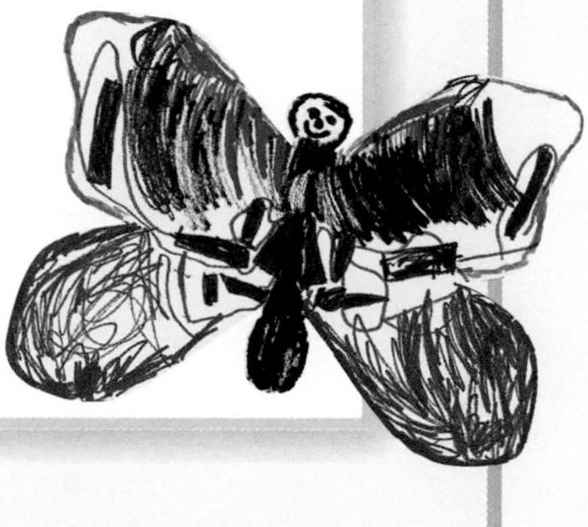

ASSESSMENT

Select two children in each guided reading group to observe. Keep anecdotal records on each child's reading performance. Consider the following questions:

- ✔ **What cues does the child use to figure out words and make meaning while reading?**
- ✔ **How well does the child retell the story?**
- ✔ **What sound-spellings or high-frequency words are causing the child difficulty?**

When completed, add the anecdotal records to the child's literacy folder for future use when grading or conferencing.

Conducting Guided Reading Groups

Meet with at least two reading groups each day. Select a book on each group's instructional reading level from the *Scholastic Guided Reading Library* or a book in your classroom library. For more information on conducting guided reading groups, see *Scholastic Guided Reading Library,* Teacher's Guide.

Setting Up Independent Centers

While meeting with each reading group, have the rest of the class work in the Independent Centers listed below. Place the appropriate center cards in the pocket chart for student reference. Rotate the cards each day. Children may also use this time to do the following:

- revise or complete writing assignments,
- complete Practice Book pages,
- write in their Journals,
- read independently.

SAMPLE MANAGEMENT PLAN FOR CENTERS

RED GROUP	BLUE GROUP	GREEN GROUP	YELLOW GROUP
Independent	ABC Center	Writing Center	Overhead Projector
Overhead Projector	Independent	ABC Center	Writing Center
Writing Center	Overhead Projector	Independent	ABC Center

TEACHER TIP

You can tell that your guided reading approaches are helping children when they:

- enjoy reading and are successful even when they are dealing with challenging texts.
- read for meaning as they problem solve.
- apply strategies while reading other texts.
- talk naturally about stories they read and share their responses.
- read to expand their knowledge and understanding.

GAY SU PINNELL

Independent Centers

Children can work in these centers while you meet with guided reading groups.

INDEPENDENT READING

Have children choose a book from the Browsing Box for their reading group. The books can be titles that children have read during guided reading or ones that correspond to their independent reading level. Ask children to read or reread the books softly to themselves. Afterward, each child can go to the Writing Center and write a retelling of the book.

WRITING CENTER

Have children go to the Writing Center and write a story about a favorite place they have visited. Suggest that they use the pronoun *I* in telling their story. Children can draw pictures to go with their stories. Allow class time for children to share their stories.

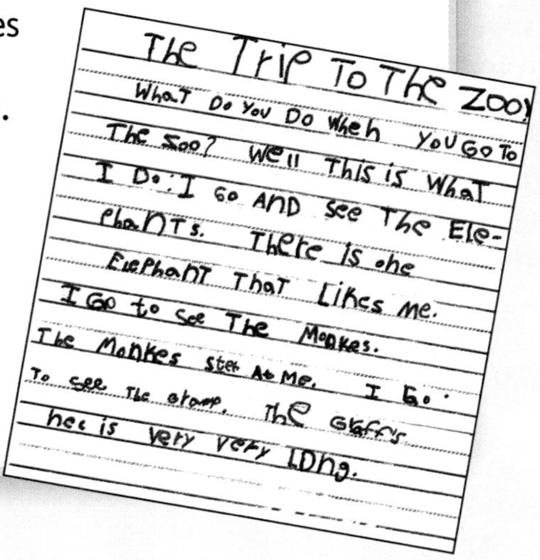

OVERHEAD PROJECTOR

Select several poems and stories, including examples of children's writing, and reproduce them on plastic transparencies. Safely secure the overhead projector in front of a white paper screen, and have children project and read them. Children can take turns pointing to the words on the transparency while their partners read.

ABC CENTER

Have children work in the ABC Center making words with magnetic or tile letters. Children can make words from a set of letters you specify, words with some of the same letters, or words with the same vowel sound. Suggest that children ask partners to tell how the words they made are alike. Be sure to include other word-building games in the center as optional activities.

WEEK 3 Words With *oa*

Spelling

WEEK 3 RESOURCES

SPELLING RESOURCE BOOK
- **Word Sort,** p. 119
- **Extra Help,** p. 120
- **Vocabulary Practice,** p. 121
- **Challenge,** p. 122
- **Proofread,** p.123
- **Student Test Form,** p. 161
- **Individual Progress Chart,** p. 162
- **Class Progress Chart,** p. 163
- **Word Sort Chart,** p. 164
- **My Words to Learn,** p. 165
- **Spelling Award Form,** p. 166

ADDITIONAL RESOURCES
- **Spelling Strategy Poster**
- **Proofreading Marks Poster**

SPELLING LIST

Words With *oa*

toad	coat
load	boat
road	

High-Frequency

was	grow

DAY 1 PRETEST/SELF-CHECK

ADMINISTER THE PRETEST

1. Do not let the **toad** hop away.
2. I carried a heavy **load** of books.
3. Be careful when you cross the **road**.
4. Anna's **coat** kept her warm.
5. I helped to sail the **boat**.
6. I **was** five in kindergarten. Now I am six.
7. I hope I **grow** tall this year!

SPELLING CONCEPT

Teach the spelling concept and present the spelling words. Explain that in some words, such as *toad* and *coat*, the long *o* sound is spelled *oa*.

WORD SORT

On the chalkboard, draw the word sort chart. Ask children to sort the spelling words on the chart.

oad	oat
toad	*coat*
load	*boat*
road	

Have children complete **Spelling Resource Book, page 119.**

DAY 2 VOCABULARY PRACTICE

BUILD VOCABULARY: RIDDLES

- Tell children that you will ask them a riddle whose answer is a spelling word. Say: *"This is an animal that hops."* *(toad)*
- Children can take turns asking each other riddles for the other spelling words.

WORD STUDY: ALLITERATION

- Write on the chalkboard: *Two tiny toads tasted two tulips.* Say the sentence aloud and ask children what they notice is the same about all the words. *(They start with the same sound, /t/.)*
- Write on the chalkboard: *Ralph ran down the street in the rain. Can Carol carry Cathy's jacket?* Ask children to replace each underlined word with a spelling word that has the same beginning sound as most of the other words in the sentence.

Have children complete **Spelling Resource Book, page 120, 121,** or **122.**

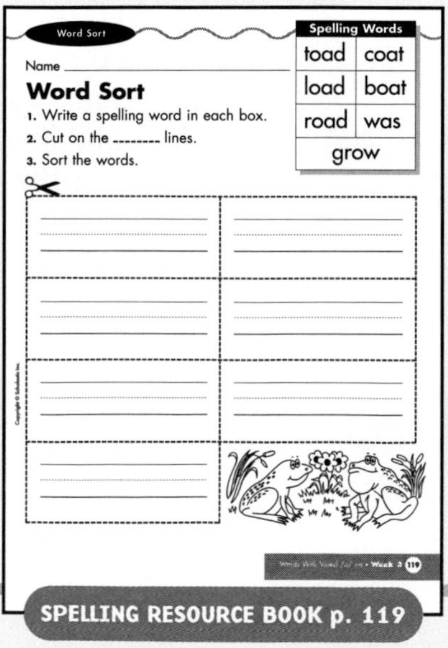

SPELLING RESOURCE BOOK p. 119

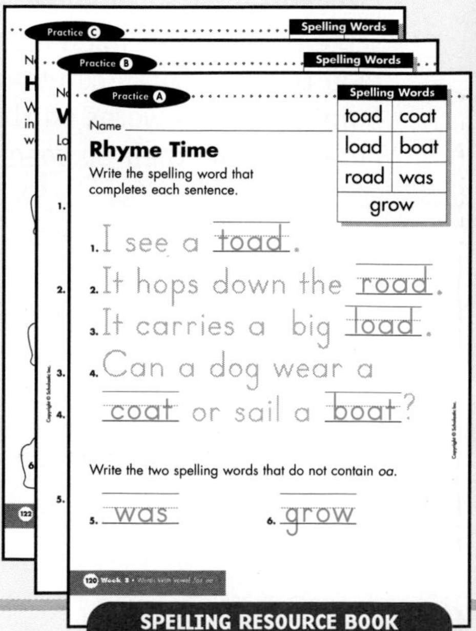

SPELLING RESOURCE BOOK pp. 120, 121, 122

DAY 3 WRITE/PROOFREAD

WRITE

- Tell children that they will write about what makes someone a good friend.
- Using a graphic organizer will help children organize information before they begin to write.

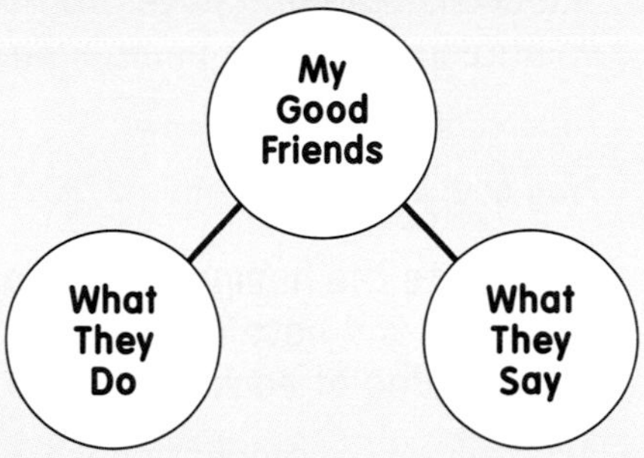

Children may:

- write a poem about a best friend.
- write a letter to a best friend telling why he or she is a good friend.

PROOFREAD

- Review the proofreading marks, using the class Proofreading Chart for reference.
- Use the following sentence for proofreading practice:

I wish ~~i~~ had my (cote.) (corrections written above: I, coat)

Have children complete **Spelling Resource Book, page 123.**

DAY 4 STUDY/REVIEW

ABC ORDER

- Review ABC order with children by writing the following groups of letters on the chalkboard. Ask children to provide the missing letters in each grouping.

_ e _ g **l _ _ o**
_ v w _ **_ _ j k**

- Write the following word groupings on the chalkboard. Ask children to put the words within each grouping in ABC order and to check their work by circling the first letter in each word.

load	*coat*	**boat**	*boat*
coat	*grow*	**was**	*coat*
road	*load*	**toad**	*toad*
grow	*road*	**coat**	*was*

TEST YOURSELF

- Review the Spelling Strategy.
- Partners can take turns providing a riddle for a spelling word and spelling it. For example, *This is an animal and it rhymes with* showed.
- Children can choose three spelling words and write them with one or two letters missing. Partners can fill in the missing letters and then write the whole word.

Children may practice for their spelling tests using the **Student Test Form, Spelling Resource Book, page 161.**

DAY 5 POSTTEST/SELF-CHECK

ADMINISTER THE POSTTEST

For the Posttest, read aloud the sentences from Day 1. Have children write each spelling word.

Then have children:

- self-check.
- record the results of their Posttest on the **Individual Progress Chart.**
- keep a list of their misspelled words in their spelling journals.

ASSESSMENT

Record the results of children's Posttests on the **Class Progress Chart, Spelling Resource Book, page 163.**

See **Handwriting Practice, page 28** for practice writing the letters *D* and *J*.

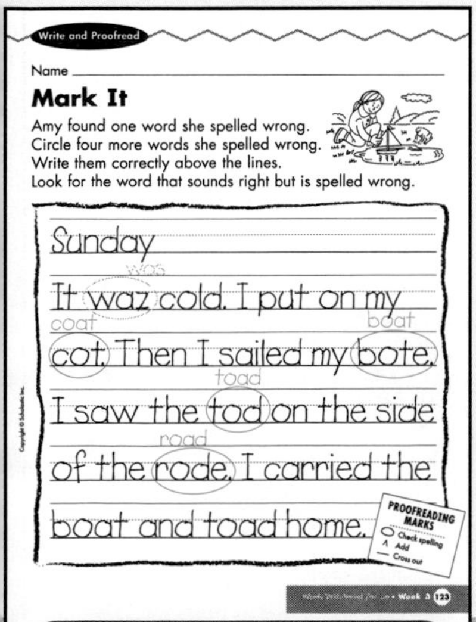

SPELLING RESOURCE BOOK p. 123

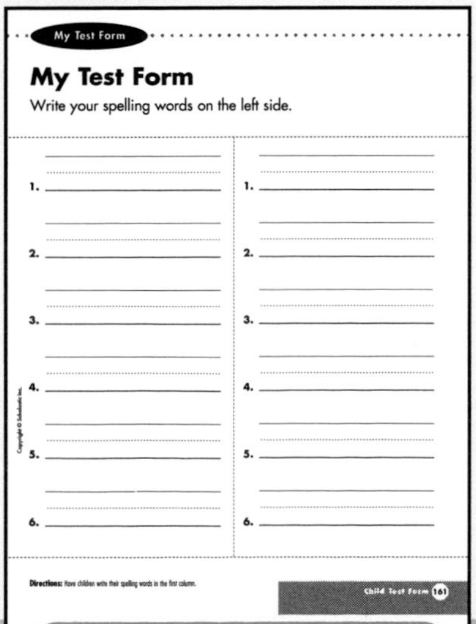

SPELLING RESOURCE BOOK p. 161

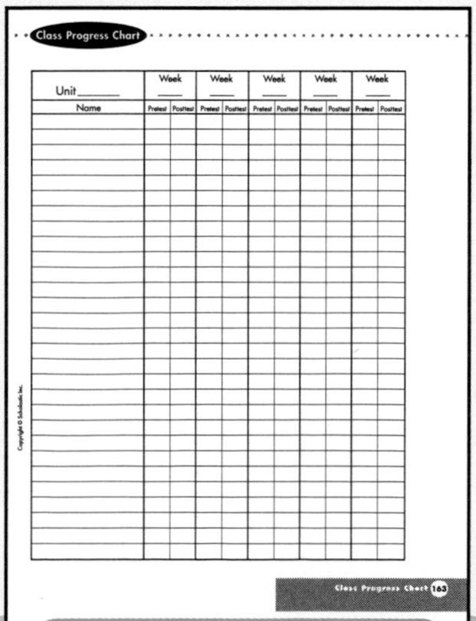

SPELLING RESOURCE BOOK p. 163

WEEK 3 Homophones

Grammar, Usage, Mechanics

OBJECTIVES

Children will explore homophones in *The Garden* and in their writing.

RESOURCES

Practice Book, p. 40
Grammar, Usage, Mechanics Resource Book, pp. 92–95

Homophones

Homophones are words that sound alike but are spelled differently and have different meanings.

MODIFY Instruction

ESL/ELD

▲ Display pairs of index cards with the following words: *sea, see; right, write; I, eye; four, for; know, no; one, won.* Review the meanings of the words with children. Then place pairs of cards below each sentence and have children choose the correct word that belongs in the blank. For example: *You can ____ with your eyes. (see/sea) I ____ how to count. (know/no).* **(CONTEXT CLUES)**

DAY 1 TEACH/MODEL

SELECTION LINK

- Write the following sentence from **Anthology page 71** on the chalkboard.

  Frog came walking by.

  Point out that the word *by* is a homophone. Explain that there is another word that sounds like *by* but is spelled differently and has a different meaning. Then write *bye* on the chalkboard and have children tell what it means.
- Write these sentences on the chalkboard underlining the homophones.

  I had a garden. *(eye)*

  The seeds must be afraid. *(bee)*

  It might take four days. *(for)*

  Have children look at the underlined word in each sentence. Ask children to think of a homophone for each underlined word. Write the homophone pairs on the chalkboard. Point out the differences in spelling and meaning.
- Ask children to list a homophone for the words *four, son,* and *two* from **Anthology page 75** and place them on a chart. Then share answers.

Homophones	
four	*for*
son	*sun*
two	*to*

DAY 2 PRACTICE

REVIEW

- Review with children that homophones are words that sound alike but are spelled differently and have different meanings.
- Write the following sentences on the chalkboard and have volunteers circle the homophone.

  Toad could not see it grow. *(see)*

  Frog could hear Toad shout. *(hear)*

  Then write the homophones *sea* and *here,* and have children tell the meaning of each.
- Ask children to dramatize homophones that have been written on cards. Have the class guess the homophone being acted out. Then have them write two short sentences with one of the pairs of homophones *sea/see* or *here/hear.* Have them underline the homophones. Then have pairs share their sentences and explain each homophone's meaning.

DAY 3 PRACTICE

RETEACH

- Review with children that homophones are words that sound alike but are spelled differently and have different meanings.
- Write the following sentences on the chalkboard. Have children write the correct form of the homophone in parentheses.

Toad reads (to, two) his seeds. *(to)*

They will not (bee, be) afraid. *(be)*

Finally (one, won) seed grew. *(one)*

Now the (hole, whole) garden grows. *(whole)*

Have children complete **Practice Book, page 40.**

DAY 4 APPLY

WRITING CONNECTION

- Review homophones with children.
- Write the words *flour* and *flower* on the chalkboard. Have children write a short sentence for each of the homophones. Then ask them to circle the homophones. Invite volunteers to share.

REVISE/PROOFREAD

- Have children search their week's poems for homophones. Have them list the homophones they used and their meanings on a chart.

Homophones	Meanings
flour	*bake with it*
flower	*in a garden*

DAY 5 ASSESS

QUICKCHECK

- Ask children to write a sentence about their day, using a homophone. You may suggest the homophones *write, right; son, sun; eye, I.*
- Write the following sentence on the chalkboard and have children identify the error.

The son is very hot.

(The sun is very hot.)

INFORMAL ASSESSMENT
OBSERVATION

✔ Did children use the correct homophone ?

✔ Did children spell the homophone correctly?

✔ Did children identify an error in using the correct homophone?

If children need additional support, use the **Reteach** lesson on **page R64.**

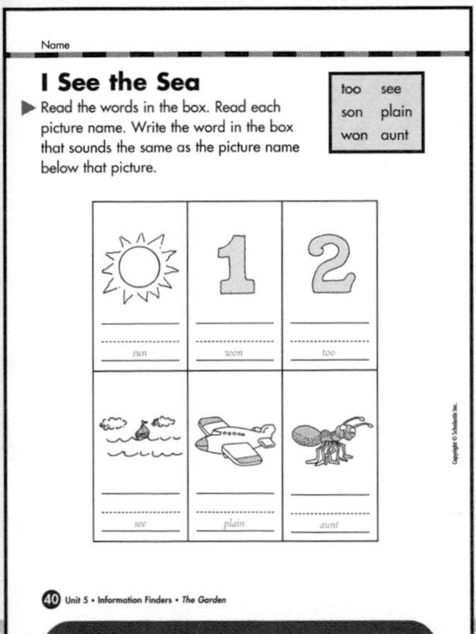
Name

I See the Sea

▶ Read the words in the box. Read each picture name. Write the word in the box that sounds the same as the picture name below that picture.

too	see
son	plain
won	aunt

40 Unit 5 • Information Finders • The Garden

PRACTICE BOOK p. 40

plane
plain

MATH

Days of Toad's Life

OBJECTIVE:
Analyze information.

MATERIALS:
Student Anthology, pp. 70–81
Chart paper

Activity

Children use pictures and text in *The Garden* to make a time line for the germination of Toad's seeds. **(VISUAL LITERACY)**

Connect to the Anthology

Ask children to go back to the story and review what happened between the time that Toad planted the seeds and the time that they started to grow.

Make New Discoveries

- Children work together to use pictures and text to figure out how many days it took for Toad's seeds to grow.
- Children draw a picture for each day and show what happened on that day.
- Children write the number of each day at the bottom of the appropriate picture, then arrange the pictures in the correct order to create an illustration time line.
- When children are finished, they can compare their time line to *The Garden* to make sure the time line is accurate.

How to Assess

Were children able to show what happened on each day and number the days in order?

SCIENCE

Frogs and Toads

OBJECTIVE:
Collect data.

MATERIALS:
Simple nonfiction books about frogs and toads
Chart paper

Activity

Children investigate frogs and toads and make charts to show what they learned. **(VISUAL LITERACY)**

Connect to the Anthology

Point out to children that although Frog and Toad look very similar, they are different animals, just as real frogs and toads are different animals.

Make New Discoveries

- Show children how to find information about frogs and toads in the books.
- Have one partner find information about frogs; the other partner can look for information about toads.
- Encourage children to write or dictate a chart such as the one below about frogs and toads.
- When the chart is complete, have partners compare the animals.

How to Assess

Were children able to collect and convey information about frogs and toads?

Frogs	Toads
live in water and on land	live on land
lay eggs	lay eggs
moist skin	dry, warty skin

SOCIAL STUDIES

Gardens in Our Town

OBJECTIVE: Make a plan.

MATERIALS: Mural paper
Crayons or markers

Activity

Children describe gardens in their city, town, or neighborhood and create a mural for a garden they would like to have in their neighborhood. **(VISUAL LITERACY)**

Connect to the Anthology

Remind children that Frog and Toad both grew flowers in their gardens. Talk with children about other things that can be grown in gardens, such as vegetables, fruits, and trees.

Make New Discoveries

- Have children brainstorm what they would grow if they had a class garden.
- Then have children draw a mural of the garden they would like to have.
- Encourage children to label as many plants on the mural as they can.
- When the mural is complete, display it in a viewing area such as a hallway or the school library.

How to Assess

Were children able to decide upon a plan for a garden and create a mural to show that garden?

THE ARTS

Music for Seeds

OBJECTIVE: Brainstorm multiple approaches.

MATERIALS: None

Activity

Children will work in groups to brainstorm a lullaby for Toad's seeds and perform it for the class.

Connect to the Anthology

Remind children that Toad sang to his seeds to help them grow.

Make New Discoveries

- Groups brainstorm words for a lullaby that Toad might sing to his seeds.
- Encourage children to set the words of their lullaby to a familiar lullaby tune such as "Rock-a-Bye Baby" or "Hush Little Baby." Encourage children to use rhyme in the lines of their new lullaby.
- Then have groups take turns singing their lullabies for the class.

How to Assess

Were children able to work together to compose new words for a familiar lullaby tune?

ASSESSMENT

Select two children in each guided reading group to observe. Keep anecdotal records on each child's reading performance. Consider the following questions:

- ✔ **What cues does the child use to figure out words and make meaning while reading?**
- ✔ **How well does the child retell the story?**
- ✔ **What sound-spellings or high-frequency words are causing the child difficulty?**

When completed, add the anecdotal records to the child's literacy folder for future use when grading or conferencing.

Conducting Guided Reading Groups

Meet with at least two reading groups each day. Select a book on each group's instructional reading level from the *Scholastic Guided Reading Library* or a book in your classroom library. For more information on conducting guided reading groups, see *Scholastic Guided Reading Library*, Teacher's Guide.

Setting Up Independent Centers

While meeting with each reading group, have the rest of the class work in the Independent Centers listed below. Place the appropriate center cards in the pocket chart for student reference. Rotate the cards each day. Children may also use this time to do the following:

- revise or complete writing assignments,
- complete Practice Book pages,
- write in their Journals,
- read independently.

SAMPLE MANAGEMENT PLAN FOR CENTERS

RED GROUP	BLUE GROUP	GREEN GROUP	YELLOW GROUP
Technology	ABC Center	Independent	Drama
Drama	Technology	ABC Center	Independent
Independent	Drama	Technology	ABC Center

TEACHER TIP

Your colleagues are a great support system, and you should:

- share descriptions of children's reading behaviors with them.
- meet with them to discuss the entire scope of a balanced literacy program.
- present and talk about samples of children's work.
- raise issues and questions that you want to discuss.
- invite them to look at how your classroom is set up for independent centers, and visit their classrooms to view their learning environments.

GAY SU PINNELL

Independent Centers

Children can work in these centers while you meet with guided reading groups.

TECHNOLOGY

Daniel's Dinosaurs is a **WiggleWorks Plus** selection. Each day have two children from each group sit together at the computer and reread the selection using **WiggleWorks Plus.** When children have finished, ask them to go to the program's Write area and write a short retelling of the story.

INDEPENDENT READING

Select several books for each reading group and place them in the appropriate Browsing Box. The books you choose can be ones that the children have read during guided reading, or they might be titles you have identified as suitable for each group's independent reading level. Tell children to select a book and read it softly to themselves. Afterward, children can gather in a small group and talk about the books they read.

DRAMA

Have children create a play based on *Daniel's Dinosaurs* or another story they choose. Children can make costumes in the Art Center, or they can use finger puppets. Children can write their plays in the Writing Center. Schedule class time for children to perform their play for the class.

ABC CENTER

Have children go to the ABC Center and build word ladders. Children can work with magnetic letters or letter tiles to construct a ladder of words. Explain that children should begin with a word they know and add or remove letters to form new words. Afterward, children can share their word ladders with partners and take turns reading the words aloud.

Spelling

WEEK 4 RESOURCES

SPELLING RESOURCE BOOK

ADDITIONAL RESOURCES

- **Spelling Strategy Poster**
- **Proofreading Marks Poster**

SPELLING LIST

Compound Words

sometime	anyone
anytime	someone
something	

High-Frequency

school	their

DAY 1 PRETEST/SELF-TEST

ADMINISTER THE PRETEST

1. Can we go to the zoo **sometime**?
2. Jack gets to go **anytime** he wants.
3. **Someone** started to laugh.
4. Has **anyone** seen my dog?
5. Will you help me with **something**?
6. Do you ride the bus to **school**?
7. I went to **their** house to play.

SPELLING CONCEPT

Teach the spelling concept and present the spelling words. Explain that a compound word is a word that is made up of two smaller words.

WORD SORT

On the chalkboard, draw the word sort chart. Ask children to sort the spelling words on the chart.

Compounds With *some*	Compounds With *any*
sometime	*anytime*
someone	*anyone*
something	

Have children complete **Spelling Resource Book, page 124.**

DAY 2 VOCABULARY PRACTICE

BUILD VOCABULARY: COMPOUND WORDS

- Review that a compound word is two small words put together. Write *someone* on the chalkboard. Ask children which two smaller words form *someone*. Ask a volunteer to draw a line between the two words.
- Children can make word puzzles by writing each compound word on a strip of paper and cutting it between the two smaller words. Then they can work together to form the compound words and use each in an oral sentence.

WORD STUDY: SYLLABLES

- Write *something* on the chalkboard. Clap each syllable as you say the word. Explain that each clap stands for one syllable. Repeat clapping and saying *something*. Ask children how many syllables are in *something*.
- Write the spelling words on the chalkboard. Ask children to clap as they say each word and identify how many syllables are in each.

Have children complete **Spelling Resource Book, page 125, 126,** or **127.**

SPELLING RESOURCE BOOK p. 124

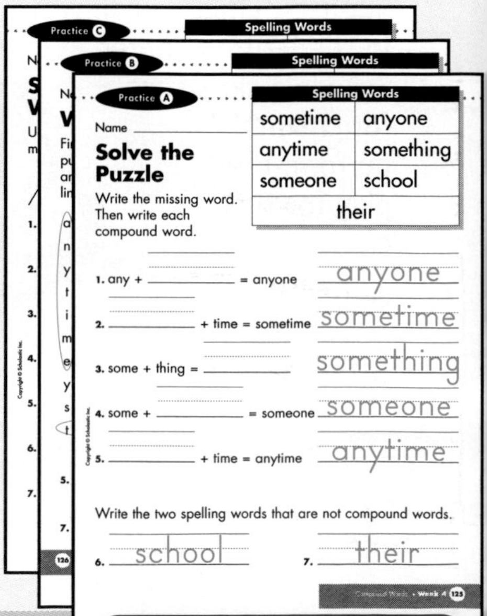

SPELLING RESOURCE BOOK pp. 125, 126, 127

DAY 3 WRITE/PROOFREAD

WRITE

- Tell children to imagine that they had a pet dinosaur. Ask them to write about what it was like, what it ate, and where it slept.
- Using a graphic organizer will help children get started.

What was your dinosaur's name?
What did it eat?
Where did it sleep?
Where is your dinosaur now?

Children may:

- write a guide about caring for a pet dinosaur.
- draw a picture of themselves with their pet dinosaur.

PROOFREAD

- Review the proofreading marks, using the class Proofreading Chart for reference.
- Use the following sentence for proofreading practice:

something you
I have (some thing) to tell (yu)?.

Have children complete **Spelling Resource Book, page 128.**

DAY 4 STUDY/REVIEW

CATEGORIZE

- Review how organizing words into categories can help you learn how to spell words.
- Write the following graphic organizer on the chalkboard. Have children write each spelling word under each heading or category in which it fits.

Compound Words			
some	thing	any	time
sometime	something	anytime	sometime
someone		anyone	anytime
something			

TEST YOURSELF

- Review the Spelling Strategy.
- Partners can take turns dictating a spelling word and spelling it using magnetic letters or a dry-erase board.
- Children can choose three spelling words and write them, replacing two of the letters with blanks. They exchange papers, fill in the missing letters, and then rewrite the words.

Children may practice for their spelling tests using the **Student Test Form, Spelling Resource Book, page 161.**

DAY 5 POSTTEST/SELF-CHECK

ADMINISTER THE POSTTEST

For the Posttest, read aloud the sentences from Day 1. Have children write each spelling word.

Then have children:

- self-check.
- record the results of their Posttest on the **Individual Progress Chart.**
- keep a list of their misspelled words in their spelling journals.

ASSESSMENT

Record the results of children's Posttests on the **Class Progress Chart, Spelling Resource Book, page 163.**

See **Handwriting Practice, page 29** for practice writing the letters *W* and *V*.

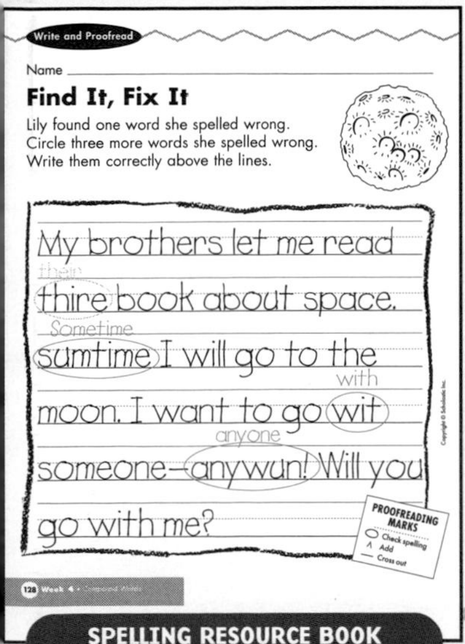

Write and Proofread
Name
Find It, Fix It
Lily found one word she spelled wrong. Circle three more words she spelled wrong. Write them correctly above the lines.
My brothers let me read
them
thire book about space.
Sometime
sumtime I will go to the
with
moon. I want to go wit
anyone
someone—anywun! Will you
go with me?
PROOFREADING MARKS

SPELLING RESOURCE BOOK
p. 128

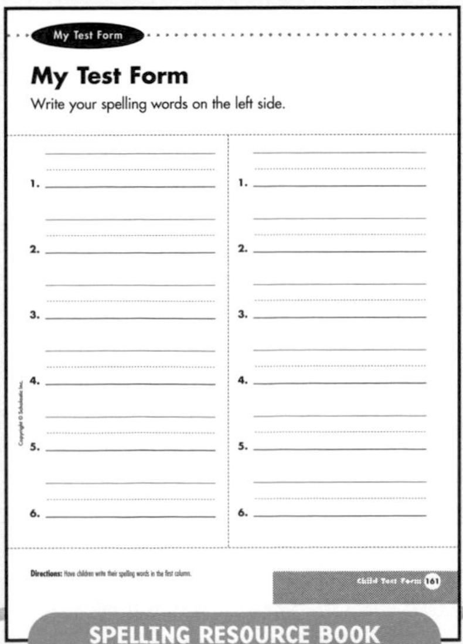

My Test Form
My Test Form
Write your spelling words on the left side.
1.
2.
3.
4.
5.
6.
1.
2.
3.
4.
5.
6.

SPELLING RESOURCE BOOK
p. 161

SPELLING RESOURCE BOOK
p. 163

WEEK 4 Verbs: Past Tense

Grammar, Usage, Mechanics

OBJECTIVES

Children will explore past-tense verbs in *Daniel's Dinosaurs* and in their writing.

RESOURCES

Practice Book, p. 54
Grammar, Usage, Mechanics Resource Book, pp. 96–99

Past-Tense Verbs

Tell children that a past-tense verb is a verb that ends in *-ed*. It tells about an action that happened in the past.

MODIFY Instruction

ESL/ELD

▲ Have English language learners brainstorm past-tense context clues, such as *yesterday, last night,* and *this morning.* Make sure that they understand the concept of past tense (past time), before practicing the *-ed* ending. Then ask children to find past-tense verbs in the story and tell when the action happened. **(CONTEXT CLUES)**

DAY 1 TEACH/MODEL

SELECTION LINK

- Write the following sentence from **Anthology page 99** on the chalkboard.

  They looked at the stingrays.

  Point out the word *looked* and explain that this is a past-tense verb. It ends in *-ed* and tells about something that already happened.

- Write these sentences on the chalkboard.

  Everything turned into a dinosaur.
  (turned)

  Mother asked him to go somewhere.
  (asked)

  They visited the aquarium.
  (visited)

  Ask volunteers to find the verbs with the *-ed* ending. Elicit from children that the action already happened. Point out that these are past-tense verbs.

- Ask children to work with a partner, list the three past-tense verbs on **Anthology page 95,** and place them on a list.

Past-Tense Verbs That End in *-ed*
directed
barked
passed

DAY 2 PRACTICE

REVIEW

- Review with children that a past-tense verb is a verb that ends in *-ed* and tells about something that has already happened.

- Write the following sentences on the chalkboard and ask children to tell which are the past-tense verbs.

  Daniel walked to school.
  (walked)

  Dinosaurs jumped out everywhere.
  (jumped)

  Daniel loved dinosaurs.
  (loved)

  Point out that in the word *love,* we dropped the *-e* to add *-ed* to make it past tense.

- Write some past-tense verbs on index cards and use those to play a modified game of charades with children. Then have children write one sentence using a past-tense verb. Have children share their sentences with a partner, circling each other's past-tense verb.

DAY 3 PRACTICE

RETEACH

- Review with children that a past-tense verb is a verb that ends in *-ed* and tells about something that has already happened.
- Write the following sentences on the chalkboard and ask children to add *-ed* to the verb in parentheses making it a past-tense verb.

Mother (open)__________ the door. *(opened)*

Fish (fill)_________ the tanks. *(filled)*

Mother (show)_________him the shark tank. *(showed)*

He (watch) _________it a long time. *(watched)*

Later, Daniel (want) _________ shark books. *(wanted)*

Have children complete **Practice Book, page 54.**

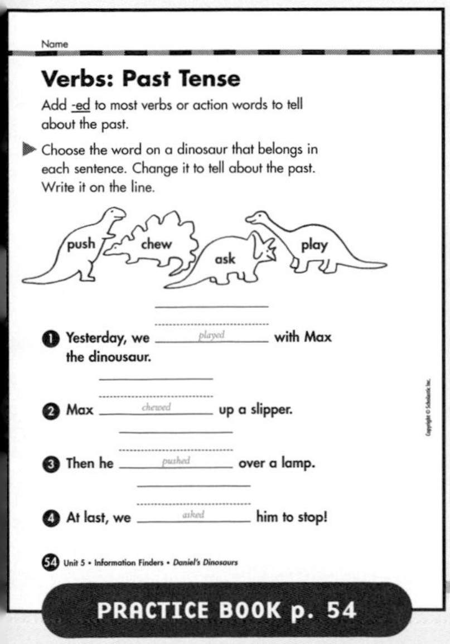
Name

Verbs: Past Tense

Add -ed to most verbs or action words to tell about the past.

▶ Choose the word on a dinosaur that belongs in each sentence. Change it to tell about the past. Write it on the line.

1. Yesterday, we ___played___ with Max the dinousaur.
2. Max ___chewed___ up a slipper.
3. Then he ___pushed___ over a lamp.
4. At last, we ___asked___ him to stop!

54 Unit 5 • Information Finders • *Daniel's Dinosaurs*

PRACTICE BOOK p. 54

DAY 4 APPLY

WRITING CONNECTION

- Review past-tense verbs with children.
- Ask children to think of a television program or movie they saw. Ask them to tell what the characters did. List the past-tense verbs that end in *-ed* on the chalkboard. Then have children write a short sentence with one of the words.

REVISE/PROOFREAD

- Have children search their week's fantasy stories for past-tense words they used and place them on the graphic organizer.

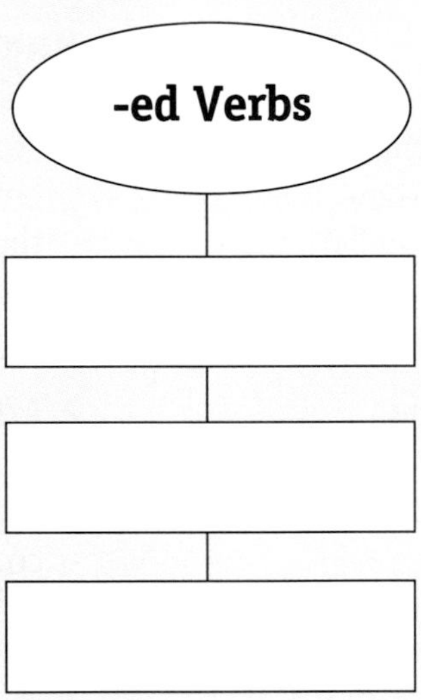

DAY 5 ASSESS

QUICKCHECK

- Ask children to write a sentence about something they did this morning, using an *-ed* past-tense verb.
- Write the following sentence on the chalkboard and have children identify the error.

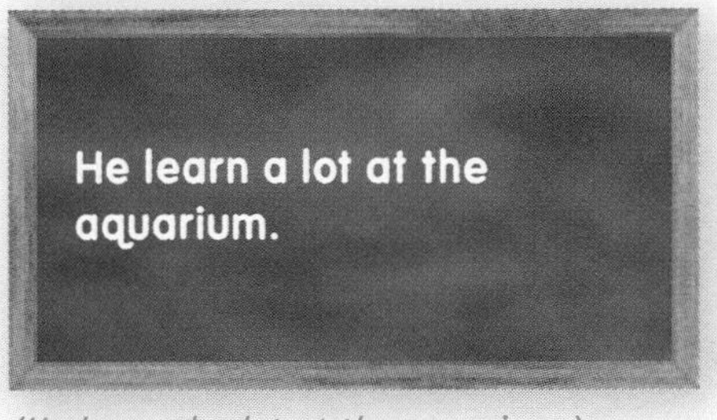

(He learned a lot at the aquarium.)

INFORMAL ASSESSMENT
OBSERVATION

✔ Did children correctly use a past-tense verb?

✔ Did children identify the verb-tense error?

If children need additional support, use the **Reteach** lesson on **page R64.**

MATH

Dinosaur Footprints

OBJECTIVE:
Use observations.

MATERIALS:
Paper
Pencils

ACTIVITY

Children estimate footprint sizes of dinosaurs pictured in *Daniel's Dinosaurs* and compare the dimensions. **(VISUAL LITERACY)**

CONNECT TO THE ANTHOLOGY

Review that there were many different dinosaurs in *Daniel's Dinosaurs*. Were they all the same size? How big do children think the dinosaurs' feet were?

MAKE NEW DISCOVERIES

- Children look through the story for the largest and the smallest dinosaurs. They then draw what they think each animal's footprint might look like, using the same scale for each.
- Ask children how many times the small footprint fits into the large one. Have children explain how they figured out their answers.

HOW TO ASSESS

Did children use observation to estimate and compare footprint sizes?

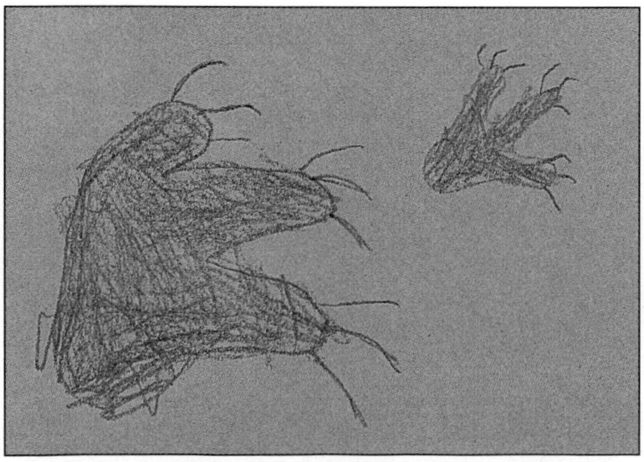

SCIENCE

Dinosaur Facts

OBJECTIVE:
Collect data.

MATERIALS:
Posterboard
Crayons or markers
Very simple nonfiction books about dinosaurs

ACTIVITY

Children investigate dinosaurs and make posters illustrating what they've learned. **(VISUAL LITERACY)**

CONNECT TO THE ANTHOLOGY

Ask children to choose one dinosaur from *Daniel's Dinosaurs* that they'd like to find out more about.

MAKE NEW DISCOVERIES

- Children who've chosen the same dinosaur can work together in small groups. Show children how to find information about their dinosaurs in the books. They can learn about the dinosaur's size, shape, what it ate, and other characteristics.
- After they've gathered the information, each group can make a poster showing facts they've collected. Display the completed posters.

HOW TO ASSESS

Were children able to collect and convey information about dinosaurs?

SOCIAL STUDIES

A Dinosaur in My Neighborhood

OBJECTIVE: Analyze information.

MATERIALS: None

Activity

Children imagine what life would be like if dinosaurs were still alive.

Connect to the Anthology

In *Daniel's Dinosaurs*, there are pictures showing people and dinosaurs together. Ask children if these pictures could be true. Are there still dinosaurs alive today?

Make New Discoveries

Generate a discussion about what life might be like if dinosaurs were still alive today. Use these questions to stimulate discussion:

- How would our towns and cities be different if dinosaurs were around? What changes might have to be made if dinosaurs walked on our streets?
- Could some dinosaurs be good pets? Why or why not? Where would they sleep at night?
- What tasks might dinosaurs be able to do to help people?

How to Assess

Were children able to analyze how life would be different if dinosaurs were still alive today?

THE ARTS

Make a Model of a Fossil

OBJECTIVE: Interpret information.

MATERIALS: Modeling clay Assortment of hard natural objects, such as shells, twigs, large seeds, or cones

Activity

Children use modeling clay to make their own fossil-like molds.

Connect to the Anthology

Point out that dinosaurs lived a long time ago. Ask children how they think scientists learned about dinosaurs.

Make New Discoveries

- Explain that one way scientists learned about dinosaurs is through fossils. Fossils are old rocks that have impressions of living things within them.
- Tell children that they can make their own model of a fossil. Demonstrate by pressing a shell or other object into softened modeling clay. Remove it to reveal the impression.
- Have children examine completed models and identify the objects that created the impressions.

How to Assess

Were children able to identify the objects that created the impressions?

ASSESSMENT

Select two children in each guided reading group to observe. Keep anecdotal records on each child's reading performance. Consider the following questions:

- ✔ What cues does the child use to figure out words and make meaning while reading?
- ✔ How well does the child retell the story?
- ✔ What sound-spellings or high-frequency words are causing the child difficulty?

When completed, add the anecdotal records to the child's literacy folder for future use when grading or conferencing.

Conducting Guided Reading Groups

Meet with at least two reading groups each day. Select a book on each group's instructional reading level from the *Scholastic Guided Reading Library* or a book in your classroom library. For more information on conducting guided reading groups, see *Scholastic Guided Reading Library,* Teacher's Guide.

Setting Up Independent Centers

While meeting with each reading group, have the rest of the class work in the Independent Centers listed below. Place the appropriate center cards in the pocket chart for student reference. Rotate the cards each day. Children may also use this time to do the following:

- revise or complete writing assignments,
- complete Practice Book pages,
- write in their Journals,
- read independently.

SAMPLE MANAGEMENT PLAN FOR CENTERS

RED GROUP	BLUE GROUP	GREEN GROUP	YELLOW GROUP
Reading Journal	ABC Center	Independent	Technology
Technology	Reading Journal	ABC Center	Independent
Independent	Technology	Reading Journal	ABC Center

TEACHER TIP

You can encourage home and family involvement by:

- inviting parents and caregivers to visit your classroom and participate in your literacy program.
- suggesting ways that family members can reinforce literacy at home.
- recommending at-home activities that give children opportunities to write.
- sending books home for family members to read with their children.
- providing instructions on how parents and caregivers can create homemade books.

GAY SU PINNELL

INDEPENDENT CENTERS

Children can work in these centers while you meet with guided reading groups.

READING JOURNAL

Ask children to work on their reading Journals. Children should record the titles of books they have read independently. Tell children to write a note about each book they list in their Journal. The notes should tell what they like about the books.

INDEPENDENT READING

Select several books that are appropriate for each leveled reading group, and place them in the individual Browsing Boxes. The books you choose can be ones that children have read during guided reading or ones that are on each group's independent reading level. Ask children to pick a book to read or reread independently. Afterward, children may enjoy drawing a picture of their favorite part of the story.

TECHNOLOGY

Each day, ask two children from each group to use the **WiggleWorks Plus** version of *The Plant Castle.* Have children reread the selection together. When they have worked through the selection, ask them to visit the program's Write area and write a brief retelling of the story.

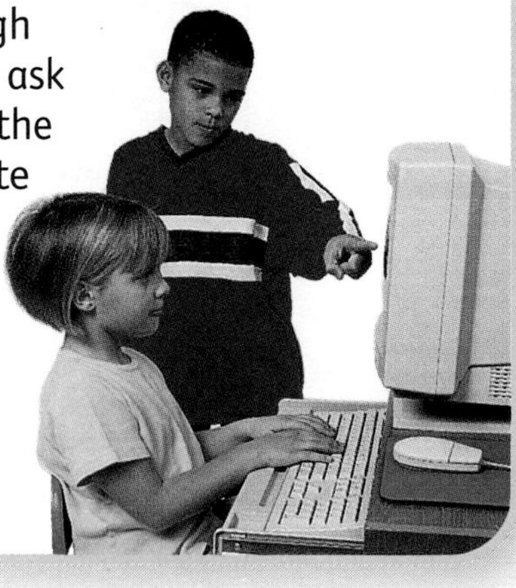

ABC CENTER

Place several word and alphabet games in the ABC Center. Include games that focus on this and previous weeks' phonics skills. The games should be fun, instructional, and challenging yet not beyond the class's current skill levels. Have children play the games with a partner or in a group. Remind children to follow the rules and play fairly.

WEEK 5 Words With *o* and *ow*

Spelling

WEEK 5 RESOURCES

SPELLING RESOURCE BOOK
- **Word Sort,** p. 129
- **Extra Help,** p. 130
- **Vocabulary Practice,** p. 131
- **Challenge,** p. 132
- **Proofread,** p.133
- **Student Test Form,** p. 161
- **Individual Progress Chart,** p. 162
- **Class Progress Chart,** p. 163
- **Word Sort Chart,** p. 164
- **My Words to Learn,** p. 165
- **Spelling Award Form,** p. 166

ADDITIONAL RESOURCES
- **Spelling Strategy Poster**
- **Proofreading Marks Poster**

SPELLING LIST

Words With *o* and *ow*

show **go**
grow **no**
snow

High-Frequency

mother **girl**

DAY 1 PRETEST/SELF-CHECK

ADMINISTER THE PRETEST

1. Where do you **go** to school?
2. Will you **show** me how to swim?
3. Flowers need sun and water to **grow.**
4. We have **no** homework today!
5. It is fun to play in the **snow.**
6. My **mother** works in that office.
7. That **girl** has a new bike.

SPELLING CONCEPT

Teach the spelling concept and present the spelling words. Explain that in some words, such as *grow,* the long *o* vowel sound is spelled *ow* and in some words, such as *go,* the long *o* vowel sound is spelled *o.*

WORD SORT

On the chalkboard, draw the chart below. Ask children to sort the spelling words in the chart.

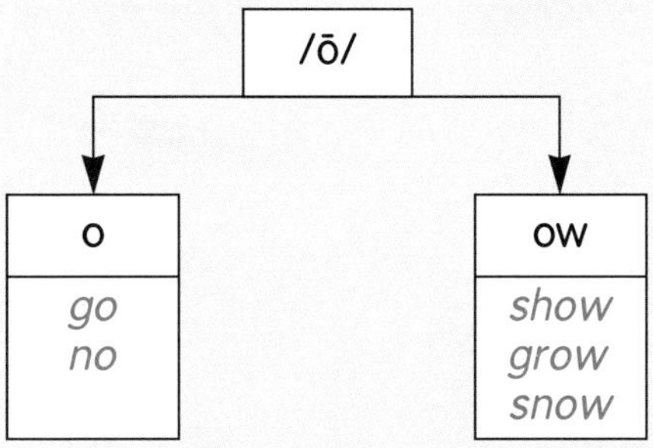

Have children complete **Spelling Resource Book, page 129.**

SPELLING RESOURCE BOOK p. 129

DAY 2 VOCABULARY PRACTICE

BUILD VOCABULARY: ACTION WORDS

- Review that action words tell what is happening, has happened, or will happen. Write on the chalkboard: *I will show you the book.* Ask children which word tells the action, or what will happen.
- Use *go, grow,* and *show* in sentences, asking children to identify the action word in each.

WORD STUDY: RHYMING

- Write *show* and *go* on the chalkboard and say each word aloud. Underline the *ow* in *show* and the *o* in *go.* Explain that both of these words have the long *o* sound even though it is spelled differently. When words end with the same sound, they rhyme.
- Write the following sentences on the chalkboard and ask children to replace the underlined spelling word with another spelling word that rhymes with it.

  I hope I no three inches this year. *(grow)*

  My dog loves to play in the show. *(snow)*

Have children complete **Spelling Resource Book, page 130, 131,** or **132.**

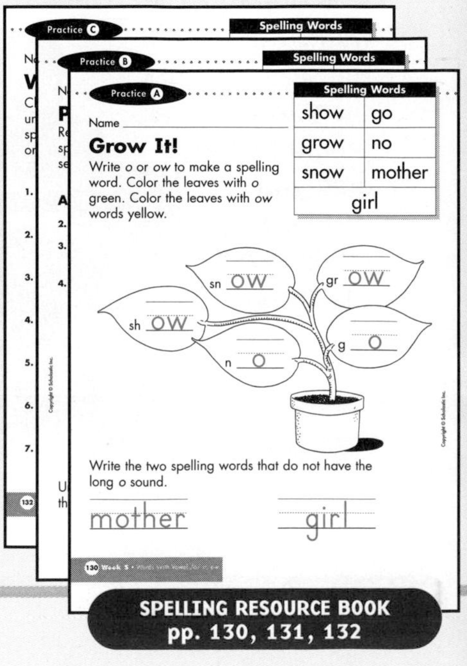

SPELLING RESOURCE BOOK pp. 130, 131, 132

DAY 3 WRITE/PROOFREAD

WRITE

- Tell children that they will write about how kindergarten and first grade are the same and how they are different.
- Using a graphic organizer will help children organize their ideas before writing.

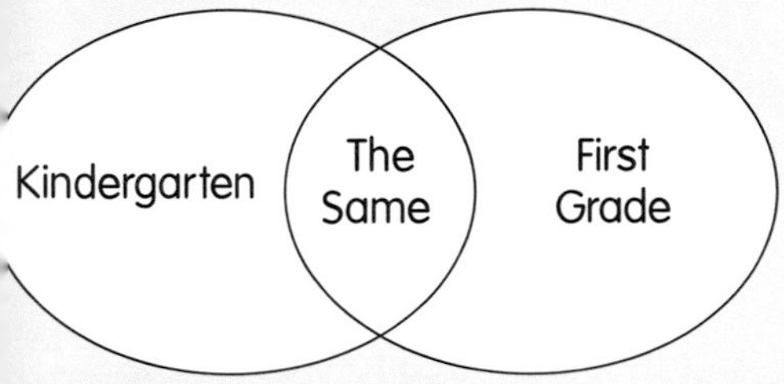

Children may:

- write a note to their kindergarten teacher that tells how first grade is different from kindergarten.
- make a list of questions they have about how second grade is different from first grade.

PROOFREAD

- Review the proofreading marks, using the class Proofreading Chart for reference.
- Use the following sentence for proofreading practice:

W more snow
~~we~~ had ~~most sno~~ than where you live~~?~~ .

Have children complete **Spelling Resource Book, page 133.**

DAY 4 STUDY/REVIEW

ADVERTISEMENTS

- Review with children the purpose of advertisements.
- Ask children to create an advertising poster inviting parents and friends to a show. Encourage them to use spelling words and illustrations in their advertisements.

TEST YOURSELF

- Review the Spelling Strategy.
- In groups of four, children can have mini spelling bees. One child dictates one word at a time to each child who in turn orally spells the word.
- Children can take turns giving simple riddles for spelling words and solving the riddles. For example, *This word is the opposite of* yes *and rhymes with* toe. *(no)*

Children may practice for their spelling tests using the **Student Test Form, page 161.**

DAY 5 POSTTEST/SELF-CHECK

ADMINISTER THE POSTTEST

For the Posttest, read aloud the sentences from Day 1. Have children write each spelling word.

Then have children:

- self-check
- record the results of their Posttest on the **Individual Progress Chart.**
- keep a list of their misspelled words in their spelling journals.

ASSESSMENT

Record the results of children's Posttests on the **Class Progress Chart, Spelling Resource Book, page 163.**

See **Handwriting Practice, pages 30–31** for practice writing the letters *Y* and *Z* and the numbers *1,2,3.*

Write and Proofread

Name

Find It, Fix It!

Jo found one word she spelled wrong. Circle five more words she spelled wrong. Write them correctly above the lines.

Jo is a grl who likes to gro plants. Her muther said there is now time. It is going to snoe. She will showe her how in the spring.

PROOFREADING MARKS

SPELLING RESOURCE BOOK p. 133

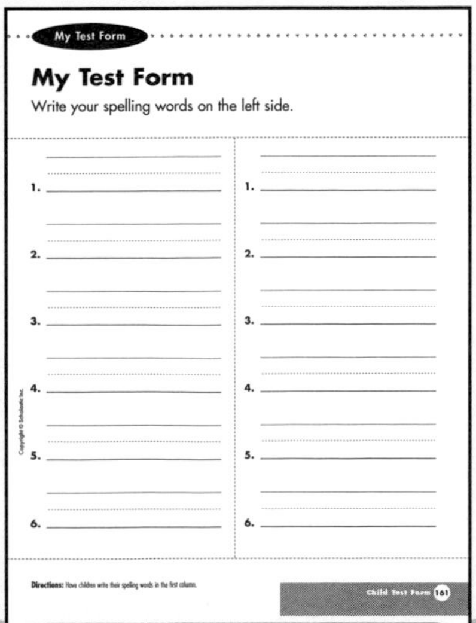
My Test Form

My Test Form

Write your spelling words on the left side.

1.	1.
2.	2.
3.	3.
4.	4.
5.	5.
6.	6.

Child Test Form 161

SPELLING RESOURCE BOOK p. 161

Class Progress Chart

Unit ___ Name	Week		Week		Week		Week		Week	
	Pretest	Posttest	Pretest	Posttest	Pretest	Posttest	Pretest	Posttest	Pretest	Posttest

Class Progress Chart 163

SPELLING RESOURCE BOOK p. 163

WEEK 5 Words That Compare

Grammar, Usage, Mechanics

OBJECTIVE

Children will explore words that compare in *The Plant Castle* and in their writing.

RESOURCES

Practice Book, p. 72
Grammar, Usage, Mechanics Resource Book, pp. 100–103

Words That Compare

Words that compare two people, places, or things end in *-er.*

MODIFY Instruction

ESL/ELD

▲ Create a set of index cards with words that compare, such as *taller, shorter, harder, softer, bigger, smaller.* Make sure children understand each word. Ask one child to choose a card from the pile and an object or use him- or herself in a comparing sentence with the word on the selected card. For example, children might say: *I am taller than Sal.* **(ORAL LANGUAGE)**

DAY 1 TEACH/MODEL

SELECTION LINK

- Write the following sentence from **Anthology page 121** on the chalkboard with another sentence containing a word that compares under it.

  We peek inside the small windows.

  Those windows are smaller than mine.

  Point out that the word *small* changes to *smaller* by adding *-er* when we compare two different windows.
- Write these sentences on the chalkboard.

  The thorns are sharper than a pin.

  The tropical room is warmer than the spring garden.

  Have children name the two things being compared in each sentence. Then have children tell which describing word compares. Point out that words that compare two things end in *-er.*
- Ask children to find words from **Anthology page 122** that could be made into a word that compares by adding *-er.* Then guide children to make the base word into a word that compares. Place these on a class chart.

My Word	*-er* Word
green	*greener*
wet	*wetter*
clear	*clearer*
tall	*taller*
high	*higher*

DAY 2 PRACTICE

REVIEW

- Review with children that a word that compares two people, places, or things ends in *-er.*
- Write the following sentence groups on the chalkboard and have children choose the correct word to complete each sentence.

  That room was (bright, brighter). *(bright)*

  That room was (bright, brighter) than the rain-forest room. *(brighter)*

  Have children name the two things being compared in the second sentence.
- Show children two items of different size in the classroom. Have children write one sentence comparing these two items, using a word that ends in *-er.* Then have children draw the two items.

DAY 3 PRACTICE

RETEACH

- Review with children that a word that compares two people, places, or things ends in *-er*.
- Write the following sentences on the chalkboard and ask children to complete the sentence with a word that compares. Remind them that words that compare two people, places, or things end in *-er*.

Trees are __________ than flowers.

A butterfly is __________ than a caterpillar.

The sun is __________ than the trees.

Some leaves are __________ than others.

Have children complete **Practice Book, page 72.**

DAY 4 APPLY

WRITING CONNECTION

- Review with children that a word that compares two people, places, or things ends in *-er*.
- Write the words *older* and *softer* on the chalkboard. For each of the words, have children write a short sentence comparing two things.

REVISE/PROOFREAD

- Have children search their week's personal narratives for *-er* words they used and place them on a chart such as the one below.

-er Word	What I Compared

DAY 5 ASSESS

QUICKCHECK

- Ask children to write a sentence comparing two toys.
- Write the following sentence on the chalkboard and have children identify the error.

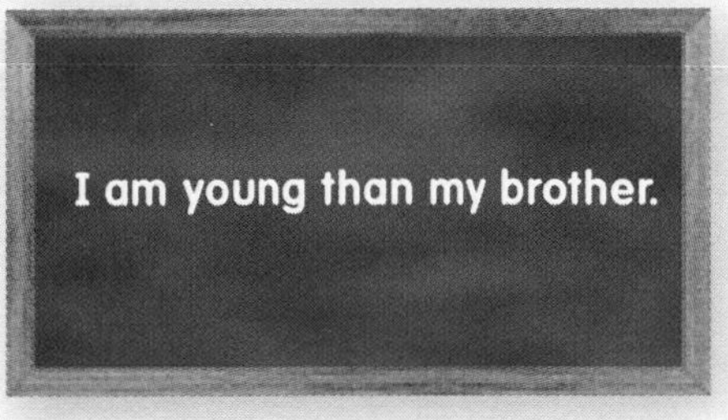
I am young than my brother.

(I am younger than my brother.)

INFORMAL ASSESSMENT
OBSERVATION

✔ Did children compare only two things using *-er?*

✔ Did children identify an error in using *-er* words to compare two things?

If children need additional support, use the **Reteach** lesson on **page R65.**

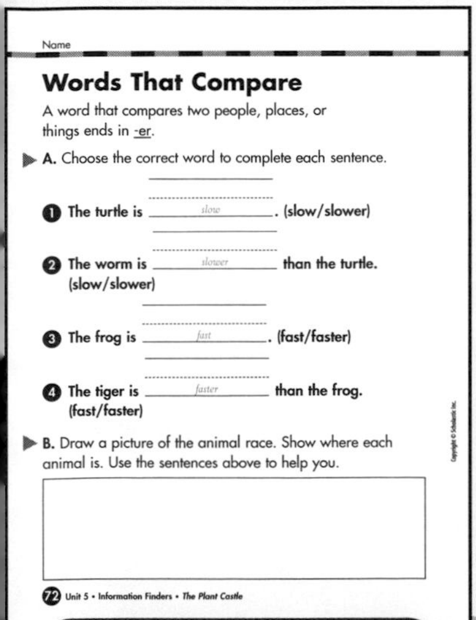
Name

Words That Compare

A word that compares two people, places, or things ends in -er.

▶ A. Choose the correct word to complete each sentence.

1. The turtle is ____slow____. (slow/slower)
2. The worm is ____slower____ than the turtle. (slow/slower)
3. The frog is ____fast____. (fast/faster)
4. The tiger is ____faster____ than the frog. (fast/faster)

▶ B. Draw a picture of the animal race. Show where each animal is. Use the sentences above to help you.

72 Unit 5 • Information Finders • The Plant Castle

PRACTICE BOOK p. 72

WEEK 5 Integrated Curriculum

MATH

Read a Garden Map

OBJECTIVE: Use charts, graphs, and visual displays.

MATERIALS: 6-inch section of string for each child

ACTIVITY

Children use the New York Botanical Garden map to compare distances between places. **(VISUAL LITERACY)**

CONNECT TO THE ANTHOLOGY

Refer to the Botanical Garden map. Discuss with children that a map shows important places and also shows how far places are from each other.

MAKE NEW DISCOVERIES

- Have children locate the Main Gate, West Gate, and Forest. Ask which gate is closer to the Forest. Children can use string to measure and compare distances.
- Ask them other questions that require measuring distances on the map. For example: *Which is closer to the Forest—the Library or the Ruth Rea Howell Family Garden?*
- Ask children to explain how they reached their answers.

HOW TO ASSESS

Were children able to use the map to compare distances between places?

SCIENCE

How Trees Change

OBJECTIVE: Note relevant details.

MATERIALS: Paper
Colored pencils or markers

ACTIVITY

Children make drawings to show the seasonal changes in local trees. (Note: This activity is most suitable in areas where trees undergo seasonal changes.) **(VISUAL LITERACY)**

CONNECT TO THE ANTHOLOGY

In *The Plant Castle,* two girls explore an arboretum. Ask children if they think the arboretum makes the trees stay the same year round.

MAKE NEW DISCOVERIES

- Ask children what season it is. Have them describe how the trees in the neighborhood look right now. Tell them to make four drawings of the same tree: one drawing for each season.
- Children should first think about how the tree looks in each season. They then make their drawings and label each drawing with the season it shows.

HOW TO ASSESS

Did children's drawings include details that showed changes in trees over the seasons?

SOCIAL STUDIES

Map the Neighborhood

OBJECTIVE: Use charts, graphs, and visual displays.

MATERIALS:
Paper
Markers, pencils, or crayons

Activity

Using the New York Botanical Garden map as a model, children make maps of their school. **(VISUAL LITERACY)**

Connect to the Anthology

Review the Botanical Garden map. Discuss how a map of your school could help visitors find their way around.

Make New Discoveries

- Each group decides whether their map will show all or part of the school and its grounds. Tell children that important places should be labeled on their maps.
- Groups can divide the project by area or by task—such as sketching, labeling, and coloring.
- You may want to display the finished maps or keep them in a school atlas.

How to Assess

Did children's maps show the relative locations of important places in the school?

THE ARTS

Fill a Greenhouse

OBJECTIVE: Use graphs, charts, and visual displays.

MATERIALS:
Reference books
Colored construction paper
Crayons
Markers
Scissors
Glue

Activity

Children make paper plants and flowers for a "greenhouse" display. **(VISUAL LITERACY)**

Connect to the Anthology

Remind children that an arboretum is a place where trees and plants grow. Point out that a greenhouse is used to protect smaller plants.

Make New Discoveries

- Each group looks through the reference books and chooses plants or flowers to make.
- Children draw, color, and cut out plants and flowers. They may also make other items that they think might be found in a greenhouse, such as watering cans, flower pots, and so on.
- The groups place their models together to form a "greenhouse."

How to Assess

Were children able to include plants and other relevant items in the "greenhouse?"

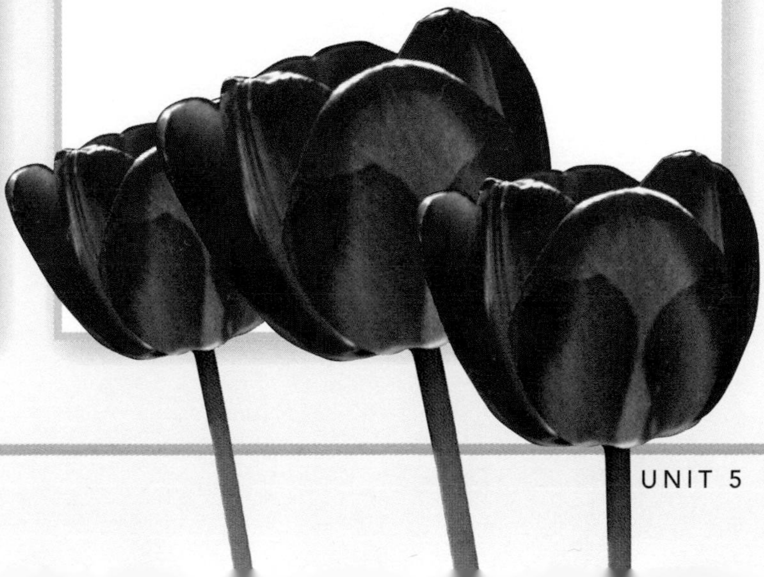

TEACHER RESOURCES

Main Idea/Details

OBJECTIVE

- Children review how details support the main idea.

MATERIALS

- Anthology, pp. 38–66
- Practice Book, p. 27

SUGGESTED GROUPING

- Pairs or small groups

SKILLS TRACE

KEY STRATEGY: TESTED
Main Idea/Details

- Introduce, p. T54
- Practice, p. T27
- Review, p. R43
- Reteach, p. R55

1 REVIEW

Remind children that the main idea of a story is what the story is mostly about. The details give more information about the main idea. Remind children that they can find the main idea in pictures and the text of the story. Tell children that they are going to review finding the main idea and the smaller details that tell about the main idea. Ask children to listen for the main idea as you read the following paragraph:

> **There are too many insects to count in the world. There are more insects than any other kind of animal. There have been insects for millions of years. They can be found everywhere—hot or cold places. There are many kinds of insects. Some insects even live in the water!**

Draw a chart like the following on the chalkboard. Help children find the main idea and supporting details of the paragraph.

Main Idea: There are too many insects to count.

Supporting Detail 1: Insects can be found everywhere.

Supporting Detail 2: more insects than any other kind of animal

Supporting Detail 3: There are many kinds of insects.

2 PRACTICE/APPLY

PUT IT IN CONTEXT Have children turn to page 38. Talk about the main idea of the cover illustration. Then have them reread pages 39–40. Ask them what the words and pictures tell about how a caterpillar turns into a butterfly.

Have pairs of children flip through the rest of the selection. Have them tell each other details about how caterpillars turn into butterflies. Then have a class discussion about the main idea of the selection. Write the main idea on the chalkboard with the details that partners noted.

3 ASSESS

DID CHILDREN:

✔ express the main idea of a selection?

✔ identify at least two supporting details?

IF NOT, TRY THIS:

See the **Reteach** lesson on **page R55.**

CHILDREN'S SELF-ASSESSMENT:

✔ Did I use words and pictures to help me understand the main idea?

For additional support, see **Practice Book page 27.**

Name
REVIEW: MAIN IDEA/DETAILS

What's the Big Idea?

▶ Read each story. Fill in the bubble next to the sentence that answers each question.

Ducks are fun to watch. I see the duck swim in the pond. It likes to play in the rain. I see the duck catch a worm.

What is the main idea of the story?
ⓐ Ducks are fun to watch.
ⓑ Ducks like worms.
ⓒ Children visit the pond.

What is a detail from the story?
ⓐ We like to swim in the pond.
ⓑ I see the duck swim.
ⓒ I see a white duck with a big nose and long feet.

The boys go to the zoo. Max runs to see the bears. Dan likes to see the giraffes. Both boys like the birds that talk.

What is the main idea of the story?
ⓐ Max and Dan are boys.
ⓑ The boys go to the zoo.
ⓒ Max sees the bears.

Unit 5 • Information Finders • I'm a Caterpillar 27

PRACTICE BOOK p. 27

SEQUENCE

OBJECTIVE

- Children review sequence.

MATERIALS

- Anthology, pp. 86–109
- Practice Book, p. 55

SUGGESTED GROUPING

- Whole class or small groups

SKILLS TRACE

KEY STRATEGY: TESTED
Sequence

- Introduce, p. T114
- Practice, p. T85
- Review, p. R44
- Reteach, p. R55

1 REVIEW

Explain to children that knowing the order of events in a story can help a reader remember and understand what happened in that story. Remind children that there is a plan they can use to help them understand the order in which events occur in a story.

> **Read carefully.**

> **Look for words that tell what happened *first, next,* and *last.***

> **Ask yourself: "Does this order make sense?"**

Write the following sentences on the chalkboard. Work together to put each event in the right sequence by writing the numeral 1 next to the event that happened first, and so on.

Mike put on his sneakers. ***(2)***

Mike put on his socks. ***(1)***

Mike tied his shoelaces. ***(3)***

2 PRACTICE/APPLY

PUT IT IN CONTEXT Have children reread *Daniel's Dinosaurs.* Then write the following sentences on the chalkboard:

Daniel and his mother went to the aquarium.

Daniel loved sharks.

Daniel loved dinosaurs.

Have children write these sentences in the sequence in which they occurred in the story. Then ask children why this sequence makes sense.

3 ASSESS

DID CHILDREN:

✔ identify the correct sequence of events for a reading selection?

✔ notice and use signal words to determine story sequence?

IF NOT, TRY THIS:

See the **Reteach** lesson on **page R55.**

CHILDREN'S SELF-ASSESSMENT:

✔ Did I retell a story in the correct sequence?

For additional support, see **Practice Book page 55.**

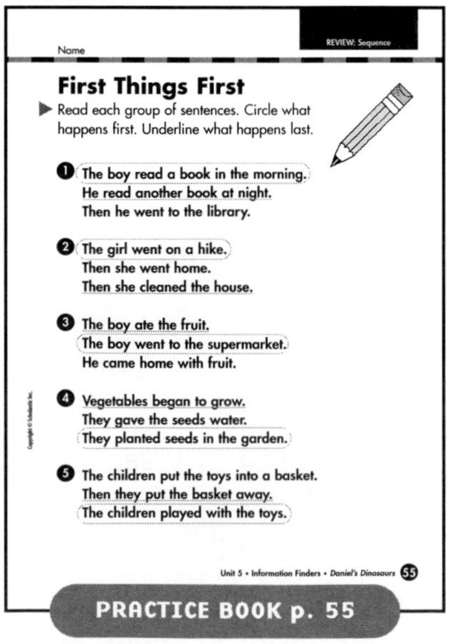
Name REVIEW: Sequence

First Things First

▶ Read each group of sentences. Circle what happens first. Underline what happens last.

1. The boy read a book in the morning.
   He read another book at night.
   Then he went to the library.
2. The girl went on a hike.
   Then she went home.
   Then she cleaned the house.
3. The boy ate the fruit.
   The boy went to the supermarket.
   He came home with fruit.
4. Vegetables began to grow.
   They gave the seeds water.
   They planted seeds in the garden.
5. The children put the toys into a basket.
   Then they put the basket away.
   The children played with the toys.

Unit 5 • Information Finders • Daniel's Dinosaurs 55

PRACTICE BOOK p. 55

SETTING

OBJECTIVE
- Children review setting.

MATERIALS
- **Anthology,** pp. 114–128
- **Practice Book,** p. 73

SUGGESTED GROUPING
- Cooperative groups

SKILLS TRACE

KEY STRATEGY: TESTED
Setting
- **Introduce,** p. T162
- **Practice,** pp. T149, T177
- **Review,** p. R45
- **Reteach,** p. R56

1 REVIEW

Remind children that the setting of a story tells the time and place it occurs. Explain that to identify the setting of a story, children should ask themselves the following questions as they read:

> **When does the story take place?**

> **Where does the story take place?**

> **What clues can I find that tell me about the setting?**

Have children turn to the first picture in the story *The Plant Castle.* Use picture clues to model using the questioning strategy described above. Help children recognize that the story begins in front of the arboretum at about two-thirty in the afternoon.

2 PRACTICE/APPLY

PUT IT IN CONTEXT Remind children that the setting of a story can change. Divide the class into cooperative groups. Have children look through the story *The Plant Castle* and make a list of the different settings within the arboretum. Remind children to ask themselves questions such as "When does this part of the story take place? Where are the children in this part of the arboretum?"

Have groups share their completed lists with each other. Check the lists with children by going through the story, scene by scene, to identify time and place.

3 ASSESS

DID CHILDREN:

✔ identify elements of setting?

✔ use a strategy to determine time and place?

IF NOT, TRY THIS:

See the **Reteach** lesson on **page R56.**

CHILDREN'S SELF-ASSESSMENT:

✔ Did I describe where and when a story takes place?

For additional support, see **Practice Book page 73.**

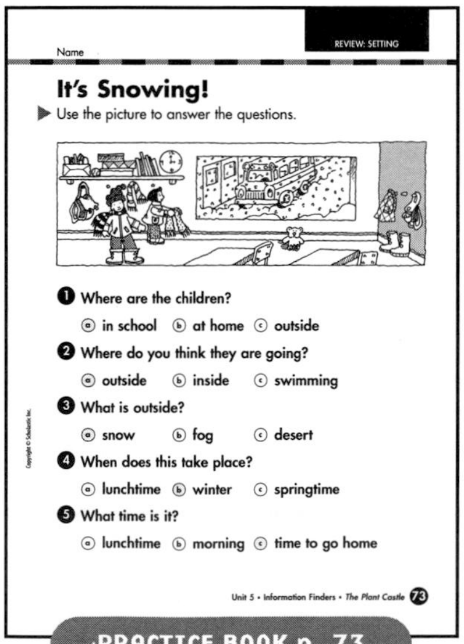
Name REVIEW: SETTING

It's Snowing!
▶ Use the picture to answer the questions.

1 Where are the children?
ⓐ in school ⓑ at home ⓒ outside
2 Where do you think they are going?
ⓐ outside ⓑ inside ⓒ swimming
3 What is outside?
ⓐ snow ⓑ fog ⓒ desert
4 When does this take place?
ⓐ lunchtime ⓑ winter ⓒ springtime
5 What time is it?
ⓐ lunchtime ⓑ morning ⓒ time to go home

Unit 5 • Information Finders • The Plant Castle 73

PRACTICE BOOK p. 73

Homophones

OBJECTIVE

- Children review homophones.

MATERIALS

- Anthology, pp. 38–66
- Practice Book, p. 28

SUGGESTED GROUPING

- Small groups or individuals

SKILLS TRACE

Homophones TESTED

- Introduce, p. T56
- Practice, pp. T39, T63
- Review, p. R46
- Reteach, p. R57

1 REVIEW

Remind children that homophones are words that sound alike but have different meanings and spellings. Write the homophones ***I, eye; no, know;*** and ***to, two*** on the chalkboard.

Ask children to say each set of words. Help them recognize that there is no difference in sound within each set. Discuss the meaning of each word, and spell each several times. Then invite volunteers to use each word in a phrase or sentence that will illustrate its meaning.

2 PRACTICE/APPLY

PUT IT IN CONTEXT Read the following sentence from the story: ***It's time to hang from a stem.*** Point out that ***to*** and ***two*** are homophones. Now write the following sentences about the story on the chalkboard, read them aloud, and explain that a homophone belongs in each sentence. Write these homophone possibilities above the sentences: ***I, eye; no, know; to, two.*** Ask children to copy the sentences and write the correct homophone in each. Encourage the use of dictionaries if children are confused in matching meaning to spelling.

_____ am a caterpillar. *(I)*

Caterpillars grow _____ be butterflies. *(to)*

We keep an _____ out for flowers. *(eye)*

The _____ of us drink nectar. *(two)*

Birds _____ we taste awful. *(know)*

So _____ bird bothers us. *(no)*

When the sentences are complete, have children read each one aloud and spell the homophone they used. Then have children name other homophone pairs and take turns using them in sentences.

3 ASSESS

DID CHILDREN:

✔ understand the term *homophone*?

✔ generate examples of homophones?

IF NOT, TRY THIS:

See the **Reteach** lesson on **page R57.**

CHILDREN'S SELF-ASSESSMENT:

✔ Did I identify a homophone?

For additional support, see **Practice Book page 28.**

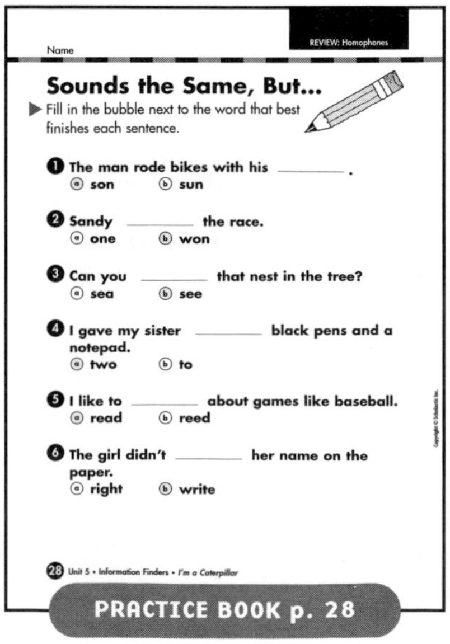
Name REVIEW: Homophones

Sounds the Same, But...

▶ Fill in the bubble next to the word that best finishes each sentence.

1. The man rode bikes with his _____.
   ⓐ son ⓑ sun
2. Sandy _____ the race.
   ⓐ one ⓑ won
3. Can you _____ that nest in the tree?
   ⓐ sea ⓑ see
4. I gave my sister _____ black pens and a notepad.
   ⓐ two ⓑ to
5. I like to _____ about games like baseball.
   ⓐ read ⓑ reed
6. The girl didn't _____ her name on the paper.
   ⓐ right ⓑ write

28 Unit 5 • Information Finders • *I'm a Caterpillar*

PRACTICE BOOK p. 28

Phonics: Words With /ô/*a*, *aw*

OBJECTIVE

- Children review /ô/*a*, *aw*.

MATERIALS

- Anthology, pp. 70–81
- Practice Book, p. 42

SUGGESTED GROUPING

- Whole class or small groups

SKILLS TRACE

Words With /ô/*a*, *aw* TESTED

- Introduce, p. T80
- Practice, pp. T95, T118, T119
- Review, p. R47
- Reteach, p. R58

❶ REVIEW

Write ***tall, call,*** and ***walk*** on the chalkboard and read the words, emphasizing the vowel sound. Isolate the sound and have children repeat it. Ask:

> **What vowel sound do you hear? (/ô/)**

> **What letter stands for this sound? (*a*)**

Point out that when the letters ***all*** and ***alk*** appear in words, the letter ***a*** stands for the vowel sound **/ô/**.

Repeat the procedure with the words ***jaw, draw,*** and ***lawn.*** Help children recognize that the letters ***aw*** also stand for the vowel sound **/ô/**. Then recite the following words and have children stand up tall and point to their jaw when they hear a word with /ô/—the same vowel sound as ***tall*** and ***jaw: law, let, paw, talk, when, drawn, wall, hall, hat, mall, awe, chalk.***

❷ PRACTICE/APPLY

PUT IT IN CONTEXT Have children turn to page 75. Ask them to read the page and stand tall when they read a word that contains the **/ô/** sound. Then write the words ***all, fall, walking, awful,*** and ***crawl*** on index cards. Display the cards and read the words with children. Then display the following incomplete sentences in the pocket chart. Read them with children. Have children place a word card in each sentence to complete it.

Toad came _____ over to the garden. *(walking)*

He saw _____ the flowers. *(all)*

He saw bugs _____ on the flowers. *(crawl)*

"The bugs could _____," Frog said. *(fall)*

"That would be _____." *(awful)*

When the sentences are complete, have children read them aloud.

❸ ASSESS

DID CHILDREN:

✔ identify the vowel sound **/ô/**?

✔ connect the letters ***a, alk, all*** and ***aw*** with the sound **/ô/**?

IF NOT, TRY THIS:

See the **Reteach** lesson on **page R58.**

CHILDREN'S SELF-ASSESSMENT:

✔ Did I identify letters that stand for the **/ô/** sound?

For additional support, see **Practice Book page 42.**

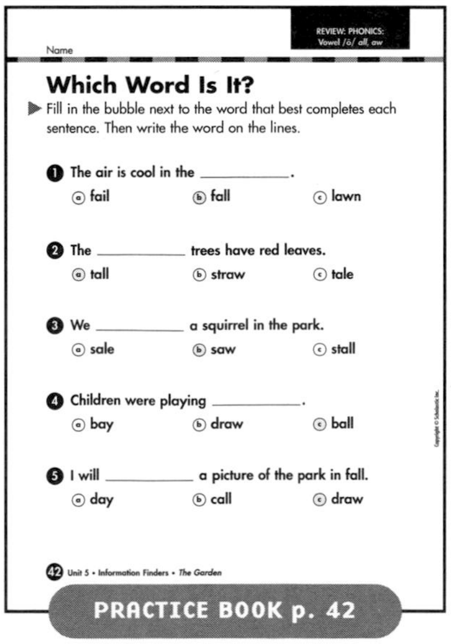
Name

REVIEW: PHONICS: Vowel /ô/ *all, aw*

Which Word Is It?

▶ Fill in the bubble next to the word that best completes each sentence. Then write the word on the lines.

1. The air is cool in the _______.
   ⓐ fail ⓑ fall ⓒ lawn
2. The _______ trees have red leaves.
   ⓐ tall ⓑ straw ⓒ tale
3. We _______ a squirrel in the park.
   ⓐ sale ⓑ saw ⓒ stall
4. Children were playing _______.
   ⓐ bay ⓑ draw ⓒ ball
5. I will _______ a picture of the park in fall.
   ⓐ day ⓑ call ⓒ draw

42 Unit 5 • Information Finders • *The Garden*

PRACTICE BOOK p. 42

PHONICS: VOWEL /ā/*ay, ai*

OBJECTIVE

- Children review vowel /ā/*ay, ai*.

MATERIALS

- Anthology, pp. 70–81
- Practice Book, p. 43

SUGGESTED GROUPING

- Small groups or individuals

SKILLS TRACE

Vowel /ā/*ay, ai* TESTED

- Introduce, p. T116
- Practice, pp. T107, T123
- Review, p. R48
- Reteach, p. R58

❶ REVIEW

Have children listen as you say the words ***may*** and ***pail*** slowly, elongating the vowel sound. Ask what vowel sound children hear in these words. Isolate the **/ā/** sound and have children repeat it after you. Then slowly blend the following words and have children clap when they hear **/ā/**: ***rain, pay, stay, gray, pail, mail, hay, say, wait.***

Write the words on the chalkboard and point to the letters ***ai*** in ***rain*** and ***ay*** in ***pay.*** Explain that both ***ai*** and ***ay*** stand for the long ***a*** vowel sound. Have children read the other words and underline the letters that stand for the long ***a*** sound.

❷ PRACTICE/APPLY

PUT IT IN CONTEXT Ask children to identify the words with ***ai*** and the long ***a*** sound. Ask other children to identify words with ***ay*** and the long ***a*** sound. Remind children that the long vowel sound heard in words such as ***may*** and ***wait*** is created with the letters ***ay*** or ***ai.*** Then write these incomplete words on the chalkboard:

s ____ ____ aw ____ ____

w ____ ____ t afr ____ ____ d

Have children copy the letters on paper and complete the words using the letters ***ay*** or ***ai.*** Challenge children to write other long a words with the ***ay*** or ***ai*** spelling.

❸ ASSESS

DID CHILDREN:

✔ identify **/ā/**—the sound of long ***a***?

✔ connect the letters ***ay*** and ***ai*** with the long *a* sound?

✔ generate words with long ***a*** spelled ***ay, ai***?

IF NOT, TRY THIS:

See the **Reteach** lesson on **page R58.**

CHILDREN'S SELF-ASSESSMENT:

✔ Did I write words with the long ***a*** sound spelled ***ay*** and ***ai***?

For additional support, see **Practice Book page 43.**

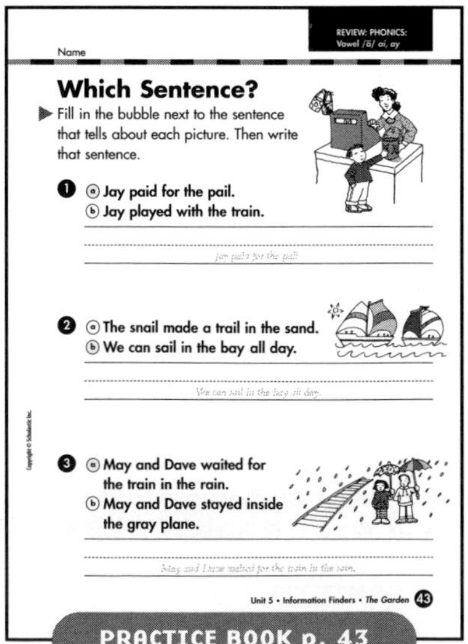
Name

REVIEW: PHONICS: Vowel /ā/ *ai, ay*

Which Sentence?

▶ Fill in the bubble next to the sentence that tells about each picture. Then write that sentence.

1. ⓐ Jay paid for the pail.
   ⓑ Jay played with the train.

2. ⓐ The snail made a trail in the sand.
   ⓑ We can sail in the bay all day.

3. ⓐ May and Dave waited for the train in the rain.
   ⓑ May and Dave stayed inside the gray plane.

Copyright © Scholastic Inc.

Unit 5 • Information Finders • *The Garden* 43

PRACTICE BOOK p. 43

PHONICS: DIGRAPHS /sh/*sh*, /th/*th*

OBJECTIVE

- Children review consonant digraphs /sh/ and /th/.

MATERIALS

- **Anthology,** pp. 86–109
- **Practice Book,** p. 56

SUGGESTED GROUPING

- Partners or individuals

SKILLS TRACE

Digraphs /sh/*sh*, /th/*th* TESTED

- **Introduce,** p. T22
- **Practice,** pp. T29, T58–T59
- **Review,** p. R49
- **Reteach,** p. R57

1 REVIEW

Write the words ***shell, ship,*** and ***wash*** on the chalkboard. Read the words, underlining the letters ***sh*** in each. Have children repeat the words after you. Follow the same procedure with ***thick, thank,*** and ***with,*** underlining the digraph ***th.*** Remind children that sometimes two letters stand for one sound. Point out that ***sh*** stands for **/sh/**—the beginning sound in ***shell*** and ***ship,*** and the end sound in ***wash.*** The letters ***th*** stand for **/th/**—the beginning sound in ***thick*** and ***thank,*** and the end sound in ***with.***

2 PRACTICE/APPLY

PUT IT IN CONTEXT Ask partners to flip through the story *Daniel's Dinosaurs* to find words with digraphs ***sh*** and ***th.*** Have them list the words they find. Then draw a Venn diagram on the chalkboard for each digraph. Have children supply words with the target sound in the initial and final positions. Encourage children to name words from the reading selection as well as other words. You may wish to use the intersection for words that have the target sound in both positions. ***(shush, thirteenth)***

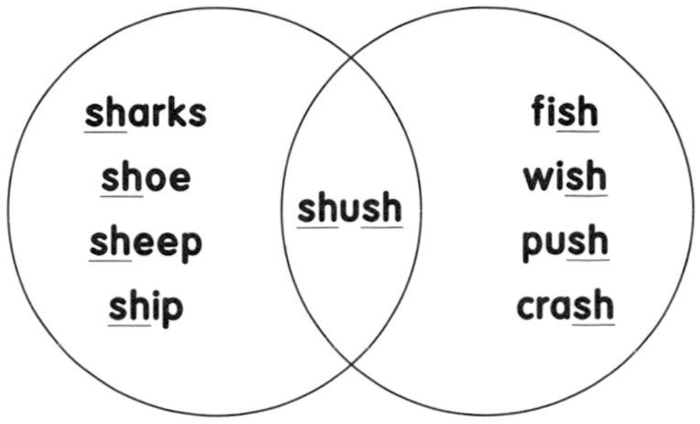

3 ASSESS

DID CHILDREN:

✔ read words with digraphs **/sh/*sh*** and **/th/*th***?

✔ connect the sounds **/sh/** and **/th/** with the letters ***sh*** and ***th***?

IF NOT, TRY THIS:

See the **Reteach** lesson on **page R57.**

CHILDREN'S SELF-ASSESSMENT:

✔ Did I find words with digraphs ***sh*** and ***th***?

✔ Did I think of words with **/sh/** and **/th/**?

For additional support, see **Practice Book page 56.**

REVIEW: PHONICS: Digraphs sh, th

Name

Match It!

▶ Match the sentence to the picture. Fill in bubble next to the word that finishes each sentence.

1. The book is ______.
   ⓐ thin ⓑ short ⓒ thick
2. I find ______ at the shore.
   ⓐ shells ⓑ shows ⓒ cloth
3. We can ______ the dog.
   ⓐ with ⓑ wash ⓒ wish
4. The baby has three ______.
   ⓐ teeth ⓑ thanks ⓒ shops
5. We ______ from the ship.
   ⓐ think ⓑ shape ⓒ fish

56 Unit 5 • Information Finders • Daniel's Dinosaurs

PRACTICE BOOK p. 56

Structural Analysis: Plurals

OBJECTIVE

- **Children review plurals formed by adding *s*.**

MATERIALS

- **Anthology**, pp. 86–109
- **Practice Book**, p. 57

SUGGESTED GROUPING

- **Whole class**

SKILLS TRACE

Plurals — TESTED

- **Introduce**, Unit 4, *Imagine That!*, p. T262
- **Practice**, Unit 4, *Imagine That!*, pp. T255, T269
- **Review**, p. R50
- **Reteach**, p. R60

1 REVIEW

Review with children that an **s** at the end of a noun, or naming word, tells that it names more than one. On the chalkboard, write the words ***cat, dog,*** and ***turtle.*** Read the words with children. Explain that to make most words mean more than one, you just add **s** to the end. Write the words ***cats, dogs,*** and ***turtles,*** and have children read the words aloud. Ask children to identify the clue that tells them that each word means more than one.

2 PRACTICE/APPLY

PUT IT IN CONTEXT Ask children to read the first few pages of the story, *Daniel's Dinosaurs*. Have them find plural nouns. Then write the following words on the chalkboard and ask children to make each word mean more than one.

book	**dinosaur**	**picture**
horse	**stingray**	**shark**
aquarium	**house**	**teacher**

After children have formed the plurals, encourage them to tell what each new word means. Then have them complete the following pattern sentence for three or four of the words: ***I like*** _____. Encourage them to illustrate each sentence they write.

3 ASSESS

DID CHILDREN:

✔ understand the concepts of one and more than one?

✔ understand the function of **s** in the formation of plural nouns?

✔ identify and form singular and plural nouns?

IF NOT, TRY THIS:

Ask children to cut out sentences with words that mean more than one from newspapers and magazines.

CHILDREN'S SELF-ASSESSMENT:

✔ Did I find naming words that are plural?

✔ Did I know how to say and write the word that means more than one of something?

For additional support, see **Practice Book page 57.**

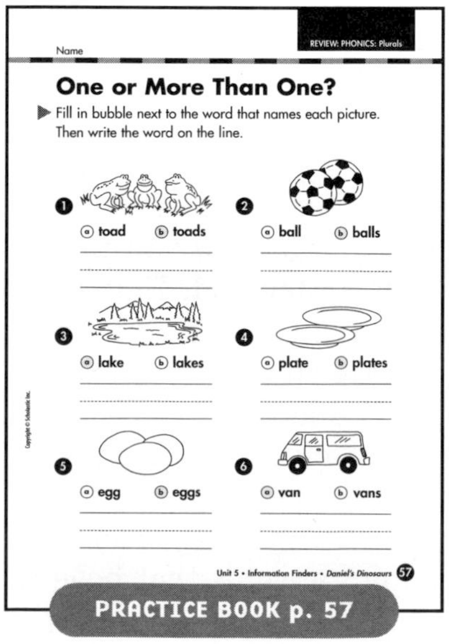
Name
REVIEW: PHONICS: Plurals

One or More Than One?

▶ Fill in bubble next to the word that names each picture. Then write the word on the line.

1. ⓐ toad ⓑ toads
2. ⓐ ball ⓑ balls
3. ⓐ lake ⓑ lakes
4. ⓐ plate ⓑ plates
5. ⓐ egg ⓑ eggs
6. ⓐ van ⓑ vans

Unit 5 • Information Finders • Daniel's Dinosaurs 57

PRACTICE BOOK p. 57

PHONICS: *s*-BLENDS

OBJECTIVE
- Children review *s*-Blends.

MATERIALS
- **Anthology,** pp. 86–109
- **Practice Book,** p. 58

SUGGESTED GROUPING
- Small groups or partners

SKILLS TRACE

s-Blends **TESTED**
- **Introduce,** Unit 4, *Imagine That!*, p. T176
- **Practice,** Unit 4, *Imagine That!*, pp. T183, T214
- **Review,** p. R51
- **Reteach,** Unit 4, *Imagine That!*, p. R60

1 REVIEW

Say the words ***small, spot,*** and ***stop,*** emphasizing the sounds for the blends ***sm, sp,*** and ***st.*** Repeat the words and have children say them with you, blending and isolating the beginning sounds.

Write the following words on the chalkboard, and read them with children.

smart	**start**	**spin**
spell	**stay**	**smile**

Explain that the two letters at the beginning of each word are blended together to make the sounds heard at the beginning of the word. Have volunteers underline the letters in each word that form the consonant blends. Encourage children to say each word again slowly, emphasizing the initial ***s***-blend.

2 PRACTICE/APPLY

PUT IT IN CONTEXT Have a volunteer read aloud page 89. Ask children to say the word that begins with ***sm, sp,*** or ***st.*** (*stories*) Then have partners cut out three slips of colored paper, writing one of the *s*-blends on each slip. Prepare pieces of paper with word endings such as ***-ell, -ile, -oke, -ay, -all, -ill, -ack.*** Have children choose a beginning blend and match it to an appropriate ending. If two or three words are possible, have children place both endings next to the blend. Encourage children to keep track of how many words they can make. Then have children use some of the completed words as responses to riddles that they create. For example, "You do this when you are happy." *(smile)*

3 ASSESS

DID CHILDREN:

✔ recognize the consonant blends ***sm, sp,*** and ***st***?

✔ read words with ***sm, sp,*** and ***st***?

IF NOT, TRY THIS:

Have children look through the unit trade books to identify other words with *s*-blends.

CHILDREN'S SELF-ASSESSMENT:

✔ Did I recognize and read the letter combinations ***sm, sp,*** and ***st*** in words?

For additional support, see **Practice Book page 58.**

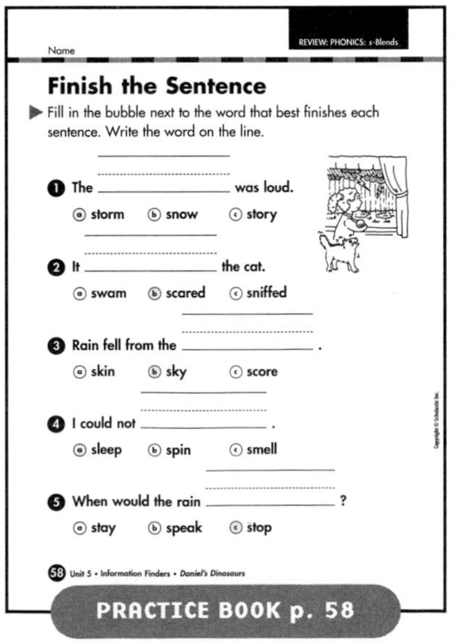
Name

REVIEW: PHONICS: s-Blends

Finish the Sentence

▶ Fill in the bubble next to the word that best finishes each sentence. Write the word on the line.

1. The ______________ was loud.
   ⓐ storm ⓑ snow ⓒ story
2. It ______________ the cat.
   ⓐ swam ⓑ scared ⓒ sniffed
3. Rain fell from the ______________ .
   ⓐ skin ⓑ sky ⓒ score
4. I could not ______________ .
   ⓐ sleep ⓑ spin ⓒ smell
5. When would the rain ______________ ?
   ⓐ stay ⓑ speak ⓒ stop

58 Unit 5 • Information Finders • *Daniel's Dinosaurs*

Copyright © Scholastic Inc.

PRACTICE BOOK p. 58

INFLECTIONAL ENDING *-ed* /d/, /t/

OBJECTIVE
- Children review inflectional ending *-ed* /d/, /t/.

MATERIALS
- Practice Book, p. 59

SUGGESTED GROUPING
- Small group or individuals

SKILLS TRACE

Inflectional Ending *-ed* /d/, /t/. TESTED
- Introduce, p. T164
- Practice, pp. T153, T171
- Review, p. R52
- Reteach, p. R59

1 REVIEW

Say the words ***asked, locked,*** and ***raced,*** stressing the final sound **/t/.** Repeat the words and have children say them after you. Ask children to listen for the final consonant sound in each word. Repeat with the words ***yelled, smelled,*** and ***bored,*** stressing the final consonant sound **/d/.**

Write the words on the chalkboard, grouping them according to the final consonant sound. Say the words with children again and have volunteers underline the letters ***-ed*** at the end of each word. Help children notice that the letters ***-ed*** can stand for the sound **/t/** as in ***asked*** or **/d/** as in ***yelled.***

ask<u>ed</u>	**lock<u>ed</u>**	**rac<u>ed</u>**
yell<u>ed</u>	**smell<u>ed</u>**	**bor<u>ed</u>**

2 PRACTICE/APPLY

PUT IT IN CONTEXT Read aloud page 87. Ask children to clap when they hear a word that ends with **/t/** or **/d/.** (*loved*) Then have children write the letters ***t*** and ***d*** on index cards. Write the words ***love, live, pass, bark, turn, stay, watch,*** and ***look*** on the chalkboard. Have children take turns adding the ending ***-ed*** to each word. Then read the new words with children. Have them hold up their ***t*** card if the word ends with the sound **/t/.** Have them hold up their ***d*** card if it ends with the sound **/d/.**

Have children use each new word in a sentence about the story *Daniel's Dinosaurs,* for example:

Daniel <u>loved</u> dinosaurs.
Two dinosaurs <u>lived</u> next door.

3 ASSESS

DID CHILDREN:

✔ identify words that end in **/t/** and **/d/**?

✔ connect the sounds with the letters ***-ed***?

✔ add ***-ed*** to words to make new words?

IF NOT, TRY THIS:

See the **Reteach** lesson on **page R59.**

CHILDREN'S SELF-ASSESSMENT:

✔ Did I identify ***-ed*** words that end in **/t/** or **/d/**?

✔ Did I add the letters ***-ed*** to the end of words to make new words?

For additional support, see **Practice Book page 59.**

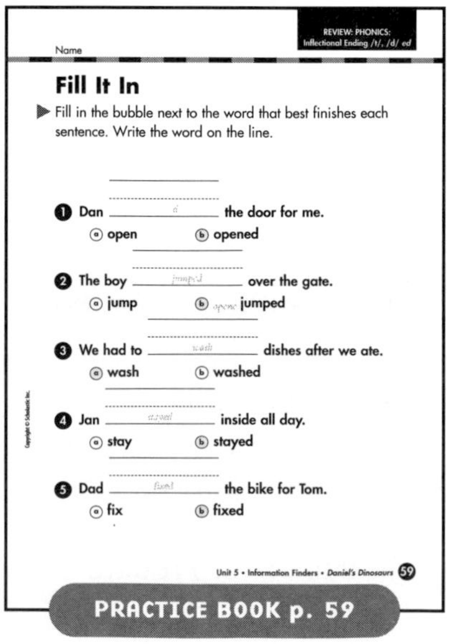
Name
REVIEW: PHONICS: Inflectional Ending /t/, /d/ -ed

Fill It In

▶ Fill in the bubble next to the word that best finishes each sentence. Write the word on the line.

1. Dan ______ the door for me. ⓐ open ⓑ opened
2. The boy ______ over the gate. ⓐ jump ⓑ jumped
3. We had to ______ dishes after we ate. ⓐ wash ⓑ washed
4. Jan ______ inside all day. ⓐ stay ⓑ stayed
5. Dad ______ the bike for Tom. ⓐ fix ⓑ fixed

Unit 5 • Information Finders • Daniel's Dinosaurs 59

PRACTICE BOOK p. 59

STUDY SKILLS: GRAPHIC AIDS: DIAGRAMS

OBJECTIVE

- Children review their use of diagrams to acquire information.

MATERIALS

- **Workshops 1, 2**
- **Practice Book**, p. 44

SUGGESTED GROUPING

- **Partners**

SKILLS TRACE

Diagrams TESTED

- **Introduce**, p. T124
- **Practice**, p. T125
- **Review**, p. R53
- **Reteach**, p. R62

1 REVIEW

Remind children that they have been working on their projects and workshops. Have them take a moment to review the diagrams they created when they made their observation logs. Have them tell what diagrams are and when they might be most useful. Encourage them to note that in addition to pictures, diagrams often include words in the form of labels. Talk about other diagrams children have made or seen and why they are useful.

2 PRACTICE/APPLY

PUT IT IN CONTEXT Have children review their Big Book of Information. Ask: *Did anyone make a diagram?* Encourage children to work with partners to look at each other's Big Book of Information. If they've included diagrams, have their partners tell them what information they are able to find and what may not be clear. If children haven't included diagrams, have them work with their partners to determine a good place for one, and figure out what kinds of information it could show.

Ask partners to make new diagrams or revise the ones already made for the Big Book of Information. Have partners share and discuss their diagrams. Ask: *If you had to teach others how to make diagrams, what would you say? What if you had to teach others how to read diagrams?*

3 ASSESS

DID CHILDREN:

✔ read and understand diagrams?

✔ make a diagram that clearly shows information, using pictures and labels?

IF NOT, TRY THIS:

See the **Reteach** lesson on **page R62.**

CHILDREN'S SELF-ASSESSMENT:

✔ Did I understand the information presented in the diagrams?

For additional support, see **Practice Book page 44.**

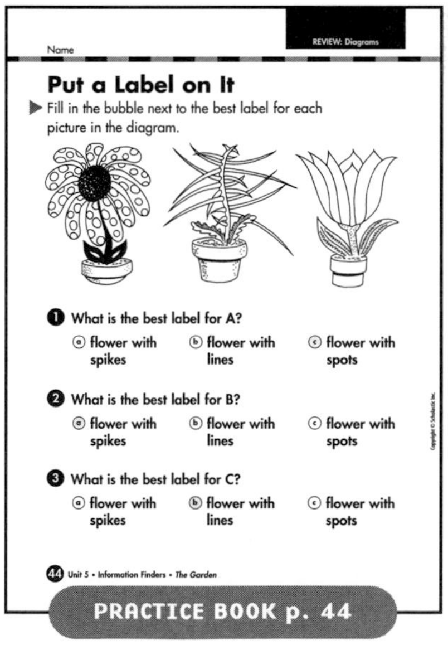
Name REVIEW: Diagrams

Put a Label on It

Fill in the bubble next to the best label for each picture in the diagram.

1. What is the best label for A?
   - (a) flower with spikes (b) flower with lines (c) flower with spots
2. What is the best label for B?
   - (a) flower with spikes (b) flower with lines (c) flower with spots
3. What is the best label for C?
   - (a) flower with spikes (b) flower with lines (c) flower with spots

Copyright © Scholastic Inc.

44 Unit 5 • Information Finders • *The Garden*

PRACTICE BOOK p. 44

Study Skills: Follow Directions

OBJECTIVE

- Children review how to follow directions for a task.

MATERIALS

- Workshop 2
- Chart paper
- Practice Book, p. 60

SUGGESTED GROUPING

- Partners or small groups

SKILLS TRACE

Follow Directions TESTED

- Introduce, p. T172
- Practice, p. T173
- Review, p. R54
- Reteach, p. R62

1 REVIEW

Ask children to recall what they learned about making a nature poster in Workshop 2. Have the class list directions for making the poster. Write the directions on chart paper, for example:

1. **Choose an environment, or a place in nature that you like.**
2. **Make a list of all the plants and animals that live there.**
3. **Imagine the plants and animals in a picture together.**
4. **Draw your nature poster.**

Talk with children about why it is important to follow directions when doing tasks such as creating posters. Ask them what would happen if the directions were not followed in order. Ask, for example: *What would happen if you tried to do Step 4 before doing Step 1?*

2 PRACTICE/APPLY

PUT IT IN CONTEXT Encourage partners to pretend that it is their job to teach kindergartners how to make a poster about their school. Ask: *What directions would you give these younger children? What tips could you give them about actually drawing the poster?*

Have partners work together to write a list of directions for the kindergarten children. Encourage them to use the directions you wrote on chart paper as a model. Then have partners trade directions with other pairs of children. Encourage them to read each other's directions and give suggestions for improvements.

3 ASSESS

DID CHILDREN:

✔ tell why it is important to follow directions in order?

✔ create concise, orderly directions?

IF NOT, TRY THIS:

See the **Reteach** lesson on **page R62.**

CHILDREN'S SELF-ASSESSMENT:

✔ Did I know why it is important to follow directions?

✔ Did I know what might happen if directions aren't followed in order?

✔ Did I write orderly directions?

For additional support, see **Practice Book page 60.**

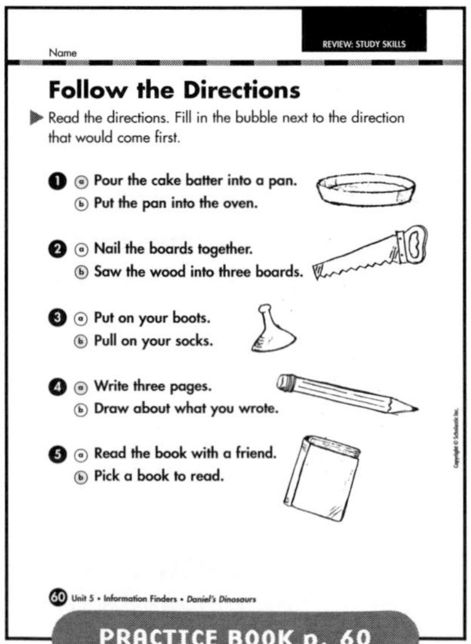
Name

REVIEW: STUDY SKILLS

Follow the Directions

Read the directions. Fill in the bubble next to the direction that would come first.

1. ⓐ Pour the cake batter into a pan. ⓑ Put the pan into the oven.
2. ⓐ Nail the boards together. ⓑ Saw the wood into three boards.
3. ⓐ Put on your boots. ⓑ Pull on your socks.
4. ⓐ Write three pages. ⓑ Draw about what you wrote.
5. ⓐ Read the book with a friend. ⓑ Pick a book to read.

60 Unit 5 • Information Finders • Daniel's Dinosaurs

PRACTICE BOOK p. 60

AIN IDEA/DETAILS

1 CONSTRUCT

Explain to children that they use the strategy of looking for the main idea when they look at billboards, watch commercials, and especially when they read a new book.

Imagine yourself outside a movie theater. There are pictures showing scenes from each movie. What can you find out about the movies by looking at the posters?

2 CONNECT

When you looked at the pictures outside the theater, they gave you some information about each movie. What kinds of details can be found on the posters? How does this information help you better understand the main idea of the poster? When you read, you can use word and picture details to give you more information about the main idea of the story.

This would be an excellent opportunity to read with children, looking for word and picture clues to support the main idea. The unit trade books are a wonderful resource for your class.

3 CONFIRM

When would you use the strategy of looking for the main idea and supporting details? How would you explain the strategy to someone?

When might it help you to look for details in words and pictures to get more information about a main idea?

SEQUENCE

1 CONSTRUCT

Imagine explaining what you do to get ready to go to school. How many steps does it take? Is the order, or sequence, almost the same each day? What are some words that help you remember the order in which things happen?

2 CONNECT

The order in which things happen is called sequence. Remembering the sequence of events in a story can help you understand and remember what you read.

Now would be a good time to read with children, working together to recognize the sequence of events. The unit trade books can provide a wonderful opportunity for reading.

3 CONFIRM

How would you explain to a friend the importance of following a sequence?

When does noticing the order, or steps involved, help you do things?

Setting

① CONSTRUCT

Suppose you wake up one Tuesday morning and it's a hot, sticky day. Your parents say, "Let's take a trip to the park! There's a lake there—we can go swimming. Afterward, we can have a picnic." What time of year is it? What clothes would you bring?

② CONNECT

Knowing the time and place in this situation is very important. It helps you know what to wear and what activities to plan. In the same way, knowing the time and place—the setting—of a story is important when you read because it helps you better understand the story.

This would be an excellent time to read with children, identifying the setting and how it affects the story. You might use the unit trade books for further reading.

③ CONFIRM

How would you explain the strategy of setting to someone? Why is it important to the enjoyment of a story?

Why does it help to know the setting for something you're going to do?

Compare/Contrast

① CONSTRUCT

Imagine that you decide to wear a purple T-shirt to school. You put on a new pair of jeans to go with it and then put your feet into your old white basketball shoes. When you walk into the classroom, you notice that your friend is also wearing a purple T-shirt with a pair of jeans. But his jeans are old and faded. He is also wearing a pair of basketball shoes, but his are red and black. A classmate walks in and sees the two of you. "Wow!" he says. "You two are dressed just alike!" Are you? How are your clothes the same? How are they different?

② CONNECT

When you decided how your clothes and your friend's clothes were alike, you compared them. When you decided how they were different, you contrasted them. You can also compare and contrast things when you read. This helps you better understand people, places, feelings, and events in a story.

Now would be a good time to read with children, comparing and contrasting people, places, feelings, and events. The unit trade books provide many opportunities to practice this skill with children.

③ CONFIRM

How would you explain to someone the difference between comparing and contrasting? How is this strategy helpful? When have you used it?

DIGRAPHS /sh/ *sh*, /th/ *th*

1 CONSTRUCT

Write the words ***she*** and ***wish*** on the chalkboard. Read the words aloud, emphasizing the consonant digraph ***sh.*** Ask children to repeat the words after you. Have them practice saying the sound by putting a finger to their lips and saying **/sh/.** Say words such as the following and ask children to say **/sh/** each time they hear the consonant digraph **/sh/*: shell, sell, keep, sheep, shoe, fish, stale, push.***

Repeat for consonant digraph ***th,*** asking children to give a "thumbs up" sign each time they hear a word with the **/th/** sound. Use words such as ***thumb, think, tell, bath, cat, with, thimble, down.***

2 CONNECT

Give children two blank index cards. Ask them to write ***sh*** on one card and ***th*** on the other. Say words that have either the **/sh/** or **/th/** sound. Ask children to hold up the card to show which sound they hear.

3 CONFIRM

Ask children to number a sheet of paper from 1 to 10. Say ten words with **/sh/** or **/th/** at the beginning or end. Have children write either ***sh*** or ***th*** to indicate which sound they hear in each word. Allow enough time for children to write their responses. Then have partners compare their answers.

HOMOPHONES

1 CONSTRUCT

Once an old sailor found a strange note in a bottle. It said, "My aunts raise ants in their basement. My cousin will only sail when there's a sale at the hardware store. I just sit around and try not to tie a knot in my fishing line!" The sailor had no idea what the words meant. Can you help figure them out?

On the chalkboard, write the homophones *aunts, ants; sail, sale;* and *not, knot.* Write the three sentences from the introductory paragraph below the words. Leave blanks for the homophones. Have children fill in the blanks with the correct homophones.

2 CONNECT

The two words in each sentence that sound alike but have different spellings and meanings are called homophones. Knowing about homophones will help keep you from getting confused when you read or listen to stories.

Now would be an excellent time for children to look for other homophones in reading selections. The trade books provide excellent reading materials for this task.

3 CONFIRM

Suppose a friend said, "I just don't understand homophones! Can you help me?" What would you say?

When have you used homophones in conversations with friends?

Words With /ô/a, aw

❶ CONSTRUCT

Have children listen carefully as you say the words ***call, all, draw, talk,*** and ***saw.*** Elongate the vowel sound as you say each word. Ask children what sound these words have in common. Guide them to recognize that all the words have the vowel sound **/ô/** as in ***saw.*** Then have children pretend to saw a piece of wood each time they hear a word with the vowel sound **/ô/**. Say words such as: ***law, jaw, sail, awe, thaw, fall, gate, hall, walk, mall, back, small.***

❷ CONNECT

Write **/ô/** words on index cards. Use the words listed above. Read the cards with children and help them recognize that the letters ***a*** and ***aw*** can stand for the vowel sound **/ô/**. Have children work in pairs. Ask them to group the words according to how the sound **/ô/** is spelled. Have them read aloud the words in each group.

❸ CONFIRM

Give children cards on which you have written the phonograms ***-all, -alk,*** and ***-aw.*** Ask partners to add initial sounds to the phonograms to make new words. Encourage children to write the new words they form and read them aloud in class.

Vowel /ā/ay, ai

❶ CONSTRUCT

Say the words ***may*** and ***mail,*** elongating the vowel sound in each word. Have children raise their hand each time they hear **/ā/**. Words include: ***hay, hot, say, pail, pat, wait, gray, tray, day, stand, gain, bait, hail.***

❷ CONNECT

Write the long ***a*** words from Construct on the chalkboard. You may want to use the words listed above. Read the words with children and help them recognize that the letters ***ay*** and ***ai*** can stand for the long ***a*** sound. Then give children two blank index cards. Ask them to write ***ay*** on one card and ***ai*** on the other. Write several sentences with long ***a*** words, spelled ***ay*** or ***ai.*** Read the sentences and have children hold up the appropriate card when they hear a word with the long ***a*** sound.

❸ CONFIRM

Give children strips of construction paper. Have them write words with the long ***a*** sound on the strips. Explain that the words should be spelled with either the letters ***ay*** or ***ai.*** Then show children how to make a chain with the word strips. Help them link the strips together and glue them so that the words show on the outside of the links. Display the chain on a classroom wall.

Vowel /ō/oa

❶ CONSTRUCT

Have children listen as you say the words ***oat, boat,*** and ***throat,*** elongating the long ***o*** vowel sound as you say each word. Then ask children to point to their throat each time they hear **/ō/**. Say words such as: ***oak, boot, toast, goat, foam, cow, coach, top, coat, soap, down, road.***

❷ CONNECT

Write the words ***oat, boat,*** and ***throat*** on the chalkboard, and underline the letters ***oa*** in each word. Help children see that the letters ***oa*** can stand for the long ***o*** sound. Then have children write the letters ***oa*** on an index card. Recite the long ***o*** words, and have children hold up their card whenever they hear a word with the long ***o*** sound.

❸ CONFIRM

Ask children to draw a large boat on paper. Then have them write words in the boat that have **/ō/**—the same vowel sound as the word ***boat.*** Encourage children to read aloud the words they wrote. Point out those that contain the ***oa*** spelling for **/ō/.**

Inflectional Ending *-ed* /d/, /t/

❶ CONSTRUCT

Recite the words ***looked, hopped,*** and ***locked,*** emphasizing the final consonant sound. Ask children what the words have in common. Help children recognize that all the words end with the sound **/t/.** Repeat with the words ***scared, played,*** and ***smelled,*** emphasizing the final sound **/d/.** Then say ***asked, bored, hatched,*** and ***yelled.*** Have children repeat each word and tell if it ends with the sound **/t/** or **/d/.**

❷ CONNECT

Write all the target words on the chalkboard. Then give children blank index cards. Have them write the letter ***t*** on one card and the letter ***d*** on the other. Read the words on the chalkboard with children. Have them hold up their ***t*** card if a word ends with the sound **/t/.** Have them hold up their ***d*** card if a word ends with the sound **/d/.**

❸ CONFIRM

On chart paper, write a list of verbs that can take the inflectional ending ***-ed.*** Read the words with children. Then have them copy each word, add the letters ***ed*** to the end of the word, and read aloud the new word they made. Have children identify whether each new word ends with the sound **/t/** or **/d/.**

VOWEL /ē/y, ey

1 CONSTRUCT

Ask children to listen carefully as you say the words ***many, very, key,*** and ***honey*** slowly, elongating the final vowel sound. Ask what sound the words have in common. Help children recognize that all the words end with **/ē/**—the long ***e*** sound. Then have children pretend to turn a key in a lock each time they hear a word that ends with **/ē/** as in ***key.*** Say words such as: ***baby, any, my, money, pretty, only, play, monkey, funny, early, ball, donkey.***

2 CONNECT

Write the words ***many*** and ***key*** on the chalkboard. Underline the letter ***y*** in ***many*** and the letters ***ey*** in ***key.*** Help children notice that the letters ***y*** and ***ey*** can stand for **/ē/.** Then write the long ***e*** words on index cards. You may want to use the target words listed above. Have children work in cooperative groups to sort the words according to how the long ***e*** sound is spelled. Suggest that children underline the letters that stand for the long ***e*** sound in each word before they sort the cards.

3 CONFIRM

Have children pick a card from each group of words that they sorted and use each word in a sentence. Then ask children to name two other words that end with the long ***e*** sound spelled ***y*** or ***ey.***

PLURALS

1 CONSTRUCT

You and your friend are getting off the bus after a trip to the city library. Each of you checked out a book. Suddenly you both realize that you don't have your books. You go back to the bus together, hoping that both books are still there. As you step outside, you hear the teacher calling, "Whose books are these?" Do you think you will find your book? Do you think your friend will find his book? What makes you think so?

2 CONNECT

When you heard the teacher ask whose books these were, you breathed a sigh of relief. When you heard /s/ at the end of the naming word *book,* it signaled that the word was naming more than one book. When you read, you'll often notice an *s* on the end of a naming word. That often means the naming word is plural. It is naming more than one thing.

This would be a good time to read with children and identify other plurals as you read. The unit trade books provide a rich variety of additional reading opportunities.

3 CONFIRM

How do you change a naming word if you want it to name more than one thing?

Vowel /ō/o, ow

① CONSTRUCT

Have children repeat the following words after you, elongating the long vowel sound /ō/ in each word: ***over, go,*** and ***low.*** Then have children put their hands over their head when they hear words with **/ō/.** Recite words such as: ***open, mop, zero, throw, row, town, hello, so, drop, know, crow.***

② CONNECT

Write the words ***go*** and ***low*** on the chalkboard. Underline the letter ***o*** in ***go*** and the letters ***ow*** in ***low.*** Guide children to understand that the letters ***o*** and ***ow*** can stand for /ō/—the long ***o*** sound. Then show children how to make an ***o*** with one hand and a ***w*** with three fingers of the other hand. Write the long ***o*** words on the chalkboard. You might want to use the target words listed above. Read the words with children, and have them use their fingers to make the letter or letters that stand for the long ***o*** sound in each word.

③ CONFIRM

On index cards, write words with long ***o*** spelled ***o*** or ***ow.*** Have children sort the cards into two piles: words in which the letter ***o*** stands for the long ***o*** sound, and words in which the letters ***ow*** stand for long ***o.*** Have children read aloud the words in each pile.

r-Controlled Vowel /är/ar

① CONSTRUCT

Recite the following words and have children repeat them after you: ***arm, car, dark.*** Ask children what sounds are the same in all the words. Help them isolate the *r*-controlled vowel sounds **/är/.** Then say words such as the following, and have children point to their arm when they hear a word that has the /är/ sounds: ***card, mat, far, yard, yawn, art, jar, star, late, farm, hard.***

② CONNECT

Write the words ***arm, car,*** and ***dark*** on the chalkboard, and have volunteers draw a line under the letters ***ar*** in each word. Guide children to see that the letters ***ar*** stand for the sounds /är/ in the words. Then have children write the letters ***ar*** on an index card. Recite the target words listed above, and have children hold up the card whenever they hear a word with the sounds **/är/.**

③ CONFIRM

Play "Start Your Cars" with children. Write the words on index cards. Give each child two or three cards. Have children pretend to drive their cars up to a "gas station" (your desk). In order to get gas and start their cars again, children must give you a card with a word that has the sounds **/är/.** If children are out of /är/ cards, they must name a word that has the /är/ sounds as in ***car*** and ***start.***

Graphic Aids: Diagrams

❶ CONSTRUCT

You just got a new set of blocks of many sizes and shapes. You want to build a beautiful tower just like the one shown on the box that the blocks came in, but you can't because the picture is all one color and it's hard to see each separate block. Then inside the box, you find a drawing of the tower that labels the blocks and shows where each one fits. How can the drawing help you?

❷ CONNECT

The picture you used to make the tower is called a diagram. Diagrams can show how something works or how it is made. They are good for showing how different parts of something fit together and what each part does. Diagrams in books can help you picture what you're reading about.

Now would be a good time to read with children, looking at diagrams together. Nonfiction books can be a helpful resource for you.

❸ CONFIRM

How would you convince a toy company to add a diagram to their instructions? Why should they do it? How would a diagram be helpful?

Follow Directions

❶ CONSTRUCT

Suppose you're walking to school. You see a sign that says, "Don't Walk." A little later, you pass a pond and notice a sign that says, "No Swimming—Danger!" What directions are these signs giving you? Why is it important to follow these directions?

❷ CONNECT

When you explain what each sign was telling you to do or not to do, you were using important skills: understanding signs and following directions. Signs show up in lots of places: on the street, in schools and libraries, at movie theaters, even at baseball stadiums! Knowing how to read signs and follow directions means that you can find things more easily and that you'll be safer.

Now would be a good time to read with children, looking for examples of signs and directions. The trade books can assist you in this activity.

❸ CONFIRM

If a friend didn't want to follow the directions on any signs, what would you tell your friend?

Name some times when you were glad that you followed directions.

WORD ORDER

RETEACH

The words in a sentence are in order. The order of the words makes sense.

PRACTICE

Write a sentence for each group of words. Begin each sentence with a capital letter. End each sentence with a period.

1. **the boy fish likes**

   ____

2. **fish in a bowl he keeps**

   ____

3. **watches sharks at the aquarium he**

   ____

4. **draws pictures fish of the boy**

   ____

5. **writes a story he about fish**

   ____

CAPITALIZING THE WORD *I*

RETEACH

Always write the word *I* as a capital letter.

PRACTICE

Write the word *I* to complete each sentence.

1. **Mom and _____ plant flowers.**
2. **_____ like flowers that are yellow.**
3. **_____ put the seeds in the ground.**
4. **My sister and _____ water the flowers.**
5. **Mom, Sis, and _____ will pick the flowers when they bloom.**

Homophones

RETEACH

Homophones are words that sound alike but have different spellings and different meanings. Words such as *to, two,* and *too* are homophones.

PRACTICE

Think about the meaning of the homophones. Choose the homophone that best completes each sentence.

1. Mom took me _____ the library. (to, two)

2. Mom and _____ got new library cards. (eye, I)

3. We looked _____ books to read. (four, for)

4. I _____ where to find children's books. (know, no)

5. Mom sees me sitting _____. (their, there)

Verbs: Past Tense

RETEACH

Action words are called verbs. Some verbs describe actions that happen now. Some verbs describe actions that have happened in the past. The ending *-ed* is often added to verbs to show that the action has already happened.

PRACTICE

Add *-ed* to each verb to make it tell about the past. Write the word in the sentence.

1. I _____ my grandmother last summer. (visit)

2. Grandmother and I _____ doing many things together. (enjoy)

3. One day we _____ to a neighbor's farm. (walk)

4. We _____ the neighbor milk his cows. (watch)

5. Then we _____ in the shade of an old oak tree. (rest)

Words That Compare

RETEACH

You can use adjectives to compare one or more people, places, or things. Add *-er* to adjectives to compare two people, places, or things. Add *-est* to compare more than two people, places, or things.

PRACTICE

Add *-er* or *-est* to compare the people, places, or things.

1. **Our city aquarium is the larg_____ in the state.**
2. **The tortoise is the old_____ animal in the aquarium.**
3. **The stingrays are small_____ than the sharks.**
4. **I stayed at the aquarium long_____ than my friend.**
5. **The little fish swam in the warm_____ water of all.**

Compound Words

❶ CONSTRUCT

Give each child an index card with a word on it that could be part of a compound word, for example: ***ball, base, foot, sun, print, hand,*** and ***light.***

Read the word on your card. Then hold the card so everyone can see it. Read the words on the other cards. Try to make a new word by putting your word together with a partner's word. What new word did you make? What is the meaning of the compound word?

❷ CONNECT

You just showed how a compound word is made up of two smaller words. If you don't know the meaning of a compound word that you read, you can try to figure it out. First look for the smaller words that make up the compound word. Then think about the meaning of each word.

Now would be a good time to look for compound words as you read with children. The trade books provide wonderful resources for additional reading.

❸ CONFIRM

How does knowing about compound words help you figure out unfamiliar words?

How might recognizing compound words help you figure out their meaning?

Name

WEEK 1

fish	waves
mouth	nose
eyes	fins

Teacher Note: The words above are story words. You may use the blank cards to add additional words.

Name

WEEK 1

more	belongs

Teacher Note: The words above are high-frequency words.
You may use the blank cards to add additional words.

Name

WEEK 2

munch	wait
grow	wet
dry	straw

Teacher Note: The words above are story words. You may use the blank cards to add additional words.

Name

WEEK 2

next	all

Teacher Note: The words above are high-frequency words. You may use the blank cards to add additional words.

Name

WEEK 3

frog	work
garden	plant
flower	seeds

Teacher Note: The words above are story words. You may use the blank cards to add additional words.

Name

WEEK 3

was	grow

Teacher Note: The words above are high-frequency words. You may use the blank cards to add additional words.

Name

WEEK 4

library	supermarket
city	office
teacher	shark

Teacher Note: The words above are story words. You may use the blank cards to add additional words.

Name

WEEK 4

school	their

Teacher Note: The words above are high-frequency words. You may use the blank cards to add additional words.

Name

WEEK 5

desert	butterfly
forest	fruits
leaves	trees

Teacher Note: The words above are story words. You may use the blank cards to add additional words.

Name

TEACHER RESOURCES

WEEK 5

mother

girl

Teacher Note: The words above are high-frequency words.
You may use the blank cards to add additional words.

Name

A	B	C	D
E	F	G	H
I	J	K	L
M	N	O	P

Name

Q	R	S	T
U	V	W	X
Y	Z	a	e
i	o	u	CAPITAL LETTERS

Name

a	b	c	d
e	f	g	h
i	j	k	l
m	n	o	p

Name

q	r	s	t
u	v	w	x
y	z	a	e
i	o	u	small letters

Name

WHAT DO YOU HEAR?

Name

TEACHER RESOURCES

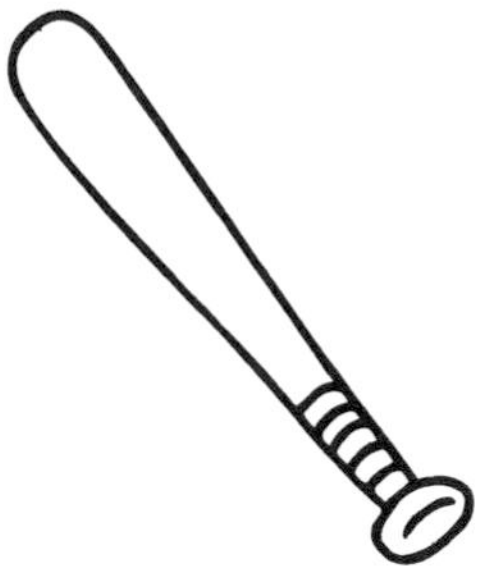

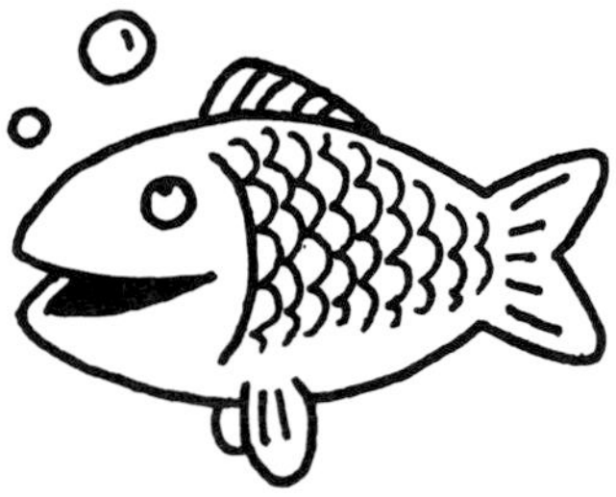

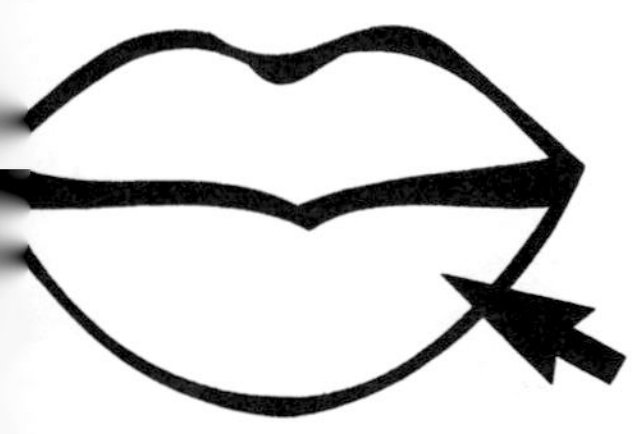

Teacher Note: The above picture cards are: bat, bee, bus, cat, coat, cup, dog, duck, fan, fish, fox, leaf, lip, log, man, moon.

Name

Teacher Note: The above picture cards are: mop, nest, nose, nut, pan, pen, pig, ring, rock, run, six, sock, sun, ten, tie, top.

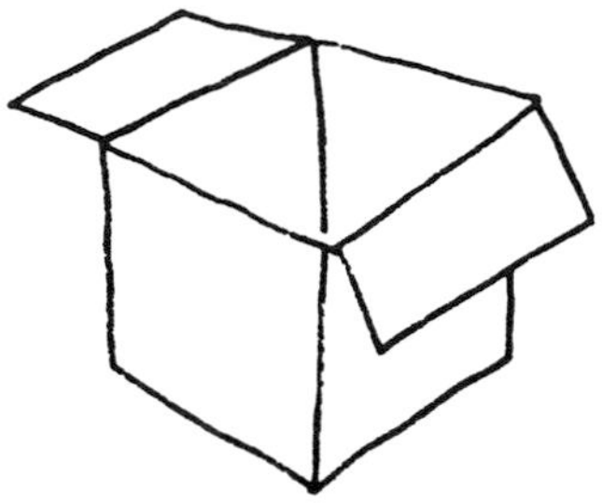
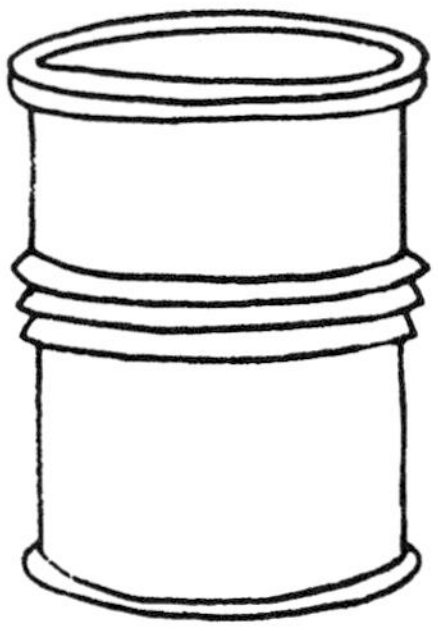

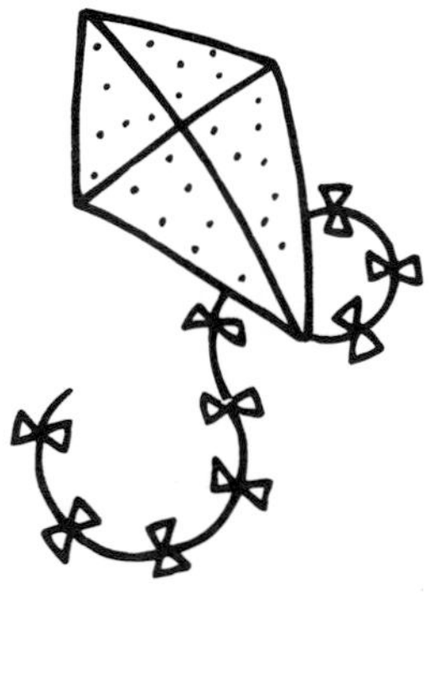
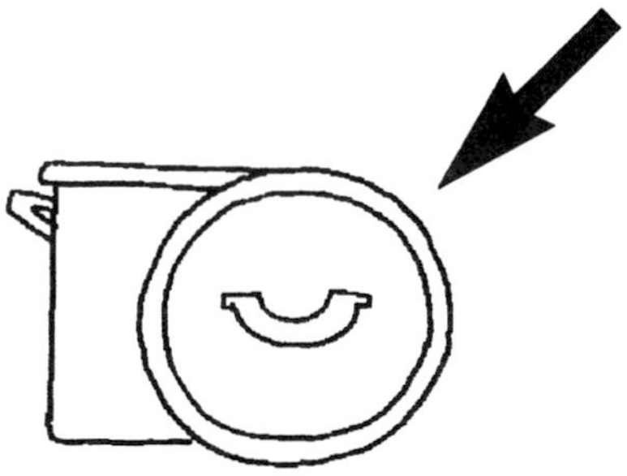

Teacher Note: The above picture cards are: bike, boat, box, can, cube, five, game, goat, hat, house, jump, key, king, kite, lid, light.

Name

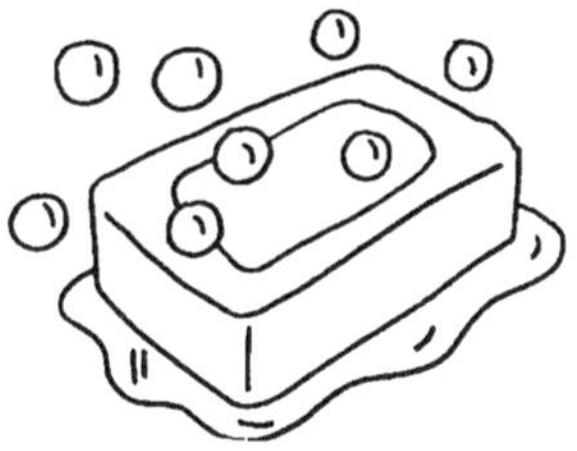

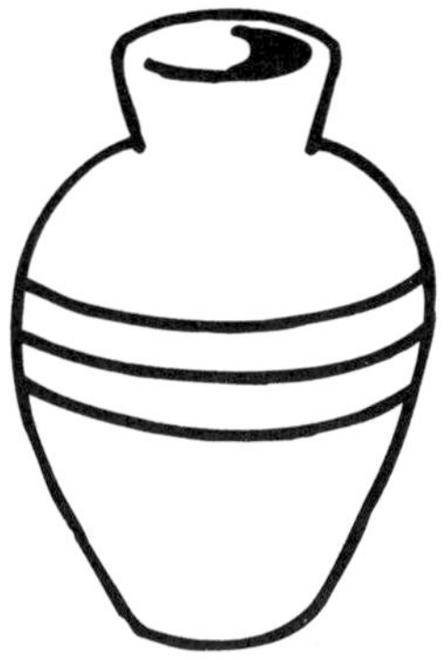

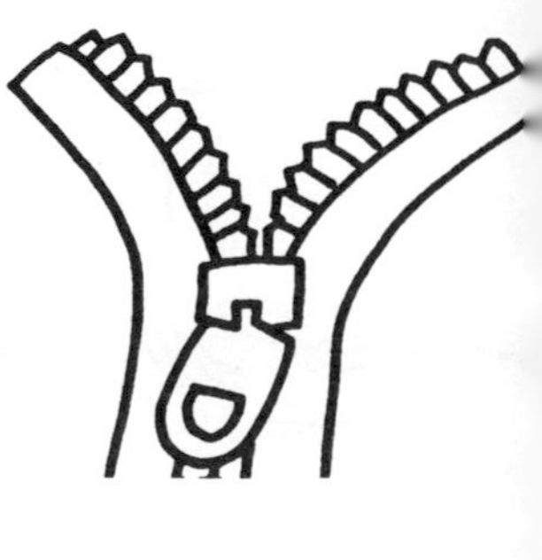

Teacher Note: The above picture cards are: map, mice, nail, net, rain, rake, rose, sit, soap, turtle, vase, vest, web, wig, yarn, zipper.

Phonics Scope and Sequence

		Student Name										
UNIT 1												
Kindergarten Transition												
WEEK 1	Phonograms *-at, -an*											
	Review Consonants in Initial Position											
WEEK 2	Phonograms *-ot, -op*											
	Review Consonants in Initial Position											
Beginning with week 3, all consonants are taught in initial, medial, and final positions.												
WEEK 3	Consonant /m/*m*											
	Vowel /a/*a*											
WEEK 4	Consonant /l/*l*											
	Consonant /t/*t*											
WEEK 5	Consonant /s/*s*											
	Vowel /o/*o*											
UNIT 2												
WEEK 1	Consonant /h/*h*											
	Vowel /i/*i*											
WEEK 2	Consonant /p/*p*											
	Consonant /f/*f*											
	Consonant /n/*n*											
WEEK 3	Consonant /k/*c*											
	Consonant /b/*b*											
WEEK 4	Consonant /w/*w*											
	Consonant /j/*j*											
	Consonant /z/*z*											
WEEK 5	Consonant /d/*d*											
	Consonant /r/*r*											
UNIT 3												
WEEK 1	Vowel /e/*e*											
	Consonant /g/*g*											
	Consonant /ks/*x*											
WEEK 2	Consonant /k/*k, ck*											
	Vowel /u/*u*											
WEEK 3	Digraph /th/*th*											
	Consonant /z/*s*											
	Consonant /y/*y*											
WEEK 4	Consonant /v/*v*											
	Consonant /kw/*qu*											
WEEK 5	Digraph /sh/*sh*											
	Mid-Year Review											

		Student Name										
UNIT 4												
WEEK 1	Final *e* (*a-e*)											
	Inflectional Ending *-ing*											
WEEK 2	Final *e* (*e-e, i-e, o-e, u-e*)											
	Vowel /ē/*ea, ee*											
WEEK 3	*l*-Blends											
	r-Blends											
WEEK 4	*s*-Blends											
	Digraph /ch/*ch*											
	Digraph /hw/*wh*											
WEEK 5	Contractions											
	Plurals											
UNIT 5												
WEEK 1	Homophones											
WEEK 2	Words With /ô/*a, aw*											
	Vowel /ā/*ai, ay*											
WEEK 3	Vowel /ō/*oa*											
	Inflectional Ending *-ed* /t/, /d/											
WEEK 4	Vowel /ē/*ey, y*											
	Compound Words											
WEEK 5	Vowel /ō/*o, ow*											
	r-Controlled Vowel /är/*ar*											
UNIT 6												
WEEK 1	Inflectional Ending *-ed* /ed/, /t/, /d/											
	Vowel /ī/*-ild, -ind*											
WEEK 2	Diphthong /ou/*ou, ow*											
WEEK 3	Vowel /ī/*igh, y*											
WEEK 4	*r*-Controlled Vowel /ûr/*ir*											
	r-Controlled Vowel /ôr/*or*											
	Words With /o͞o/*oo*, /o͝o/*oo*											
WEEK 5	*r*-Controlled Vowel /ûr/*er, ur*											

Grade	K	1	2	3	4	5
Reading						
Print Awareness						
recognize that print messages represent spoken language and convey meaning	•	•				
knows print moves left-right, top-bottom	•	•				
understands that written words are separated by spaces	•	•				
know the difference between individual letters and words	•	•				
know the difference between capital and lower-case letters	•	•				
know the order of the alphabet	•	•				
recognize conventions of capitalization and punctuation	•	•				
understand that spoken words are represented in written language by specific sequences of letters	•	•				
recognize parts of a book	•	•	•	•	•	•
recognize that there are correct spellings	•	•	•	•	•	•
recognize distinguishing features of paragraphs			•	•	•	•
Phonological Awareness						
divide sentences into individual words	•	•	•			
identify, segment, and combine syllables	•	•	•	•		
produce and distinguish rhyming words from non-rhyming	•	•	•	•		
identify and isolate initial and final sounds	•	•	•	•		
blend sounds	•	•	•	•		
segment one-syllable words into individual phonemes clearly producing beginning, medial, and final sounds	•	•	•	•		
Letter-Sound Relationships						
name and identify each letter of the alphabet	•	•				
understand that written words are composed of letters that represent sounds	•	•				
learn and apply letter-sound correspondences of:						
consonants (beginning, middle, end)	•	•	•			
short vowel sounds	•	•	•			
phonograms/word families/patterns	•	•	•			
digraphs		•	•	•	•	•
blends		•	•	•	•	•
long vowel sounds		•	•	•	•	•
diphthongs		•	•	•	•	•
variant vowels		•	•	•	•	•
blend initial letter-sounds with common vowel spelling patterns to read words	•	•	•	•		
decode by using all letter-sound correspondences within regularly spelled words	•	•	•	•	•	•
use letter-sound knowledge to read decodable texts	•	•	•	•		

Scope and Sequence

Grade	K	1	2	3	4	5
Word Identification						
decode by using all letter-sound correspondences within a word	•	•	•	•	•	•
use common spelling patterns to read words	•	•	•	•	•	•
use structural cues to recognize compounds, base words, and inflectional endings		•	•	•	•	•
use structural cues to recognize prefixes and suffixes			•	•	•	•
use root words and other structural cues to recognize derivational endings			•	•	•	•
identify multisyllabic words by using common syllable patterns			•	•	•	•
recognize high-frequency irregular words	•	•	•	•	•	•
use knowledge or syntax and context to support word identification and confirm meaning	•	•	•	•	•	•
read regular and irregular words automatically		•	•	•	•	•
locate meanings, pronunciations, and derivations of unfamiliar words using dictionaries, glossaries, and other sources		•	•	•	•	•
Fluency						
read regularly in independent-level materials		•	•	•	•	•
read regularly in instructional-level materials		•	•	•	•	•
read orally from familiar texts		•	•	•	•	•
self-select independent-level materials		•	•	•	•	•
read silently for increasing amounts of time		•	•	•	•	•
demonstrate characteristics of fluent and effective reading		•	•	•	•	•
adjust reading rate based on purpose		•	•	•	•	•
read aloud		•	•	•	•	•
Text Structures/Literary Concepts						
distinguish different forms of texts	•	•	•	•	•	•
understand simple story structure	•	•	•	•	•	•
distinguish fiction from nonfiction	•	•	•	•	•	•
distinguish fact from fantasy	•	•	•	•	•	•
distinguish among types of text	•	•	•	•	•	•
distinguish between roles of the author and illustrator	•	•	•	•	•	•
identify text as narrative or expository			•	•	•	•
compare communication in different forms	•	•	•	•	•	•
understand and identify literary terms	•	•	•	•	•	•
analyze characters	•	•	•	•	•	•
identify importance of setting	•	•	•	•	•	•
recognize and analyze story problem/plot and resolution	•	•	•	•	•	•
judge internal consistency or logic of stories and texts		•	•	•	•	•
recognize that authors organize information in specific ways		•	•	•	•	•

• = direct instruction ▒ = mastery

GRADE	K	1	2	3	4	5
identify purposes of different types of texts	•	•	•	•	•	•
recognize the distinguishing features of genres		•	•	•	•	•
describe the author's perspective or point of view			•	•	•	•
Variety of Texts						
read fiction, nonfiction, and poetry for pleasure and information	•	•	•	•	•	•
use graphs, charts, signs, captions and other informational texts to acquire information	•	•	•	•	•	•
read classic and contemporary works	•	•	•	•	•	•
read from print a variety of genres for pleasure and information	•	•	•	•	•	•
read from electronic sources a variety of genres for pleasure and information	•	•	•	•	•	•
read to accomplish various purposes		•	•	•	•	•
select varied sources, i.e., nonfiction, novels, textbooks, newspapers and magazines for information and pleasure		•	•	•	•	•
read for varied purposes, i.e., to be informed, entertained, appreciate writer's craft, and discover models for writing		•	•	•	•	•
Vocabulary Development						
discuss meanings and develop vocabulary through meaningful/concrete experiences	•	•	•	•	•	•
develop vocabulary by listening and discussing selections read aloud	•	•	•	•	•	•
identify words that name persons, places or things, and actions	•	•	•	•	•	•
use dictionaries, glossaries, technology, and context to build word meanings and confirm pronunciation		•	•	•	•	•
demonstrate knowledge of synonyms, antonyms and multiple-meaning words		•	•	•	•	•
draw on experiences to bring meanings to words in context		•	•	•	•	•
use thesaurus, synonym finder, dictionary and software to clarify meanings and usage				•	•	•
determining meanings of derivatives by applying knowledge of root words and affixes			•	•	•	•
use curricular content areas and current events to study words			•	•	•	•
Comprehension						
use prior knowledge and experiences	•	•	•	•	•	•
establish purposes for reading	•	•	•	•	•	•
retell or act out the order of events in stories	•	•	•	•	•	•
monitor own comprehension		•	•	•	•	•
draw, discuss, and describe visual and mental images		•	•	•	•	•
make and explain inferences, i.e., determining important ideas, causes and effects, making predictions, and drawing conclusions		•	•	•	•	•
identify similarities and differences in topics, characters, problems, and themes	•	•	•	•	•	•
produce summaries of text selections		•	•	•	•	•
represent text information through story maps, graphs, charts, outline, time line, or graphic organizer	•	•	•	•	•	•

Scope and Sequence

Grade	K	1	2	3	4	5
distinguish fact from opinion			•	•	•	•
practice different kinds of questions and tasks, including test-like questions		•	•	•	•	•
use cause and effect, or chronology to locate and recall information		•	•	•	•	•
determine main idea and supporting details	•	•	•	•	•	•
paraphrase and summarize text	•	•	•	•	•	•
draw inferences and support with text evidence and experience		•	•	•	•	•
find similarities and differences across texts in treatment, scope, organization		•	•	•	•	•
answer different types and levels of questions, i.e., open-ended, literal, and interpretative; multiple-choice, true-false, and short-answer	•	•	•	•	•	•
Literary Response						
listen to stories read aloud	•	•	•	•	•	•
participate actively during a read aloud of predictable and patterned selections	•	•	•	•		
respond through talk, movement, music, art, drama, and writing	•	•	•	•	•	•
describe how illustrations contribute to text	•	•	•	•	•	•
connect, compare, and contrast ideas, themes, and issues across texts	•	•	•	•	•	•
demonstrate understanding of informational texts through writing, illustrating, demonstrations	•	•	•	•	•	•
support interpretations or conclusions with examples from text		•	•	•	•	•
offer observations, make connections, react, speculate, interpret, and raise questions in response to text	•	•	•	•	•	•
interpret texts through journal writing, discussion, enactment, and media	•	•	•	•	•	•
support responses by referring to relevant aspects of the text and own experiences	•	•	•	•	•	•
Inquiry/Research						
identify and form relevant questions for research	•	•	•	•	•	•
use pictures, print, and people to gather and answer questions	•	•	•	•	•	•
draw conclusions from information gathered	•	•	•	•	•	•
locate and use important areas of the library/media center	•	•	•	•	•	•
use alphabetical order to locate information		•	•	•	•	•
recognize and use parts of a book to locate information	•	•	•	•	•	•
use multiple sources to locate information that addresses questions			•	•	•	•
interpret and use graphic sources of information, i.e., charts, graphs, and diagrams	•	•	•	•	•	•
demonstrate learning through productions and displays	•	•	•	•	•	•
organize information in systematic ways		•	•	•	•	•
use compiled information and knowledge to raise additional unanswered questions				•	•	•
use text organizers to locate and organize information			•	•	•	•
summarize and organize information from multiple sources by taking notes, outlining ideas, or making charts			•	•	•	•

• = direct instruction   ▢ = mastery

GRADE	K	1	2	3	4	5
Culture						
connect own experiences with life experiences, language, customs, and cultures of others	•	•	•	•	•	•
compare experiences of characters across cultures	•	•	•	•	•	•
compare text events with own and other readers' experiences	•	•	•	•	•	•
determine distinctive and common characteristics of cultures through wide reading	•	•	•	•	•	•
articulate and discuss themes and connections that cross cultures	•	•	•	•	•	•
LISTENING/SPEAKING						
determine purposes	•	•	•	•	•	•
respond to directions and questions	•	•	•	•	•	•
participate in rhymes, songs, conversations and discussions	•	•	•	•	•	•
listen critically to interpret and evaluate	•	•	•	•	•	•
listen to stories and other texts read aloud	•	•	•	•	•	•
identify musical elements of literary language	•	•	•	•	•	•
connect experiences and ideas with those of others	•	•	•	•	•	•
compare language and oral traditions that reflect customs, regions, and cultures	•	•	•	•	•	•
choose appropriate language for audience, purpose, and occasion	•	•	•	•	•	•
use verbal and nonverbal communication when making announcements, directions, introductions	•	•	•	•	•	•
ask and answer relevant questions, and contribute	•	•	•	•	•	•
present dramatics	•	•	•	•	•	•
gain control of grammar	•	•	•	•	•	•
learn vocabulary of school	•	•	•	•		
use vocabulary to describe ideas, feelings, and experiences	•	•	•	•	•	•
support spoken language using props	•	•	•	•	•	•
retell by summarizing or clarifying	•	•	•	•	•	•
eliminate barriers to effective listening	•	•	•	•	•	•
understand major ideas and supporting evidence	•	•	•	•	•	•
interpret messages, purposes, and perspectives	•	•	•	•	•	•
identify and analyze persuasive techniques			•	•	•	•
distinguish between opinion and fact				•	•	•
monitor own understanding		•	•	•	•	•
listen to proficient models of oral reading	•	•	•	•	•	•
describe how language of literature affects listener	•	•	•	•	•	•
assess language choice and delivery				•	•	•
identify how regional labels/sayings reflect regions and cultures				•	•	•
demonstrate skills that reflect interviewing, reporting, requesting and providing information		•	•	•	•	•

Scope and Sequence

Grade	K	1	2	3	4	5
use effective rate, volume, pitch, tone	●	●	●	●	●	●
give precise directions and instructions in games and tasks	●	●	●	●	●	●
clarify and support with evidence, elaborations and examples		●	●	●	●	●
WRITING						
Penmanship/Capitalization/Punctuation						
write own name and other important words	●	●				
write each letter of alphabet, capital and lowercase	●	●				
use phonological knowledge to map sounds to letters, in order to write messages	●	●	●	●	●	●
write messages left to right, top to bottom	●	●	●	●		
gain control of pencil grip, paper position, beginning strokes, posture, letter formation, appropriate size, and spacing	●	●				
use word and letter spacing and margins		●	●			
use capitalization and punctuation, i.e., names, first letters in sentences, periods, question marks, exclamation marks, proper nouns, abbreviations, commas, apostrophes, quotation marks, contractions, possessives	●	●	●	●	●	●
write legibly by selecting cursive or manuscript, as appropriate		●	●	●	●	●
Spelling						
write with proficient spelling of: CVC, CVC silent e, one syllable with blends		●	●	●	●	●
inflectional endings: plurals, verb tenses, drop final e when endings are added			●	●	●	●
single-syllable words with r-controlled vowels, final consonants		●	●	●	●	●
orthographic patterns, i.e., consonant doubling, dropping e, changing y to i			●	●	●	●
use resources to find correct spellings, synonyms, and replacements			●	●	●	●
use conventional spelling of familiar words in final drafts		●	●	●	●	●
spell multisyllabic words using regularly spelled phonogram patterns			●	●	●	●
write with more proficient spelling of contractions, compounds, and homonyms		●	●	●	●	●
open and closed syllables, consonant before -le, and syllable boundary patterns			●	●	●	●
spell words ending in -tion and -sion				●	●	●
spell accurately in final drafts		●	●	●	●	●
Composition/Process						
dictate messages	●	●	●			
write labels, notes, and captions for illustrations, possessions, charts, and centers	●	●	●	●	●	●
write to record ideas and reflections	●	●	●	●	●	●
generate ideas before writing on self-selected topics	●	●	●	●	●	●
generate ideas before writing on assigned topics	●	●	●	●	●	●
develop drafts		●	●	●	●	●
use available technology to compose text	●	●	●	●	●	●
revise selected drafts for varied purposes		●	●	●	●	●
revise drafts for coherence, progression, and logical support of ideas		●	●	●	●	●

● = direct instruction ▢ = mastery

GRADE	K	1	2	3	4	5
edit for appropriate grammar, spelling, punctuation, and features of polished writings		•	•	•	•	•
demonstrate understanding of language use and spelling by bringing pieces to final form and "publishing"		•	•	•	•	•
proofread own writing and that of others		•	•	•	•	•
select and use reference materials and resources for writing		•	•	•	•	•
Purposes						
dictate messages	•	•	•			
write labels, notes, and captions for illustrations, possessions, charts, and centers	•	•	•	•	•	•
write to record ideas and reflections	•	•	•	•	•	•
write to express, discover, record, develop, reflect, and refine ideas, and to problem solve	•	•	•	•	•	•
write to communicate with a variety of audiences	•	•	•	•	•	•
write in different forms for different purposes	•	•	•	•	•	•
write to influence			•	•	•	•
write to inform	•	•	•	•	•	•
write to entertain	•	•	•	•	•	•
exhibit an identifiable voice in personal narratives and stories			•	•	•	•
choose the appropriate form for own purpose for writing				•	•	•
use literary devices, i.e., suspense, dialogue, figurative language			•	•	•	•
Grammar/Usage/Mechanics						
use nouns and verbs in sentences	•	•	•	•	•	•
compose complete sentences and use appropriate punctuation	•	•	•	•	•	•
use singular and plural forms of regular nouns		•	•	•	•	•
compose sentences with interesting elaborated subjects				•	•	•
edit writing toward standard grammar and usage		•	•	•	•	•
use correct irregular plurals			•	•	•	•
use singular and plural forms of regular nouns, and adjust verbs for agreement		•	•	•	•	•
compose elaborated sentences and use appropriate punctuation				•	•	•
use regular and irregular plurals correctly			•	•	•	•
write in complete sentences, varying the types			•	•	•	•
employ standard English usage, subject-verb agreement, pronoun referents, and parts of speech		•	•	•	•	•
use adjectives and adverbs		•	•	•	•	•
use prepositional phrases to elaborate written ideas				•	•	•
use conjunctions to connect ideas				•	•	•
use apostrophes in contractions and possessives		•	•	•	•	•
use objective-case pronouns accurately			•	•	•	•

Scope and Sequence

GRADE	K	1	2	3	4	5
Evaluation						
identify the most effective features of a piece by using student and teacher criteria		•	•	•	•	•
respond constructively to others' writing	•	•	•	•	•	•
determine how own writing achieves its purposes		•	•	•	•	•
use published pieces as models	•	•	•	•	•	•
review collection of own work to monitor growth		•	•	•	•	•
apply criteria to evaluate writing		•	•	•	•	•
review a collection of written works to determining its strengths and weaknesses, and to set goals		•	•	•	•	•
Inquiry/Research						
record/dictate questions for investigating	•	•	•	•	•	•
record/dictate own knowledge	•	•	•	•	•	•
take simple notes from sources		•	•	•	•	•
compile notes into outlines, reports, summaries			•	•	•	•
frame questions, to direct research		•	•	•	•	•
organize prior knowledge with graphic organizer	•	•	•	•	•	•
take notes from various sources			•	•	•	•
summarize and organize ideas		•	•	•	•	•
present information in various forms	•	•	•	•	•	•
evaluate own research and raise new questions				•	•	•
Connections						
collaborate with other writers		•	•	•	•	•
correspond with peers or others by e-mail or conventional mail				•	•	•
VIEWING						
Representing/Interpretation						
describe illustrator's choice of style, elements, and media	•	•	•	•	•	•
interpret events and ideas from maps, charts, graphics, video segments, and technology presentations	•	•	•	•	•	•
Representing/Analysis						
interpret and evaluate visual image makers	•	•	•	•	•	•
compare-contrast print, visual, and electronic media	•	•	•	•	•	•
Representing/Production						
select, organize, and produce visuals to complement and extend meanings	•	•	•	•	•	•
produce communications using technology	•	•	•	•	•	•

• = direct instruction   = mastery

Skills and Strategies

Reading Skills and Strategies*

Emergent Literacy

Comprehension/Thinking Strategies

References to the book you're in are in blue. Each unit in Grade 1 is identified by the initials of its theme.

PV	·	Personal Voice: Hello!
PS	·	Problem Solving: Problem Patrol
TW	·	Teamwork: Team Spirit
CE	·	Creative Expression: Imagine That!
MI	·	Managing Information: Information Finders
CI	·	Community Involvement: Hometowns

* Boldface page references indicate full skill lesson.

Index

Phonics

Index

Phonological Awareness

Index

Writing and Language Arts Skills and Strategies

Conventions of Language

Daily Language Practice

Index

Instruction in Oral Language/Listening, Speaking, Viewing

Listening

Speaking

Viewing

Integrated Language Arts

Research and Study Skills

Index

Integrated Curriculum Activities

The Arts

Math

Science

Social Studies

Index

INSTRUCTIONAL ISSUES

Assessment

Baseline Assessment

Classroom Management Forms

Comprehension Check/Think About Reading

Formal Assessment

Informal Assessment

Portfolio

Tested Skills

Cultural Connections

Index

Grouping Strategies

Classroom Management

Cooperative/Small Groups

Individuals

Partners

Whole Class

Modify Instructions

ESL/ELD

Extra Help

Gifted & Talented

Real-life Connections

Journal

Mentors

Places

Projects

Strand Connections

Workshops

Technology

Listening Center Audiocassettes

Other Technology

Presentation Tools

Scholastic Network

Videos

WiggleWorks Plus

Literature

Genre

Drama

Fiction

Myths, Legends, Fables, and Tales

Nonfiction

Poetry

Sources and Text Types

Titles, Authors, and Illustrators

TEACHER'S EDITION

Acknowledgments

Grateful acknowledgment is made to the following sources for permission to reprint from previously published material. The publisher has made diligent effort to trace the ownership of all copyrighted material in this volume and believes that all necessary permissions have been secured. If any errors or omissions have inadvertently been made, proper corrections will gladly be made in future editions.

Cover: Fred Bavendan/Minden Pictures

Back Cover: R. Faris/Corbis

Book Cover Credits: Cover from AN ALPHABET OF DINOSAURS by Peter Dodson, paintings by Wayne D. Barlowe, black-and-white illustrations by Michael Meaker. Paintings copyright © 1995 by Wayne D. Barlowe. Line art copyright © 1995 by Michael Meaker. Published by Scholastic Inc. Cover from ANIMAL TRACKS by Arthur Dorros. Illustrations copyright © 1991 by Arthur Dorros. Published by Scholastic Inc. Cover from DEAR MR. BLUEBERRY by Simon James. Illustrations copyright © 1991 by Simon James. Published by Scholastic Inc., by arrangement with Simon & Schuster Books for Young Readers, Simon & Schuster Children's Publishing Division. Cover from LOST! by David McPhail. Illustrations copyright © 1990 by David McPhail. Published by Scholastic Inc., by arrangement with Little Brown & Company, Inc. Cover from OWL AT HOME by Arnold Lobel. Illustrations copyright © 1975 by Arnold Lobel. Published by Scholastic Inc., by arrangement with HarperCollins Publishers Inc. Cover from THREE DAYS ON A RIVER IN A RED CANOE by Vera B. Williams. Copyright © 1981 by Vera B. Williams. Published by Scholastic Inc., by arrangement with William Morrow & Company, Inc.

Sentence Strips: Text for sentence strips adapted from DEAR MR. BLUEBERRY by Simon James. Copyright © 1991 by Simon James. Published by Scholastic Inc., by arrangement with Simon & Schuster Books for Young Readers, Simon & Schuster Children's Publishing Division. All rights reserved.

Workshop and Project Cards: Workshop 1: Front of Card: "My Ranger Notebook" observation log form from *Super Science® Red.* Teacher's Edition, September 1992. Copyright © 1992 by Scholastic Inc. reprinted by permission. *SUPER SCIENCE* is a registered trademark of Scholastic Inc. Back of card: Photos: br: Chip Henderson for Scholastic Inc.; bc: Francis Clark Westfield for Scholastic Inc. Illustrations: John Holm. **Workshop 2:** Front of Card: "Home Sweet Home" poster copyright © 1992 by Scholastic Inc. Supplement to *Scholastic News,* April 1992 edition. Photos: (poster): tidal wave: © Superstock/Four By Five; Kids: © Superstock/Four By Five; Hot air balloons: © George Ancona/International Stock Photo; foliage: © Gary Braasch; Boy digging: © John Griffin/The Imageworks; zebras: © Superstock/Four By Five; Large photo: © NASA. Back of card: Photos: br: Chip Henderson for Scholastic Inc.; bl: Francis Clark Westfield for Scholastic Inc.; © Franklin Viola/Comstock, Inc.; walrus: © Dan Guravich/Photo Researchers, Inc.; seal: © Tom & Pat Leesen/Photo Researchers, Inc.; puffin: © Joan W. Warden/Picture Perfect. Illustrations: John Holm. **Project:** Front of Card: "Seahorses" is excerpted from (How Living Things Grow) by Dwight Kuhn. Copyright © 1993 by Dwight R. Kuhn. Published by Scholastic Inc. Photos: cr: © Paul A. Zahl/Photo Researchers, Inc.; cl: © IKAN/Peter Arnold, Inc.; br: Chip Henderson for Scholastic Inc.; bc: Francis Clark Westfield for Scholastic Inc. Illustrations: John Holm.

Photography and Illustration Credits

Photos: Photo Stylists: Gayna Hoffman, Shawna Johnston. p. T23: Ken O'Donoghue for Scholastic Inc. p. T69: Clara Von Aich for Scholastic Inc. p. T71: Jean Marzolla for Scholastic Inc. p. T81: Ken O'Donoghue for Scholastic Inc. p. T97: Ken O'Donoghue for Scholastic Inc. p. T117: Ken O'Donoghue for Scholastic Inc. p. T121: Clara Von Aich for Scholastic Inc. p. T130: Ken O'Donoghue for Scholastic Inc. p. T135: Arnold Lobel for Scholastic Inc. p. T143: Ken O'Donoghue for Scholastic Inc. p. T165: Ken O'Donoghue for Scholastic Inc. p. T172: Clara Von Aich for Scholastic Inc. p. T178: Ken O'Donoghue for Scholastic Inc. p. T233: Clara Von Aich for Scholastic Inc. p. T235: Clara Von Aich for Scholastic Inc. p. T275: Clara Von Aich for Scholastic Inc. p. T276: © Art Gingert/Comstock, Inc. p. T283: Clara Von Aich for Scholastic Inc. p. T296: Clara Von Aich for Scholastic Inc. p. R2: Gay Su Pinnell for Scholastic Inc. p. R3: Clara Von Aich for Scholastic Inc. p. R6: © Franklin Viola/Comstock, Inc.. p. R7: Clara Von Aich for Scholastic Inc. p. R8: © Zig Leszczynski/Animals, Animals. p. R9: © Jack Zehrt/FPG International. p. R14: Richard Lee for Scholastic Inc. p. R18: Gay Su Pinnell for Scholastic Inc. p. R19: Ken O'Donoghue for Scholastic Inc. p. R24: Ken O'Donoghue for Scholastic Inc. p. R25: Ken O'Donoghue for Scholastic Inc. p. R26: Gay Su Pinnell for Scholastic Inc. p. R30: Clara Von Aich for Scholastic Inc. p. R32: © Peter Gridley/FPG International. p. R33: © Townsend P.Dickinson/Comstock, Inc. p. R34: Gay Su Pinnell for Scholastic Inc. p. R35: Ken O'Donoghue for Scholastic Inc. p. R39: Clara Von Aich for Scholastic Inc. p. R40: John Lei for Scholastic Inc. p. R41: © R.R. Lee/SuperStock.

Upfront pages: All reduced facsimiles of Student Anthologies, Teacher Editions, ancillary components, and interior pages are credited, if necessary, in their original publication format. p. T8: Chip Henderson for Scholastic Inc. p. T9 Maryellen Baker for Scholastic Inc.

Illustrations: p. T21: Nathanial Fisher for Scholastic Inc. p. T35: Nathanial Fisher for Scholastic Inc. p. T57: Ben Lloyd for Scholastic Inc. p. T62: Nathanial Fisher for Scholastic Inc. p. T79: Gayna Hoffman for Scholastic Inc. p. T79: Shawna Johnston for Scholastic Inc. p. T124: Shawna Johnston for Scholastic Inc. p. T129: Kathy Reynolds for Scholastic Inc. p. T129: Lee Rodman for Scholastic Inc. p. T143: Ben Lloyd for Scholastic Inc. p. T145: Ariana Johnston for Scholastic Inc. p. T169: Shawna Johnston for Scholastic Inc. p. T177: Gayna Hoffman for Scholastic Inc. p. T178: Ben Lloyd for Scholastic Inc. p. T187: Gayna Hoffman for Scholastic Inc. p. T189: Gayna Hoffman for Scholastic Inc. p. T225: Nathaniel Fisher for Scholastic Inc. p. T247: Ava Deluca-Verley for Scholastic Inc. p. T247: Colin Williams for Scholastic Inc. p. T249: Lee Rodman for Scholastic Inc. p. R15: Gayna Hoffman for Scholastic Inc. p. R16: Deborah Drummond for Scholastic Inc. p. R17: Liz Carr for Scholastic Inc. Kevin Neal for Scholastic Inc. Maurice Thomas for Scholastic Inc. Shawna Johnston for Scholastic Inc. p. R27: Deborah Drummond for Scholastic Inc. Brad Johnston for Scholastic Inc. p. R35: Deborah Drummond for Scholastic Inc.

Credits and Acknowledgments

Reduced Student Pages

Acknowledgments

Grateful acknowledgment is made to the following sources for permission to reprint from previously published material. The publisher has made diligent efforts to trace the ownership of all copyrighted material in this volume and believes that all necessary permissions have been secured. If any errors or omissions have inadvertently been made, proper corrections will gladly be made in future editions.

Table of Contents: From DANIEL'S DINOSAURS by Mary Carmine, illustrated by Martin Baynton. Illustrations copyright © 1990 by Martin Baynton. Reprinted by permission of Ashton Scholastic Ltd., New Zealand. "Fish Faces" from FISH FACES by Norbert Wu. Copyright © 1993 by Norbert Wu. Reprinted by permission of Henry Holt and Co. "I'm a Caterpillar" from I'M A CATERPILLAR by Jean Marzollo. Text copyright © 1997 by Jean Marzollo. Illustrations copyright © 1997 by Judith Moffat. Reprinted by permission of Scholastic Inc."Caterpillars" from CRICKET IN A THICKET by Aileen Fisher. Copyright © 1963 by Aileen Fisher. Copyright renewed © 1991 by Aileen Fisher. Used by permission of Marian Reiner for the author. "Frog and Toad Together. 'The Garden'" from FROG AND TOAD TOGETHER by Arnold Lobel. Copyright © 1971 by Arnold Lobel. Reprinted by permission of HarperCollins Publishers. "Tommy" from BRONZEVILLE BOYS AND GIRLS by Gwendolyn Brooks. Copyright © 1956 by Gwendolyn Brooks Blakely. Reprinted by permission of HarperCollins Children's Books, a division of HarperCollins Publishers. "Daniel's Dinosaurs" from DANIEL'S DINOSAURS by Mary Carmine, illustrated by Martin Baynton. Text copyright © 1990 by Mary Carmine. Illustrations copyright © 1990 by Martin Baynton. Reprinted by permission of Ashton Scholastic Ltd., New Zealand. "I Can Read With My Eyes Shut" from I CAN READ WITH MY EYES SHUT by Dr. Seuss. TM and copyright © 1978 by Dr. Seuss Enterprises, L.P. Reprinted by permission of Random House, Inc. "The Plant Castle" from THE PLANT CASTLE by Pat Mora, illustrated by Gerardo Suzan. Copyright © 1996 by Scholastic Inc.

Photography and Illustration Credits

Photos: pp.6tl, 6mr, © Gerard Lacz/Animals Animals; pp.7br, 34br, 34tl, Maryellen Baker for Scholastic Inc.; p.35bl, Chip Henderson for Scholastic Inc.; pp.36–37, © Ron Dalquist/Superstock; pp.36br, 37br, 37c, © Norbert Wu; p.69, © Ellen Warner; p.85, Harper Collins; p.113, Courtesy Scholastic New Zealand; p.131, © Valerie Santiago; p.132br, © David Young Wolff/ Tony Stone Images; p.135br, © Michael P. Gadomski/ PhotoResearchers.

Cover: Fred Bavendan/Minden Pictures

Back Cover: R.Faris/Corbis

Illustrations: pp.4–5:Karen Barbour for Scholastic Inc. pp.6–7: Jackie Snider. pp.82–83:Tungwai Chau for Scholastic Inc. pp.67–68:Doran Potka for Scholastic Inc. p.129:Paul Miesel for Scholastic Inc. p.130:Gerard Suzan

Illustrated Author Photos: pp.37, 69, 85, 113, 131: David Franck for Scholastic Inc.